STERLING
Education

Psychology for Educators

Essential Principles

3rd edition

3   2   1

ISBN-13: 979-8-8855722-6-2

Sterling Education materials are available at quantity discounts.

Contact info@sterling–prep.com

Sterling Education
6 Liberty Square #11
Boston, MA 02109

STERLING
Education

Understanding psychological principles is essential for educators because they work closely with students from diverse backgrounds experiencing a wide range of emotional, mental, and behavioral challenges. Psychology plays a crucial role in shaping effective teaching practices and enhancing student learning. Knowledge of psychology enhances educators' ability to provide holistic learning, connect with their students, and navigate the complex emotional landscape of an educational setting.

This book provides thorough coverage of psychology topics, teaching the foundational theories and concepts necessary for understanding human behavior. The material is clearly presented and systematically organized for learning important principles and relationships, providing comprehensive learning.

From the early theories on human mind to the modern neuropsychology perspectives, readers will develop a better understanding of all major psychological theories, principles and approaches that elucidate multidimensional concepts of emotion, behavior and cognition. They will learn about historically significant psychology researchers, biological basis of human behavior, basic principles of consciousness and cognition, what drives human emotions and motivations, all major groups of psychological disorders, as well as how early childhood psychological development affects human behavior.

Experienced psychology and sociology instructors, researchers, and clinicians prepared this learning material to build knowledge and skills crucial for understanding psychology. Our editorial team reviewed and systematized the content for targeted and effective learning so readers can significantly improve their understanding of the subject.

We wish you great success in your mastering of psychology!

240212akp

Featured on

 **FOX** ◉CBS  NBC

Chemistry

Physics

Cell and Molecular Biology

Organismal Biology

American History

American Law

American Government and Politics

Comparative Government and Politics

World History

European History

Psychology

Sociology

Environmental Science

Human Geography

Visit our Amazon store

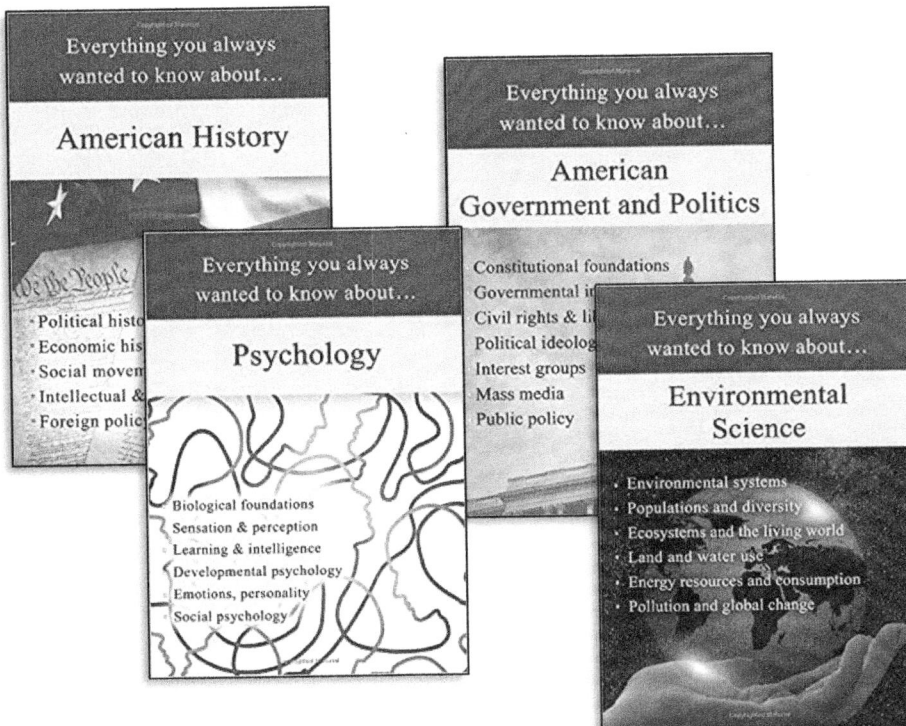

Table of Contents

Table of Contents (*continued*)

Table of Contents (*continued*)

Table of Contents (*continued*)

CHAPTER 4: LEARNING (*continued*)

Table of Contents (*continued*)

Table of Contents (*continued*)

CHAPTER 5: COGNITION & STATES OF CONSCIOUSNESS (*continued*)

Table of Contents (*continued*)

Table of Contents (*continued*)

Table of Contents (*continued*)

Table of Contents (*continued*)

Table of Contents (*continued*)

Table of Contents (*continued*)

Table of Contents (*continued*)

Table of Contents (*continued*)

CHAPTER 1

History & Approaches

Since its emergence in 1879, the field of psychology has undergone many changes in its progression to contemporary times. Theories and research methodologies have experienced significant revisions over the decades. While some areas not part of the discipline and originate from its "introspective" past can be considered "unscientific," experimental psychology is a science because it adheres to rigorous methods to investigate phenomena that increase understanding of behavior and mental processes.

Incorrect perceptions of psychology often originate from the media and popular culture. While a science, researchers' perspectives can influence the approach used and the resulting explanation of phenomena. Therefore, solid knowledge of major psychological approaches is critical for a comprehensive understanding of the discipline and future practice.

History of Psychology

Perspectives shaping psychology

Philosophers and scientists have been trying to understand the human mind since the beginning. Initially, it was believed that evil spirits caused psychological problems. In 5,000 B.C., trephining (i.e., chipping holes in a patient's skull to allow evil spirits to escape) was used to treat these problems.

As humans became more scientific, so did the understanding of psychological problems.

Science emerges from empiricism (i.e., knowledge through experience) and determinism (i.e., cause-and-effect relationships governing events), and while many sciences, including biology, physics, astronomy, and chemistry, developed during the 1600s, psychology developed later.

Early explanations for abnormal behavior often involved supernatural or religious reasoning.

What made up the mind was often tied to the soul. While psychology today is empirical and deterministic, before the 1600s, psychology's focus was philosophical.

Thus, while science grew in the 1600s, psychology did not become a scientific discipline until the late 1800s.

Painting of a surgeon removing part of a skull (17th century)

Classical perspective

Philosophical influences in psychology date to 430 B.C. when Hippocrates attempted to explain moods, emotions, and behaviors. He theorized that moods, emotions, and behaviors were caused by an excess or lack of *body fluids*, which he called humour.

Hippocrates believed these humours were blood, yellow bile, black bile, and phlegm. This theory persisted for years, though Galen, sometime in the second century A.D., expanded on this theory and allowed for the "mixing" of the four humours, which could result in any of nine "temperaments."

Galen assigned a temperamental category to each humour:

> *sanguine* (blood)
>
> *choleric* (yellow bile)
>
> *melancholic* (black bile)
>
> *phlegmatic* (phlegm)

Hippocrates, the Greek physician

Sanguine temperament is associated with air and is thought to include carefree, pleasure-seeking, talkative, and sociable people. People with this temperament make friends easily and struggle with being forgetful and seeing things all the way through.

Choleric temperament tends to be excitable, restless, and impulsive. This temperament is usually associated with fire. These individuals are known for getting things done efficiently, being strong-willed, and good at planning.

Melancholic temperament is associated with Earth and is believed to encompass the traits of cautiousness, introversion, and seriousness. Individuals are thought to be at risk for moodiness and depression and prefer to do things independently.

Phlegmatic temperaments are calm, caring, tolerant, and private. This temperament is usually associated with water. Individuals are likely to be content with themselves, be consistent in their habits, and have faithful friends.

Philosophical perspective

Nicholas Culpeper (1600s) wrote about the humours as governing principles in health that also had astrological correspondences. Culpeper believed that this influenced personality and that while some people had only one temperament, others had a mixture, with one temperament being primary and the other being secondary.

Alfred Adler, Erich Adickes, and Ernst Kretschmer created theories based on the four temperaments, which shaped modern conceptions of temperament and personality.

Nicholas Culpeper, an English physician

In 1637, René Descartes theorized that animal spirits, produced in the blood, are responsible for causing the body to move and behave. He postulated that the pineal gland was the seat of the soul and directed the animal spirits, as this was where all thoughts were formed. He believed that because infants had innate abilities to move, some knowledge had to be inborn in humans.

Descartes asserted that nerves were hollow tubes filled with animal spirits flowing through the body and responsible for all functions, including memory and behavior. His descriptions of animal spirits are remarkably similar to the modern understanding of the nervous system.

Contrary to Descartes, in 1690, the English philosopher and physician John Locke proclaimed that infants are born as tabula rasa or "blank slates." He stated that children's experiences determine the types of adults they become, with their thoughts, emotions, and abilities. Locke postulated that the sources of all ideas are sensations and reflections.

Natural selection perspective

In the late 1800s, much research was being conducted in laboratories that propelled psychology to become a scientific discipline. In the 1850s, Gustav Fechner began to examine sensation and perception and founded psychophysics (the study of the link between the mental representation of the world and physical work).

Fechner asked individuals to hold weights of different mass in each hand and then, while slowly adding equal weights to each hand, would ask individuals to identify which added weight they perceived as heavier.

Surprisingly, individuals cited the weight added to the hand initially holding less weight as heavier. Fechner went as far as to develop an equation calculating the perceived change. He also studied this perceived change phenomenon for loudness and brightness.

Charles Darwin influenced the field of psychology with his *theory of natural selection*. Darwin believed that behaviors, in addition to physical traits, were subject to *genetic influence* and, thus, *natural selection*.

Sir Francis Galton, a cousin of Darwin, believed that behaviors were subject to natural selection and heritability. He purported that genetics explained all the psychological differences among people. Galton began to measure these differences and noted that the closer the relative was to a person, the more similar the traits tended to be.

Galton concluded that the English government should encourage intelligent or talented individuals to have children, and people who did not possess these traits (e.g., criminals, those with mental disabilities) should be kept out of the English gene pool.

Galton contributed to what became the psychology field by pioneering statistical methods to measure and study behavior. Some of these methods are used in modern psychology.

Medical influences

The then-growing field of medicine influenced the development of psychology.

Franz Josef Gall created a map of the head, which he used to assign distinctive characteristics such as intelligence, moral character, and other personality traits. He believed that the shape and bumps on the head indicated these characteristics.

Franz Joseph Gall, German Physician and Anatomist

Gall referred to his technique as *phrenology*. While his theory has not withstood rigorous testing, it was important as the first theory to assert that brain areas control different behaviors and traits, now known as *brain localization*.

Building on this, Paul Broca and Karl Wernicke, both physicians, identified brain areas that control speech areas. Broca had a patient nicknamed Tan, so named because "tan" was the only word he could speak after suffering a stroke, though he could understand speech well.

When Tan died, Broca performed an autopsy and discovered an area on the left side of the brain that was damaged; this area is *Broca's Area* and responsible for speech production.

Similarly, Wernicke had a patient who had brain damage that resulted in his speaking in made-up or unusual words. When performing the autopsy, Wernicke identified an area in the left brain responsible for speech comprehension, known as *Wernicke's Area*.

Franz Mesmer inadvertently introduced the concept of *psychosomatic medicine*. He believed that metallic fluids in the body were the cause of disease and insanity, and by using magnets, he could redirect these fluids. Mesmer used trance-like states to treat his patients (these *trances* are *hypnosis*). The medical community rejected Mesmer's claims, concluding that the patient's belief in the treatment caused healing; thus, *psychosomatic medicine* was born.

Notes for active learning

.

Theoretical Approaches to Behavior

Structuralism

Before the later 1800s, human behavior was explained philosophically or by experimentation. It was not called psychology because the field was not formed. However, all had significant influences on the creation of the field of psychology and approaches taken to explain behavior.

In 1879, a German physician, physiologist, and psychologist, Wilhelm Wundt, established the first experimental laboratory devoted to psychological phenomena. Two years later, he founded the first academic journal in psychology.

Wundt believed psychology should focus on discovering the essential mental components of perception, consciousness, thinking, emotions, and mental states. Wundt labeled his perspective *structuralism* as he was primarily interested in the mind's structure (or building blocks).

Introspection was used by Wundt to uncover the fundamental mental components of the mind. His introspection technique required a research participant to describe in detail what they had experienced when exposed to various stimuli. Wundt believed that these descriptions revealed the building blocks of the mind.

Wundt's *structuralism* was not without critics. Some scientists opposed introspection, stating that it was not a scientific technique. Others noted that people have difficulty describing specific inner experiences. Thus, some building blocks might be left out or not accurately defined.

About four years after Wundt established his laboratory, G. Stanley Hall established the first psychological laboratory in the U.S. at Johns Hopkins University and founded the *American Journal of Psychology*. He was the first president of the American Psychological Association.

Functionalism

Like Wundt and Hall, William James established his laboratory at Harvard University. James's approach to psychology differed significantly from Wundt's. James believed psychology should focus on how behavior functions (i.e., *functionalism*), allowing people to adapt to their environment rather than considerations of the mind's structure. For example, James might have been interested in how fear prepares the mind to cope with emergencies. His approach is.

James used a *stream-of-consciousness* technique to study functionalism, where individuals would express their thoughts and reactions to events. James, unlike Wundt, examined thoughts (reactions) as a continuous flow rather than their fundamental pieces.

Functionalism replaced *structuralism* as the predominant theory about the mind and behavior.

Wilhelm Wundt, a German physician

Behaviorism

During the first half of the 20th century, psychology in America was not dominated by functionalism but rather the novel approach called *behaviorism*. Behaviorism rejected the idea that the emphasis of psychology should be on the mind's inner workings. Instead, it believed that psychology should focus on observable behavior that could be measured objectively.

Edwin Twitmyer was the first to describe the process of *classical conditioning*. He set up experiments initially to study reflexes. In his studies, he had a machine that would ring a bell just before it tapped a research participant's patellar tendon (just below the kneecap), causing the individual's kicking reflex to engage.

One day, the machine malfunctioned, and the bell rang without a tap on the patellar tendon. Twitmyer observed that the participant's leg kicked anyway. Twitmyer presented his findings at the American Psychological Association Conference. However, it received a lukewarm response, likely because it did not fit in with the existing work in psychology in the U.S.

Around the same time Twitmyer was conducting his experiments, Ivan Pavlov conducted a series of experiments that revealed dogs could learn to anticipate food at the sound of a bell after the bellringing had been initially paired with food. He named this process *classical conditioning* and won the 1904 Nobel Prize for his experiments.

Ivan Pavlov, Russian physiologist

In the U.S., John B. Watson emphasized that psychology should focus on environmental changes that produce observable behaviors. Watson believed that thoughts and other internal events were too subjective and had no place in the science of psychology. Not only were internal events too subjective, but according to Watson, all behavior could be explained through conditioning. Thus, internal events were unnecessary to the study of psychology.

Watson is famous for saying, "give me a dozen healthy infants, well-formed, and my own specified world to bring them up in, and I'll guarantee to take anyone at random and train him to become any type of specialist I might select – doctor, lawyer, artist, merchant-chief and, yes, even a beggar-man and thief, regardless of talents, penchants, tendencies, abilities, vocations and race of his ancestors."

Watson's most famous experiment was with Little Albert, showing fear could be a conditioned response. Later, Watson was employed in advertising, where he applied behaviorist principles. Today's advertising agencies still use techniques introduced by Watson.

Principles of operant conditioning

B.F. Skinner, an American psychologist, believed that only observable behaviors should be studied. Skinner devoted much of his career to studying animals and their behavior in response to rewards and punishments.

Skinner's work was primarily done with animals in boxes (i.e., Skinner Boxes), where an animal would be rewarded for a particular response (e.g., pecking a lever in the case of pigeons) and receive nothing for giving undesired responses. Skinner would vary when the reward was given so the animals could be observed to learn a pattern.

Skinner's work led to the formation of the *principles of operant conditioning*. He believed that human behavior was much like animal behavior and was influenced by drives for rewards and motivation to avoid punishment.

Behaviorism was criticized for rejecting free will. Psychologists opposed to behaviorism believe humans can use *free will and reasoning* to make a decision that may be contrary to the innate drive for reward (or motivation to avoid punishment).

Psychoanalytic and psychodynamic

Early approaches to explaining behavior focused on using research methods of the existing sciences to understand behavior. Later approaches expanded on this and began using techniques unique to psychology to understand behavior. Further attempts were made to find new ways to explain and treat psychological disorders.

The father of psychoanalytic theory, Sigmund Freud, believed that while the conscious mind (i.e., the part of the mind one is aware of) is essential, the most crucial part of the human experience is what is happening in the unconscious mind (i.e., the part of the mind one is unaware of).

Freud believed that within the unconscious mind were urges to fulfill sexual and aggressive impulses. He stated that these were usually from early childhood and not remembered by the conscious mind.

However, these unfulfilled impulses could influence the individual (e.g., causing an individual to feel depressed, restricting the use of a part of one's body). Freud believed that the therapist's purpose was to uncover these unconscious impulses to help the patient cope with them more effectively and eventually decrease the symptoms being experienced. Freud's work had little scientific backing, with most of his theory being based on his observations and musings.

Neo-Freudians

Psychologists (many of whom were trained by Freud) continued to build on his theory as "Neo-Freudians." The Neo-Freudians helped to shape psychodynamic theory as it is today.

Neo-Freudians disagreed with Freud's assertion that childhood events determined adult personality and paid greater attention to social factors and the effects of society on personality development.

Carl Jung, a student of Freud's, rejected Freud's view that unconscious sexual urges were the most important aspect of psychology. Jung instead believed that humans have a collective unconscious, a standard set of images, feelings, and ideas inherited from ancestors, and a personal unconscious, which are the experiences, ideas, and feelings unique to the individual.

Jung believed humans have *archetypes* (i.e., universal symbols) in their *collective unconscious*. He cited art, literature, and religion as evidence of this. For example, the mother archetype can be found in all religions, many examples of art worldwide, and diverse types of literature. However, there is little evidence to suggest that the collective unconscious exists.

Karen Horney is regarded as the first feminist psychologist. She outright rejected several of Freud's notions, including that women have penis envy. She asserted that instead of being envious of the male anatomy, women were envious of the independence, status, and freedom they were often denied.

Horney believed *social relationships* were crucial in developing their personality. In particular, she believed the child's relationship with their parents was essential to personality development.

Karen Horney, feminist psychologist

Alfred Adler moved further from Freud's theory, asserting that humans are primarily motivated by striving for superiority. Adler believed that all humans sought out self-improvement and perfection. Further, because humans are social beings, he thought they were motivated by social interest and desire to improve others.

Adler stated that when an adult has been unable to overcome feelings of inferiority developed as a child, that adult has an inferiority complex. He stated that the inferiority complex should be the focus of psychotherapy.

Finally, Erik Erikson believed that personality develops over a lifespan. Evolving personality radically differs from Freud, who believed that personality is developed by the end of childhood.

Erikson proposed a developmental model where the individual has a particular crisis to overcome at each phase in life. Erickson stated that it was the *outcome of each crisis* that determined personality.

Humanistic

Until the 1950s, the view of humans was that there was no free will. Behaviorism posited that humans were a product of classical and operant conditioning, and psychoanalysis claimed that unconscious urges were responsible for behavior and symptoms. In response to these perspectives, humanistic psychology was created.

Two of the founders, Carl Rogers and Abraham Maslow, believed that humans did have free will, and rather than the focus being placed on what is wrong with humans (as in psychoanalysis), the focus should be on people striving to be the best they can be.

Humanists believe humans are innately good and strive to lead productive and fulfilling lives. In treatment, Rogers and Maslow focused on helping individuals grow to their full potential.

Maslow postulated that humans have needs that can be arranged in a hierarchy, with the primary motivation being to strive to improve and move up the hierarchy. Maslow arranged his hierarchy into a pyramid named *Maslow's Hierarchy of Needs*.

Maslow noted that basic needs, such as food, clothing, and shelter, must be satisfied before the individual can reach the next level. At the top of Maslow's hierarchy is self-actualization.

Maslow stated that all humans strive for this, though few will reach it. Self-actualization is when people are fulfilled and have reached their highest potential. Maslow stated that this was unique to every individual.

Rogers focused on the *self* and *ideal self*. Rogers believed that a person's self-concept (i.e., perception of who one is) comes from interactions with others. This self-concept encompasses who one thinks they are (i.e., self) and who one wishes one were (i.e., ideal self).

Rogers posited that when there is a gap between the self and the ideal self, individuals may demonstrate psychological issues, such as depression. He stated that humans are born with a need for acceptance, sympathy, and love from others, which he referred to as a need for positive regard. Rogers stated that it was the therapist's job to provide unconditional positive regard to patients trying to overcome the gap between the self and their ideal self.

Sociocultural

In the early 1900s, there was an interest in how people influence the behavior of others.

Specifically, Norman Triplett focused his research (1898) on social influences and conducted one of the first formal experiments in this area.

He found that individuals ride bicycles faster in the presence of others as compared to when they are alone. This work, while published, did not gain much popularity until the 1940s.

Norman Triplett, an American psychologist

However, in the 1940s, Triplett's research gained traction when research on social influences boomed, with psychologists collaborating with sociologists. This research focused on trying to understand how ordinary people could become horrific prison camp guards (e.g., in Nazi-controlled Germany) and how propaganda influences people (significant concerns during World War II). From this collaboration, the field of social and personality psychology was born.

Kurt Lewin is cited as the founder of *modern social psychology*. His primary research focus was on race relations in the United States. Through his research, he discovered that behavior is a function of the individual and the environment. Lewin found that one can expect different behaviors because of the differences between individuals and situations.

For example, if a person is typically talkative and outgoing, how might that person act at a wedding? Moreover, might that person react differently at a funeral? The answer is likely yes, showing that individual personality traits, situations, and expected behavior are essential.

Contemporary approaches

Contemporary approaches to psychology recognize that there is not one reason or explanation for the behavior but that a combination of factors best explains it.

There is greater recognition of how psychology overlaps with the other sciences (e.g., biology) and of the many different things that can be meant when one says they study "psychology."

Evolutionary

As biology has gained a greater understanding of genetics and genetic influences on health, illness, traits, etc., psychologists have begun to look for genetic explanations for behavior and personality. Evolutionary psychologists explore how behavior is influenced by genetics.

For example, one explanation for why humans sleep at night instead of during the day is that their eyes do not see well in the dark. By being inactive and lying still during the night, humans had a greater chance of survival. If they were up wandering around at night, they may step off the edge of a cliff or get devoured by a predator.

Biological

Advances in biology and neurology have expanded the biological perspective in psychology. In clinical neuropsychology and behavioral neuroscience, emphasis is placed on the biological factors that cause psychological disorders or determine behavior.

For example, there are structural changes in the brain (e.g., increased ventricle size) in patients with schizophrenia. A clinical neuropsychologist is interested in studying how these structural changes contribute to the symptoms.

Behavioral neuroscientists may be interested in how emotions are related to physical sensations in healthy individuals and individuals with a disorder.

Cognitive

Behaviorism was the predominant approach in the U.S. during the first half of the 20th century.

However, European psychologists focused on *thought* and *thought processes*, creating the field of *cognitive psychology*.

Hermann Ebbinghaus is credited with completing the first studies focusing on memory. Using himself as his research subject, he memorized lists of made-up words and then tried to recall the lists over time.

Ebbinghaus plotted his results as *forgetting curves*, which showed that most of what is learned is forgotten quickly, but then forgetting slows, and the remaining information is retained.

Hermann Ebbinghaus, German psychologist

Biopsychosocial

Biopsychosocial approach is among the newest in psychology, emphasizing the biological, psychological, and sociocultural factors influencing health and illness.

Biological factors include *brain structure*, *hormones*, and *pharmaceuticals.*

Psychological factors:

thought processes, emotions, personality, and subjective experiences.

Sociocultural factors:

gender, ethnicity, family, peers, and culture.

For example, when considering the causes of depression, one might consider family history, neurotransmitters, and history of brain injury, which are biological explanations of depression.

For psychological explanations of depression, it would be essential to consider what a person tells themselves (e.g., "I am worthless").

Sociocultural factors for depression include family support, personality characteristics, and recent bereavement. Clinically, three categories of factors contribute to depression symptoms.

Subfields in Psychology

Subfields in psychology are defined by their approach, focus, constructs, and questions they seek to answer about behavior.

Biological psychologists seek to find connections between biological factors (e.g., brain structure, hormone levels, neurotransmitters) and behaviors. They often receive advanced training in neuroscience to understand these factors and their effects on behavior.

Clinical psychologists are interested in the diagnosis and treatment of psychological disorders. Some clinicians study psychological disorders in addition to (or instead of) treating psychological disorders.

Cognitive psychology concerns higher mental processes. They study memory, reasoning, decision-making, thinking, language, and problem-solving processes.

Counseling psychologists, like clinical psychologists, can provide treatment. However, these psychologists tend to focus more on educational, social, and career adjustment problems rather than psychological disorders.

Educational psychology studies human learning. This field studies how humans learn and retain information and the role that individual differences play.

Developmental psychology focuses on how humans grow and change from conception to death. Areas of growth and change studied include thought processes, physical development, moral development, sense of self, and emotions.

Experimental psychology examines processes: sensation, perception, learning, thinking, and memory. Research uses humans or animals.

Human factors psychology focuses on applying psychological principles to work environments. Ergonomics, safety, product design, and human-computer interaction are studied by human factors psychology. For example, *goals* of efficiency and safety in work environments.

Industrial-organizational psychology focuses on human behavior in the workplace. Companies hire industrial-organizational psychologists to evaluate and apply psychological theories to workplace situations to increase productivity, employee satisfaction, safety, and well-being.

Personality psychology studies the consistency in human behavior over time. Practitioners examine the traits and characteristics that differentiate people.

Psychometrics is concerned with psychological measurement, including theory and technique.

Social psychology seeks to understand how people's behaviors, thoughts, and feelings are affected by others. The "others" may be present, imagined to be present, or implied to be present.

Psychology in education

Understanding psychological principles is essential for educators because they work closely with students from diverse backgrounds experiencing a wide range of emotional, mental, and behavioral challenges.

Knowledge of psychology enhances educators' ability to provide holistic learning, connect with their students, and navigate the complex emotional landscape of an educational setting.

Psychology plays a crucial role in shaping effective teaching practices and enhancing student learning. There are several compelling reasons why psychology is essential in the education field.

Understanding learning processes

Teachers and education professionals interact with students and families from diverse backgrounds, each with unique emotional states. Understanding common psychology principles gives educators insights into how people acquire and retain knowledge. By applying psychological principles, they can implement various learning methods and tailor their teaching approaches to meet the diverse needs of students.

Instructional improvement

By analyzing the social, emotional, and cognitive processes involved in learning, educators may contribute to improving instructional methods. They can explore how the timing of introducing new information affects retention, the role that culture plays in processing new ideas, the impact of language on skills and knowledge, instructional differences between in-person and remote learning, and many other educational processes. By understanding factors that influence student motivation, teachers can design effective lessons and foster a positive learning environment.

Individual differences

Not every student learns the same way. Being able to identify and appreciate individual differences in learning styles, cognitive abilities, and emotional factors allows educators to adapt their teaching strategies to accommodate diverse learners.

Mental health awareness

Teachers and education professionals encounter students with various emotional and mental health challenges. Basic psychology knowledge and specialized training programs equip them with the ability to identify signs of mental and emotional distress, offer support, and collaborate with mental health professionals.

Stress management

Education is a very demanding profession, sometimes involving stressful situations. Knowledge of psychology can help teachers and education administrators stay organized, manage emotions, and maintain a healthy perspective. Recognizing and understanding their own mental well-being empowers educators to promote successful learning outcomes for all students.

CHAPTER 2

Biological Bases of Behavior

Understanding the links between biology, physiological processes, and behavior is essential for studying psychology. In pursuit of this understanding, extensive research has been conducted on the brain using evolving brain imaging technologies.

Important discoveries have been made concerning brain regions' structures and associated functions. Insights have been gained concerning the functions of the central and peripheral nervous systems. Other research discoveries highlighted the structures, functions, and importance of neurons.

Neuroscience aids psychologists and psychiatrists in developing an understanding of how an excess (or deficit) of certain neurotransmitters is connected to physical and mental disorders (e.g., Parkinson's disease, dopamine deficiency), as well as how specific pharmaceutical agents act in their patients.

Effects of the Nervous System on Behavior

Behaviors

Behavior is the internally coordinated responses (actions or inactions) of organisms (individuals or groups) to *internal* or *external stimuli*.

Behaviors are *innate* (instinctual) or *learned*.

Behavior is an action of an organism that *changes its relationship* to its environment.

Behavior provides *outputs* from organisms to the environment.

Brain structure

Vertebrate brains are at the anterior end of the *dorsal tubular nerve cord*.

Brain consists of outer grey matter (i.e., *cell bodies*) and inner (subcortical) white matter nerve fibers (i.e., *axons*), many covered in myelin sheaths (e.g., oligosaccharides).

Brain has three regions: *forebrain*, *midbrain*, and *hindbrain*.

It has four ventricles, including two lateral ventricles.

> *Cerebrum* is associated with the two lateral ventricles
>
> *Diencephalon* is associated with the third ventricle.
>
> *Brain stem* and *cerebellum* are associated with the fourth ventricle.

Informational pulses executed in the nervous system allow people to perform daily functions.

Information processing occurs in the *central nervous system* (CNS), a mass of nerve cells.

Central core is formed by the *diencephalon* (location of the third ventricle), consisting of the thalamus, several large nuclei, and the hypothalamus.

Hypothalamus is the *command center* for neural and endocrine coordination. It forms the third ventricle floor below the thalamus and next to the pituitary gland.

Hypothalamus maintains homeostasis and many regulatory functions, such as osmoregulation and thermoregulation. It is an integrating center regulating hunger, sleep, thirst, water balance, body temperature, and blood pressure. It controls the *pituitary gland* and links the *nervous and endocrine systems*. The hypothalamus regulates ADH (*anti-diuretic hormone*) secretions via neuro-secretory cells.

Thalamus has two masses of grey matter on the sides and roof of the third ventricle. It is the last portion of the brain for sensory input before the cerebrum. Thalmus is a central relay for sensory impulses traveling from the body or brain to the cerebrum.

Besides olfaction, the thalamus channels sensory impulses to specific regions of the cerebrum for interpretation.

Pineal gland, which secretes the *melatonin* hormone, is in the diencephalon.

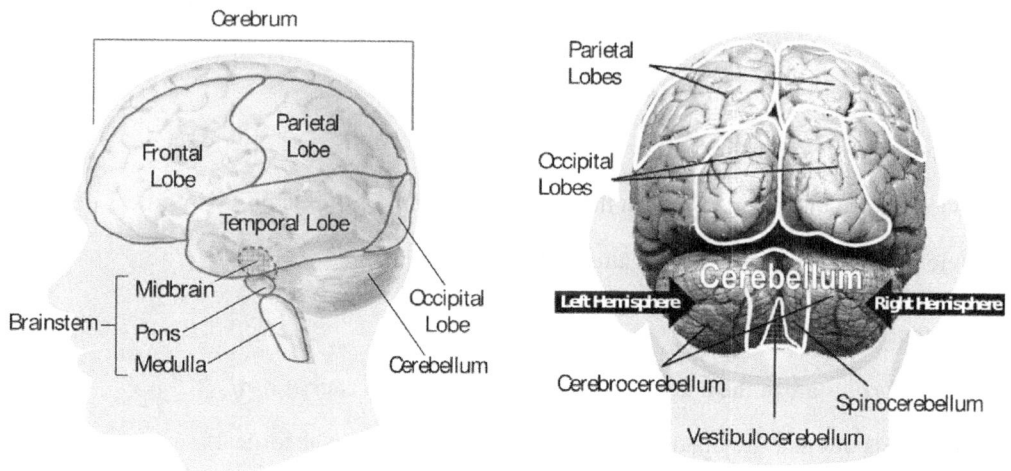

Generalized structure of the human brain

Forebrain

Forebrain lies above the brainstem and cerebellum and is the most evolutionary advanced brain region. It is the largest and most crucial brain region, with components responsible for several activities. The forebrain receives sensory input from the midbrain and hindbrain and regulates their output.

Cerebrum (or *telencephalon*) is the largest component of the forebrain, comprising most of the forebrain and responsible for the higher thought processes necessary for memory, language, speech, intelligence, and creativity. It is the last center receiving sensory input and integrating it to command motor responses.

Grey matter of the outer part of the cerebrum is the cerebral cortex, the brain region receiving information from the thalamus and lower brain regions.

White matter is in the inner portion of the cerebrum.

Cerebrum has two hemispheres connected by the *corpus callosum*, a thick nerve bundle.

Each hemisphere is divided into the:

> *frontal lobe* (involved in conscious thought and voluntary skeletal muscle movement),
>
> *parietal lobe* (sensory information for temperature, touch, pressure, and pain),
>
> *temporal lobe* (processing auditory information and smell), and
>
> *occipital lobe* (processing visual information).

Midbrain

Midbrain is a collection of cell bodies that receive incoming signals from the spinal cord and various brain regions. It participates in smooth movement, temperature control, and visual and auditory-motor reflexes integration.

Brainstem has the *midbrain, pons,* and *medulla oblongata*. It contains the *reticular formation*, a bundle of axons responsible for motor functions and cardiovascular and respiratory control. Besides acting as a relay station for tracts passing between the cerebrum and spinal cord (or cerebellum), the midbrain has reflex centers for *visual, auditory,* and *tactile responses*.

Brainstem connects the brain to the central nervous system by connecting the cerebrum to the spinal cord. This part of the brain is evolutionarily the oldest structure and smallest region of the brain, which has developed over time into the two other components. The brainstem is primarily concerned with life support and essential functions such as movement, while evolved brain areas perform more advanced processes.

Hindbrain

Hindbrain is in the posterior brain region, which unconsciously regulates organ systems. It regulates lung and heart functions, even during sleep, and coordinates motor activity.

Pons functions with the medulla to regulate breathing rate. It contains bundles of axons between the cerebellum and CNS and has reflex centers concerned with head movements responding to visual or auditory stimuli.

Medulla oblongata lies between the spinal cord and pons, anterior to the cerebellum. It contains vital centers for regulating heartbeat, breathing, and vasoconstriction. It contains reflex centers for vomiting, coughing, sneezing, hiccupping, and swallowing. Medulla oblongata has nerve tracts that ascend (or descend) between the spinal cord and the brain's higher centers.

Cerebellum is separated from the brain stem by the fourth ventricle. It is in two portions and joined by a narrow median portion. It integrates impulses from higher centers to coordinate muscle actions, maintain equilibrium and muscle tone, and sustain normal posture.

Cerebellum receives information from the eyes, inner ear, and muscles to indicate position; it integrates that information and sends impulses to the muscles to maintain balance. The cerebellum assists in learning new motor skills (e.g., sports or playing the piano).

Human hands require a substantial proportion of the *primary motor area* for precise movements.

Ventral to the primary motor area is a pre-motor area that organizes motor functions before the primary area sends signals to the cerebellum.

Lateralization of cortical functions

Most evidence of lateralized brain function stems from understanding how brain damage affects performance on cognitive tasks. Paul Broca, a 19th-century neurologist, first studied a patient's inability to produce speech following brain damage. His patient was Leborgne, who understood most of what was said to him, and though he could only utter the word "tan," he was able to drink and eat, leading Broca to discard the theory of motor impairment.

Leborgne's brain was damaged in the lower rear portion of the frontal lobe, a lower front portion of the parietal lobe, and an upper part of the temporal lobe. Broca concluded that frontal lobe damage affected speech production.

Aphasia is the partial (or total) loss of ability to articulate ideas due to brain damage.

Broca's Area is to the lower rear portion of the frontal lobe, adjacent to the motor cortex.

Paul Broca, neurologist

Korbinian Brodmann examined brain cells with strains to recognize chemical differences between various areas. Brain areas defined by cytoarchitectonic characteristics are *Brodmann's area*. There are 52 recognized Brodmann's areas in the brain.

In 1871, Carl Wernicke reported a language disorder called *Wernicke's aphasia,* characterized by excessive fluent speech, made-up words, and a lack of comprehension despite intact hearing.

Women are more vulnerable to aphasia after severe damage to the frontal lobe. Men are more vulnerable to aphasia after damage to the parietal and temporal lobes. There are similar sex differences in *apraxia* (i.e., impairment in voluntary movement).

Carl Wernicke, German psychiatrist

In the Wernicke-Geschwind model, Broca's area stores the motor representation of speech, while Wernicke's area stores the auditory representation of speech sounds.

Arcuate fasciculus fibers connect these areas. This model is considered oversimplified.

Methods for studying the brain

Electroencephalogram (EEG) uses sensors (i.e., electrodes) to measure brain electrical activity.

Computerized tomography (CT) uses computer-enhanced X-rays to produce images of specific brain regions.

Magnetic Resonance Imaging (MRI) uses magnetic fields, producing more detailed images than CT scan images.

Functional MRI (fMRI) portrays the differences in activity in various brain regions.

Positron Emission Tomography (PET) tracks radioactive markers injected into the bloodstream.

Neuronal communication and behavior

Neurons consist of a cell body and branching fibers. A neuron consists of dendrite fibers that receive information and axon fibers that pass the information along to other neurons and various muscular glands.

Myelin sheath is a layer of fatty tissue that insulates the axons and increases the transmission speed of their impulses. An action potential is initiated when the excitatory signals minus the inhibitory signals exceed the intensity of the threshold (or the minimum value).

After receiving signals, an action potential is started by moving charged ions (e.g., Na^+ and K^+) in and out of axon membrane channels. Nerve cells communicate by firing.

47

Neurotransmitters and behavior

Neurotransmitters are chemical messengers released in the brain, allowing communication between neurons. Neurotransmitters can excite or inhibit neurons. There are at least 50 identified neurotransmitters.

Neurotransmitters include acetylcholine, norepinephrine (adrenaline), dopamine, serotonin, and gamma-aminobutyric acid (GABA). Each neurotransmitter directly or indirectly affects neurons in specific brain regions, affecting behavior.

Acetylcholine and norepinephrine are *excitatory* neurotransmitters, while serotonin and GABA are *inhibitory* neurotransmitters, and dopamine may function as either, depending on where it acts and which receptor site it binds to.

Schizophrenia is a severe mental illness caused by *gene-environment interactions* leading to psychopathology. It causes disturbances in thinking, emotional reactions, and behaviors. It is characterized by positive symptoms or psychotic behaviors (e.g., delusions and hallucinations) and negative symptoms (e.g., flat affect, inability to experience pleasure, and lack of engagement in daily activities). *Chlorpromazine* and *Clozapine* block dopamine receptors in the brain to ease symptoms and aid the patient in being functional.

Depression affects about 3.5% of the human population. In depression, there is an excess of inhibition signals that control mood, thought, pain, and other sensations. Antidepressants are used to treat depression. These antidepressants affect norepinephrine and serotonin levels in the brain and aid in correcting abnormal neurotransmitter activity.

Prozac is a selective serotonin reuptake inhibitor (SSRI) that reestablishes the level of serotonin needed to function at an average level. SSRIs inhibit the reuptake of excess serotonin at the synaptic gap, increasing neurotransmitter activity in the synaptic cleft. This increased serotonin activity helps alleviate depressive symptoms.

Alzheimer's disease affects about four million Americans. This progressive brain disease causes memory loss and dementia, and eventually, the affected individuals cannot properly care for themselves. It is caused by the loss of cells that secrete acetylcholine in the basal forebrain. The basal forebrain is the portion of the brain that controls sensory and associative information processing and motor activities. There is no known treatment for this disease.

Generalized Anxiety disorder (GAD) causes excessive worry, which in turn interferes with daily tasks and functioning. Research has portrayed generalized anxiety disorder as involving many neurotransmitter systems in the brain, including norepinephrine and serotonin.

Attention-deficit/hyperactivity disorder (ADHD) causes hardships in attention, overactivity, impulse control, and distractibility. Dopamine and norepinephrine imbalances are strongly related to ADHD.

Effects of the Endocrine System on Behavior

Behavioral endocrinology

Behavioral endocrinology studies the interaction between hormones and behavior. Hormones are like neurotransmitters but can travel *via* the blood throughout the body. Hormones influence behaviors involving aggression, mating, and parenting.

Testosterone, estrogen, cortisol, and oxytocin are hormones influencing behavior and are vital to specific behaviors in the animal kingdom.

For example, sea slugs have an egg-laying hormone (ELH) that causes them to lay eggs. ELH excites the reproductive tract and causes egg expulsion, even if the sea slug has not mated. Hormones directly control the process of molting. Behaviors like these are instinctual, as they are innate and inherited.

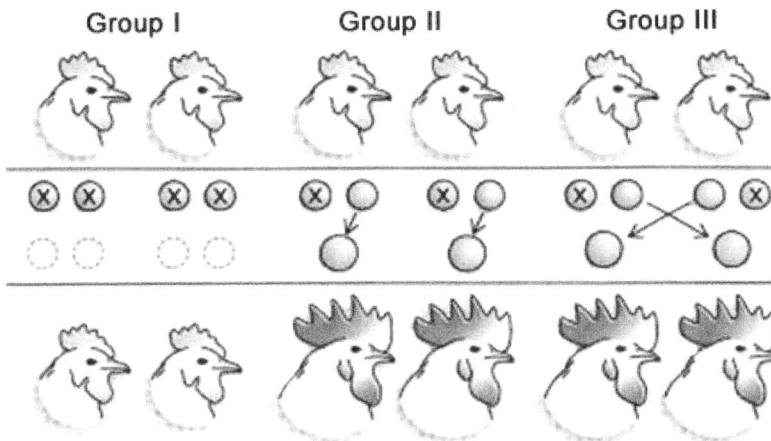

In what is considered the first endocrinological experiment, Arnold Berthold castrated three groups of birds. The first group was castrated with testes removed. The second group had testes removed, but one of each bird's testes was re-implanted into their abdominal cavity. The birds in the third group had their testes removed, and one testis from a different bird was transplanted into their abdominal cavities.

Birds in the first group were smaller than average and did not engage in typical rooster behavior.

Birds in the second and third groups were of average size and engaged in typical behaviors.

Berthold concluded that no specific nerves direct testicular function and proposed that there must be a "secretory blood-borne product," hormones.

Major hormones of behavior and emotions

Testosterone is an *androgenic steroid hormone* influencing aggressive and assertive behaviors. Evidence often cited for this claim is that males who tend to produce more testosterone are more aggressive than females, even across species. In humans, males produce ten times more testosterone than women and are convicted of violent crimes at a similarly higher rate, although some argue that this is due to socialization.

During puberty, when blood concentrations of androgens rise, aggressive behaviors tend to increase. Researchers have found that males and females with heightened levels of testosterone smile less than their low-testosterone counterparts, which suggests that testosterone is implicated in dominant behavior, distinct from aggressive behavior.

Estrogen

Estrogens are steroid hormones associated with female sexual and reproductive development. Although present in males, estrogens exist at much higher rates in females. They are vital in sexual behavior, as well as in mental health and eating patterns. In non-human mammals, a peak in estrogen induces estrus prior to ovulation. Female non-human mammals have no mating desire when not experiencing this peak in estrogen.

Estrogen is essential for mental health, although the exact influence and mechanisms are unknown. Mice that displayed obsessive-compulsive-like rituals decreased these behaviors when their estrogen levels were raised.

Women suffering from postpartum depression display symptom reduction after estrogen levels are stabilized. Estrogen has been theorized to influence eating behaviors, particularly binge eating behaviors. Estrogen replacement has been shown to suppress binge eating in female mice. Symptoms in women with *bulimia nervosa* fluctuate with their menstrual cycle, suggesting that estrogen levels may contribute to this disorder.

Cortisol

Cortisol is a steroid hormone associated with fight-or-flight behavior. Levels of cortisol increase during stress. Cortisol increases blood pressure and blood sugar levels and suppresses the immune system. Cortisol redistributes glucose to the brain and major muscles during a fight-or-flight situation. This can be seen as an adaptive process, as individuals experiencing this fight-or-flight response can behave quickly and efficiently to ensure survival.

Epinephrine

Epinephrine (also known as adrenaline) is a hormone produced by the adrenal glands and plays an essential role in the fight-or-flight response. It increases blood flow to muscles, cardiac output, and blood sugar level. The major emotion related to epinephrine is fear. If high amounts of the hormone are produced frequently (e.g., in response to stress), it may lead to poor sleep, anxiety and increased potential for heart damage.

Threat: an attack, harmful event, or threat to survival

Brain: the brain processes the signals- beginning in the amygdala, and then the hypothalamus

ACTH: pituitary gland secretes adrenocorticotropic hormone

Cortisol released   Adrenaline released

Physical Effects

Heart rate increase   Bladder relaxation   Tunnel vision

Shaking   Dilated pupils   Flushed face

Dry mouth   Slowed digestion   Hearing loss

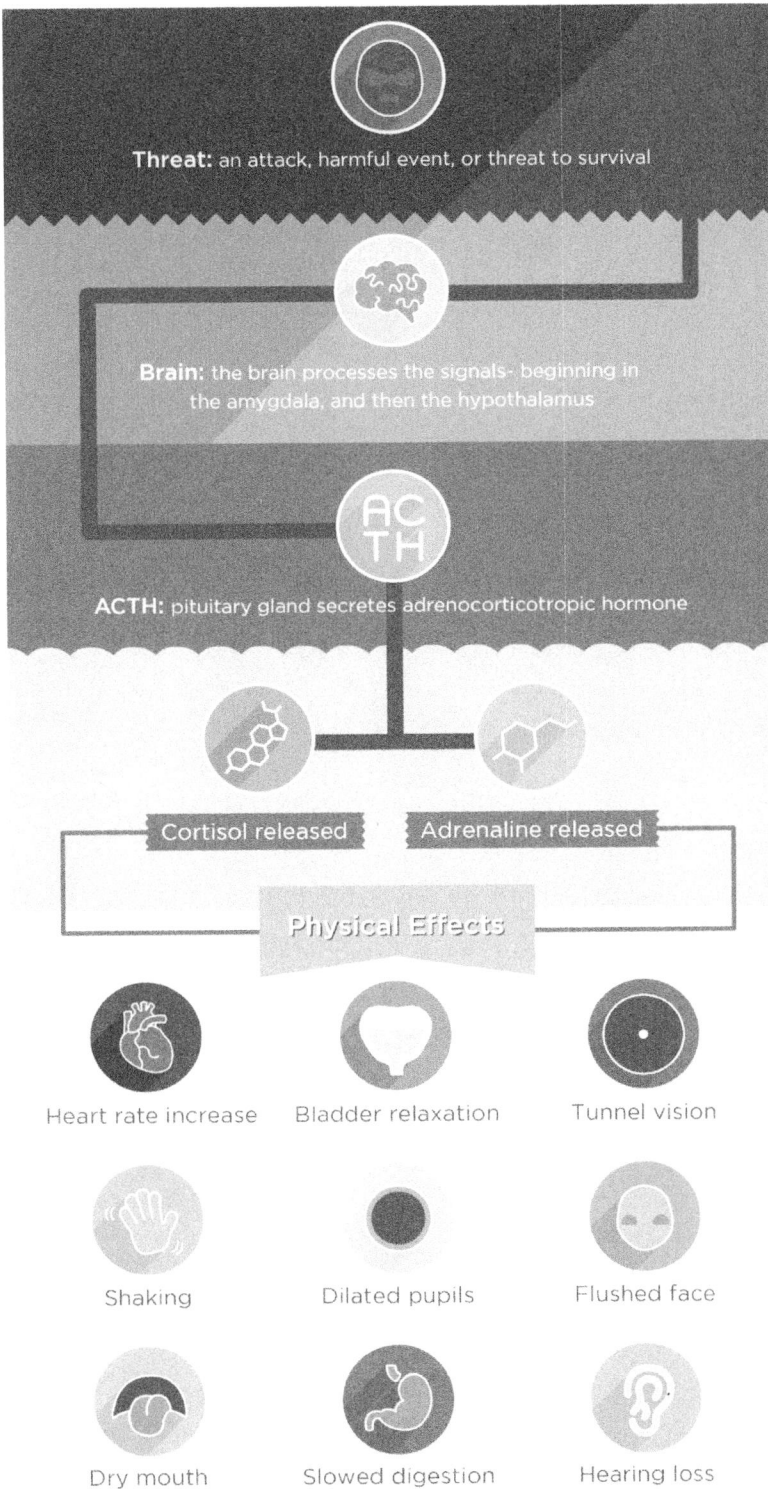

The fight-or-flight response involves the sympathetic nervous system

Oxytocin

Oxytocin is a peptide hormone that triggers lactation and social bonding, particularly influential in parenting behavior. Female rats receiving antagonists after giving birth do not behave in the typical maternal way. Oxytocin increases bonding by individuals with similar characteristics. It is vital for forming monogamous pair bonding in certain animals.

Behavioral Genetics

Temperament, heredity, and genes

Temperament is the aspect of personality believed to be innate (rather than learned) due to its emergence in infancy. Temperament is persistent throughout childhood and adulthood.

Behavioral genetics studies genetic factors underlying differences in temperaments. Genetic factors are determined by examining *heredity* and characteristics (i.e., traits) transmission from parent to offspring. These traits and characteristics are controlled by *genes* (or functional units) comprised of DNA that provide instructions for the creation of proteins.

Behavioral geneticists ask *mechanistic questions* that are answered by describing how an organism is biologically organized and equipped to behave.

Twin studies assess temperament differences in people with the same genetic makeup (DNA) to determine the effects of genes on temperament. It has been concluded that if identical twins are raised in dissimilar environments, as in the case of adoption, but share certain traits, those traits result from the influence of their shared genetic makeup and not the environment.

Adopted children can be compared to their adoptive parents to determine the role of environment on temperament. Studies using this method, however, have been criticized because there is evidence that peers rather than parents exert environmental influence.

Migratory bird studies provided early evidence that behavior has a genetic component. In an experiment by Andreas Helbig, German blackcaps fly southwest to Spain and northwest Africa. In contrast, Austrian blackcaps fly southeast to Israel and northwest Africa.

Helbig hypothesized that bird hybrids would fly an intermediary path if this behavior were genetically controlled. Indeed, hybrids in a funnel cage left directional marks intermediate to the parent birds' flight paths.

Adaptive value of traits and behaviors

Adaptive value is a trait, behavior, or characteristic positively affecting an organism's survival.

Behavioral ecology studies behavior and explains specific behaviors that increase fitness.

Behavior is the coordinated responses to internal and external stimuli; an organism's action changes its relationship to the environment. Since genes influence behavior, behavior evolves.

Behavioral ecologists examine behavior by asking *survival value questions* and determining how behavior helps animals exploit resources, avoid predators, or secure a mate.

Altruism is behavior benefiting another at its expense and is observed across many species.

While altruism may not initially appear to be an adaptive property, it has a genetic benefit known as *inclusive fitness,* the reproductive success of an individual plus close relatives.

Altruism helps relatives who can reproduce to survive. Squirrels, for example, sound an alarm when a predator approaches, putting themselves at risk to save many relatives.

Kin selection is an instance of inclusive fitness, which combines the number of offspring produced with the number an individual can produce by supporting others, such as siblings. Kin selection is the evolutionary strategy that favors the reproductive success of an organism's relatives, even at a cost to the organism's survival and reproduction.

Kin altruism is altruistic behavior whose evolution is driven by kin selection. Examples include honeybees that do not reproduce but leave that function to their relatives and the adoption of orphans within animal populations.

Social behavior is adaptive for many species. Some animals are solitary and join with a species member only to reproduce, while some pair, bond, and cooperate in raising offspring.

Sociobiology studies social behavior from an evolutionary and biological perspective. It is based on a reproductive cost-benefit analysis of the value of living in a society comprised of members organized cooperatively extending beyond sexual and parental behavior.

There are benefits and costs to living in a social group. Societies will only evolve if the benefits of reproductive success outweigh the disadvantages. Social groups such as herds, flocks, and schools provide concealment and defense against predators, thus increasing the chances of survival of the organisms within them. Packs are adaptive, enabling members to work together to trap prey. Lions, for example, work together to catch larger prey, such as buffalo.

Packs are adaptive, enabling members to work together to trap prey.

Dominance structures within social groups minimize fighting for food and mates. Dominance is determined by a confrontation where one animal gives way to another.

Agonist behavior (aggression and submission) is adaptive and originates from competition for food, mates, and territory. It is ritualized, so injuries and time spent in contests are minimized.

Territoriality (i.e., possession and defense of territory) is adaptive to ensure adequate food and a place to mate.

Mate selection can be viewed through a behavioral, ecological lens.

Reproductive behavior of males and females is adaptively related to anatomy and physiology.

Males, for example, produce sperm in great quantity and compete with males to inseminate many females. Females produce few eggs and are selective about mates.

Good genes hypothesis suggests selectivity promotes survival because females tend to select males with adaptive traits.

Run-away hypothesis asserts that females choose desirable traits because they are initially adaptive. However, these traits can become exaggerated until they become disadvantages. For example, selecting a mate due to brightly colored feathers makes an organism easily found by a predator.

Notes for active learning

Genetic and Environmental Influences on Behavior

Heredity and environmental interplay

Genetic and environmental factors combine to produce behavior. On average, genetics and the environment influence an organism's behavior. Note that these influences vary by trait and are challenging to quantify.

For example, the bidirectional nature of genes and the environment is illustrated by *phenylketonuria* (PKU). PKU is an inherited disorder that causes intellectual disability from the abnormal breakdown of the amino acid *phenylalanine*. A single gene controls PKU. Infants with this gene fed a diet low in phenylalanine did not develop an intellectual disability. This example illustrates the importance of the interaction between genes and the environment rather than the individual influence of each.

Gene-environment interaction models have been proposed for most psychopathologies.

Orchid/dandelion hypothesis is a recent proposal about the nature of depression. It states that groups of children can survive in good or unpleasant environments with little consequence because of their genetic makeup. These children are *"dandelions,"* which flourish anywhere. Another group of children is "orchids," which excel when placed in positive environments but become depressed in poor environments.

Orchid/dandelion hypothesis explains how genes contributing to depression persisted during evolution. Children with this environmental sensitivity are hypothesized to thrive when placed in positive environments, making it likely that their genes will be passed on.

Regulatory genes and behavior

Central dogma of molecular biology states that a DNA segment (i.e., a gene) encodes for ribonucleic acid (RNA), which then codes for one of 20 amino acids (i.e., building blocks of proteins). Proteins are considered the intermediate point between genes and behavior.

Regulator genes are genes that control the expression of one or more genes. About 95% of genes are regulator genes and do not code for proteins. Regulation occurs during transcription, post-transcription, and translation. Gene regulation does not directly affect the genetic code but regulates how proteins are encoded.

Environmental factors modulate gene expression and gene regulation. The human genome mapping (30,000 putative genes) has helped recognize the modulatory of gene expression. One field of interest that examines the interaction between nature and nurture is *epigenetics.*

Epigenetics studies changes in gene expression due to environmental factors. A recent study showed that childhood abuse could affect genetic expression, highlighting the implications of parental care on the epigenetic regulation of hippocampal glucocorticoid receptor expression.

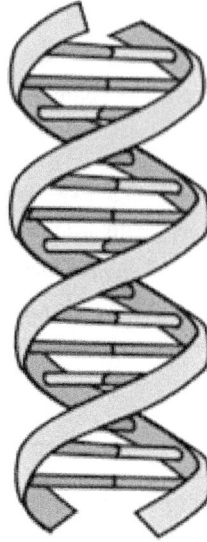

DNA molecule contains the individual's genetic code

Genetically based behavioral variation

Even within a species, genetic and behavioral variation can be observed.

The feeding behavior of garter snakes is an example. Steven Arnold tested garter snakes from different locations and found that inland garter snakes only fed on frogs and fish, refusing to feed on slugs. Coastal populations of garter snakes, however, readily fed on slugs.

Hybrid garter snakes showed an intermediate acceptance of slugs. Observation showed smell receptors and tongue flicks were indicated as physiological differences underlying this behavior.

Interactions between genes (internal) and the environment (external) cause behavioral variation.

Behavioral variation can be affected by epigenetics, which are molecular factors changing gene expression but *do not* change the DNA sequence (i.e., not inheritable by offspring).

Relationship matrix

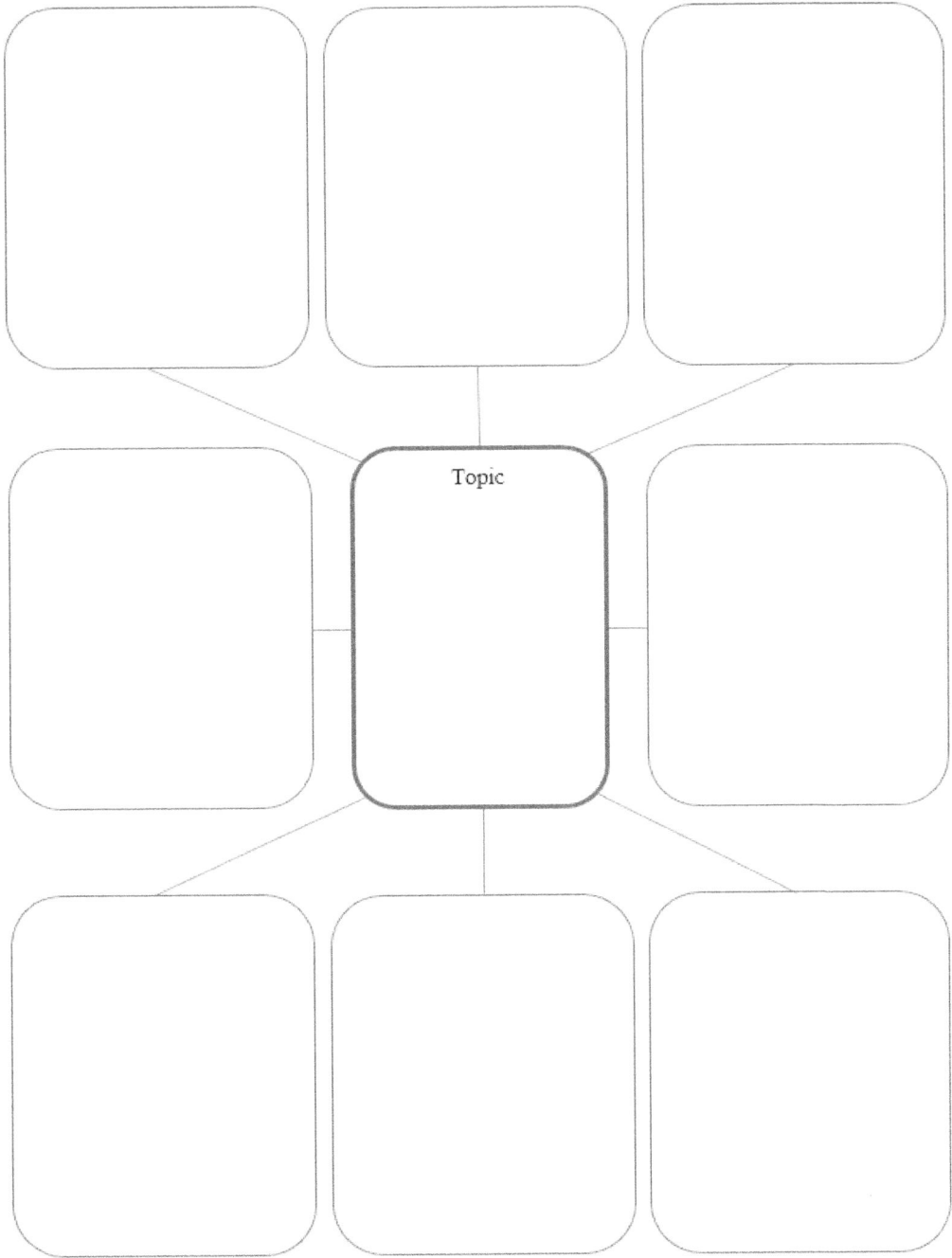

Topic

Notes for active learning

CHAPTER 3

Sensation & Perception

Sensation is the effect of environmental stimuli on sensory organs. Perception is a cognitive process and effect of sensory input interpretation; it can be dramatically shaped by top-down and bottom-up processing. Combined, sensation and perception provide the basis for every organism's awareness of its environment.

Senses share common properties, which use thresholds, adaptation, and transduction. The senses are varied, and each possesses its structures and functions. For example, vision is processed by the eyes and brain, while the ears and brain process hearing.

Sensation

Psychophysics

Psychophysics was founded in the mid-1800s by Gustav Theodor Fechner, a German physicist, psychologist, and philosopher. His experiments started the field of psychophysics and the broader field of experimental psychology.

Psychophysics is the quantitative study of the relationship between physical and psychological events. More specifically, it studies stimuli and resulting sensations and perceptions that they bring about. The primary areas of study within psychophysics are threshold, Weber's law, signal detection theory, and sensory adaptation.

Threshold

Threshold is the intensity that must be *exceeded* for a reaction.

Sensory threshold is the weakest stimulus detected 50% of the time.

Absolute threshold is the weakest stimulus detected with a certain percentage (often 50%) when there is initially no stimulus.

For example, a typical hearing test emits beeps with increasing volume. Test-takers indicate when they hear a beep. This test seeks to measure the subject's absolute threshold for hearing, which is why there is initially no sound.

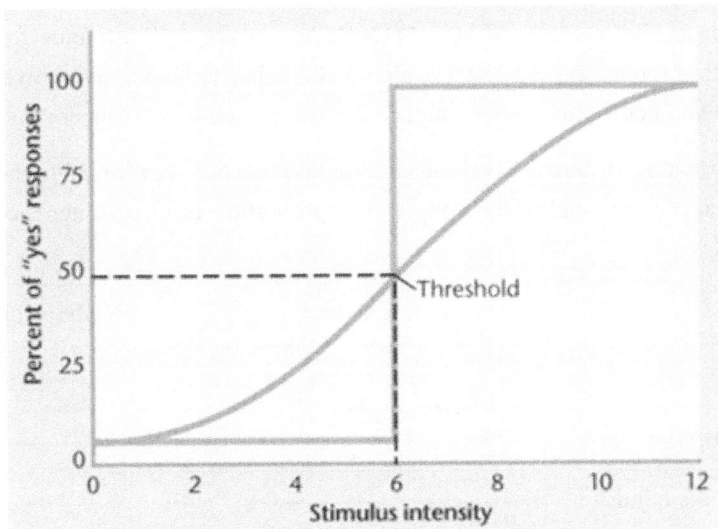

Sensory threshold vs. stimulus intensity

Differential threshold is the level at which an organism can perceive a change in an already-detected stimulus and detect it half of the time. It is the magnitude of the intensity change between the original and final stimuli.

For example, when a person notices an increase in room temperature. The differential threshold is the point at which this temperature difference is detected and subtracted by the original temperature.

Terminal threshold is the upper limit at which a stimulus can no longer be detected.

For example, if one touched a hot stove, the pain would be felt instead of heat because the terminal threshold for temperature has been exceeded.

The highest pitch that a person can hear is the *terminal threshold for pitc*h.

Weber's law

Initially proposed for weightlifting, *Weber's law* (German physician Ernst Heinrich Weber, founder of experimental psychology) posits that the differential threshold for an individual is dependent on *proportion,* not the amount.

For example, if a weightlifter notices when one pound is added to the ten-pound weight that he was lifting, then according to Weber's law, he would notice when two pounds are added to a twenty-pound weight.

For this reason, Weber's law is the *law of just noticeable differences.*

Weber's law was later applied to sensation. Although it does not hold entirely true for sound or extremely high or low-intensity stimuli, Weber's law is generally accurate for sight, touch, taste, and smell. A typical experiment in which Weber's law is supported involves having a test subject judge two lines, with one line longer. This is repeated with a longer set of lines.

Findings show that the difference in these larger lines must be proportional to the smaller lines for participants to notice that one is longer. The proportion of change necessary to notice a difference varies.

	Left is shorter	Right is longer
Obvious	—	——
Less obvious	————	————
Hard to distinguish	————	————

Law of just noticeable differences applies to other senses. A dog, for example, can detect much more subtle change in smell than humans.

Signal detection theory

Signal detection theory aims to uncover the internal and external mechanisms contributing to sensation and perception. It posits that detecting a given stimulus is partly dependent on the intensity of the stimulus. For example, a loud noise is more likely to be detected than a soft noise, and a temperature change of 10 °F is more likely to be detected than a change of 2 °F.

Signal detection theory proposes that the psychological state of the individual or animal experiencing the stimuli affects how it is perceived.

For example, someone walking alone at night in a bad neighborhood will likely experience a soft noise that is subjectively louder than if they had heard the same noise during the day. This significant theory notes that past experiences and expectations can influence our perception.

Signal detection theory has applications for understanding sensation by laboratory experiments.

Researchers often begin perception experiments with a *signal detection test*. In each test trial, a stimulus is presented (or withheld). The participant indicates whether they perceived a stimulus.

Receiver operating characteristic curve is plotted with repeated trials, providing information to the researchers on detecting various stimuli. This curve provides a unique baseline for each participant and allows researchers to study perception more accurately.

Sensory adaptation

Sensory systems are constantly recalibrating with feedback from the environment.

Sensory adaptation occurs when a constant stimulus is presented over time, and receptors respond by decreasing sensitivity. This ability of receptors to adapt is in sensory receptors, excluding *pain receptors*.

For example, a person does not notice the sensation of clothes on their skin because skin receptors have adapted to this constant stimulus by reducing their sensitivity.

Similarly, a friend's house may have a specific smell. However, the people living in the house often cannot detect it because they have been sensing it over time, and their olfactory receptors have adapted.

Sensory adaptation occurs in the visual system. When in the dark, the concentration of the light-sensing chemical in rods and cones of the eye increases, leading to increased sensitivity and the ability to see better.

Dark adaptation occurs in cones within ten minutes, while rods need thirty minutes.

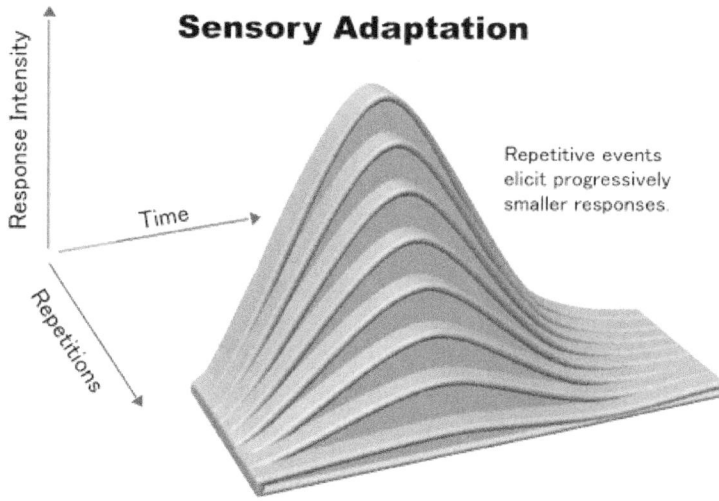

Sensory Adaptation

Response Intensity

Time

Repetitions

Repetitive events
elicit progressively
smaller responses.

Sensory adaptation decreases responses intensity of responses to repeating stimuli

Sensory Receptors

Stimulus

Type (or *modality*) is the first aspect of a stimulus. The stimulus is primarily coded for by the type of receptor that it activates. For example, taste is coded for by taste receptors, while odor receptors code for smell.

Intensity is when an increased stimulus produces a larger receptor potential, leading to higher action potential frequencies. Stronger stimuli affect a *larger area* and recruit *more receptors*.

Location is the site of the stimulated receptor.

Acuity is location precision and is negatively correlated with *convergence* in ascending neural pathways, the size of the *receptive field*, and *adjacent receptive field overlap*. Response and receptor density are highest at the center of the receptive field. Acuity is increased by *lateral inhibition*; excited neurons reduce the activity of adjacent neurons.

Duration is the fourth aspect of a stimulus with rapid and slow adapting receptors.

> *Rapid adapting receptors* respond at the stimulus onset but slow gradually during the remainder of the stimulus.

> *Slow-adapting receptors* respond at (or near) the initial firing level during stimulus duration.

Rapid adapting receptors are critical for signaling rapid change, while *slow adapting receptors* are essential for signaling slow changes.

Types of sensory receptors

Sensory receptors are nerve endings that respond to an internal or external stimulus.

Three classifications of sensory receptors: *receptor complexity*, *location*, and *stimulus detected*.

Complex receptors are encapsulated nerve endings with physical specialization (e.g., eyes).

Less complex receptors are free nerve endings; dendritic terminal ends have no specialization.

Exteroceptors are at or near the skin's surface, respond to stimuli on the body's surface, and code for tactile sensations, vision, hearing, smell, and taste.

Interoceptors respond to stimuli from the body, visceral organs, and blood vessels. For example, receptors within the GI tract carry signals to the brain relating to feelings of hunger. Interoceptors are associated with the *autonomic nervous system* (i.e., *rest and digestion*).

Proprioceptors respond to internal stimuli occurring in skeletal muscles, tendons, ligaments, and joints and detect the position of body parts.

Receptors are classified by the type of stimuli detected; receptors have five categories.

Mechanoreceptors respond to touch and pressure; rapid-adapting or slow-adapting receptors. They respond to pressure deeper in the dermis.

Photoreceptors respond to light.

Thermoreceptors respond to temperature and temperature changes. For example, one type of thermoreceptor responds to increases in temperature, while another responds to decreases.

Chemoreceptors respond to taste, smell, and changes in blood chemistry. They are found universally in animals, and chemoreception is among the most primitive senses.

Nociceptors respond to pain and tissue damage.

Mechanoreceptors	• Respond to touch and pressure
Photoreceptors	• Respond to light
Thermoreceptors	• Respond to temperature
Chemoreceptors	• Respond to taste, smell, and changes in blood chemistry
Nociceptors	• Respond to pain and tissue damage

Skin contains many receptors close to the surface (i.e., boundary of dermis and epidermis).

Proprioceptors, mechanoreceptors, photoreceptors, thermoreceptors, chemoreceptors, and nociceptors are *somatic sensors* in the *somatosensory system.*

Sensory pathways

Sensory unit is a single neuron and its receptor endings. When stimulated, a sensory unit activates its neuron's receptive field within the brain.

For example, when the receptive field of a retina's cells is stimulated, associated neurons in the visual cortex of the occipital lobe are activated so sensory input can be interpreted.

Specific pathways are needed for each of the senses and types of stimuli.

Ascending pathways carry sensory information through the spinal cord to higher brain levels. Via these pathways, information from taste cells is transmitted to the *parietal lobe*, from the eyes to the occipital lobe, and information from the ears is transmitted to the temporal lobe.

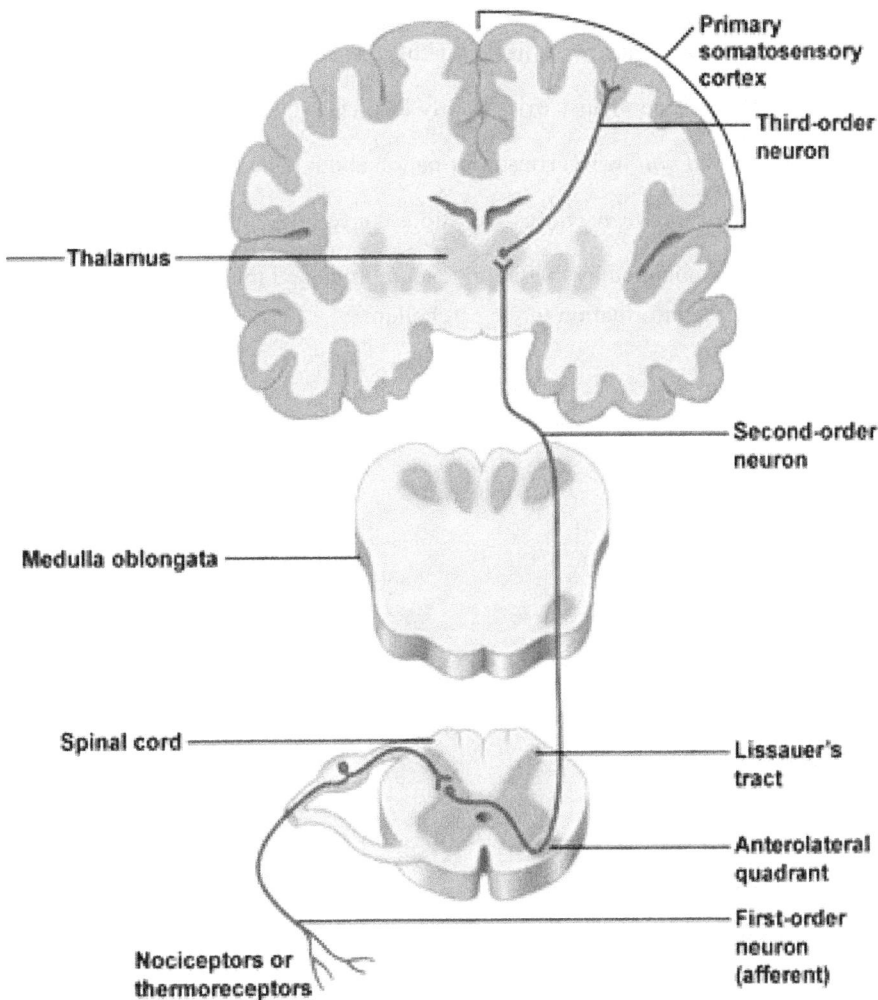

Ascending pathway with afferent, second and third-order neuron

Ascending pathways for tactile (or *touch*) sensations are the *posterior column pathway*, *anterolateral pathway*, and *spinocerebellar pathway*.

- *Posterior column pathway* carries delicate touch, vibration, pressure, and proprioceptive (position of body regions) sensations from the skin and joints.

  Information is transmitted to the postcentral gyrus of the cerebral cortex via first-order, second-order, and third-order neurons.

- *Anterolateral pathway* (*spinothalamic trac*t) carries pain, temperature, and poorly localized touch sensations.

  Information flows from the skin through the ventral posterolateral nucleus in the thalamus to the somatosensory cortex of the postcentral gyrus.

  Spinothalamic tract has two adjacent pathways: anterior and lateral pathways.

    Anterior pathway carries poorly localized touch sensations.

    Lateral pathway carries information about pain and temperature.

- *Spinocerebellar pathway* carries sensations concerning limb and joint position.

  Information is obtained by the Golgi tendon organ and muscle spindles, which then convey the information to the cerebellum.

Hearing

Ear structure and function

Human ear has three main parts: the *outer, middle,* and *inner*.

Outer ear is common when referring to the ear. It has a *pinna* and an *auditory canal*.

Pinna (or *auricle*) is the visible part of the external ear; it directs and amplifies sound waves.

Auditory canal is the ear's opening, lined with fine hairs that filter the air. It has modified sweat glands that secrete earwax (or *cerumen*) to guard against foreign matter.

Middle ear cavity is filled with air and has three small bones known collectively as *ossicles*.

Ossicle bones are the *malleus* (or hammer), *incus* (or anvil), and *stapes* (or stirrup).

Ossicles convert vibrations in *eardrum* (or *tympanic membrane*) into fluid waves in inner ear.

Auditory tube (or *eustachian tube*) extends from the middle ear to the pharynx to equalize pressure within the tympanic cavity with ambient air pressure.

Oval window (or *vestibular window*) is a membrane-covered middle and inner ear opening.

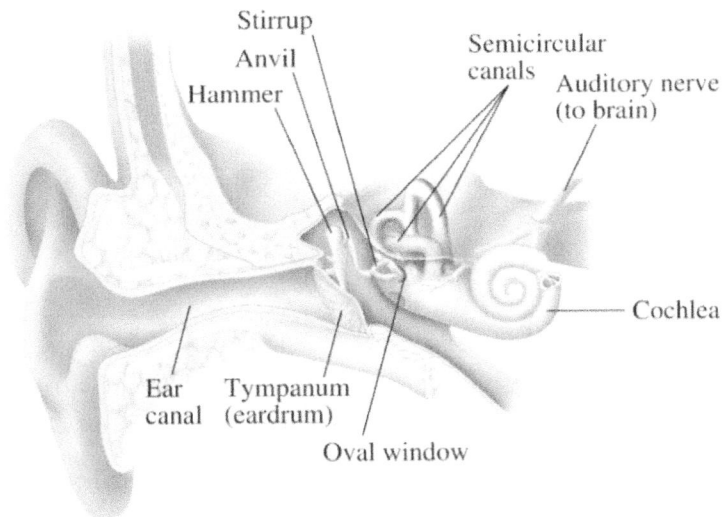

Ear structure with anatomical references

Inner ear contains the *bony labyrinth*, a hollow cavity in the skull's temporal bone.

Bony labyrinth has two main functional parts: the *cochlea* and *vestibular system*.

Cochlea is spiral-shaped and houses the cochlear duct, which contains the *organ of Corti*.

Organ of Corti has hair cells called *stereocilia*.

Afferent neurons from *stereocilia* hair cells form the *cochlear nerve*.

Upper compartment of the cochlea is the *scala vestibuli*, a fluid-filled cavity that conducts sound vibrations to the *cochlear duct*.

Cochlear duct converts vibrational energy into electrical energy and sends signals to the brain.

Vestibular system of the bony labyrinth has three perpendicular semicircular canals critical for the sense of balance.

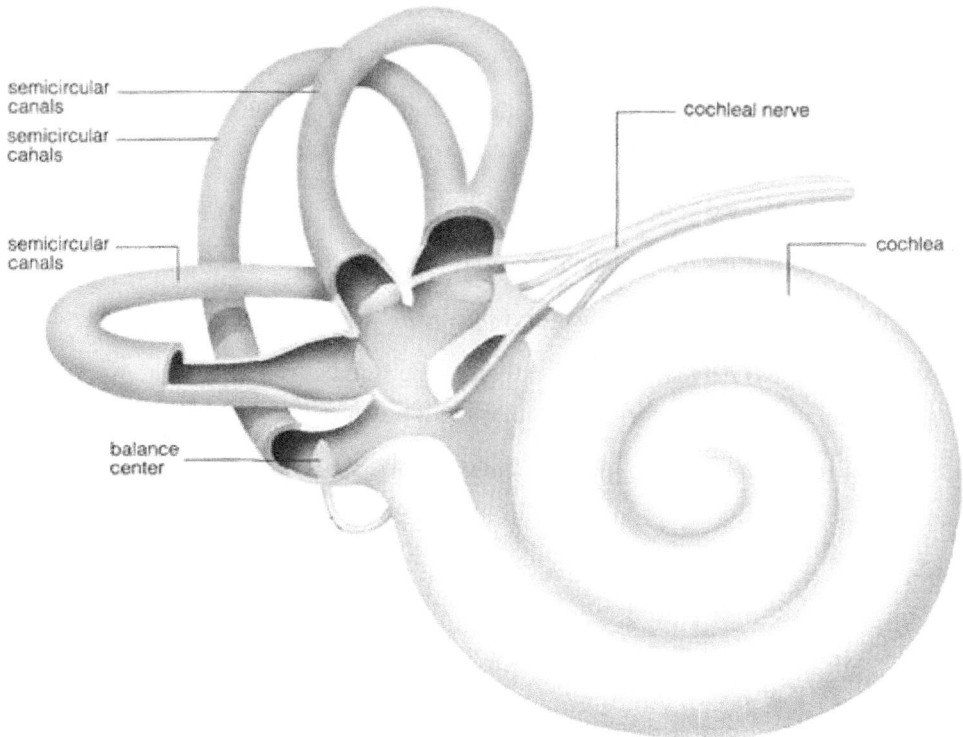

Vestibular system of the bony labyrinth

Sensory reception by hair cells

Hearing begins when sound waves enter the *auditory canal*, hitting the *tympanic membrane* (eardrum) and causing it to vibrate. These vibrations then move to the ossicles.

Sound is amplified about twenty times by the size difference between the *tympanic membrane* and the *oval window*.

Stapes strike the *oval window membrane*, passing pressure waves to the fluid in the cochlea.

When the stapes strikes the membrane of the oval window, pressure waves move from the vestibular canal to the tympanic canal and across the *basilar membrane*, the base for these hair cells, causing the *round window* to bulge, exciting *stereocilia*, which bend from the vibration of the basilar membrane.

Stereocilia bending generates nerve impulses in the *cochlear nerve* that travel to the brain stem.

Auditory processing

Nerve impulses from the cochlear nerve into the brainstem reach the cerebral cortex's auditory areas, and the information is interpreted as sound.

Sound interpretations occur via the *primary auditory pathway*, which initiates in the cochlea and moves through the *vestibulocochlear nerve* to the *superior olivary complex*.

Neurons carry impulses to the *mesencephalon*, a major structure forming the midbrain.

Primary auditory cortex finally receives the message.

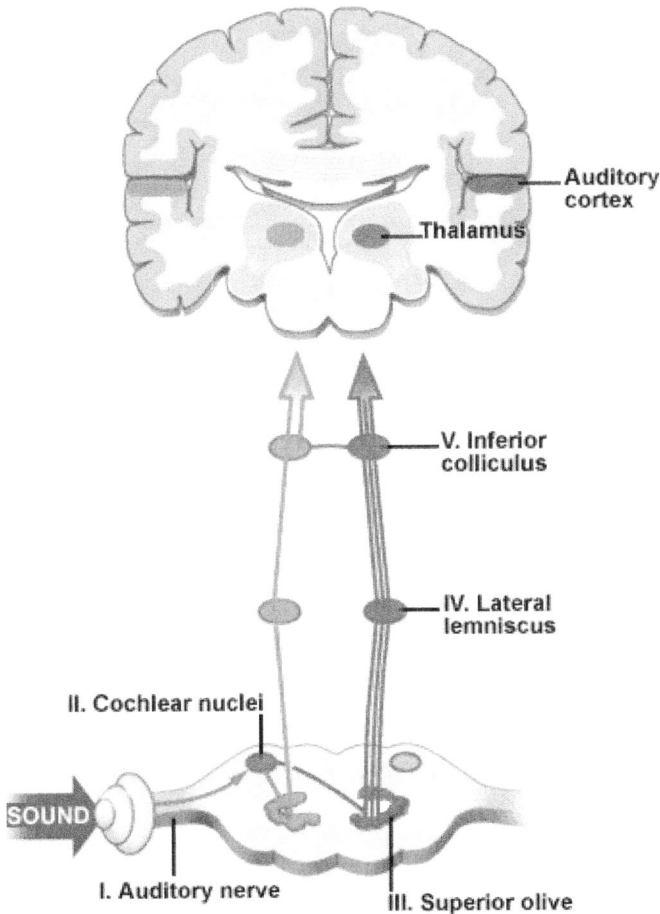

Auditory pathway

Organ of Corti is varied in structure so that different areas are sensitive to different *pitches*.

Nerve fibers from regions result in various activations, producing pitch sensation.

Organ of Corti's narrow base detects *high pitch*, while the wide tip detects *low pitch*.

Magnitude of vibrations detects sound *volume*. Increased stimulation of receptors is interpreted as louder, while decreased stimulation is softer.

Brain detects tone based on the *distribution of hair cells stimulated*, allowing differentiation of sounds (e.g., piano *vs.* violin) even if the instruments play the same tune with the same volume.

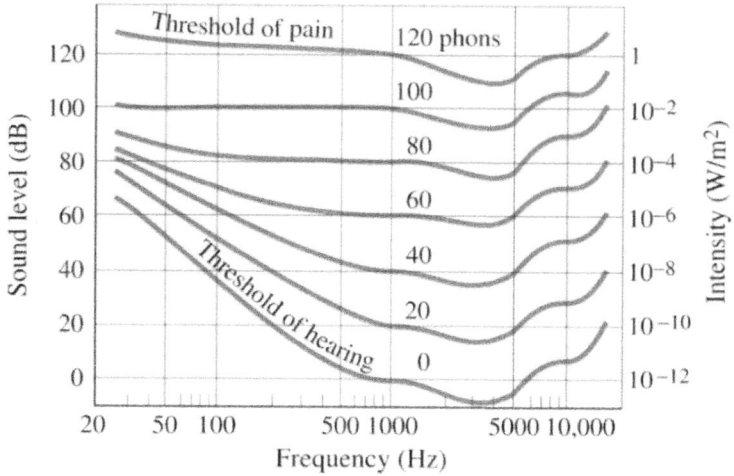

Sound level vs. frequency produces sound with various intensities

Vision

Eye structure and function

Human eye is an elongated sphere measuring 2.5 cm in diameter. Although many consider it like a camera, the eye is a considerably more complex network of interconnected parts.

Orbit contains the eye, a pear-shaped structure formed by several bones.

Sclera is the outer, white, fibrous layer that covers most of the eye for protection.

Cornea is the transparent part of the sclera at the front of the eye. It can be conceptualized as the *"window of the eye,"* which focuses light on the retina and acts as a protective covering.

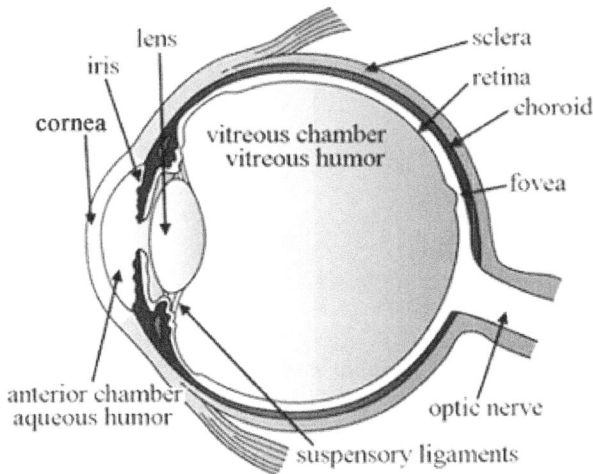

Pupil is the black circle in the middle of the eye that dilates and constricts in response to light. Pupil size determines the amount of light entering the eye.

Choroid is the deep brown inner layer of the eye, containing blood vessels and pigments that absorb stray light rays.

Choroid thickens to form a ring-shaped ciliary body, which becomes the *iris*.

Iris is the pigmented area (e.g., eye color) around the pupil, controlling the amount of light entering by dilating and constricting the pupil with the *papillary sphincter* and *dilator muscles*.

Stimulation of the sympathetic nerves dilates the pupil to let in more light when the environment is dark. In contrast, stimulation of the parasympathetic nerves constricts the pupil to allow less light in bright environments.

Lens is behind the iris and aids in focusing refracted light onto the retina. It divides the eye into two chambers: the *aqueous humor* and the *vitreous humor*.

Aqueous humor nourishes the cornea and fills the anterior cavity.

Blocking of outflow of the aqueous humor results in increased pressure in the eye, or *glaucoma*.

Vitreous humor is jelly-like, protecting the eye's shape and filling the posterior cavity.

Lens focuses light onto the retina by thickening (to focus on nearby objects) and thinning (to focus on distant objects).

Retina is a thin layer of tissue behind the lens that interprets visual stimuli. The retina contains blood vessels and cells that sense light. Specifically, it contains the *fovea centralis*, which produces color vision in daylight. Considerable processing occurs in the retina before an impulse is sent to the brain.

Myopia (or *nearsightedness*) is seeing objects well when close but not when away. Myopia is often due to an elongated eyeball that focuses a distant image in front of the retina. Radial keratotomy surgically cuts and flattens the cornea to correct this issue.

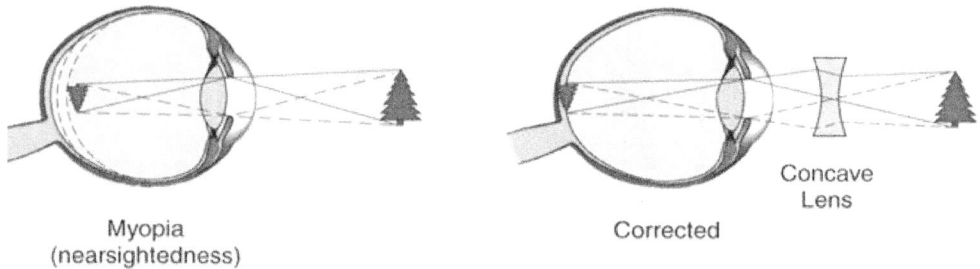

Myopia
(nearsightedness)

Concave
Lens

Corrected

Myopia or nearsightedness

Hyperopia (or *farsightedness*) is seeing objects well when far away but not close. It is often due to a shortened eyeball that focuses images behind the retina.

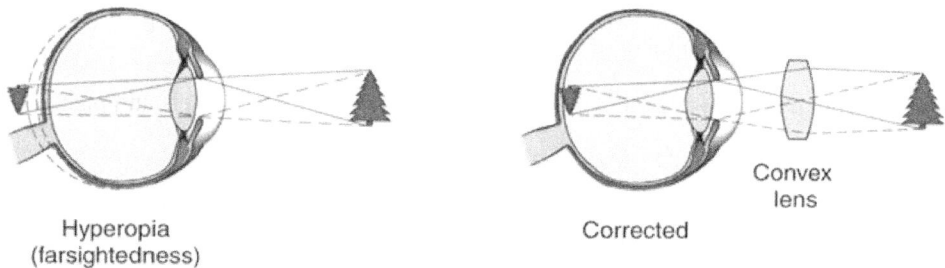

Hyperopia
(farsightedness)

Convex
lens

Corrected

Hyperopia or farsightedness

Astigmatism occurs when the cornea or lens is uneven, causing images to become blurry.

Cataracts are when the lens becomes opaque due to new cells forming within it. Diminished light enters through the lens.

Presbyopia is vision loss when (often due to age) the lens loses elasticity and cannot assume a spherical shape, causing near vision to be lost.

Light receptors

Vision begins when light becomes focused on photoreceptors in the retina.

Photoreceptor cells sense light. In their simplest form, photoreceptors only detect the presence and intensity of light.

Human vision is much more complex. Photoreceptors on the back of the retina pick up photons of light via the 130,000,000 rods and cones.

Photoreceptors sense light because they contain *photopigments*, which absorb light.

Four photopigments are rhodopsin, blue-sensitive, green-sensitive, and red-sensitive pigments.

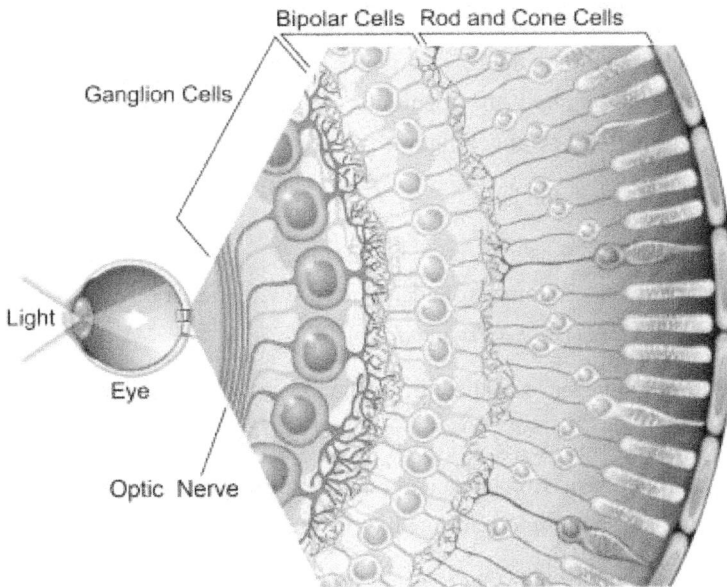

Cross-section of ganglion, bipolar, rod, and cone cells

Photopigments are contained within two types of photoreceptors: rods and cones.

Rods and cones have an outer segment joined to an inner segment by a stalk.

Outer segment has stacks of *lamellae*, membranous disks with many rhodopsin molecules.

Rhodopsin has protein *opsin* and pigment *retinal* (or *chromatophore*) derived from vitamin A.

Cones are responsible for *sharp* and *color vision*. They are primarily located in the *macula*, an extremely sensitive area of the retina. Specifically, cones are in the *fovea*, an area within the macula.

Three types of cones contain blue, green, or red pigment composed of rhodopsin and opsin, with varying structures of opsin allowing for the absorption of different wavelengths of light.

Intermediate colors stimulate combinations of cones; the brain interprets the combined nerve impulses as one of 17,000 hues.

Humans and other primates are the only animals with color vision ability.

Rods are responsible for peripheral and night vision. They are more sensitive to light than cones but do not provide detailed or color images. When a rod absorbs light, rhodopsin splits into opsin and retinal, leading to the closure of ion channels in the rod cell plasma membrane. This produces signals that result in impulses to the brain.

Rods are grouped outside the macula in the periphery of the retina.

Visual image processing

Light rays enter the eye through the *cornea*, which bends them due to its curved surface so they can freely pass through the pupil (the opening in the center of the iris with the ability to dilate and constrict depending on how much light is passing through).

Light rays then pass through the lens.

Ciliary muscle controls the lens's shap*e*, which relaxes when viewing distant objects, causing the lens to flatten. The lens becomes rounder when viewing near objects where light rays must bend more. This change is *visual accommodation*.

Light rays pass through the lens and the vitreous humor to focus on the retina. Due to refraction, the image on the retina is inverted 180 degrees, later corrected in the brain.

Once the light has been sensed by rods and cones within the retina, this sensory information must be transmitted to the brain to translate into vision.

Retina has three layers of neurons that transmit information:

> *rods and cones* near the choroid,
>
> *bipolar cells*, and
>
> *ganglion cells*.

Since only rod and cone cells are light-sensitive, light must penetrate the ganglion cells.

When a rod absorbs light, rhodopsin splits into opsin and retinal, a cascade reaction and closure of ion channels in the rod cell plasma membrane. This stops the release of inhibitory molecules from the rod's synaptic vesicles, which starts signals that result in impulses to the brain.

Rods and cones synapse with bipolar cells, creating a hyperpolarization that activates the retinal (the pigment molecule) and causes it to change shape.

After retinal is activated, it returns to its resting shape, and the photoreceptor cell is depolarized.

Bipolar cells pass information to ganglion cells; through this process, *integration occurs*.

Many rods can synapse with a single ganglion cell, resulting in indistinct vision.

Each cone cell, however, only synapses with one ganglion cell, resulting in clear vision. There are more rods and cones than nerve fibers leaving ganglionic cells.

Receptive field rod cell stimulation causes ganglion cells to be weakly stimulated or (remain neutral).

If the receptive field *center* is lit, the ganglion cell is *stimulated*.

If only the *edges* of the receptive field are lit, the ganglion cell is *inhibited*.

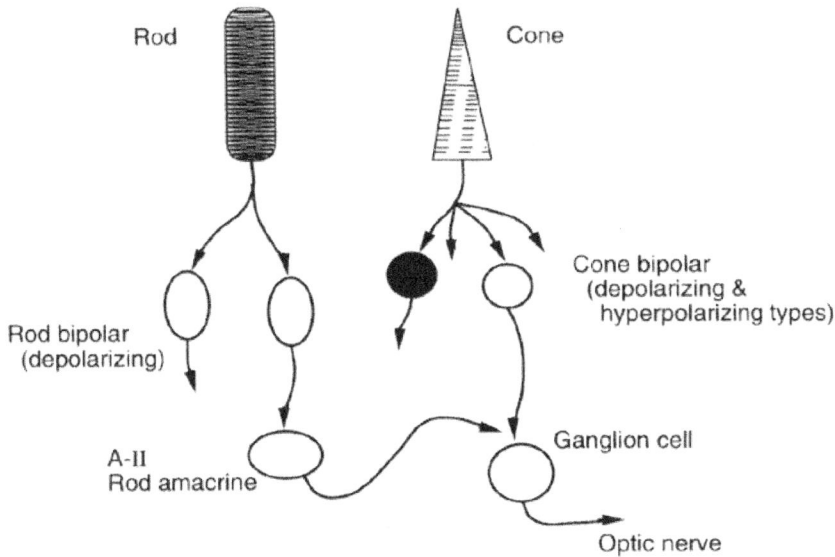

Rods and cones generate signals transmitted via the optic nerve

Visual pathways in the brain

Historically, visual perception was believed to encompass only what was seen externally by the eye. It was believed that these external stimuli directly produce a perception in the brain.

However, it is now known that information from the eye is simply a physiological process; significant processing of the signals that the eye receives occurs in the brain.

Ganglion cells produce an action potential for these signals to reach the brain, the first step in the pathway from the eye to the brain.

Axons from the ganglion cells come together to form the *optic nerve*.

Optic nerve is a pathway that crosses to the opposite side of the brain at the *optic chiasm*.

Thus, information from the right side of the visual field is sent to the left half of the brain, and information from the left side of the visual field is sent to the right half of the brain.

Blind spot is where the optic nerve passes through the retina and lacks rods and cones. The brain combines information from both eyes to compensate for this blind spot.

Information from the optic nerve travels through the optic tract and terminates in the lateral geniculate nucleus in the thalamus.

Information is then sent from the thalamus to the visual cortex in the occipital lobe. Here, a visual association area compares new visual information with old information.

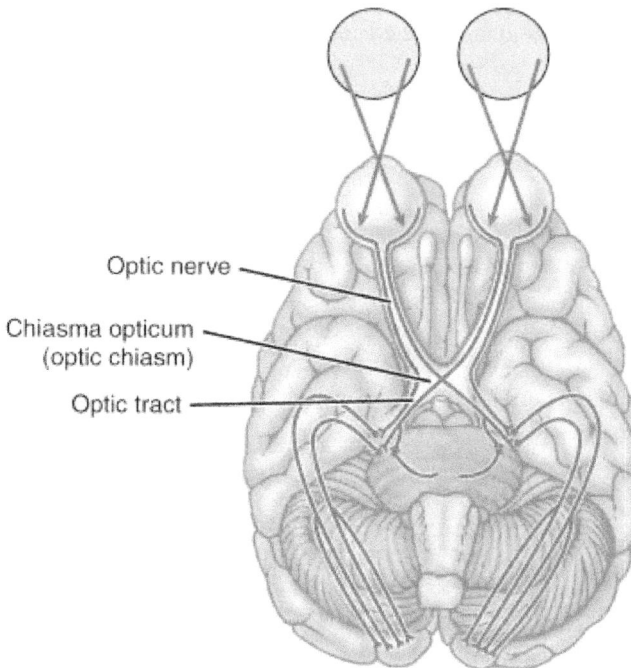

Optic nerve

Chiasma opticum (optic chiasm)

Optic tract

Vision reception and transmission via the optic nerve

Once visual information has been transmitted through this pathway; the brain can process the inverted image from the retina and make it appear upright. The brain combines the images from each eye to form a 3D image used to judge distance.

Parallel processing

Parallel processing is the brain's ability to simultaneously process differing-quality stimuli, helping people perceive the world in a unified way rather than disjointed pieces.

Information is divided into *color, motion, shape,* and *depth of field*.

Each component is analyzed individually by the brain, and new information is compared with stored memories to identify better the stimuli being processed.

These four components (i.e., color, motion, shape, and depth) are then integrated to form a complete image without analyzing each component individually.

It is hypothesized that before these separate processes integrate, they are stored as memories to aid in recognizing the image.

Parallel processing is rooted in cognitive psychology, which studies mental functions and views the brain as analogous to a complex computer.

Parallel processing concept applies beyond sensation to other cognitive psychology processes: *attention*, *memory*, *perception*, *language*, and *metacognition.*

Feature detection

Feature detection is how the brain filters visual information for important objects. It can be conceptualized as focusing on common elements across various aspects of an object.

For example, seeing ten cats, each a distinct size and color, the brain knows they are all cats.

Similarly, regardless of font, one can identify the letter "a" below.

a a a a a a a

Feature detection identifies common elements for processing

It is hypothesized that this process is done via *feature detectors*, specialized neurons in the visual cortex that code for certain features such as lines, angles, and movements.

Feature detection occurs for distinctive features simultaneously, a type of parallel processing. It passes information to higher-level brain cells, which then process it to form a complete image.

An alternative hypothesis to feature detection proposes that groups of cells, rather than individual cells, function as a network to detect certain features.

Notes for active learning

Smell

Olfactory cells

Olfactory cells are modified bipolar neurons located in the *epithelium* (mucous membrane) on the roof of the nasal cavity. Olfactory cells are *chemoreceptors* because they detect chemicals.

Humans have about 40 million olfactory cells that detect over one trillion odors.

Olfactory cells are covered in tufts of long, non-motile cilia that contain receptor proteins for an odor molecule. Each *olfactory cell* contains only *one type of odor receptor*.

There are approximately 1,000 distinct types of odor receptors.

When chemicals enter the nostrils, they are trapped in the mucus of the nasal cavity, where they then dissolve. These molecules then bind to receptors on the cilia, causing cell depolarization and creating an action potential.

Axons of olfactory receptor cells of the same specificity synapse together. Information is passed to the olfactory cortex within the limbic system through a specific pathway in the brain.

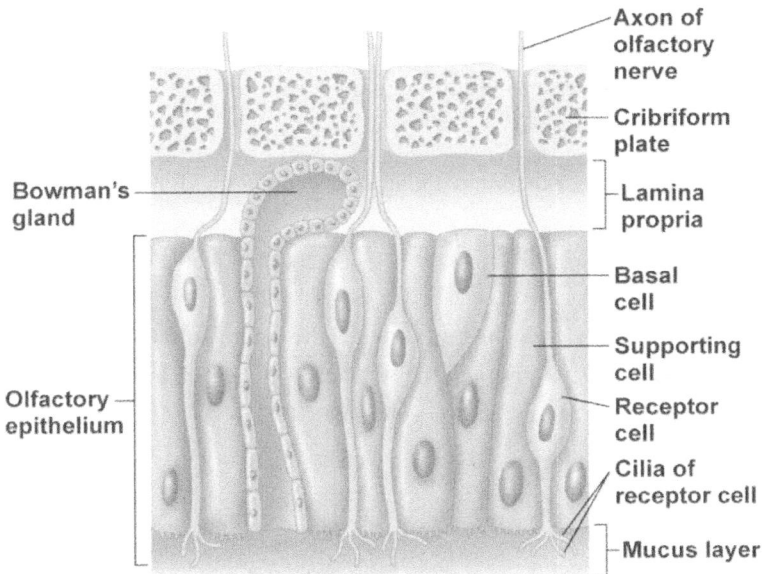

Olfaction and associated cells

Sense of taste supplements the sense of smell, as the same substances often stimulate the receptors for taste and smell.

When one loses the sense of taste from a cold, this is often due to losing the sense of smell.

Pheromones

Pheromones are chemicals secreted in sweat and other bodily fluids that influence the organism's body, secreting them and other organisms around. Pheromones are crucial in the behavior of many animals, particularly for sex, fear, and food.

Pheromones participate in mate attraction; some organisms can release pheromones that attract potential mates from over two miles away. Pheromones have a role in territory marking; dogs and cats spray their pheromone-filled urine on objects.

Research suggests that pheromones influence human behavior. A study by Martha McClintock suggested that women's menstrual cycle could be sped up or slowed down, depending on the pheromones women are exposed to. The methodology of this study has been questioned. It is hypothesized that women prefer the smell of men with genetically coded immunity (i.e., innate immunity), which is different from them and results in disease-resistant children.

Olfactory membranes and *vomeronasal organs* detect pheromones in non-human animals. In adult humans, the vomeronasal organ appears shrunk or absent, suggesting that humans can sense pheromones through the regular olfactory process.

Olfactory pathways in the brain

Olfactory pathway is not well understood; however, once the cilia detects sensory information, it gets transferred to the olfactory bulb through openings in the cribriform plate, a part of the skull at the top of the nasal cavity.

Olfactory bulb is at the base of the brain and in direct contact with the limbic system.

Connection of the olfactory bulb with the limbic system is hypothesized as to why smells are associated with emotions and memories.

Information in the olfactory bulb moves through the lateral olfactory tract to the primary olfactory cortex, then travels through the thalamus, where interneurons relay it to the orbitofrontal cortex for conscious smell perception.

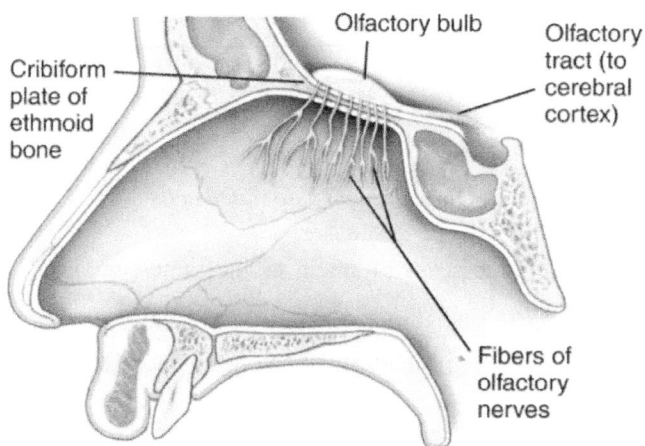

Other Senses

Somatosensation

Somatosensation is the broad sensory system of touch, specifically temperature, pain, vibration, and body position; the types of receptors that are part of the somatosensory system include nociceptors, thermoreceptors, proprioceptors, and mechanoreceptors, as previously described.

In general, a somatosensory pathway has *three long neurons.*

The first neuron's cell body is in the *dorsal root ganglion* of the spinal nerve.

The second neuron's cell body is in the *spinal cord* or *brainstem*. Axons of these neurons cross to the opposite side of the spinal cord or brainstem and usually terminate in the thalamus.

The third neuron usually has its cell body in the *ventral posterior nucleus* (VPN) of the thalamus, and it ends in the *lateral postcentral gyrus* in the *parietal lobe* of the cerebral cortex, where the processing aspect of somatosensation primarily occurs.

Taste

Sense of taste is instrumental from an evolutionary perspective. Foods that are potentially harmful taste bitter, while high-calorie foods taste sweet, thus increasing an organism's chance of survival. This sense begins with *taste buds*, as they contain the receptors for taste.

Taste buds are primarily on the tongue, specifically along the walls of *papillae*, with small elevations on the tongue's surface. Isolated taste buds are on the surfaces of the hard palate, pharynx, and epiglottis, contained by *epithelium*.

Taste buds contain multiple taste cells, each opening at a taste pore, where food particles dissolve in saliva contact taste receptors.

Taste receptors detect five elements of taste: sweet, sour, salty, bitter, and umami (i.e., savory).

Taste buds are concentrated in tongue regions, and elements organize into independent pathways. The brain takes a weighted average of taste messages to form the perceived taste.

Taste is *chemoreception* because chemical signals are transduced into action potentials.

Elongated taste cells contain hair-like *microvilli* with receptor proteins, which sense certain chemicals with microvilli, releasing neurotransmitters to signal to the brain.

Primary sensory axons for taste run through the facial, glossopharyngeal, and vagus nerves.

This information is primarily transmitted to the gustatory cortex in the neocortex. Taste information then moves through the thalamus and is received by two regions of the frontal lobe: the insula and the frontal operculum cortex.

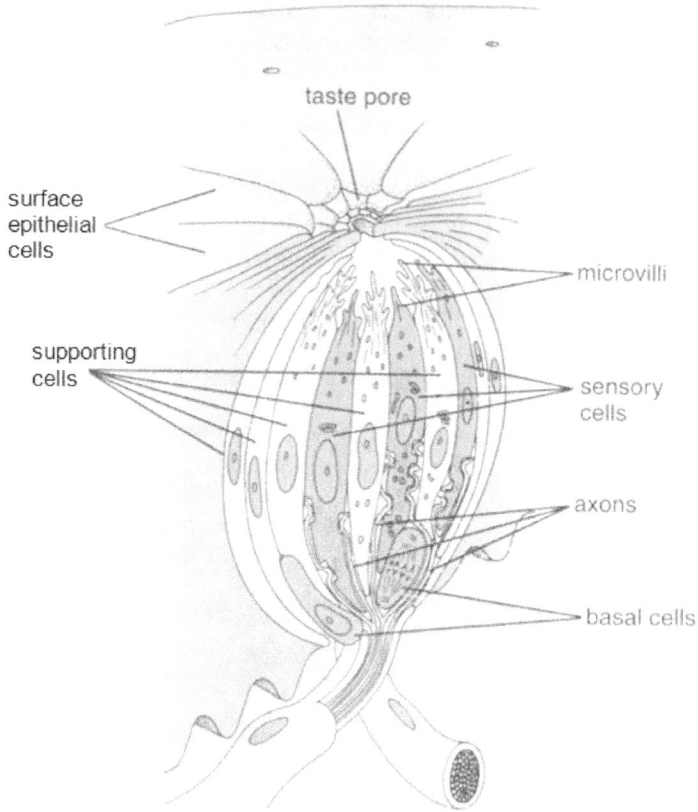

Taste pores initiate taste sensation

Kinesthetic sense

Kinesthetic sense (or *proprioception*) is the body's perception of position, including the movement of joints, muscles, and tendons.

Even with eyes closed, the brain can sense where various body parts are.

Kinesthetic sense provides constant feedback to the brain about muscles and relative position.

Much of this information is subconscious and without awareness.

Proprioceptors provide sensory information about joint angle, muscle length, and muscle tension. Information from the body is transmitted from these proprioceptors to the parietal cortex of the brain, where information about the position of body parts can be interpreted.

The channel through which this information transmission occurs has yet to be discovered, although it is hypothesized to be a similar pathway to that of touch.

Vestibular sense

Vestibular sense is the awareness of balance and spatial orientation.

Sensory information primarily originates in the inner ear, but visual and proprioceptive information is also used.

Processes for the sense of balance include *dynamic* and *static equilibrium*.

Dynamic equilibrium refers to the rotational movement of the head and utilizes the semicircular canals. The enlarged bases of the canals are *ampullae*.

Fluid within the canals causes the stereocilia of the hair cells to bend.

Vestibular nerve carries this information to the brain.

Dynamic and static equilibrium

Static equilibrium detects vertical and horizontal movement of the head relative to gravity.

Static equilibrium uses the utricle and saccule of *maculae* (i.e., mechanoreceptors) within them.

Utricle and *saccule* are tiny membranous sacs with hair cells.

Utricle is sensitive to horizontal movements, while *saccule* is sensitive to vertical movements. Small carbon granules resting on a gelatinous membrane with hair cells are displaced during movement, bending the hair cells and indicating the direction of movement.

Information from static and dynamic equilibrium hair cells is transmitted to the *parietal lobe*.

Parietal lobe integrates sensory information from other body areas to provide a complete sense of movement and balance.

Notes for active learning

Perception

Top-down processing

The brain uses top-down and bottom-up processing to integrate and understand stimuli.

Top-down processing is when perceptions form from larger concepts to specific information.

Top-down processing (*concept-driven processing*) is outside conscious awareness when an incomplete image or word (e.g., the image below) forms by filling in the missing details.

Top-down processing affects sensation. For example, if a boy enters a pizza shop and smells something ambiguous, he will likely identify it as the smell of pizza because of expectations.

When expectations or prior knowledge influence perception, top-down processing occurs.

Top-down processing (or concept-driven processing) permits the mind to complete the image

Bottom-up processing

Bottom-up processing occurs in the direction opposite top-down processing. This process starts with sensory information and then moves to higher-level processing.

Bottom-up processing is known as *data-driven processing*.

For example, if one accidentally places their hand on a hot stove, the reaction will be to pull away quickly without consciously deciding.

Processing moved directly from the stimulus (e.g., pain) to action (e.g., retracting hand); therefore, bottom-up processing occurred.

Debate surrounds how sensory systems rely on top-down processing *vs.* bottom-up processing. Researchers have thus turned to neurobiology to answer these questions.

Specific brain regions have more bottom-up connections, and others have more top-down connections.

Primary visual cortex contains primarily bottom-up connections.

Fusiform gyrus (part of temporal and occipital lobes) may be involved in top-down processing.

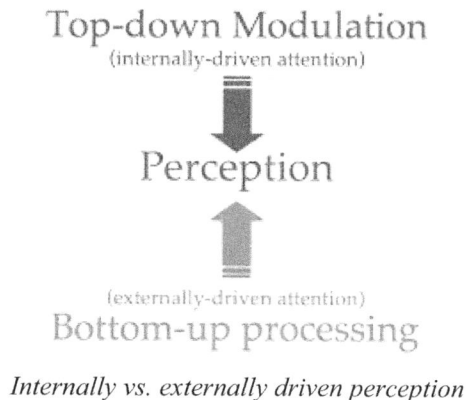

Top-down Modulation
(internally-driven attention)

Perception

(externally-driven attention)
Bottom-up processing

Internally vs. externally driven perception

Perceptual organization

An organism's environment is three-dimensional; thus, a three-dimensional approach is needed to understand it.

Eyes measure three dimensions: height, width, and depth.

Organisms conceptualize these properties by processing sensory information within the brain.

For example, the brain uses many rules and principles to determine the depth of an object.

One rule concerns *relative size*, meaning smaller objects tend to be perceived farther away.

Interposition means that objects that block other objects are perceived as closer.

Relative clarity is the principle that objects with a clear image are perceived as closer than objects with a hazy image. Objects higher in the visual field are perceived as farther away.

Parallel lines appear to converge with distance, giving the perception of depth. The brain uses shading to inform depth perception; dimmer objects often seem farther away.

Brain uses rules and principles to determine an object's motion. The images of objects traveling toward the eye appear to grow, while the images of objects traveling away appear to shrink.

Phi phenomenon is an optical illusion whereby one perceives a continuous motion between objects flashing at a certain speed.

Form perception is identifying a form despite a new image being displayed on the retina. During visual processing, information is formatted to draw out relevant and detailed information from a stimulus. Although this process is not fully understood, it occurs in *ventral* and *dorsal streams*.

Constancy is the ability to perceive objects as unchanging, even when the retinal image changes. For example, people identify their friends even when seeing them from different angles and do not think they have transformed into different people just because they have turned around.

Gestalt principles

Gestalt [German, to *shape* (or *form*)] refers to an *organized* or *unified whole*.

Gestalt psychology posits that *the whole is greater than the sum of its parts*, thus emphasizing *top-down processing*.

Gestalt psychology seeks to understand how organisms perceive meaning out of meaningless stimuli, particularly visual stimuli.

Several Gestalt principles describe how humans perceive "wholes" from parts.

Gestalt principles are categorized into *similarity, continuation, closure, proximity*, and *figure*.

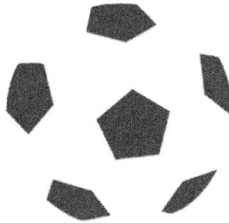

Gestalt principles complete the image

Similarity principle is that when an image has similar elements, these elements are integrated into groups, and each group is perceived as a single unit.

Principle of continuation is that groups aligned tend to be perceived as wholes.

Closure principle states that when an image is incomplete, if enough of the image is present, the mind fills in the gaps, and the image is perceived as a whole.

Proximity principle is that items tend to be perceived as a single group when close.

Figure principle is the tendency to differentiate an object from its surroundings by perceiving the object as a figure and the surroundings as a background.

Relationship matrix

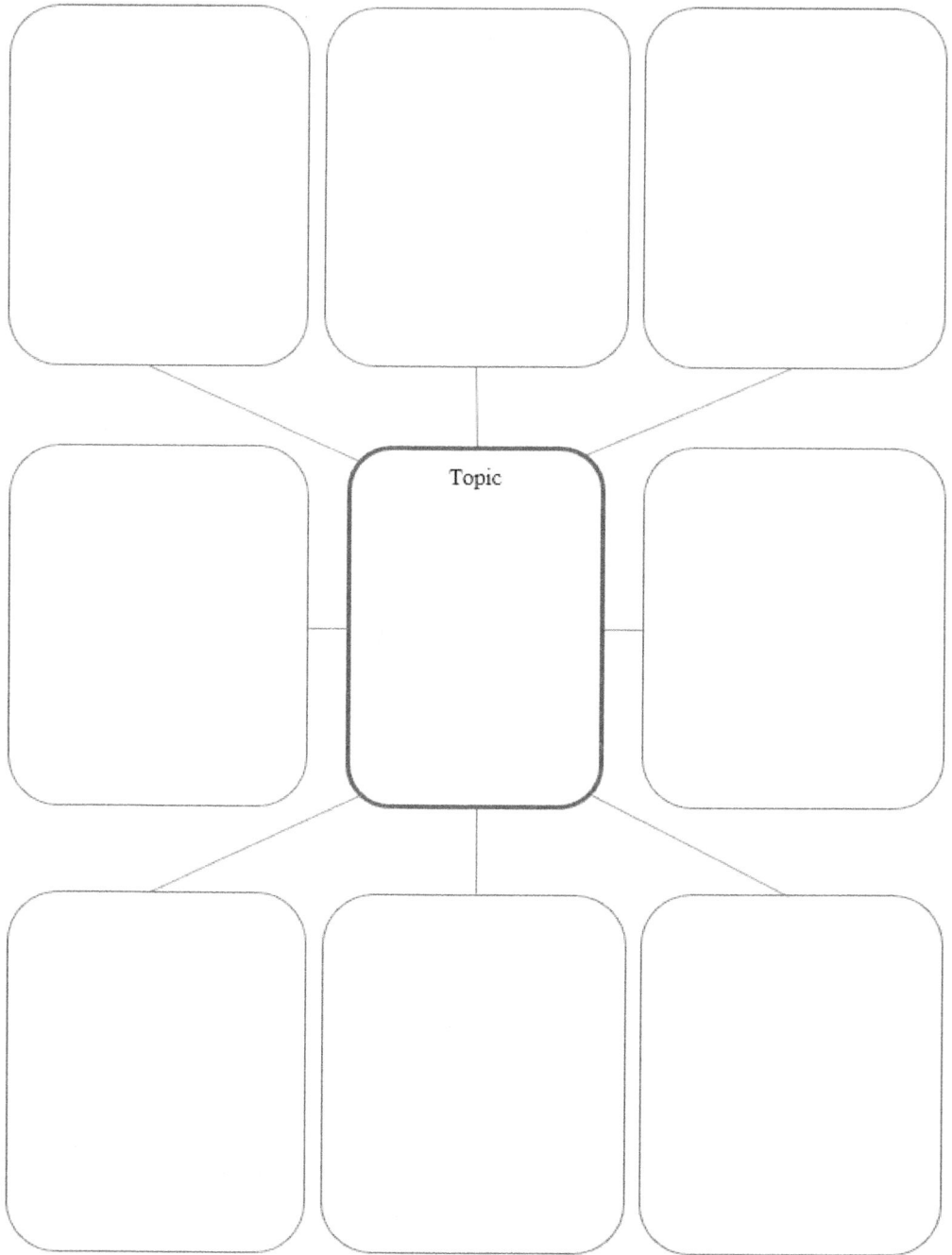

Topic

Notes for active learning

Notes for active learning

CHAPTER 4

Learning

Changes in behavior can be learned or unlearned. Conversations about learning are evoked in exploring the differences between the types of behavior change. This process can be categorized as classical conditioning, operant conditioning, and observational learning.

Biological bases of behavior expose hereditary influences for learning. Common learning phenomena are recognized in the everyday experiences of pet training (*operant conditioning*) and phobia development (*classical conditioning*).

Classical and operant conditioning have many associated concepts: acquisition, contingency, discrimination, extinction, generalization, punishment, reinforcement, and spontaneous recovery. Research on cognition and animals' biological predispositions toward learning has contributed significantly to the field.

Associative Learning

Cognitive processes in associative learning

Two types of associative learning are classical conditioning and operant conditioning.

Classical and *operant conditioning* are under the category of *behavioral psychology.*

Behaviorism focuses on observing behavior and its consequences.

Cognitive psychology uses a different approach. The brain is considered, and the discipline studies how thoughts affect people's views and behavior.

Cognitive psychologists do not posit that learning is solely due to stimulus pairing and reinforcement, although they acknowledge that these are components of the learning process. For example, Wolfgang Kohler observed that when his chimp was challenged to reach a fruit hanging from the ceiling, the chimp was eventually able to reach the fruit using various props in the room. The chimp stacked boxes to reach the fruit and then used a stick to obtain it.

In this case, the chimp combined and used previously learned behaviors to solve the problem.

Chimps combine and use previously learned behaviors to solve the problem.

Insight learning

Insight learning is when previously learned behaviors are combined in innovative ways.

Stacking boxes and using the stick was reinforced for the chimp because the chimp could obtain the fruit. When a new situation was presented where the fruit was out of reach, the chimp combined the two reinforced behaviors to obtain the desired result (e.g., retrieving the fruit).

For example, insight learning is observed when someone wants to hang a picture on the wall, pulls a chair over to where the picture needs to be placed, gets on the chair, and places the picture where desired.

Latent learning

Latent learning is when learning is not expressed as an observable behavior until required.

Unseen behaviors may become available, when necessary, in *latent learning*. For example, a child driven to school by her parents learns the school route. One day, when her parents cannot drive her to school, she can navigate her way to school independently on a bike.

Conditioning does not only refer to behavioral learning.

In *operant conditioning*, certain behaviors are reinforced, and the probability of repeated behavior increases. Cognitively, reinforcement provides the expectation of a future reinforcer.

Thinking prospectively participates in this type of learning. Expectation might be present in stimulus generalization. For example, if students are rewarded for raising their hands before speaking in one class, they may expect this behavior to be reinforced in other classes.

Biological processes of associative learning

Learning is a change in behavior due to experience. Many outside factors affect learning, but it is constrained biologically. For example, chimpanzees communicate via sign language but not vocally because they lack fully developed vocal cords.

Associative learning is understood through stimuli essential for the organism's survival. Not all reinforcers are equally effective.

Consider food aversion. Suppose someone becomes nauseous after eating chocolate; even though the cause of nausea might not be solely due to the chocolate, they develop a strong aversion to the taste and smell of chocolate. Aversion to chocolate goes against the principles of associative learning because it occurs after one instance, and the aversion lasts for an extended period, sometimes indefinitely.

Researchers have tried to condition organisms to associate the feeling of nausea with factors like sound and light, but thus far, they have been unsuccessful. It is argued that learning occurs more rapidly if biologically relevant to the organism.

Learning is a process that causes physical changes to the central nervous system.

Different regions of the brain participate in learning. For example, the cerebellum is responsible for learning motor tasks, and the amygdala for fear responses.

Learning and memory are interconnected as synaptic connections following memory formation.

Incoming information is initially stored as *short-term memory,* lasting from seconds to hours, and then can be permanently transformed into *long-term memory* via *consolidation.*

Classical Conditioning

Conditioned learning

Classical conditioning is when a conditioned stimulus is *paired* with an unconditioned stimulus to produce a conditioned response.

In classical conditioning (as opposed to operant conditioning), there is *no* voluntary or conscious control over whether a behavioral response occurs following the pairing of stimuli.

Classical conditioning behaviors are not maintained by consequences but by the continuous association of specific stimuli.

Classical conditioning elements

Learning is a durable change in behavior brought about by experience.

Associative learning occurs when an organism learns that events are connected or when a response becomes associated with a particular stimulus.

Classical conditioning (one form of associative learning) is when a stimulus that initially had no response associated with it becomes paired with a stimulus that elicits a response. This pairing results in the stimulus that initially had no response eliciting the same response as the stimulus it was paired with.

Classical conditioning was accidentally discovered by Ivan Pavlov, who was initially studying the digestive system of dogs. Pavlov observed that after repeated pairing of a bell ringing and food, the dogs started to salivate at the sound of the bell, even when there was no food.

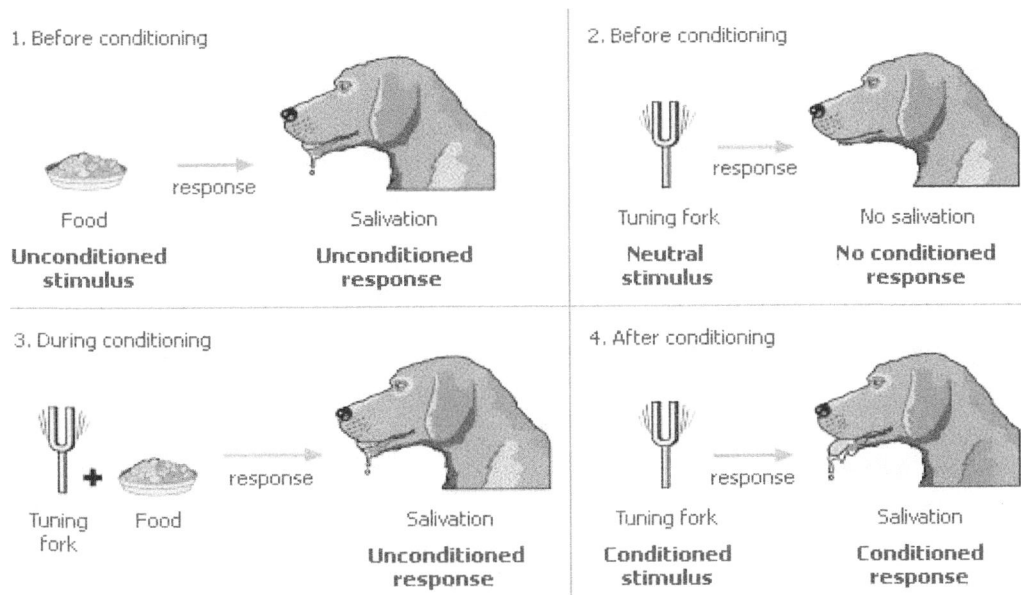

1. Before conditioning

Food
Unconditioned stimulus

response

Salivation
Unconditioned response

2. Before conditioning

Tuning fork
Neutral stimulus

response

No salivation
No conditioned response

3. During conditioning

Tuning fork   Food

response

Salivation
Unconditioned response

4. After conditioning

Tuning fork
Conditioned stimulus

response

Salivation
Conditioned response

Classical conditioning with food as unconditioned stimulus

In this experiment, food was the *unconditioned stimulus* because it naturally elicited a response from the dogs; this response did not have to be learned. Salivation at the food presentation was the *unconditioned response*, as it did not have to be learned.

The sound of the bell changed from a *neutral stimulus* to a *conditioned stimulus* through the learning process. Salivation in response to the bell is the *conditioned response*, as it must be learned through conditioning. Note that behaviors learned through classical conditioning are not maintained by their consequences but rather by paired associations.

Classical conditioning process is prominent in the development of phobias and anxiety.

For example, in a famous "Little Albert" experiment, Watson and Rayner demonstrated that classical conditioning elicits a phobic reaction in a previously neutral stimulus. Little Albert was a nine-month-old infant who initially showed no response to a white rat. However, he started to cry whenever a hammer was struck against a steel bar. Over seven weeks, the white rat and loud noise were *repeatedly paired*. After seven weeks, Little Albert displayed a fearful response to the white rat, even when the loud noise was not present.

The white rat was originally a *neutral stimulus* and became a *conditioned stimulus*. Crying in response to this conditioned stimulus was the conditioned response. Albert's crying in response to the loud noise (unconditioned stimulus) was the unconditioned response.

Forward, delay and trace conditioning

Forward conditioning is learning at the fastest rate. In forward conditioning, the start of the conditioned stimulus comes before the start of the unconditioned stimulus to signal that the unconditioned stimulus will follow.

Delay conditioning and *trace conditioning* are examples of forward conditioning.

Delay conditioning is when the conditioned stimulus is active and overlaps with the unconditioned stimulus's activity.

Trace conditioning is when the conditioned stimulus and unconditioned stimulus do not overlap. Instead, the conditioned stimulus begins and ends before the unconditioned stimulus is active.

Trace interval is the period with no stimulus.

For example, when a buzzer sounds for five seconds, and a second later, a puff of air is shot into a person's eye, and they blink. After multiple pairings of the buzzer and a puff of air, the person blinks at the sound of the buzzer.

Simultaneous conditioning is conditioned and unconditioned stimuli, active and inactive.

From the example, ringing the buzzer and blowing a puff of air simultaneously would mean the conditioned and unconditioned stimuli coincided.

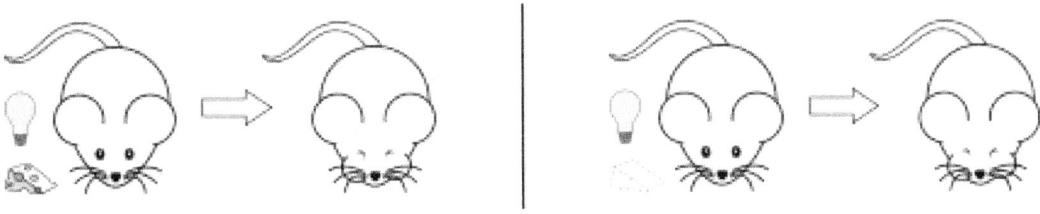

Simultaneous conditioning uses active and inactive stimuli

Higher-order conditioning

Second-order and *higher-order conditioning* is a two-step process.

First step is presenting a neutral or conditioned stimulus (#1), which signals an unconditioned stimulus through forward conditioning. A second neutral stimulus, or conditioned stimulus (#2), is paired with the conditioned stimulus (#1) and comes to produce its unique conditioned response.

For example, bell ringing is paired with food until the bell sound elicits salivation. If the light is paired with a bell, the light elicits salivation.

Bell sound is the *conditioned stimulus* (#1), and food is the *unconditioned stimulus*.

Light is the *conditioned stimulus* (#2) once paired with the *conditioned stimulus* (#1).

Backward and temporal conditioning

Backward conditioning is when the conditioned stimulus immediately follows an unconditioned stimulus. The conditioned response for the conditioned stimulus proves to be inhibitory. This occurs because the conditioned stimulus acts as a signal that the unconditioned stimulus has ended rather than as a signal that the unconditioned stimulus is about to surface. Here, the puff of air into an individual's eye could be followed by the sound of the buzzer.

Temporal conditioning is when an unconditioned stimulus is presented at regular time intervals. Conditioning occurs when the conditioned response happens shortly before each unconditioned stimulus. Here, an organism's biological clock serves as the conditioned stimulus.

Zero contingency procedure is when the conditioned stimulus is paired with the unconditioned stimulus; however, this unconditioned stimulus can be present at other times. If this occurs, it is assumed that the unconditioned stimulus can occur without the conditioned stimulus.

Consequently, the conditioned stimulus does not predict the unconditioned stimulus per se, the conditioning does not occur, and the conditioned stimulus does not necessarily produce a conditioned response. This finding suggests that the component of associate learning known as *prediction*, rather than the pairing of a conditioned and unconditioned stimulus, precedes conditioning. This finding had a significant impact on later conditioning research.

Acquisition and extinction

Acquisition (in classical conditioning) is when the conditioned response is first established and gradually strengthened. Acquisition occurs at the first instance that an organism displays a conditioned response to a previously neutral stimulus.

Extinction is the process of a conditioned response being decreased or discontinued. In classical conditioning, extinction occurs when a previously conditioned stimulus is no longer paired with an unconditioned stimulus. Once Pavlov discontinued the bell ringing and food pairing, for example, the dogs stopped salivating in response to the sound of the bell.

Spontaneous recovery is the re-emergence of a previously extinguished conditioned response after a period of rest. This renewed conditioned response is usually much weaker than the conditioned response before extinction. Spontaneous recovery sometimes occurs when the organism is returned to the environment in which the conditioned response was acquired.

Stimulus generalization is when a stimulus similar to the conditioned stimulus elicits the same conditioned response. This occurs when similar stimuli are not themselves conditioned. In the Little Albert experiment, for example, Little Albert developed a fear not only of white rats but of all furry animals, including cats and dogs.

Stimulus discrimination is differentiating between a conditioned stimulus and similar stimuli.

For example, if Pavlov's dogs had not salivated in response to a novel bell sound, this would be a form of stimulus discrimination.

Operant Conditioning

Operant behaviors

Operant conditioning is associative learning in which behavior is modified by its antecedents (i.e., before trained behavior) and consequences.

Operant conditioning is distinguished from classical conditioning (respondent conditioning) because operant conditioning uses *reinforcement and punishment.*

Operant behavior relies on the environment and is maintained by its antecedents and consequences, while classical conditioning involves the conditioning of reflexive (reflex) behaviors elicited by prior associations.

Operant conditioning was initially studied by Edward Thorndike and popularized by B.F. Skinner and experiments with lab rats.

Operant conditioning focuses on the antecedents and consequences of behavior and their effect on the rate of behavior. It is used widely in applied behavior analysis, an evidence-based therapy primarily used for children with autism and in the treatment of anxiety disorders.

Types of reinforcement

Reinforcement is anything that increases behavior. It is unrelated to the person's intention to change their behavior.

For example, suppose a teacher praises a student for turning in homework on time, and this behavior decreases. In that case, praise acts not as a reinforcement but a punishment.

Similarly, a teacher who does not allow a student to go outside for recess after the student is disruptive would reinforce the disruptive behavior if the student becomes more disruptive.

Positive reinforcement is the addition of a stimulus to increase it after a behavior occurs.

For example, if the hand-raising behavior increases, positive reinforcement occurs when a child is presented with a sticker every time they raise a hand in class.

Negative reinforcement involves taking away a stimulus to increase a behavior.

For example, a teacher may cease teaching when a child is disruptive. Removing the lesson negatively reinforces the tantrum-throwing behavior if the tantrums increase in response.

In positive and negative reinforcement, the words positive and negative do not mean *good* or *bad* but the *presentation* or *removal* of a stimulus.

Dog training using positive reinforcement

Primary reinforcers (e.g., food, water, and pleasure) are naturally reinforcing.

Conditioned reinforcers are reinforcers that are not naturally reinforcing for organisms.

Stimuli become reinforced by association with primary reinforcers *via* classical conditioning.

For example, if a student receives a token for good behavior in class and can convert it into candy, the token becomes a *conditioned reinforcer*, as it becomes associated with candy.

Premack Principle should be considered before selecting a specific reinforcer because the person receiving the reinforcer must be considered.

For example, if a child likes chocolate ice cream but hates dance class, the parent can use chocolate ice cream as the reinforcer to encourage the child to attend dance class; *more probable behaviors reinforce less probable behaviors.*

Reinforcement schedules

Rate at which behavior occurs depends largely on when it is reinforced.

Four reinforcement schedules: fixed-ratio, variable-ratio, fixed-interval, and variable-interval.

Fixed-ratio schedule of reinforcement is when a reinforcer is presented after a behavior occurs a set number of times.

For example, on a fixed-ratio (FR) schedule, a rat receives a food pellet after pushing a lever ten times.

Fixed-ratio schedule of reinforcement results in a steady increase in behavior, with a brief pause after each reinforcer is delivered.

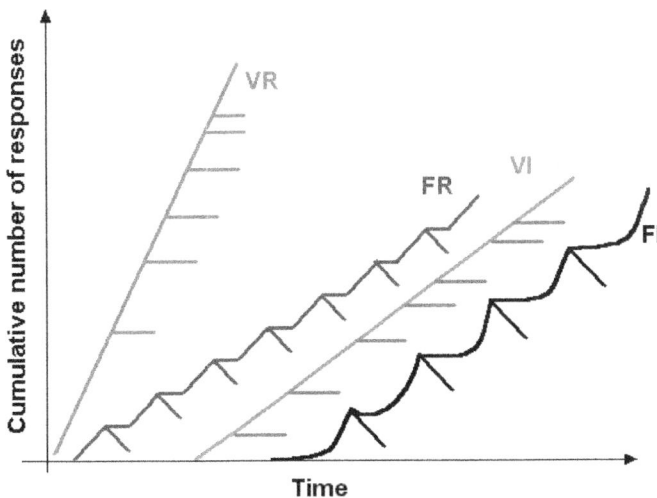

Variable-ratio (VR), fixed-ratio (FR), variable-interval (VI), and fixed-interval (FI)

Variable-ratio schedule of reinforcement is when behavior is reinforced after an unpredictable number of responses.

For example, variable-ratio (VR) is when a rat receives a food pellet after pushing a lever ten times, then five times, and then again after four times.

On a variable-ratio schedule, *behavior increases rapidly at a steady rate*. For example, lottery games are often based on this schedule of reinforcement.

Fixed-interval schedule of reinforcement is when a reinforcer is presented following a behavior after a fixed amount of time has elapsed.

For example, a fixed interval (FI) is when a rat receives a food pellet the first time it presses a lever after a one-minute interval.

Receiving a paycheck after working two weeks is an example of a fixed-interval (FI) schedule of reinforcement.

Fixed-interval schedules are considered the *weakest schedule of reinforcement.*

Variable-interval schedule of reinforcement is when a reinforcer is presented after the first response, following a variable amount of time.

For example, variable interval (VI) is when a rat is presented with a food pellet after pushing a lever after one minute, then after two minutes, and again after three minutes.

Variable interval reinforcement schedule results in a *steady increase in behavior.*

Shaping and extinction

Shaping is the process of reinforcing small approximations of the desired behavior. It is used when the desired behavior does not occur or occurs less frequently than desired. When shaping a behavior, the desired behavior is broken into small steps and then reinforced individually.

For example, shaping is often used in dog training and teaching autistic children to speak. A pet trainer reinforces the head-turning behavior when teaching a pet to spin around. Once the dog consistently turns its head, the trainer only rewards the dog for turning its head and taking a step. Once the dog does that consistently, the trainer rewards the dog for turning its head and taking two steps, etc. Reinforcement of the small steps that make up spinning in a circle continues until the dog spins in a full circle.

Another example, when teaching a child with autism to say the word "cookie," a behavioral therapist would reinforce after the child makes a "c" sound, then a "coo" sound, then a "cook" sound, and finally would reinforce only after the child says the word "cookie."

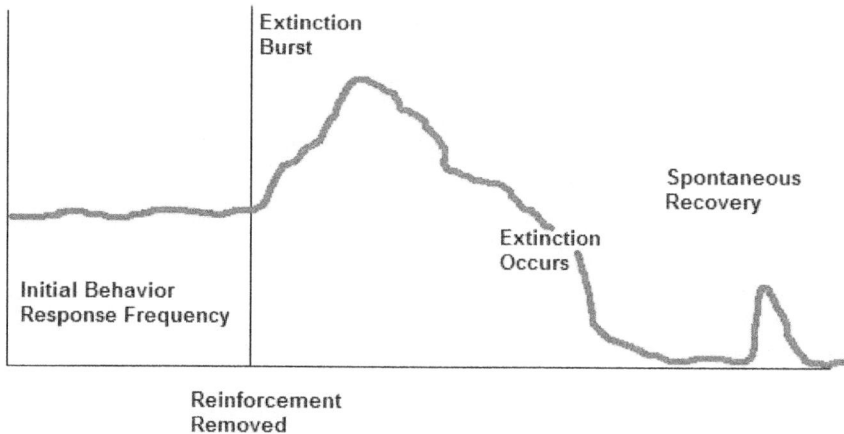

Extinction graph with outcomes relative to reinforcement

Extinction (operant conditioning) is stopping reinforcement of a previously reinforced behavior.

Extinction for operant conditioning differs from extinction for classical conditioning. For extinction to be effective, all *reinforcement of undesired behaviors* must stop.

Thus, in a clinical setting, it is essential to ensure that parents and teachers are aware of the extinction process.

Shortly after the start of the extinction process, an *extinction burst* occurs.

An extinction burst is a *temporary increase in undesired behavior*.

B.F Skinner accidentally discovered extinction burst when a pellet dispenser jammed during an experiment that involved a rat pressing a lever to receive food. Skinner found that the rat initially pushed the lever at a greater rate when it stopped receiving reinforcement. After a while, the lever-pressing behavior declined and eventually stopped.

B.F. Skinner, American psychologist

When using extinction to get a dog to stop begging for food at the dinner table, all family members must be willing to stop giving the dog food, or a variable schedule of reinforcement will be created, and the behavior will be strengthened. Initially, the dog will increase the begging behavior. After the extinction burst has peaked, the begging behavior will decline and eventually stop altogether.

Punishment

Punishment *decreases* behavior. As with reinforcement, whether something is considered punishment depends on its effect on the rate of behavior.

Positive punishment is when a stimulus causes a decrease in behavior. For example, receiving a speeding ticket is a *positive punishment* if the speeding behavior subsequently decreases.

Negative punishment occurs when a stimulus is removed, and a behavior decreases. For example, removing a child's television after they swear is a *negative punishment*.

Behavior analysts and animal trainers tend to avoid using punishment, as it has been hypothesized to increase aggression and may lead to other problematic behaviors.

When punishment is used in behavior analysis (or animal training), it is usually done only when extinction alone has failed to reduce a behavior.

Punishment is generally used in conjunction with the reinforcement of *incompatible behavior*.

For example, a teacher with a child in class who hits classmates sitting next to him may punish hitting behavior while reinforcing hand-folding. Note that successful punishment may become negatively reinforcing for the punisher.

	Positive (+) To add, present, provide	Negative (-) To remove, take away
Reinforcement – behavior INCREASES	**Positive Reinforcement** Stimulus *provided* contingent on the behavior, increasing behavior.	**Negative Reinforcement** Stimulus *removed* contingent on the behavior, *increasing* behavior.
Punishment – behavior DECREASES in the future	**Positive Punishment** Stimulus is **PROVIDED** contingent on the behavior, leading to a **DECREASE**.	**Negative Punishment** Stimulus is **REMOVED** contingent on the behavior, leading to a **DECREASE** of the behavior.

Positive vs. negative reinforcement/punishment

Trial-and-error learning is operant conditioning, combining punishment and reinforcement.

If a response is desirable, organisms increase this behavior (reinforcement).

If a response is undesirable, organisms avoid this behavior (punishment).

Escape and avoidance learning

Escape learning is when an individual performs a behavior to terminate an aversive stimulus. Escape behavior then becomes negatively reinforced as it increases in rate due to removing a stimulus. Escape conditioning has a large role in the maintenance of many psychopathologies.

Individuals with social anxiety may, for instance, leave (escape) a highly social environment, resulting in the removal of anxiety. Although this anxiety reduction may seem temporarily beneficial, the escape behavior becomes reinforced and is more likely to recur in the future.

Avoidance learning is escape behavior. If a signal is given before the aversive stimulus is activated, the organism will learn to engage in escape behavior proactively. For example, a person with social anxiety who has learned to escape highly social and anxiety-producing situations may begin to avoid these situations altogether.

Avoidant behavior is self-reinforcing, meaning that the reinforcer (relief) occurs whether the aversive stimulus is avoided. Since avoidance learning is self-reinforcing, avoidance behavior will often perpetuate without intervention.

Exposure therapy is used for the individual with social anxiety who avoids social situations. Exposure therapy involves exposing the individual to the previously avoided stimuli to break the escape pattern, thus decreasing the fear response.

Associative learning comparisons

	Classical Conditioning	**Operant Conditioning**
Response	Involuntary, automatic	Voluntary, operates environment
Acquisition	Associating events where the conditioned stimulus announces the unconditioned stimulus	Associating response with a consequence (reinforcer or punisher)
Extinction	Conditioned response decreases; conditioned stimulus is repeatedly presented alone	Responses decrease when reinforcement stops (after the initial temporary increase)
Cognitive processes	Individuals develop the expectation that conditioned stimulus signals the arrival of unconditioned stimulus	Subjects develop expectation that a response will be reinforced or punished; exhibit latent learning without reinforcement
Biological predisposition	Natural predispositions constrain what stimuli and responses can easily be associated	Organisms learn behaviors like instincts; unnatural behaviors instinctively drift toward them

Associative learning comparisons of classical vs. operant conditioning

Animal Behavior

Sensitive periods

Certain behaviors must occur during a *critical period* to be learned by humans and animals.

Imprinting is learning associated with a *sensitive period*.

Imprinting is a *phase-sensitive type of learning* (learning occurring at a particular age or life stage) that is rapid and *independent of the consequences* of behavior.

For most animals that imprint, the sensitive period occurs within 13-16 hours of life.

For example, chicks, ducklings, and goslings follow the first moving object they see after hatching. These animals usually imprint on their mother but can imprint on any moving organism or object, including humans.

Song learning in birds involves a sensitive period. Work by Peter Marler shows that young birds learn to sing in part from older birds. Songs heard outside of the sensitive period do not affect the birds. These birds' brains are primed to respond to acoustic stimuli during the sensitive period; the birds can even learn other species' songs due to the strength of social influence.

In humans and animals, vision is learned during a critical period. The brain regions processing vision develop from signals from the eyes. One experiment showed this by sewing one eye of a cat shut immediately after birth. Only vision in the open eye developed; the sewn-up eye did not develop normally and could not sense visual stimuli. In humans, it is essential to treat babies born blind as soon as possible to ensure that the critical period for vision is not missed.

Cycles of behavior

Circadian rhythms are the daily physiological and behavioral cycles. These include any biological processes that tend to reoccur every 24 hours.

Circadian rhythms have been observed widely in cyanobacteria, fungi, plants, and animals.

These rhythms are driven by a *circadian clock*, an internal mechanism that receives input from external cues and provides an output that regulates behavior. The circadian clock is driven primarily by input from sunlight but is affected by temperature, eating and drinking patterns, and social interactions.

Nocturnality is a pattern of animal behavior characterized by activity during the night and sleeping during the day. Nocturnal creatures have specific adaptations to thrive on this sleep pattern. They have advanced senses of hearing, helping them avoid predators and communicate.

They often have larger corneas, allowing more light to enter their eyes in the dark.

Communication

Communication is any action by a sender that influences the behavior of a receiver. Often, these signals benefit both the sender and the receiver.

Four types of communication are *chemical*, *auditory*, *visual*, and *tactile*.

Four types of communication used by animals are chemical, auditory, visual, and tactile

Chemical communications are chemical signals (e.g., pheromones, urine, and feces).

Pheromone is a chemical released to cause a reaction in another member of the same species.

Pheromones that trigger reversible behavioral changes are *releaser pheromones*, while those that cause long-term behavioral changes are *primer pheromones*.

Chemical communication is often used in mating and territory marking. Female moths attract males with tail gland pheromones, while cats mark their territory with urine.

Auditory communication stems from sound. It is faster than chemical communication and can be modified by volume, pattern, duration, and repetition.

Like chemical communication, auditory communication is often used in mating and marking territories. Whale songs, for example, have six basic themes for mating and group identification.

Birds have various songs for distress, courting, and marking territory. Language is the ultimate auditory communication, and complex language is restricted to humans.

Non-human primates are limited to about 40 vocalizations with limited meaning.

Chimpanzees cannot advance beyond the level of a two-year-old child, even when raised in an environment identical to that of an infant.

Grammar appears to exist exclusively in humans.

Visual communication is often used by active daytime animals. It is generally for defense and courtship displays, which are exaggerated and performed to clarify the meaning.

Visual communication between males uses threat postures, which may prevent fighting. These behaviors include baring teeth to display aggression and lying supine to display submission.

Bees use visual communication to convey information about food sources. A bee that locates a source of pollen returns to the hive and performs a dance indicating the distance and direction of the source from the hive.

Tactile communication occurs when one animal touches another. Tactile communication is used for feeding, mating, and grooming. For example, gull chicks peck at their parent's beak to display hunger and to prompt the parent to feed them.

Male leopards will nuzzle the female's neck to stimulate her willingness to mate.

In primates, grooming cleans the skin or coat of another and creates social bonds.

Tactile communication is used for feeding, mating, and grooming

Many animal species have mate-selection rituals referred to as "courtship."

Courtship may involve a combination of chemical, auditory, visual, and tactile communications (e.g., complicated dances, touching, vocalizations, displays of beauty, or fighting prowess).

Animal courtships often occur out of sight of humans and are among the least documented animal behaviors.

Habituation

Non-associative learning is when a particular organism is exposed to only one type of stimulus. It reflects the relatively permanent change in the response strength towards a single stimulus due to repeated exposure. It is considered the simplest way of learning.

Two types of non-associative learning are *habituation* and *sensitization*.

Habit is a behavior performed continuously and repeatedly until it becomes automatic.

Habituation is a learned behavior that allows animals to disregard meaningless stimuli by diminishing response to a frequently repeated stimulus; it is *stimulus-specific*.

Habituation is *short-term habituation* and *long-term habituation*.

Short-term habituation lasts minutes or hours. For example, the stimulus is presented at short intervals every 15 seconds. Response to the stimulus decreases quickly with repetition, and response strength recovers after a period without stimulus.

Long-term habituation lasts for days or weeks. It involves repeatedly induced short-term habituation, with an extended period between each session. The individual remains habituated to the stimulus for days or even weeks.

Habituation differs from *extinction* because behaviors that decrease in extinction are learned, while the behaviors that decrease in habituation are innate. Sea anemones, for example, will disregard repeated "feeding" stimulation with a stick.

Sensitization

Sensitization is where an individual becomes more responsive to the stimulus with each repeated stimulus presentation. Instead of having the ability to tune out the stimulus or avoid reacting in general, the stimulus tends to have a more profound effect.

For example, when someone tries to fall asleep, the sound of water dripping from a faucet becomes more difficult to ignore.

Sensitization may cause an individual to respond strongly to similar stimuli. For example, as an individual leaves a rock concert and an ambulance passes by with loud sirens, the siren seems louder than usual and more painful as the person's ears have become sensitized to rock music.

Sensitization is only temporary and does *not* cause long-term behavioral changes.

Insight and spatial learning

Insight learning is learning by reason and rationality. It is a form of problem-solving that occurs suddenly through understanding the relationship between distinct aspects of a problem.

Insight learning is a sudden realization that is distinct from cause-and-effect problem-solving.

For example, apes presented with a problem requiring them to use objects in new ways to receive food are believed to use insight learning to solve the problem. Insight learning manifests as a spontaneous occurrence and is a noteworthy phenomenon in the learning process.

Spatial learning (i.e., associative learning) is how animals encode environmental information.

In spatial learning, animals associate attributes of a landmark with reward.

For example, wasps can associate pinecones with the location of their nest and become lost when the pinecones are removed.

Innate and inherited behaviors

Innate behavior (or *instinct* and *inborn behavior*) is the inherent inclination of organisms towards a particular complex behavior the organism is "*programmed to do.*"

Fixed action patterns are the simplest instinctive behaviors in which a short to medium-length sequence of actions, without variation, is conducted in response to a clearly defined stimulus.

Behavior is instinctive if performed without being based upon *prior experience* (in the absence of learning) and *expresses innate biological factors*.

Inherited behaviors develop because they increase fitness across generations. In mammals, care for offspring by female parents is believed to be an innate behavior.

Some innate behaviors require maturation, making them appear learned.

For example, birds appear to fly through observational learning, but in laboratory settings, they can fly on their first try, even without seeing another bird fly. In this example, the flight behavior is innate, but the ability to fly requires physical maturation.

Fixed action patterns (or *behavioral patterns*) are behaviors performed similarly and elicited by a sign stimulus. Behavioral patterns are believed to be innate, although recent research has questioned this belief; many behaviors formerly thought to be fixed action patterns are found to have developed after practice.

One example of a behavioral pattern occurs in Kelp gull chicks, who beg for food from parents by pecking at a red spot on their mothers' beaks. In a lab setting, the chicks peck at any beak model initially but only at models resembling their parents later, suggesting that behavior patterns are *not entirely* innate.

Notes for active learning

Observational Learning

Social learning

Most advanced organisms, including humans, do not only learn through direct experience.

Observational learning (*social learning* or *vicarious learning*) is a form of learning relevant to humans and animals. In observational learning, learning occurs through observing the behavior of others. It is the learning that occurs by watching and imitating others.

Observational learning was identified in 1961 in an experiment conducted by Albert Bandura. In this experiment, children in one group observed an adult playing aggressively with a Bobo doll; children in another group observed an adult playing non-aggressively with the same doll.

Children in the group who had observed the adult playing aggressively with the doll were likelier to play aggressively than those in the other group. Another study found that monkeys born in a laboratory do not fear snakes until they are shown a video of other monkeys with a fear response to snakes.

Modeling

Modeling is a fundamental mechanism of observational learning. Here, the observer sees the action being performed by another. As time passes, the same observer imitates that particular action. Children usually engage in activities like "playing house" or "superhero."

Most children play the role of mom or Superman based on their observed models. An adult's appearance is modeled after the appearance of other members of society; for example, an adult's dress, walk, and talk are all similar to that of his or her acquaintants.

Modeling is not just limited to humans. Lions participate in modeling. Lionesses take their cubs out when hunting, and the cubs observe and can then hunt based on what they have observed.

Mirror neurons

Mirror neurons have been identified in various brain regions, including the premotor cortex, supplementary motor area, primary somatosensory cortex, and inferior parietal cortex.

For example, in monkeys, mirror neurons fire when the monkey performs a particular task and when the monkey observes another monkey performing a task.

Humans have mirror neurons, although their function is unknown.

Some investigators propose that mirror neurons are activated by connecting the sight and action of a particular movement; they are programmed to mirror.

Other researchers believe mirror neurons aid in observing and help imitate observed actions.

Disorders of the mirror neuron mechanism may be related to autism spectrum disorders.

Vicarious emotions are proposed to involve mirror neurons in humans.

Vicarious emotions include *empathy*, the emotional reaction based on another's emotional condition (or understanding) of another from the other's frame of reference.

Observational learning and behavior

Observational learning connects social organisms such as humans. Humans form and behave similarly throughout development; however, this mimicking has flaws. Individual differences are present between humans.

Personality differences and psychological disorders can affect observational learning.

Research on observational learning has focused on violence, suggesting that observing violence can increase the overall behavioral pattern of violent acts.

However, individuals who observe violence do not always become violent, and *cognitive processes* (i.e., thinking and reasoning) have a vital role in how individuals choose (or not choose) to learn through *observation*.

Therefore, observations *influence* but do *not dictate* behavior in humans.

Relationship matrix

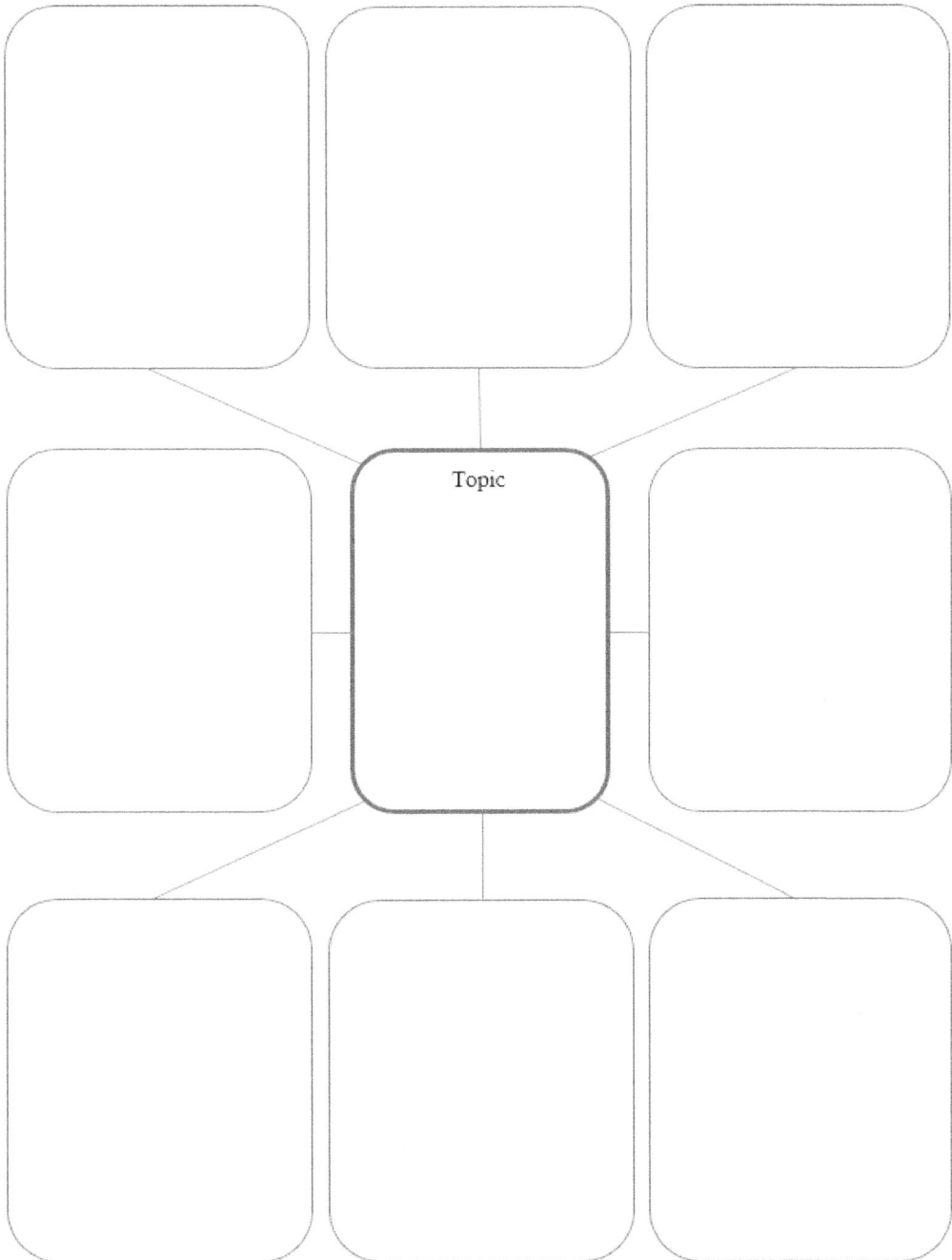

Topic

Notes for active learning

CHAPTER 5

Cognition & States of Consciousness

Cognition is learning, remembering, retrieving, and using information for communication and problem-solving. Consciousness is prominent in discussions of sensation.

Defining consciousness can be challenging. Researchers facilitate the process by constructing individual definitions to explore *states of consciousness* and associated concepts.

Understanding cognition and states of consciousness, such as sleep and sleep cycles, dreams, hypnosis, circadian rhythms, and psychoactive drug effects, is of primary importance to psychology researchers.

Attention

Selective attention

Attention is a state of focused awareness on a subset of the available perceptual information. It is the ability to focus and concentrate on a task. It is the allocation of processing resources.

Selective attention poses a difficulty in attending to more than one activity simultaneously.

Trying to address one task over the other requires selective attention.

Selective attention is observed by the classic *Stroop effect*, in which participants asked to identify the ink color of the word describing another color (e.g., when the word "blue" is printed in red) are slower and more prone to errors than when the word and ink color match.

Reading is an *automatic process*, and color naming is a *controlled process*.

Automatic reading interferes with a person's ability to selectively attend to ink color.

For example, in the dichotic listening task, the participants listen to two messages simultaneously. One message goes to each ear. As they listen, they are asked to ignore one of the messages and repeat the words from the other message.

Not much processing occurs with the unattended message. However, participants can identify the message as a human voice or noise and whether the voice is male or female, but the information is limited. They cannot tell what language the voice was speaking or report any of the words spoken, even if the same word was repeated repeatedly.

Treisman's *Shadowing Study* highlights that humans cannot focus on multiple stimuli simultaneously. It shows what can draw attention, such as hearing an individual's name in the unattended ear. However, when attention is drawn to the unattended ear, information is lost from the attended ear. This phenomenon is known as the *cocktail party effect*.

Someone cannot focus on more than one task without one of the activities suffering.

"Cocktail party effect" is when information is lost from the attended ear because attention is drawn to the unattended ear.

Bottleneck theory and early selection

Bottleneck theory describes the bottleneck mechanism that limits the amount of information that can be attended to simultaneously.

Bottleneck controls what information gets through, what is selected, and when selection occurs.

Researcher Donald Broadbent proposed that in *early selection*, physical characteristics of messages are used to select one message for processing, while other information is ignored.

Attenuation *vs.* late selection

Anne Treisman proposed that in *attenuation*, physical characteristics select one message for complete processing, and others are only partially processed. J. Anthony and Diana Deutsch proposed that in *late selection*, messages get through, but only one response can be made.

Treisman and Geffen tested *attenuation* and *late selection*. Dichotic listening and detecting target words in either channel (where an individual taps upon detection) were performed.

Detection was much worse in the unattended channel, thus supporting the *attenuation principle*.

Detection should not be a late selection problem since all the information gets to the subject.

Interference and capacity theory

As mentioned, attending to more than one stimulus at once is difficult.

Interference is when a person tries to focus on two stimuli simultaneously and makes multiple responses rather than one response to multiple stimuli.

Capacity theory is that limited cognitive resources are available for mental tasks. Nonetheless, theories suggest that *only one cognitive process* can coincide even with multiple resources.

Automatic processing does not require divided attention. An example would be driving a car, listening to the radio, and carrying on a conversation at the same time.

Controlled processing requires divided attention.

Feature integration theory

Feature integration theory addresses attention and perceptual processing.

Individuals may process inputs in parallel (or simultaneously) with *divided attention* or process parts of the scene serially (i.e., one at a time), requiring *focused attention*.

Overall, more demanding processing is required when objects are more complex.

Experiments support the *feature integration theory*. People must focus on a stimulus before synthesizing it into a meaningful pattern. Individuals focus on complex incoming information, including visual and auditory stimuli, to synthesize it into a meaningful pattern.

Cognition

Information-processing model

Information-processing model describes how the human mind translates sensory information. This model compares the mind to a computer information processing system. The mind performs a string of mental computations based on various mental representations. Incoming information is exposed to processes well beyond simple stimulus-response patterns.

The mind receives information through attention mechanisms, working memory processes that actively manipulate the incoming information, and long-term memory that passively holds the incoming information for future use.

As children grow, their brains develop, leading to higher-order processing and sensory-driven responses to incoming information. This model focuses on a continuous development pattern rather than having distinct steps like Piaget's theory of cognitive development.

Piaget's cognitive development

Jean Piaget's *theory of cognitive development* states that there are specific stages that children go through in which their intellect and ability to understand relationships evolve. The stages outlined by Piaget are fixed for children, regardless of their country of origin, ethnicity, or native language. However, the age range at which children achieve them is flexible and can vary from child to child.

Jean Piaget, Swiss developmental psychologist and philosopher

Sensorimotor stage occurs between birth and the age of two years. Infants begin to understand information entering their senses, and their ability to interact with the outside world evolves. The child learns to manipulate objects even though they cannot understand and process the permanency of objects when not within present sensory perception. Once an object is removed from view, the child cannot understand that the object still exists.

Towards the end of this stage, children can achieve the concept of *object permanence*. For example, after object permanence has developed when a mother leaves the room, the child understands that she will probably return, giving the child a sense of security.

Cognitive development stages

Preoperational stage is the second stage of Piaget's cognitive development theory and is when a child achieves object permanency from two to seven years old. Language development occurs rapidly. Children learn to interact with their environment through words and images.

Egocentrism is when children believe that everyone sees the world in the same manner as them, which is distinctive in this stage. Children do not understand perspectives and believe that inanimate objects have the same ability they do to perceive visuals, feelings, sounds, and touch.

Conservation is understanding that quantity does not change even if the shape changes, which is a primary focus in this stage of development.

For example, if a short and wide glass of water is poured into a tall and thin glass, the child perceives that the taller glass has more water because of its height. They cannot understand the concept of reversibility and focus on a single aspect of a stimulus, a phenomenon of *centration*.

Concrete operations stage is the third of Piaget's cognitive development theory. It involves children from the ages of seven to about twelve. There is a slight decrease in *centristic thought* and an increased ability to focus on more than one aspect of a specific stimulus.

At this stage, the child can process the concept of grouping, knowing that small and large dogs belong to the same category. Another example is that pennies, quarters, and dollar bills are all part of the larger category of money. This concept of grouping can only be applied to tangible objects. Other objects that have not been seen or touched remain elusive since the ability of abstract thinking has yet to develop.

Formal operations are the fourth and final stage of Piaget's cognitive development theory. Children at this stage are from the age of twelve and up. The child develops a more abstract view of the world. They can apply reversibility and conservation concepts to real and imagined situations. They have a more holistic understanding of the world and cause and effect.

When children enter their teenage years, they can develop their view of the world around them. Most children reach this stage, but those who do not have *lower intellectual capacities*.

Cognitive changes in late adulthood

Piaget's theory of cognitive development posits that the onset of formal operational thinking proceeds up to the age of twenty-five. Expanding these findings, researchers have focused on cognitive development after this age.

Constructive development framework (CDF) states that the development of *post-formal operational thinking* in an adult is exemplified primarily by *dialectical thinking*.

Dialectical thinking is the search for truth through reasoned argumentation with a framework of four classes of thoughts: *process, context, relationship*, and *transformation*.

Process class of thought is how things in our systems emerge, evolve, and eventually disappear.

Context is the class of thought that describes how things are part of the structure of a larger, more stable, and more organized whole. Contextualization of distinct parts within a whole gives rise to various points of view.

Relationship class of thought describes how things that are part of a larger whole are related and the nature of their common ground.

Transformation class of thought describes how living systems undergo constant development and transformation (potentially a synthesis of the previous form of organization) and are subject to influencing human agency.

In late adulthood, cognition becomes more focused, and the elderly make the most of their cognitive abilities through goal-oriented processing. Older individuals focus on activities that take minimal cognitive effort but produce maximum results to conserve cognitive resources.

As individuals enter late adulthood, their memory begins to fail, and they have difficulty remembering events, names, and complex concepts. Although their problem-solving abilities deteriorate with time, their decision-making abilities are usually faster and more focused.

Older adults who continue stimulating their minds through conservation and educational activities experience a slower decline in cognitive abilities than those who remain stagnant.

Culture and cognitive development

Lev Vygotsky developed *the sociocultural theory of cognitive development,* which proposes that children's cognitive skills evolve from interactions with their surrounding culture involving parents, teachers, and other community members.

To comprehend the role of culture in cognitive development, Vygotsky proposed that it is imperative to study cognitive development from four interrelated perspectives.

Four perspectives: *micro-genetic, ontogenetic, phylogenetic,* and *socio-historical frameworks.*

> *Micro-genetic framework* is cognitive development in brief periods (i.e., minutes and seconds).

> *Ontogenetics* changes over a lifetime.

> *Phylogenetics* is a change over evolutionary periods.

> *Socio-historical framework* is cultural changes (e.g., values, norms, traditions, and technology).

Lev Vygotsky, a Soviet psychologist

Principles of cultural influence are embedded in *sociocultural theory of cognitive development.*

First principle of cultural influence is that cultures vary in the institutions and settings they offer to facilitate children's development and in how they assess their cognitive development.

Second principle of cultural influence is that unless these variations are considered part of the child's cultural contexts, the child's cognitive development is seriously underestimated.

Vygotsky suggested that children are born supplied with necessary mental functions. These functions include memory, sensation, perception, and attention. Mental functions are influenced by the culture they are subjected to, and the culture transforms them into new mental processes and higher cognitive abilities over time.

Initial cognitive competence comes from interactions with adults and other knowledgeable people within the child's culture. The myriad tasks a child must learn, such as learning and speaking a new language, are far too complicated to learn in isolation. Vygotsky proposed that most tasks are learned through guidance and encouragement from the culture surrounding the child. The child's cognitive development is influenced and shaped as the child participates in cultural activities and observes adults engaging in those cultural activities.

Vygotsky's theory posits that children's cognitive development is enhanced through proper interactions. For example, a structured learning environment, in which the child is provided with aid and instruction uniquely parallel to the child's current abilities, can fuel development.

Cooperative and interactive learning exercises are vital during this process, as is monitoring the child's progress very closely.

As the child gains ability, more cognitive responsibility should be given. Unlike Piaget's theory, which emphasizes that peers are the primary change agents in a child's cognitive development,

Vygotsky's theory proposes that adults are the most important source of guidance.

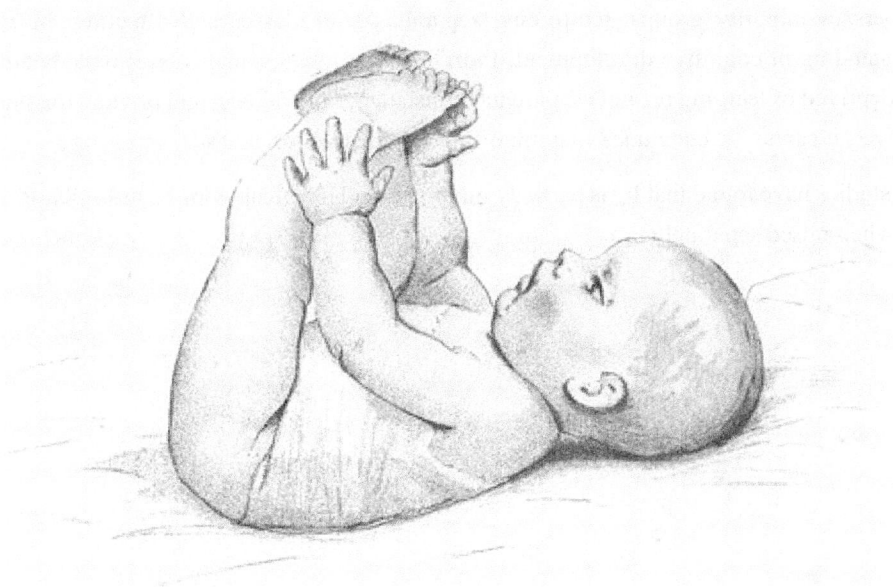

In Vygotsky's theory, children's cognitive development is enhanced through the right interactions, in which they are provided with aid and instruction that are appropriate to the child's current abilities.

Heredity and environment influence cognitive development

Cognitive development combines *heredity* and *environmental forces.*

Heredity is inherited developmental instructions transmitted to offspring via the genetic code.

Environment includes *external surroundings* and *social* and *cultural influences.*

Interactions between heredity and the environment can be visualized as paths for development.

In the earlier stages of life, development is heavily based on heredity. As life continues, the number of path options increases, and the influence of the environment increases.

It is difficult to accurately distinguish the influences that heredity and the environment have on human characteristics. Individuals with similar genetic makeup, such as close relatives, usually live in similar environments. Consequently, when similarities in IQ are within one family, it is difficult to differentiate whether these similarities arose from heredity or the environment.

However, extensive research has found that both heredity and the environment are crucial in cognitive development and intelligence.

Many researchers propose that heredity sets an individual's IQ's upper and lower bounds.

Physical and behavioral experiences about an individual's quality of life may affect intellectual development. Many researchers argue that the *environment* determines IQ.

Historically, the race and intelligence controversy has encouraged discrimination against members of minority groups, reinforcing separate social classes and affecting the general understanding of cognitive development. Individuals in lower social classes have historically been deprived of learning resources, parental assistance, role models, and privacy for studying. However, it cannot be concluded that minorities score lower on IQ tests.

Twin studies have found that IQ is partially inherited, and identical twins have similar IQ scores even when raised separately.

Biological factors that affect cognition

Hippocampus is vital in creating memories.

Eric Kandel and colleagues have shown that individuals with a damaged hippocampus lose the ability to form *explicit memories* but can form *implicit memories*.

Eric Kandel, Austrian psychologist and neuroscientist

Evidence shows that the *amygdala* is central in storing emotional memories because some emotions prove experiences. Specific memories have emotional significance and are remembered better or are harder to forget. For example, individuals with post-traumatic stress disorder (PTSD) have problems getting rid of traumatic memories because they are heavy emotional experiences.

Clive Wearing study researched the effects of brain damage on memory. The procedure was to examine Clive's amnesia through qualitative and quantitative processes. The qualitative process consisted of interviews with Clive's wife, Deborah. Deborah Clive was asked about her husband's amnesia, and she described Clive writing in his diary, "9:00 AM just woke up," and several moments later, writing, "9:01 AM just woke up," demonstrating severe amnesia.

In Clive's case, the MRI showed damage to the frontal and temporal lobes. However, the hippocampus was the most affected part of his brain, where memory and learning functions are localized. Qualitative interviews discovered that memories are distributed in several brain regions, not just the hippocampus.

For example, Clive could still play the piano, illustrating that the brain areas related to procedural memory and the cerebellum were unaffected.

Types of problem-solving

Problem-solving strategies include *trial and error*, *algorithm* (or a step-by-step process), and *heuristics* (or mental shortcuts).

For some problems, a combination of these strategies is used to formulate a solution.

For example, an algorithm strategy is used while changing a tire until an individual notices a missing wrench. In the meantime, other tools will be used, and the best possible solution will be sought using trial and error.

Problem-solving strategies are used *consciously* at certain times and *unconsciously* at others.

Individuals might not be actively thinking about a particular problem. However, while in the shower or during mundane activities, a person might get insight or inspiration, known as *insight.*

Theories on problem-solving

Gestalt theory states that problem-solving occurs through a *flash of insight*.

Insight is when a problem solver transitions from a state of not knowing to a state of knowing.

During insight, problem solvers *envision the problem* that *enables the solution.*

Gestalt psychologists conceptualize insight as schemas where the respective parts fit together.

Additionally, it involves sudden reorganization of visual information to make it fit to solve problems. It involves simply restating the problem, thus making it easier to solve. It removes various mental blocks and finds a mental analog (or similar problem) the analytical person already knows how to solve.

Information processing theory states that a problem can be represented as a problem space or a representation of the initial state, goal state, and all possible intervening states and a search heuristic. This process is seen as a strategy for moving through the problem space from one state of the problem to the next. The problem begins in the initial given state, where the analytical person applies an operator that generates a new state until the goal is reached.

For example, a common search heuristic is a *means-ends analysis*, where the problem solver seeks to *apply an operator* that will satisfy the problem solver's current goal; if a constraint blocks the application of the operator, then a goal is set to remove that constraint.

Information processing theory informs educational programs aimed at teaching strategies for problem-solving.

Barriers to effective problem-solving

Humans are not always careful and logical when making decisions. Usually, humans do not put in enough time and effort to make decisions; they write off the problem or situation as trivial, lack the time necessary to solve the problem, or can find no clear and logical path to solve it.

Mental shortcuts (or *heuristics*) increase the efficiency of deciding. Mental shortcuts are helpful but can lead to errors in judgment.

Representativeness heuristic is the tendency to think about the likelihood of a particular event occurring based on typical mental representations of those events.

Availability heuristic is the tendency to make judgments based on how readily available the information is in a person's memory. If the memory is readily available, a person might think that the idea is more common than it is.

Belief bias is the tendency to judge arguments based on personal beliefs rather than using sound logic. Once preexisting beliefs are formed, they resist change through *belief perseverance.*

Belief perseverance is the tendency to maintain beliefs despite contrary evidence.

Confirmation bias is a barrier in problem-solving that occurs when individuals search for information that supports their preconceived notions rather than information that disproves them. This bias prevents people from considering the problem from multiple perspectives.

People approach problems from a *biased perspective*. In this sense, the decision will be erroneous. A one-sided rather than holistic view of the situation might lead the problem solver to an incorrect solution.

Overconfidence is an overestimation of the accuracy of knowledge and judgments. It may develop through a frequent utilization of intuitive heuristics and a tendency to confirm preconceived notions.

Framing influences how the information is presented. For example, people buy the meat in the grocery store labeled as 75% lean versus the meat labeled as 25% fat.

Fixation is the inability to see problems from a fresh perspective and is an obstacle to problem-solving. Fixation occurs due to a *mental set.*

Mental set tends to fixate on solutions that have worked in the past, even though these solutions may not be adequate for the current problem.

Functional fixedness tends to perceive the functions of objects as fixed and unchanging.

Notes for active learning

Consciousness

States of consciousness

Consciousness is an individual's awareness of themself and their surroundings. It is selective attention to information and processing one thing at a time.

Pre-consciousness is information a person is unaware of but can be accessed with attention.

Unconsciousness is information that cannot be accessed, including primitive beliefs and patterns that drive behavior.

Alertness

Alertness is the state of active attention using high sensory awareness, such as being watchful and prompt to meet danger or emergency. It often manifests itself in being quick to perceive and act. This is related to both psychology and physiology.

An alertness deficiency manifests from some conditions, including narcolepsy, attention deficit disorder, chronic fatigue syndrome, depression, Addison's disease, and sleep deprivation, with a pronounced lack of alertness graded as an altered level of consciousness.

People who have to be alert during their jobs, such as air traffic controllers or pilots, often face challenges maintaining their alertness.

Research shows that retaining a constant level of alertness is rare, if not impossible, for people engaged in attention-intensive and monotonous tasks. If people working in safety-related fields (e.g., transportation) have attention deficits, this may have severe consequences (e.g., air traffic controllers and nuclear power plant operators).

Circadian rhythms

Circadian rhythm is an animal's 24-hour biological clock, which can be negatively affected by changes in normal behavior patterns, such as tiredness after long travel periods (i.e., *jet lag*).

Body temperature and awareness change throughout the day and night; therefore, taking a test or studying during a circadian peak is advised. Jet lag negatively affects rhythms.

If all light cues and clocks are hidden, humans adapt to a 25-hour day; however, bright lights reset an individual's natural clock.

Suprachiasmatic nucleus, *pineal gland*, and melatonin hormone affect circadian rhythms.

Hypothalamus is a small brain section that influences the glandular system.

Suprachiasmatic nucleus is the internal clock regulating waking up and falling asleep.

Brain's waves change according to the specific stage of the sleep cycle.

Sleep cycles

Sequence from drowsiness to deep stage IV sleep usually takes about an hour.

Adaptive theory of sleep proposes that animals and humans evolved sleep patterns to avoid predators by sleeping when predators are most active.

Restorative theory of sleep proposes that it is necessary for physical health, replenishing biomolecules, and repairing cellular damage.

Electroencephalogram (EEG) measures stages of sleep. Individuals lying awake and relaxed before sleep show *slow alpha waves*.

Delta sleep can occupy up to forty percent of children's sleep

Sleep stages

There are five stages of sleep, and 60-90 minutes are needed to pass through all five stages.

First four stages of sleep are NREM (non-REM), and the last is REM sleep.

Stage one is experienced as one falls asleep and is a transition stage between being awake and being asleep. It usually lasts one to five minutes and occupies 2-5% of a typical night of sleep.

In stage one, the eyes roll slightly and consist of *theta waves*, which are slow-moving, high amplitude, and low frequency.

Additionally, there are brief periods of *alpha waves*, like those present while awake.

Stage two follows and is considered the baseline of sleep, part of the 90-minute cycle, and occupies 45-60% of sleep time.

Stages three and *four* are *delta* (i.e., *slow wave*) sleep and lasts 15-30 minutes.

Slow wave sleep is when brain activity slows dramatically from the *theta rhythm* of stage two, much slower *delta* waves, and the waves' height (i.e., *amplitude*) increases dramatically.

Stage four sleep is the deepest, with predominant EEG (*electroencephalogram*) activity of low frequency (1–4 Hz) and high-amplitude fluctuations of *delta waves*. It is the most restorative. Sleep-deprived brains crave delta sleep.

In children, delta sleep occupies up to forty percent of sleep time, which causes children not to wake up or stay in "dead asleep" states most of the night.

Stage five is *REM sleep.* REM (*rapid eye movement*) sleep is active and accounts for 20-25% of a typical night of sleep. Breathing, heart rate, and brain wave activity quicken.

REM sleep is when vivid dreams occur.

During REM, the body is essentially paralyzed, while the genitals become aroused with morning erections from the final REM stage.

Babies are in REM more than adolescents and adults.

From REM, a person returns to stage two.

Dreaming

Dreams are images, emotions, and thoughts that pass through a sleeping person's mind.

Manifest content is the remembered storyline of a dream, while *latent content* is the underlying meaning of a dream.

Under Freud's *wish fulfillment theory*, dreams are the key to understanding our inner conflicts. They highlight the ideas and thoughts hidden in one's unconscious mind. The theory poses that dreams represent wish-fulfilling attempts, where one acts out their unconscious desires.

Wish fulfillment theory includes latent and manifest content, where manifest content is the *literal storyline* of the dream, and latent content is the *unconscious meaning* of it.

Ego protects individuals from information in the unconscious mind, called "*protected sleep.*"

Information processing theory is that dreams sort and process memories experienced daily. REM sleep increases after stressful events.

Activation-synthesis theory (i.e., physiological function theory) is that during the night, the brainstem releases random neural activity, and dreams function to make sense of that activity.

REM rebound is the tendency for REM sleep to increase following REM sleep deprivation. When a person has not slept well for a week and then sleeps for ten hours, that person will dream more frequently.

Sigmund Freud, Austrian neurologist, and founder of psychoanalysis

Daydreaming (the term) is used frequently in contemporary society. The question scientists ask is why humans take part in such an activity. Daydreaming may help people prepare for future events; it nourishes social development and can substitute for impulsive behavior.

Sleep-wake disorders

Insomnia is a recurring problem of falling or staying asleep. Insomnia is not defined by the number of hours slept every night. It affects about 10% of the population.

Narcolepsy is uncontrollable sleep. One suffering from this disorder lapses directly into REM, usually in times of stress or joy. This disease affects less than 0.001% of the population.

Sleep apnea is temporary breathing cessation during sleep and consequent reawakening. It is as common as insomnia. This disorder affects attention, memory, and energy levels and prevents deep sleep. Overweight men tend to be at a higher risk of being affected by sleep apnea.

Night terror is a sleep disorder characterized by high arousal and a sensation of being terrified. It occurs in stage four, early in the night. These arousals are often not remembered.

Sleepwalking (or *somnambulism*) is a sleep disorder affecting 10% of people at least once. It occurs mainly during deep, non-REM sleep, usually in stage three or four, early at night. Some symptoms or features of sleepwalking include ambulation or moving about during sleep.

The onset of this disorder typically occurs in pre-pubertal children. It is challenging to arouse the person during an episode, usually followed by amnesia. Other medical and psychiatric disorders can be present but do not account for the condition. The ambulation is not due to other sleep disorders such as REM sleep behavior disorder or night terrors. Fatigue persists, and stress and anxiety levels are high during this time.

Sleepwalking may include sitting up and appearing awake while asleep, getting up and walking around, or complex activities such as moving furniture, going to the bathroom, dressing, undressing, and similar activities. Some individuals even drive a car when they are asleep. The episode can be brief, lasting a few seconds, thirty minutes, or longer.

One common misconception is that a sleepwalker should not be awakened. It is not dangerous to awaken a sleepwalker; however, the person will be confused and disoriented briefly. A misconception is that a person cannot be injured when sleepwalking. Injuries caused by tripping and loss of balance are common among sleepwalkers.

Hypnosis and meditation

Hypnosis is comparable to relaxation, where physical and mental health components must be addressed together. Researchers propose that hypnosis is a deep state of relaxation, where the mind is more focused, and the connection between thoughts, emotions, and behaviors is vivid.

Contrary to widely held belief, hypnosis is not magical and cannot cause individuals to do anything against their judgment or moral beliefs.

Hypnotherapists are licensed professionals who use hypnosis as part of the treatment regimen for various psychological disorders. It is rarely the primary form of treatment but is beneficial when used with relaxation and talk therapy for a more comprehensive treatment plan.

Posthypnotic amnesia is forgetting events that occur while under hypnosis.

Posthypnotic suggestion claims that a hypnotized person behaves in a certain way after hypnosis ends.

Role theory states that during hypnosis, people act out the roles of a hypnotized person because they are expected, suggesting that hypnosis is a social phenomenon.

Hypnotic suggestibility is the ability to be hypnotized. It is greater in people with rich fantasies, who can focus intensely on a single task for a long time and follow directions well.

State theory states that hypnosis is an altered state of consciousness.

Dissociation theory was conceptualized by Ernest Hilgard, who hypothesized that hypnosis causes a *voluntary split in consciousness*. One level responds to the hypnotist's suggestions, and the other retains awareness of reality.

In the ice water bath experiment, subjects in a state of hypnosis felt pain but did not report it. This experiment suggested the presence of a hidden observer. There seems to be a level of consciousness that monitors what is happening, while another level obeys the hypnotist.

Meditation is a powerful mechanism that slows brain processes and quiets thoughts, the cessation of thoughts. If the goal is to relax and turn off the mind, then meditation is a helpful tool to ease stress and anxiety.

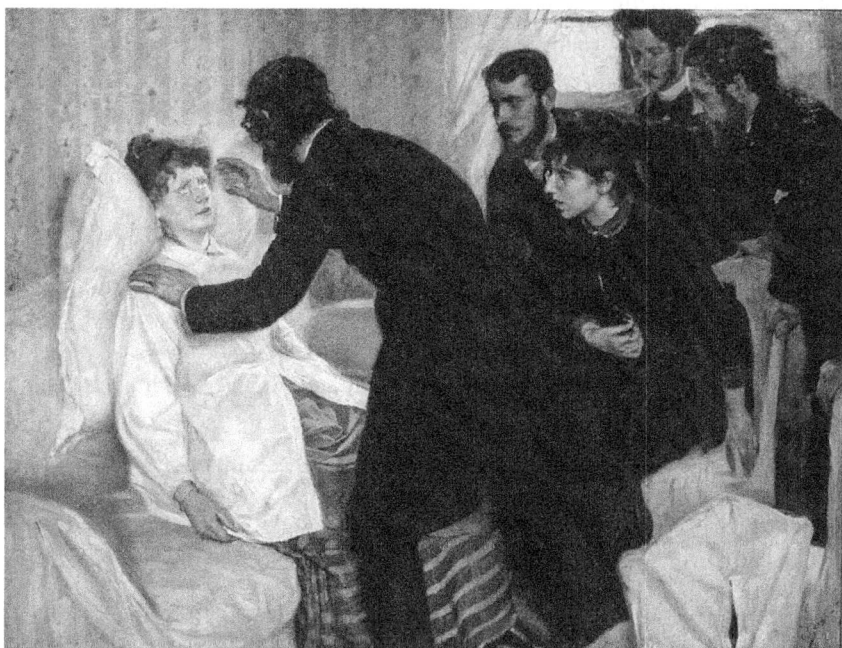

Painting of a hypnotic session

Consciousness-altering drugs and substances

Psychoactive drug is a consciousness-altering chemical that affects mood and perception.

Psychoactive drugs are in food and drinks, including chocolate, coffee, soda, alcohol, and over-the-counter medications (e.g., Aspirin, Tylenol). These drugs affect consciousness by influencing the function of neurotransmitters at the synapses of the central nervous system.

Some psychoactive drugs are agonists and mimic the functionality of a neurotransmitter; some are antagonists and block the action of a neurotransmitter, and some work by blocking the reuptake of neurotransmitters at the synapse.

Tolerance is caused by a physiological change when more of the same drug is needed for the same effect; failure to increase dosage accordingly can lead to symptoms of withdrawal.

Psychoactive drugs include depressants, stimulants, and hallucinogens.

Depressants slow bodily and cognitive functions.

Stimulants arouse body and cognitive functions.

Hallucinogens distort perceptions or evoke sensation without any sensory input.

Alcohol is a depressant that slows the sympathetic nervous system, disrupts memory processing and reduces self-awareness.

Alcohol is associated with almost 60% of crimes. From a macro perspective, it is the worst legally available and readily accessible substance.

Barbiturates are depressants and tranquilizers. They are usually taken to sleep, yet REM sleep is reduced. A synergistic effect can occur when this drug is taken with other drugs.

Opiates are depressants derived from the poppy plant and are agonists for endorphins.

Opiates are physically addictive as they rapidly change brain chemistry and create tolerance and withdrawal symptoms. Examples of opiates are heroin and morphine.

Addiction comes quickly, and withdrawal symptoms are severe.

Stimulants speed up bodily and cognitive processes by affecting the autonomic nervous system and producing a sense of euphoria. Caffeine, cocaine, amphetamines, and nicotine are stimulants that disturb sleep, reduce appetite, increase anxiety, and cause heart problems.

Hallucinogens cause changes in the perception of reality, including sensory hallucinations, loss of identity, and vivid fantasies.

LSD (*lysergic acid diethylamide*), peyote, psilocybin, mushrooms, and marijuana are hallucinogens. LSD is associated with PTSD and schizophrenia.

Reverse tolerance occurs when the second dose is less than the first but can cause greater effects and linger in the body for weeks.

Drug addiction and the reward pathway in the brain

One critical pathway in understanding the effects of drugs on the brain is the *reward pathway*.

Reward pathway involves many brain regions, including the ventral tegmental area, the nucleus accumbens, and the pre-frontal cortex. When activated by a rewarding stimulus like food, water, and sex, information travels from the ventral tegmental area to the pre-frontal cortex.

Cocaine provides a prime example of how drugs interfere with the regular activity of the brain. When an individual snorts, smokes, or injects cocaine, it travels to the brain via the bloodstream.

Even though it reaches all brain areas, its euphoric effects are controlled in a few specific areas, especially those associated with the reward pathway.

Information is transmitted in the brain by neurotransmitters (e.g., dopamine).

Under normal conditions, dopamine is released by a neuron in the synapse and binds to specialized proteins, known as dopamine receptors, on the neighboring neuron. After the signal is sent to the neighboring neuron, dopamine is transported back to the neuron, from which another specialized dopamine transporter protein releases it.

Drugs of abuse can negatively affect the process of *neurotransmission*.

Cocaine blocks the removal of dopamine from the synapse by binding dopamine transporters. This results in a build-up of dopamine in the synapse, which causes the continuous stimulation of receiving neurons, responsible for the euphoria experienced by cocaine users.

Memory

Encoding

Memory is the persistence of learning over time by storing and retrieving information.

Encoding is the processing of information in the memory system.

Automatic processing and *effortful processing* are the two ways of encoding information.

> *Automatic processing* is the unconscious encoding of incidental information. Space, time, and word meanings are encoded without effort, automatic with practice.

> *Effortful* encoding requires conscious effort.

Rehearsal is the common effortful processing technique. After sufficient rehearsal, what was effortful may become automatic.

Factors affecting encoding

Next-in-line effect states that individuals rarely remember what has been said or done if it has occurred immediately preceding the need to use information.

Information acquired minutes before falling asleep is rarely remembered.

However, information gained an hour before sleep is well remembered.

Ears register recorded information played while one is sleeping but is not remembered.

Spacing effect states that individuals encode better after studying or practicing over time.

Serial positioning effect is an individual's tendency to recall the first and last items in a list.

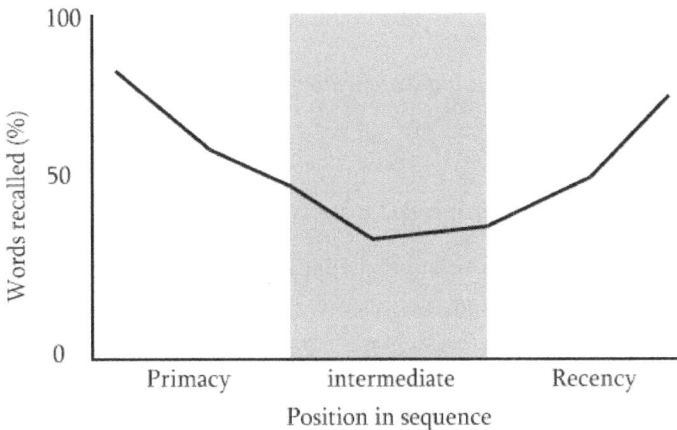

Serial position effect

Three types of encoding are *semantic*, *acoustic*, and *visual*.

> *Semantic encoding* is the encoding of *meaning*, such as the meaning of words.

> *Acoustic encoding* is the encoding of *sounds*, especially the sounds of various words.

> *Visual encoding* is the encoding of *picture images*.

Research found *semantic* encoding to be the most effective for ascertaining meaning.

Self-reference effect states that people remember better when used to describe themselves. One example of this phenomenon can be seen with the use of adjectives.

Processes that encode memories

Many strategies exist to enhance the encoding process.

Imagery (or *mental pictures*) is a strategy to enhance the encoding process.

Chunking is the organization of items into familiar, manageable units.

Often, these processes occur automatically.

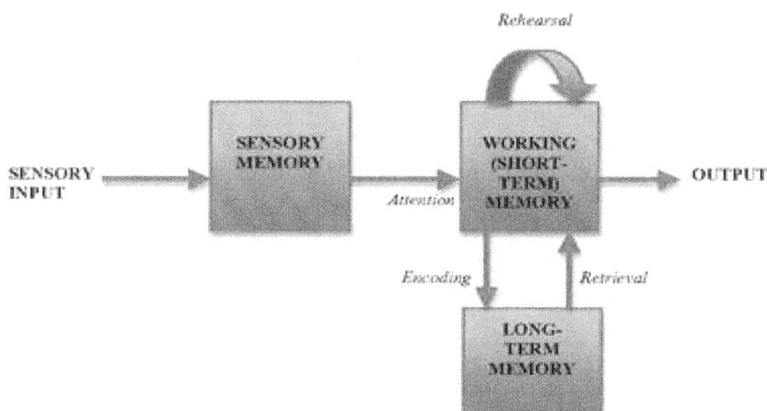

Model of memory systems

Memory storage

Memory storage is the retention of encoded material over time.

Sensory memory is the first stop for any external stimuli. It contains all the information the senses process for less than a second.

George Sperling's experiment flashed a 3×3 grid for one-twentieth of a second. Participants had to recall one of the rows immediately afterward, which was indicated by a matched tone.

Participants could recall everything perfectly, which suggests that the entire grid system must be held in sensory memory for a split second.

Iconic memory is a momentary sensory memory of visual stimuli, a photograph-like quality lasting about a second.

Echoic memory is for auditory stimuli. Even when not paying attention to someone, one can still recall the last few words in the past three or four seconds.

Selective attention determines which sensory images get encoded.

Short-term or working memory holds everything an individual is currently thinking. If the individual does not use short-term memory, it usually fades within 10 to 30 seconds.

Working memories refer to the memories that individuals are currently working with and are aware of. The capacity is limited to seven items. Individuals can recall digits better than letters.

Long-term memory is an individual's permanent storage. It is unlimited; once the information is there, it usually remains indefinitely.

Memories are *not* electrical and *do not* reside in a specific part of the brain.

Episodic memory is memories of specific events stored in sequential order.

Semantic memories are general knowledge stored as facts, meanings, or categories.

Procedural memory is performing skills stored sequentially and challenging to describe with words.

Explicit memories are conscious memories of facts or events.

Implicit memories are unintentional, and individuals might not even realize they have them.

Eidetic (or *photographic memory*) is rare and uses compelling and enduring visual images.

Semantic networks and spreading activation

Semantic network theory states that the brain forms memories by connecting meanings and context with meanings already in memory.

Spreading activation searches associative networks, neural networks, or semantic networks. The process is initiated by labeling a set of source nodes (e.g., concepts in a semantic network) with weights (or "*activation*") and then iteratively propagating (or spreading) that activation to nodes linked to the source nodes.

Activation originates from alternate paths and terminates when two paths reach the same node.

Brain research shows that several brain areas are essential in semantic processing.

Recall, recognition, and relearning

Retrieval refers to getting information out of memory so that an individual can utilize it.

Recall retrieves memory using external cues, including logical structures, partial memories, narratives, or clues.

For example, recall is when a person takes an exam; this involves remembering parts of the information and then reconstructing the rest based on partial memories.

Recognition matches a current event (or fact) with something in memory. Here, an individual identifies information after experiencing it again, for example, by taking a multiple-choice exam and recognizing the correct answer among the choices.

Re-learning is the process of learning something already learned. It is easier to understand and retrieve information in the future and strengthen memories.

Retrieval cues

Retrieval cues carry forward the recovery of lost memories. Retrieval cues are most important for *prospective memory* (or memory about a future event). Cues can be an object (or scent) that reminds a person of something related.

For example, when trying to memorize the parts of the brain, it helps to use a brain model with parts that can be disassembled and reassembled since auditory, visual, and tactile sensations are identified as cues.

Cued recall is a process used by researchers to study these effects. Subjects are given pairs of words to study. The experimenter gives participants one word to cue the recall of the word with which it was paired.

Stronger links between the words increase the subject's recall of the pair.

When mental and physical cues are not immediately available to generate them independently, a fruitful strategy is to take cues from hierarchies, associations, and schemas, which, as mentioned before, are the many ways the information is organized in long-term memory.

Mood-congruent memory proposes a greater likelihood of recalling an item when the person recognized their mood when the event occurred. For example, depressed people will recall sad memories from the past.

Moods affect how an individual interprets other people's behaviors.

State-dependent memory is the recall of events encoded states of consciousness.

Processes that aid retrieval

Priming is a mechanism of *association* used to retrieve information.

Priming effect is when people respond faster (or better) to an item if a similar item precedes it. It is an involuntary and unconscious phenomenon consisting of repetition and semantic priming.

Repetition priming means recognizing a face or word is easier and quicker if an individual has recently seen that same image or word.

Semantic priming is recognizing someone quickly if seen with someone associated with them.

Retrieval is affected by the order in which the information is presented.

Primacy effect states that individuals are more likely to recall items at the beginning of a list.

Recency effect is demonstrated by the ability to recall items at the end of a list.

Serial position effect suggests that the recall of a list is affected by the order of items.

Context effect helps individuals put themselves in the context they experienced when encoding the information.

Tip-of-the-tongue phenomenon is the temporary inability to remember information.

Flash-bulb memories are vivid recollections of striking events because of the elevated level of surprise and emotional arousal these events create. They are powerful because of the relevance of concurrent events encoded as contextual information and memory.

William James, the psychologist who identified the tip-of-the-tongue phenomenon

Déjà vu is that eerie feeling of having experienced something before. During this phenomenon, the current situation cues a similar experience, tricking the mind into thinking they are the same.

Forgetting

Encoding failure is the inability to encode information properly. Consequently, the information does not enter long-term memory.

Retrieval failure is when the memory is encoded and stored but cannot be accessed.

Motivated forgetting is when narratives are revised consciously or unconsciously. One example of this mechanism is *repression.* In psychoanalytic theory, repression is the primary defense mechanism for banishing anxiety-arousing thoughts and feelings from consciousness.

Aging and memory

Normal aging is associated with a memory decline and is referred to as age-related memory loss or age-associated memory impairment. Studies comparing the effects of aging on several types of memory, including semantic memory, episodic memory, short-term memory, and priming, found that *episodic memory* is the most impaired due to *normal aging*. Aging also causes some short-term memory impairment.

Source information is an episodic memory impairment with aging. This type of information involves where and when the information was learned. Knowing the source of information can be helpful in daily decision-making.

Episodic memory is supported by networks spanning frontal, temporal, and parietal lobes. The interconnections within the lobes enable distinct aspects of memory.

Effects of grey matter lesions have been extensively studied, but less is known about the interconnecting fiber tracts.

With aging, degradation of white matter structure is observed, further focusing attention on the critical white matter connections.

Additionally, associative learning, a component of episodic memory, is affected by aging.

Reasons have been proposed for the elderly using fewer effective ways to encode and retrieve.

Disuse is when adults tend not to use memory strategies as they move further away from the educational system.

Diminished attentional capacity hypothesis suggests that older people engage in less self-initiated encoding due to reduced attentional capacity.

Memory self-efficacy is the lack of experience older people have, such as losing confidence in their memory performance, leading to poor results.

A postmortem research examination of five brains of elderly people classified as "super-aged," having above-average memory, presented a possible biological explanation for memory deficits in aging. The study found that these individuals had fewer fiber-like tangles of *tau protein* than those seen in typical elderly brains. However, a similar amount of amyloid plaque was found.

Memory dysfunctions

Alzheimer's disease is a progressive neurodegenerative disease in which connections mediating cell-to-cell communication in the brain are damaged. It is the most common form of *dementia.*

Wernicke-Korsakoff syndrome is a neurological disease caused by *thymine* (or Vitamin B_1) deficiency. It is usually associated with heavy alcohol consumption.

Symptoms include oculomotor malfunctions, cerebellar dysfunction, and altered mental states. It is characterized by severe amnesia, disorientation, frequent confabulation, or making up of information to compensate for poor memory retrieval.

Those afflicted have impaired short-term memory and experience difficulty learning new information or tasks.

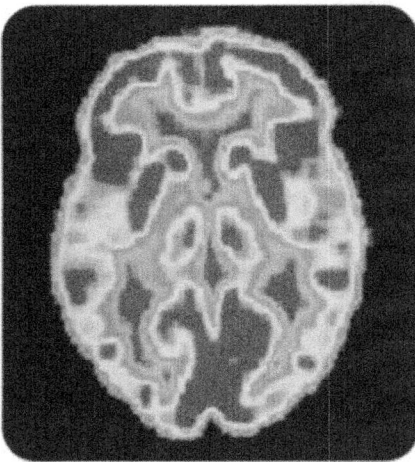

PET Scan of Normal Brain   **PET Scan of Alzheimer's Disease Brain**

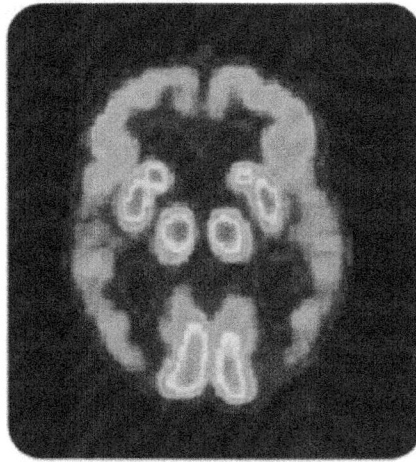

PET scans of a healthy brain versus the brain of a person with Alzheimer's disease

Stress affects memory

Cortisol is a hormone produced in the adrenal glands in response to psychological and physiological stress.

However, too much cortisol is released during long-term stress, affecting immune functioning and memory processing.

Excessive cortisol inhibits the brain from *forming* or *accessing* existing memories.

Sapolsky performed a study that demonstrated that prolonged stress could damage neurons in the hippocampus, but this can be reversed if normal cortisol levels are restored.

Long-term stress can cause irreversible damage.

Robert Sapolsky, an American biologist

Lupein observed elderly persons for five years to study the effect of cortisol on memory and found that about 30% of people had high cortisol levels.

Elderly with high cortisol levels have more memory loss and significant hippocampus atrophy.

Decay

Decay occurs when a person does not use memory or its connections for a long time.

Re-learning effect is when relearning information takes less time and effort than learning.

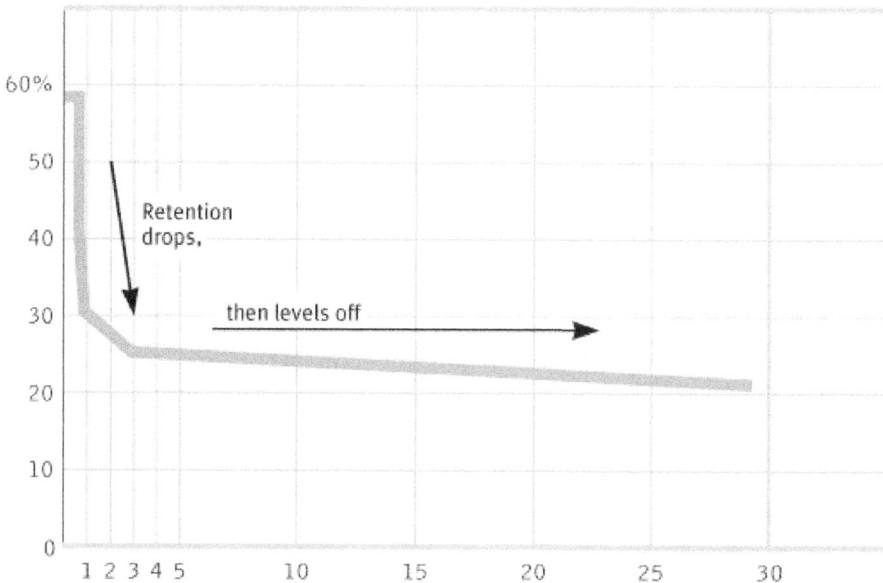

Ebbinghaus Forgetting Curve plots the percentage of list retained when relearning vs. days.

Interference

Interference is when information in memory competes with what someone is trying to recall.

Retroactive interference is learning that interferes with the recall of older information.

Proactive interference is older information interfering with the recall of recent information.

Memory construction and source monitoring

People tend to alter memories as they encode or retrieve them. Expectations, schemas, and environment may alter their memory formation and retrieval process.

Source amnesia is the inability to recall the origin of an event that has been experienced, heard, read about, or imagined.

Source monitoring is an unconscious mental test humans perform to determine if a memory is factual and accurate, comes from a dream, or is imagined. Individuals use many sources to determine the source of a memory or an idea.

Physical, linguistic, and categorical information about people and objects determines reality in certain situations, such as determining that the person we see walking toward us is a longtime friend and not a character from a movie.

External source monitoring focuses on sources that are in an individual's environment. For example, recalling which professor gave an exam yesterday.

Internal source monitoring focuses on internal factors, such as when individuals try to distinguish between what they said aloud and what they thought to themselves.

Source monitoring errors occur for many reasons, such as brain injury, aging, depression, and cognitive biases.

Neural plasticity

Neural plasticity is the formation of neural connections, which allows neurons to repair, regrow, and adapt after injury or disease. This process varies by age, with children experiencing rapid formation of neural connections, which is ongoing throughout life.

Neural plasticity is affected by *heredity* and the *environment.*

Memory and *learning* are closely related but independent.

Memory is previously acquired information.

Learning is the *acquiring of knowledge* (or skills).

Long-term potentiation

Long-term potentiation (LTP) is the signal transmission that strengthens the response of the post-synaptic nerve cells by forming additional synapses. It is essential for neural plasticity.

Early phase (within 1 hour): CaMKII and PKC are activated, independent of protein synthesis.

Late phase requires gene transcription in the postsynaptic cell. Gene transcription and mRNA translation occur, and the number of AMPA receptors increases, increasing the size of the synaptic connection (depending on protein synthesis).

Long-term potentiation starts with the rapid stimulation of CAI neurons in the hippocampus.

Glu and D-serine bind to NMDA receptors. Ca^{2+} flows into the cell, and Ca^{2+} binds to calmodulin. CaMKII is activated, which phosphorylates AMPA receptors. Permeability of Na+ ions increase, which increases the cell's sensitivity to depolarization.

Gene expression and protein synthesis increase, and finally, synaptic connections strengthen.

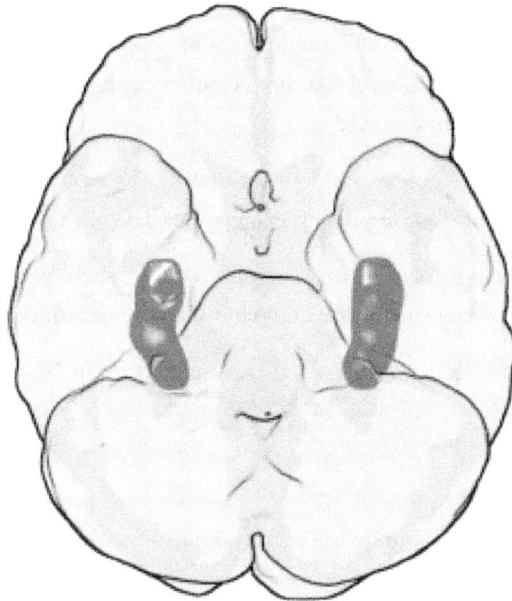

Long-term potentiation (darkened spots) was discovered in the hippocampus

Milner and Scoville research study

Henry Gustav Molaison is an important patient in the history of neuroscience. Since the age of seven, he had epilepsy caused by a head injury. As he grew, seizures got worse, and surgery was his only hope for relief.

Pioneering brain surgeon William Scoville proposed to remove the part of the brain that was causing the seizures. Henry agreed to the operation, and in 1953, Scoville performed *bilateral medial temporal lobe resection*, removing a portion of Henry's temporal lobe, including the hippocampus and amygdala regions.

After recovering from the surgery, Henry suffered from severe amnesia. He knew his name and family and could remember his childhood but had gaps in his memory of the last 11 years leading up to the surgery. More importantly, Henry had severe anterograde amnesia. He lost the ability to form new memories and forgot everything that happened to him in seconds.

Henry's severe side effects of the surgery interested a young researcher, Brenda Milner, who conducted a case study on Henry Molaison and compared her findings with Dr. Scoville's medical procedures. Her research was published in 1957 and is a widely cited neuroscience study that changed the understanding of the brain and memory. Milner continued testing Henry Molaison and published more findings between 1962 and 1972, supporting the existence of procedural memory.

Henry became a full-time research subject at the Massachusetts Institute of Technology (MIT) under the supervision of Suzanne Corkin, who analyzed original MRIs that revealed missing regions of the temporal lobe, hippocampus, and surrounding areas. These brain areas use specific neurotransmitter pathways in memory, including acetylcholine, vital in learning and episodic memory.

Hippocampus transforms *episodic memories* from *short to long-term memories*. Since Henry could retain some memories, it was hypothesized that the hippocampus does not store memories but processes them.

Medial temporal region within the hippocampus is central for *long-term memory storage* and using knowledge in everyday situations.

Henry and other amnesia patients have deficits in some memories but not others, which is evidence that the brain has multiple memory systems supported by different brain regions.

Henry Molaison died in 2008 at the age of 82. His much-researched brain was removed and scanned using MRI. It was sliced into 2401 70-micrometer sections mounted onto slides for neuroscientists to map the human brain.

Notes for active learning

Language

Language development theories

Learning perspective argues that children imitate what they see and hear and learn from punishment and reinforcement. B.F. Skinner proposed that adults shape children's speech by reinforcing infants' babbling that sounds almost like words.

Nativist perspective states that humans are biologically programmed to gain knowledge. Noam Chomsky proposes that humans have a *language acquisition device (LAD),* which contains knowledge of grammatical rules common to all languages. It allows children to understand the rules of the language they hear.

Noam Chomsky, American linguist and scientist

Chomsky developed *transformational grammar*, *surface structure*, and *deep structure*.

Transformational grammar transforms a sentence.

Surface structure includes words that are written.

Deep structure is the underlying syntactic representation of a sentence.

Interactionist theory states that a combination of social and biological factors causes language development. Interactionists believe that language learning is heavily influenced by children's desire to communicate with others; children are born with powerful brains that mature slowly and predispose them to acquire new understandings that they are motivated to share with others.

Collaborative learning model has the foremost interactionist theorist, Vygotsky, who posits that conversations with adults help children cognitively and linguistically.

Stages of language development

Phonemes are the smallest unit of sound used in language. English has about 44 phonemes.

Morphemes are the smallest units of meaningful sound represented as words or parts of words. Language consists of phonemes that make up morphemes, which add to words.

Syntax is the order in which words are spoken or written.

Babies proceed through the same stages of language development, independent of what language they are first exposed to and use.

Babbling is the first stage and occurs around six months of age. It represents experimentations with phonemes. Babies in this stage can produce any phoneme in any language.

Holophrastic stage is the next stage when babies speak in single words (or holophrases).

Telegraphic speech is the third stage, when toddlers combine words they can say into simple commands. The meaning is clear, but there is no syntax present.

Children learn grammar and syntax rules by misapplication at beginning stages of development.

Influence of language on cognition

Individuals can think in words, but often, the thinking occurs in mental pictures.

Linguistic relativity hypothesis proposed by psychologist Benjamin Whorf states that the structure of a human language affects how an individual conceptualizes their world.

Based on the concept that every language uniquely describes and conceptualizes the world, the hypothesis states that an individual's native language limits their cross-cultural understanding.

Every human language portrays the values of the place and culture from which it came, and various philosophers and linguists have long debated how this affects and shapes the mentality of people who speak a different language.

Brain areas that control language and speech

Brain's left hemisphere is responsible for language and speech. It is the dominant hemisphere, and the right hemisphere is vital in interpreting *visual information* and *spatial processing*.

About one-third of left-handed individuals have speech functions on the brain's right side. Left-handed individuals may need more complex testing to determine if their speech center is on the left or right side before brain surgery.

Aphasia is the impairment of language affecting production, comprehension, reading, or writing due to brain injury, commonly caused by stroke or trauma.

Broca's area is located in the left portion of the frontal lobe. If this area of the brain is damaged, the individual will have difficulty moving the tongue or facial muscles to make the sounds of speech. The individual can still understand spoken language but has significant difficulty speaking and writing, especially within specified lines; this is *Broca's Aphasia*.

Wernicke's Area is in the left temporal lobe. Damage to this area causes *Wernicke's Aphasia*.

The affected individual may speak in long sentences without meaning, add unnecessary words, and even create novel words. They can make speech sounds but have difficulty understanding speech and, therefore, are unaware of their mistakes.

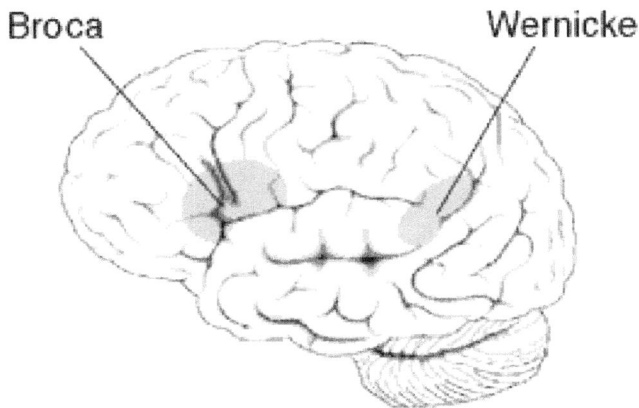

Broca's and Wernicke's areas

Relationship matrix

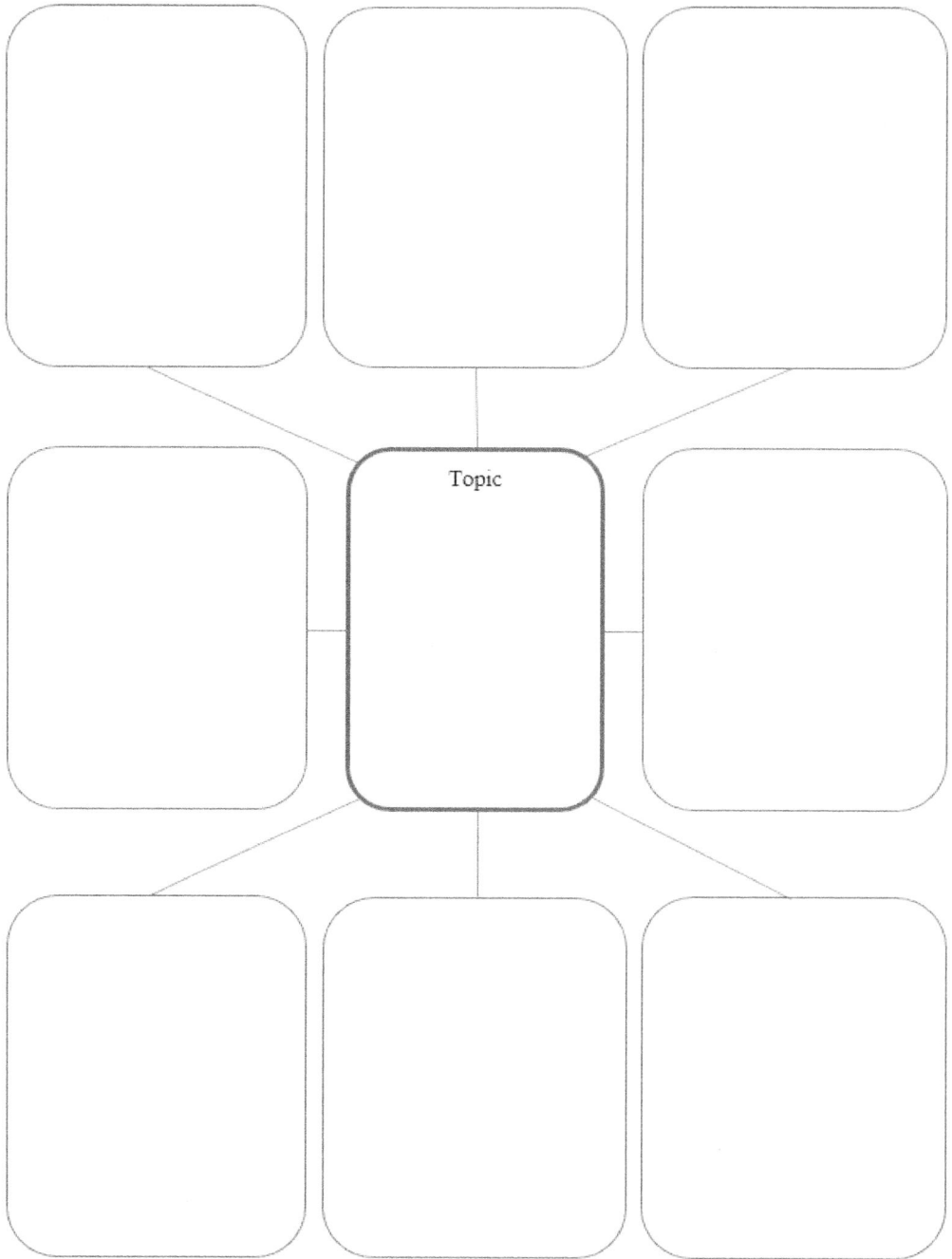

Topic

Notes for active learning

Notes for active learning

CHAPTER 6

Motivation & Emotion

To better understand emotion, researchers focus on exploring the influence of biological and cultural factors and the motivation of biological and social factors. Human behavior illustrating theories of motivation can be divided into primary and secondary motives. Behaviors can be triggered by environmental cues and neural or hormonal mechanisms involved in various motivational states.

Conflicting behaviors and motives reveal complex brain functions. In analyzing the link between physiology and experienced emotions, established theories of James–Lange, Cannon–Bard, Schachter–Singer, and opponent-process theories offer interesting and sometimes divergent explanations.

Emotions

Three components of emotion

Emotions refer to states of mind arising spontaneously in response to a stimulus.

Emotions differ from *moods* in that emotions are typically short and have a clear cause, while moods can last for an extended period and are not always in response to stimuli.

Affect refers to the experience of emotion in a brief period; it also describes an individual's expression of emotion.

Psychologists typically study emotions in three domains: cognition, physiology, and behavior.

Cognitive component

Cognitive component of emotions is the thoughts that arise during an emotional experience.

Research suggests that cognitions have a bidirectional relation with emotions; specific thoughts can cause an emotional experience, and a person's emotional state can influence their thoughts.

For example, thinking about an upcoming test may lead to anxiety. Additionally, anxiety can lead a person to think about all the details of the worst-case scenario in different situations.

Cognitive therapy (CT) is when individuals with various psychopathologies are instructed to evaluate their cognitions and analyze the emotions that result from them.

Aaron Beck, recognized as the father of cognitive therapy, termed cognitions that contribute to negative emotions as "automatic thoughts."

Cognitive theorists propose that reflection on these automatic thoughts can reduce their effect on emotions.

Physiological component

Physiological component of emotions refers to bodily changes during an emotional experience. Changes in sympathetic and parasympathetic nervous systems elicit responses. Neurological changes contribute to the physiological aspects of emotions.

Physiological responses correlated with emotional experiences include changes in heart rate, blood flow, facial expression, and pupil dilation.

Emotions may not have unique physiological patterns; *fear and excitement share* the same physiological responses.

The physiological responses associated with emotions prepare an individual's body to engage in a specific action. Fear, for example, is associated with pupil dilation, which allows the eye to take in the maximum amount of visual information in an emergency.

Behavioral component

Emotions can be described as states of behavioral readiness. Although emotions do not cause behaviors, their presence increases the likelihood that certain behaviors will occur.

For example, anger is correlated with aggressive behavior, and anxiety is correlated with avoidant behavior. The behavioral component accounts for the adaptive nature of emotions.

Behavioral component of emotions refers to the outward expression of emotions. How people perceive emotional cues and experiences of others influences how they interact with them.

For example, when someone looks angry or acts aggressively, others may be more likely to stay away from that person.

Universal emotions

There is debate over how many basic emotions exist and what those emotions are.

Emotions are typically organized according to the facial expressions that coincide with them. Theories classifying human emotions suggest between four and eight basic emotions.

Research by Paul Ekman in Papua New Guinea showed that emotions and their representation as facial expressions are consistent across cultures, suggesting that they are innate rather than learned responses.

Ekman initially identified six basic emotions across all cultures and labeled them universal. Contempt was added later as the seventh universal emotion.

Paul Ekman, an American psychologist

Fear

Fear occurs when there is a perceived threat of danger. Fear is associated with the fight-or-flight response, which involves escaping or defending against the perceived threat. Physiologically, fear is associated with the activation of the sympathetic nervous system, resulting in an increased heart rate, rapid breathing, muscle tension, and constriction of blood vessels. Fear is primarily associated with the amygdala. It is easily conditioned in humans and animals; some theorize that this is why phobias are so common.

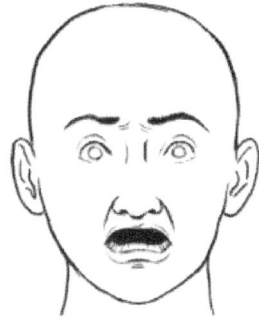

Fear is associated with anxiety, which arises when threats are perceived to be uncontrollable or unavoidable. Anxiety describes chronic worry not associated with a specific stimulus. Fear and anxiety are subjectively negative emotions.

Anger

Anger is a negative emotion by subjective reports and social appraisal. Physical correlates of anger include increased heart rate, blood pressure, adrenaline levels, and blushing. Note that the physiological response to anger is like fear; some theories propose that anger is used to mask fear unconsciously. Anger is often felt when one's boundaries have been violated or when reality does not align with expectations.

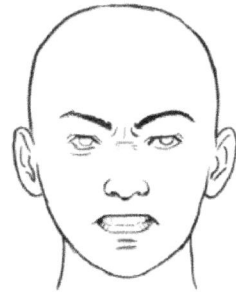

Behaviorally, anger is associated with aggression, which refers to overt action intended to harm another individual. Anger is associated with increased risk-taking. Relaxation skills are taught to reduce anger levels in people who have trouble with anger management.

Happiness

Happiness is a pleasurable emotion resulting from attaining a subjective goal. Happiness is often associated with higher levels of energy and sociability. Physiologically, happiness is associated with lower levels of cortisol and an increased heart rate. Dopamine participates in the regulation of happiness.

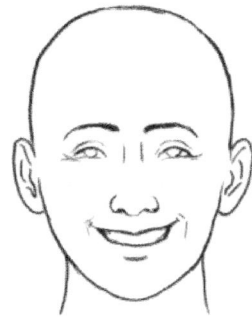

Positive psychology is a discipline in psychology concerned with studying and promoting happiness. Research suggests that 50% of an individual's happiness is genetically determined.

Martin Seligman, an American psychologist, theorized that humans are happiest if they possess five measurable elements of well-being: positive emotion, engagement, relationships, meaning, and achievement (PERMA).

Surprise

Surprise, the briefest of emotions, results from an unexpected event. When surprised, one's attention is directed to the unexpected event. After the initial reaction, the surprise changes to a different emotion depending on the cause of the surprise.

For example, if the surprising stimulus is a spider, the surprise is likely to be followed by fear. If the surprising stimulus is finding a twenty-dollar bill, surprise will be followed by happiness.

Physiologically, a surprise is a startled response. It is not necessarily experienced as pleasant or unpleasant. Surprise is associated with activation of the sympathetic nervous system only when the unexpected event is deemed threatening.

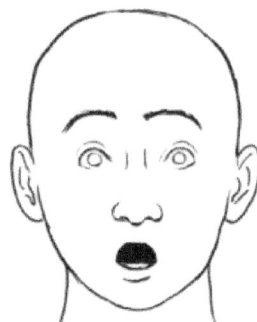

Contempt

Contempt is a social emotion felt when one believes to be superior to someone else.

Behaviorally, contempt is characterized by the rejection (or exclusion) of another. Contempt is often felt when another is viewed as easily controllable, and the two parties lack intimacy. It is often felt in conjunction with anger (or may follow anger). There is evidence that this emotion is used to regard the actions of others as incompetent.

Paul Ekman did not initially identify contempt as a universal emotion, but it was added later. Findings on contempt are less clear than on other emotions, causing some experts to be skeptical of contempt's status as a universal emotion.

Disgust

Disgust is a rejection response protecting the body from potentially harmful contaminants.

In North America, nine domains eliciting disgust exist: food, body products, animals, sexual behavior, death, gore, poor hygiene, interpersonal contamination, and moral offenses.

Studies have found that females are more sensitive to disgust than males. Disgust is a defensive emotion emphasizing the difference between humans and animals.

Another hypothesis proposes that disgust is a food-related emotion that evolved to protect humans from disease.

Interestingly, some of the nine domains found to elicit disgust can be viewed in terms of their pathogenic natures.

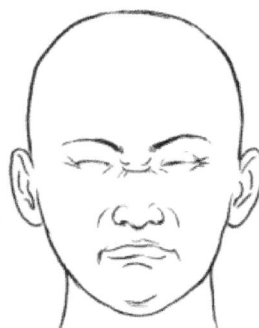

Sadness

Sadness is primarily associated with a perceived loss and is often described as a "sinking" feeling. Behavioral correlates of sadness include becoming lethargic, withdrawn, and isolated.

Physiologically, sadness is not fully understood but is associated with decreased heart rate. Chronic sadness can lead to poor cardiovascular health and increase the chances of dying after a heart attack.

Excessive sadness is characteristic of depression. One type of treatment for depression, cognitive therapy, focuses on the cognitive components of sadness to reduce its intensity.

Someone receiving cognitive therapy for depression would be taught to recognize cognitions that contribute to sadness (e.g., "I'm not good at anything") and produce evidence to contradict these thoughts. They are taught to replace cognitions associated with sadness with more neutral thoughts (e.g., "I am good at some things; I can improve in the areas I am not yet as good in.")

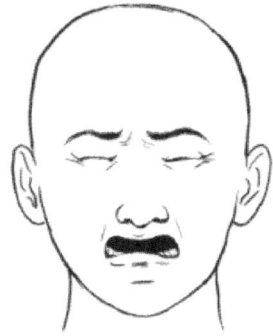

Adaptive role of emotion

Emotions play a functional role in the lives of humans and other animals. As early as 1872, Charles Darwin theorized that emotions evolved and adapted over time. Since then, research has developed to detail how specific emotions evolved and their functions.

Different emotions prepare the body for behavior in numerous ways.

Emotions like fear and anxiety allow the body to react automatically.

For example, if a car swerves onto the sidewalk, individuals on the sidewalk will move out of the way due to their fear response and not any thought processes per se.

Individuals typically avoid stimuli that result in negative emotions by seeking out situations associated with positive emotions. In this way, positive emotions like joy, pride, and happiness motivate future behavior. Individuals will repeat behaviors associated with positive emotions.

For example, emotions provide intrinsic rewards for adaptive behaviors, such as finding food and having sex.

Emotions and emotional expression are crucial interpersonally. In humans, the emotional cues of others influence our interactions with them.

For example, infants were placed on safety glass with a visual cliff in the middle of the surface. The infants' mothers stood at the opposite side of the visual cliff and were instructed to display fear, sadness, anger, interest, or joy. Approximately 75% of the infants crossed when the mother displayed joy or interest; none crossed when the mother displayed fear.

Notes for active learning

Emotion Theories

James–Lange theory

James-Lange theory of emotions was independently proposed by psychologist William James and physiologist Carl Lange. This theory states that physiological responses to stimuli are the basis for emotions. Thus, emotion is a secondary response to a physiological trigger.

According to this theory, the brain receives input regarding muscle tension, heart rate, perspiration, and other physiological processes and interprets these responses as a particular emotion. This theory proposes that emotions are the subjective experiences of physiological reactions. Thus, James and Lange believed that without physical arousal, emotions would not exist.

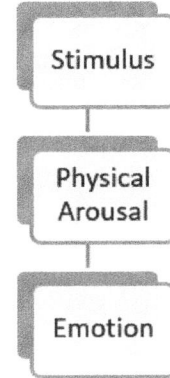

Cannon–Bard theory

Cannon-Bard theory of emotions was proposed in the late 1920s by William Cannon and his doctoral student Philip Bard. Cannon and Bard disagreed with the James-Lange theory and proposed that emotions and physiological reactions coincide as separate entities.

Cannon and Bard believed that the James-Lange theory did not account for people being physiologically aroused without experiencing emotions, such as when exercising. Since different emotions can have the same physiological arousal pattern, Cannon and Bard believed that physiological arousal cannot precede emotions, but the two exist separately. For example, fear and anger have similar physiological profiles but are experienced as different emotions.

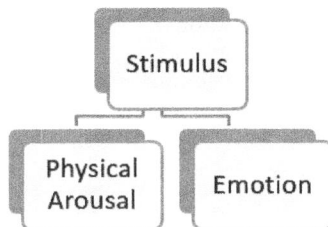

Cannon and Bard cited research on animal behavior to support their theory.

For example, dogs with spinal cord and vagus nerves separated from their bodies showed no change in emotional behavior, suggesting that emotions are not just physiological responses.

William Cannon, American merchant and politician

Schachter–Singer theory

Schachter-Singer theory of emotions was devised by researchers Stanley Schachter and Jerome E. Singer. It states that emotions result from the interaction of cognitive and physiological factors.

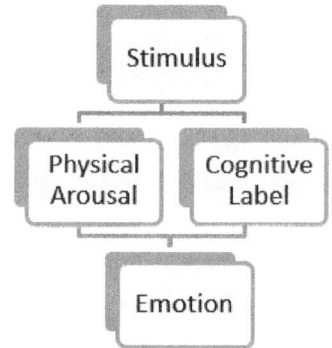

Thus, cognition provides a framework within which an individual can understand their physiological response.

Stanley Schachter showed that individuals would label a state of physiological arousal based on the cognitions available to them (via prompts and suggestions).

Additionally, individuals will not label cognitions as emotions if physiological arousal is absent, suggesting that physiological arousal and cognition must be present for an individual to experience an emotion.

This theory emphasizes the role of *past emotional experiences*. According to this theory, past experiences of emotion provide a framework for individuals to label their emotions.

Biological Processes in Perceiving Emotions

Brain regions generate and experience emotions

Basal ganglia are groups of nuclei found on the sides of the thalamus. They are connected to the thalamus in the limbic system. The basal ganglia are vital for cognitive function by enabling various cognitive and emotional programs to be stored in other cortical areas.

Orbitofrontal cortex (OFC) participates in the decision-making aspect of emotion. It controls an individual's engagement in reinforced and punished behaviors. It is involved in motivational behavior such as eating and drinking. Damage to the orbitofrontal cortex is often associated with impulsivity, suggesting that this area *modulates goal-directed behavior*.

Prefrontal cortex (PFC) is associated with the experience and regulation of emotions. The prefrontal cortex integrates cognition and emotion. Individuals with depression display abnormally low activity in their prefrontal cortex.

Ventral striatum is activated by stimuli associated with reward. This area is the primary site of rewarding feelings elicited by dopamine.

Insular cortex (or *insula*) is linked to the social emotions of disgust and empathy and is involved in processing others' emotions. It processes physiological information to form an experience of emotion. It is integral to experiencing pain and conscious desires.

Though typically associated with motor control, research proposes that the *cerebellum* may be central to *regulating emotions*.

Limbic system and emotions

Limbic system structures are related to emotion.

Amygdala is composed of two round structures involved in emotions and motivation. It is associated with fear and aggression and linked to fear conditioning. It activates the *sympathetic nervous system* (i.e., *fight-or-flight response*) and increases arousal.

Thalamus primarily relays information among brain regions. Thalamus lesions are associated with difficulties in emotional reactivity due to the thalamus' connections with other limbic system regions. Additionally, the thalamus participates in the *regulation of sleep*.

Hypothalamus is located below the thalamus and participates in expressing emotions. It *processes fear* and engages in *defensive behaviors* resulting from fear.

Hippocampus is primarily involved in creating new memories and is easily affected by long-term stress. Atrophy of the hippocampus has been found in patients who have post-traumatic stress disorder, schizophrenia, and depression.

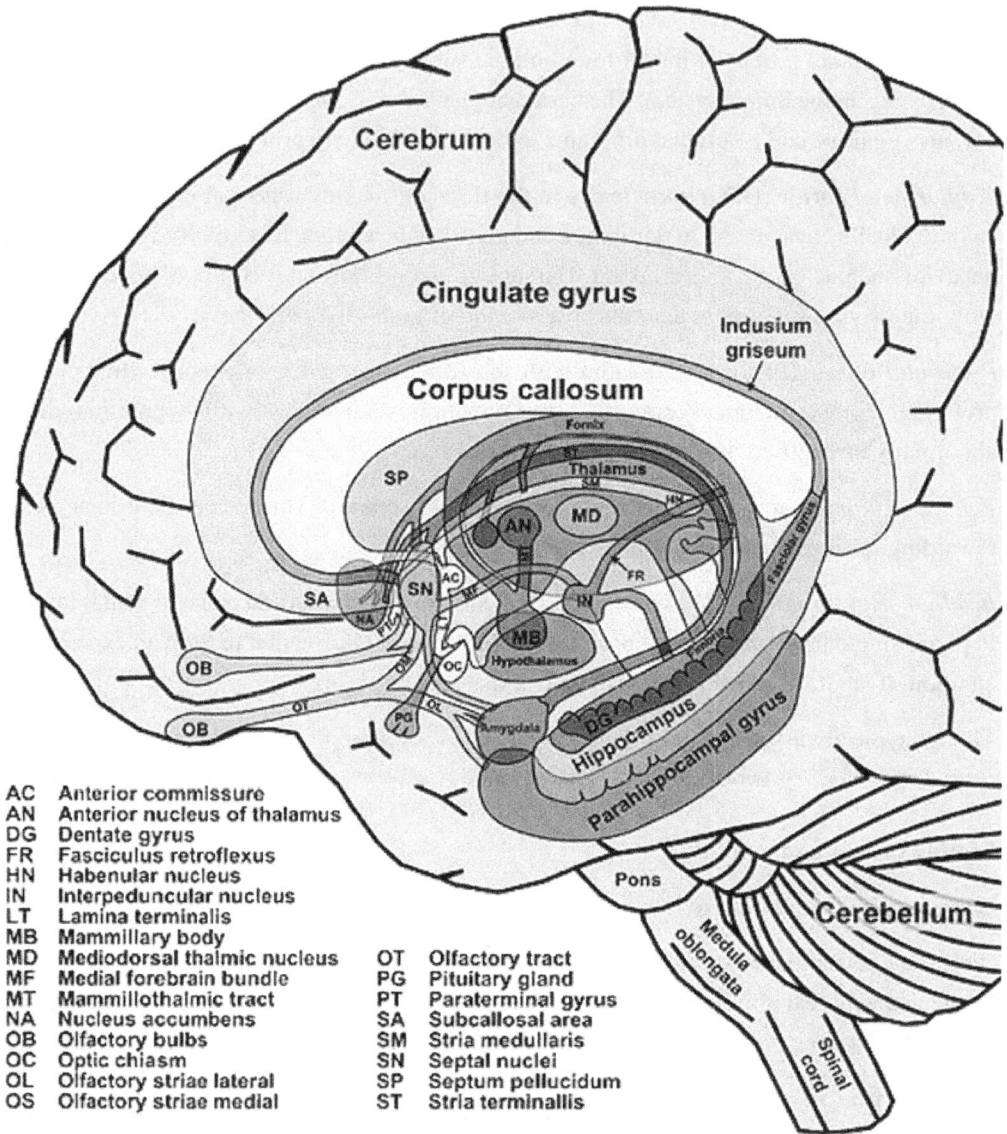

AC	Anterior commissure
AN	Anterior nucleus of thalamus
DG	Dentate gyrus
FR	Fasciculus retroflexus
HN	Habenular nucleus
IN	Interpeduncular nucleus
LT	Lamina terminalis
MB	Mammillary body
MD	Mediodorsal thalmic nucleus
MF	Medial forebrain bundle
MT	Mammillothalmic tract
NA	Nucleus accumbens
OB	Olfactory bulbs
OC	Optic chiasm
OL	Olfactory striae lateral
OS	Olfactory striae medial

OT	Olfactory tract
PG	Pituitary gland
PT	Paraterminal gyrus
SA	Subcallosal area
SM	Stria medullaris
SN	Septal nuclei
SP	Septum pellucidum
ST	Stria terminallis

Limbic system and nearby brain structures

Autonomic nervous system and emotions

Autonomic nervous system (ANS) is part of the peripheral nervous system and regulates bodily organs such as heart rate, respiratory rate, sexual arousal, digestion, and pupillary response.

Autonomic nervous system responses are involuntary and without conscious intervention.

Autonomic nervous system is divided into the

> *sympathetic nervous system*

> *parasympathetic nervous system*

Both branches are constantly activated to maintain homeostasis.

Sympathetic nervous system is associated with the *fight-or-flight* (e.g., fear, stress) response.

For example, the sympathetic nervous system dilates the pupils to increase the amount of light entering the eye. It increases blood flow to the muscles by increasing heart rate, dilating the skeletal muscles, and inhibiting digestion, making the body more efficient during an emergency. Lung bronchioles dilate, allowing more oxygen intake with each breath. These physiological responses prepare the body for action, whether for *fight* or *flight*.

Parasympathetic nervous system (rest and digest) decreases blood pressure, slows heart rate, and promotes digestion. It restores homeostasis with *relaxation and tranquility*.

	Parasympathetic *Body at rest*	**Sympathetic** *Emergencies*
Eyes	Constricts pupils	Dilates pupils
Heart	Beats more slowly	Beats faster and stronger
Lungs	Constricts airways	Relaxes airways, breathe more deeply
Digestion	Stimulates digestion	Inhibits digestion
Muscles	Reduces blood flow to skeletal muscles	Increases blood flow to skeletal muscles

Physiological markers of emotion

Emotions are characterized by their physiological responses (signatures of emotion).

These functional responses prepare the body to engage in different behaviors and result from the interaction between the *peripheral nervous, endocrine, limbic,* and other brain regions.

For example, anger is characterized by its association with the *sympathetic nervous system.* Thus, when experiencing anger, an increase in blood pressure and heart rate can be expected. This response prepares the body for aggressive behavior like attacking and defending.

The physiological responses of individual emotions are not unique.

For example, anger and fear are characterized by similar central nervous system arousal; when experiencing both emotions, heart rate, perspiration, and blood pressure increase. Emotions are *more than* just their physiological markers.

Recent theories of emotions have conceptualized physiological responses as existing on a continuum. These theories sort emotions by their distribution among two or more dimensions.

Wilhelm Wundt, the father of modern psychology, proposed that emotions can be described in three dimensions, how:

> *pleasurable* they are
>
> *arousing* they are
>
> *straining* they are

Most modern theories incorporate *valence* (i.c., the emotional value associated with a stimulus) and *arousal* as two dimensions of emotions.

Wilhelm Wundt, father of modern psychology

Motivation

Motivation directs behavior

Motivation is derived from the Latin word *movere,* meaning *to move.*

Motivation is a need (or desire) that energizes and directs behavior; initiating, guiding, or maintaining goal-directed behaviors.

Motivation theories, which explore the processes that explain why and how human behavior is activated, are considered one of the most critical areas of study in organizational behavior.

Despite the extensive research conducted in this area, no unified, universally accepted theory of motivation exists.

So far, research on motivation has found it to be multidimensional, dynamic, and fluctuating; it can be modified or influenced by social interactions and is a crucial component of change.

Factors that influence motivation

Factors influencing motivation can be intrinsic (internal) or extrinsic (external), and they can have biological underpinnings and sociocultural influences.

Several theories of motivation have been proposed, each focusing on a different aspect of or reason for what motivates goal-oriented behavior.

Early theories of motivation focused on instincts, and psychologists suggested that humans were programmed to behave in specific ways as a response to motivational cues.

However, in the early twentieth century, researchers began to examine the possibility of different explanations for differential motivation in individuals.

Some psychologists, such as Freud, focus on internal drives, while others, such as Bandura, focus on external factors, the effect of learning from the environment, and how reinforcement contingencies influence individual behavior.

Other psychologists took a third approach, examining cognitive processes and how cognitive schema about the past and future influences behavior, motivating behavior in a certain way.

Theories of motivation

Since many theories of motivation suggest the influence of several distinct factors, they are categorized into two schools of motivation theory:

> *content theories of motivation*
>
> *process theories of motivation*

Content theories (or *needs theories of motivation*) represent the earliest theories in the field and suggest that needs are the primary factors affecting motivation. An example of this type of theory would be Maslow's hierarchy of needs model.

Process theory of motivation focuses on how human needs change.

Instinct

Evolutionary perspective on motivation asserts that behaviors are not made consciously but have an instinctual base.

Instincts (or impulses) represent the capacity of an organism to conduct complex behaviors automatically without conscious awareness.

Instinctual theory assumes innate, automatic, involuntary forces and unlearned behavior patterns present when elicited by specific stimuli.

For example, cats tend to arch their backs when faced with an imminent threat.

Many instinctual behaviors are observed in humans.

For example, most instinctual behaviors can be observed as reflexes in babies, such as a sucking response to obtain food, a crying response to express distress or some need, a grasping response while exploring objects in the environment, and the ability to convey feelings and thoughts through body language, even unconsciously.

Although there is a premise that instinctive behaviors are hereditarily based, they seem to be influenced by the forces of natural selection.

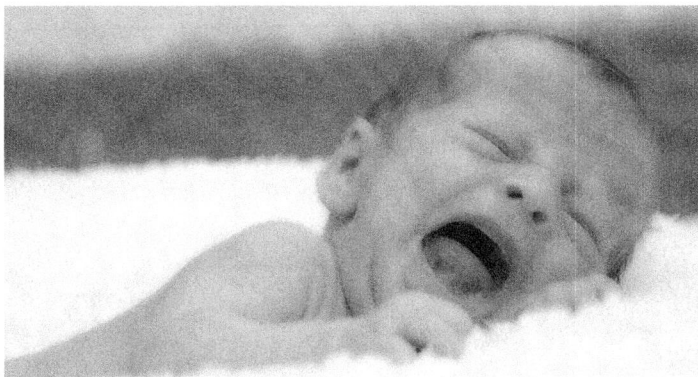

Most instinctual behaviors are baby reflexes (e.g., crying to express distress or needs).

Arousal

According to the optimal arousal perspective, individuals are motivated by attempting to reach an optimal state of arousal or activation.

Research has found that individuals perform best at a *moderate level* of arousal.

Arousal theory in humans is observed in introverts and extroverts, where the level of arousal may affect whether a person is motivated to interact with others.

> *Extroverts* may have a lower level of cortical arousal and are, therefore, more likely to seek arousal than introverts.

> *Introverts* are believed to have higher levels of cortical arousal and, therefore, do not require as much external stimulation from their environment.

Critics of arousal theory argue that one of the major limitations of this model is that it can only focus on internal influences of behavior and can provide us with only half the picture.

Drives

Drive reduction theory suggests that drives and needs motivate behavior.

Drive is a specific state of arousal following a physiological need.

Negative feedback systems exist to maintain *homeostasis* between drives and needs.

Drive reduction theory proposes two types of drives—primary and secondary.

Primary drives are innate and result from biological needs.

Secondary drives are learned from operant conditioning or association with primary reinforcers.

For example, a person feels hunger by simply smelling or seeing food, even if they have eaten. Supermarkets utilize this insight by providing food samples or generating food smells within the supermarket, so the smell might motivate people to buy it.

Critics of drive-reduction theory assert that it only focuses on observing internal physiological environments, yet external factors have a crucial role in motivation.

Another limitation of drive reduction theory is that it does not explain some behaviors, usually driven by *curiosity*.

Unreasonable curiosity creates danger and does not necessarily result in drive reduction.

Needs

Need is required because it is essential for the individual and tends to be satiated following a drive or behavioral response that is goal-oriented toward meeting this need.

Maslow prioritized needs from

1) *biological,*

2) *social,* and

3) *ultimately spiritual.*

Biological needs include food, water, oxygen, sleep, hygiene, sexual and stress release.

Safety needs include security, comfort, and peace of mind.

Attachment need is the desire to belong, affiliate, love, and be loved.

Esteem needs include self-efficacy, self-esteem, a sense of worthiness, and respect from others.

Cognitive needs include the desire for knowledge and understanding.

Self-actualization needs include developing and fulfilling one's potential, having meaningful goals, and being able to fulfill them in life.

Transcendence is a recently acknowledged need and refers to desires for spirituality, religion, or identification with a higher being (or source) for guidance.

Human Behavior Motivations

Incentive theory

Physiological need creates an aroused tension, which is the drive that motivates an organism to satisfy it. The need is usually to maintain *homeostasis*.

Individuals are not only pushed by their needs but are pulled by incentives, which are positive or negative environmental stimuli that motivate behavior.

Incentives are the stimuli that individuals are drawn to by learning. Some stimuli are associated with rewards, and others with punishment. Individuals are motivated to seek rewards and avoid behaviors associated with no rewards or negative consequences.

Individual differences in behavior across settings and people have underlying value systems traditionally associated with specific incentives or rewards.

A classic example of incentive theory in humans is the drive toward the incentive of monetary compensation or recognition.

People work and excel at what they do because they want to receive remuneration or recognition from others; regardless of whether the task is unpleasant, the incentive fuels the behavior.

Nonetheless, incentives may not motivate action, as people may not place the same value on different rewards or incentives and might lack sufficient motivation for unpleasant tasks.

Social, cognitive, and physiological factors influence an individual's motivation.

Incentive theory of motivation proposes that people must believe the reward is obtainable for it to be a motivating factor.

For example, if a runner does not believe they will meet a marathon's time requirements, they might find it so challenging to attain this goal that it is not realistically attainable, and consequently, they do not put effort into achieving the abandoned goal.

Cognitive, expectancy, and need-based theories

Cognitive-based theory of motivation focuses on the *intrinsic* (internal) or *extrinsic* (external) motivating factors that influence an individual's decision-making and behaviors.

Research shows intrinsic motivating factors are more effective at motivating certain behaviors.

Cognitive-based theory proposes that motivation is not innate but instead persistent behavioral patterns resulting from interaction with different environmental stimuli. There is a high emphasis on *expectations* regarding the possible outcomes of *goal-directed behavior*.

Expectancy-value theory is cognitive motivation theory that posits that the amount of effort put into a task depends on the degree to which the person expects to succeed. Therefore, the value of a task is considered along with attainment value, intrinsic value, and costs.

Need-based theory of motivation (proposed by Maslow) focused on the human hierarchy of needs, from physiological ascending to self-actualization. According to Maslow's theory of motivation, needs higher in the hierarchy cannot be met before lower needs have been met.

ERG theory and two-factor theory

Needs theories evolved to include the *ERG theory* (proposed by Clayton Alderfer) and the *Two-Factor* theory (proposed by Frederick Herzberg).

ERG theory is a modification of Maslow's five hierarchically organized needs and proposes that basic human needs group into three categories:

> *Existence*
>
> *Relatedness*
>
> *Growth*

Two-factor theory proposed by Herzberg focuses on what satisfies and dissatisfies individuals, especially in the workforce.

Two-factor theory distinguishes:

> *Motivators* (e.g., public success, responsibility, recognition) give positive satisfaction from intrinsic conditions.
>
> *Hygiene factors* (e.g., working conditions, salary, safety, and job security) characterize the environment in which an individual works and affect satisfaction.

For example, the lack of a constant office temperature or inappropriate background noise levels are hygiene factors which affect a person's motivation.

Paralleling Maslow's theory, *existence* corresponds to physiological and basic safety needs, *relatedness* to social needs and need for belonging, and *growth* to self-actualization and esteem.

This theory is more flexible than Maslow's theory, as it recognizes that more than one need can operate at a specific time and does not rank these needs in any order.

Biological and sociocultural motivators

Behavior may be motivated by *integrating biological* and *sociocultural factors*.

Diathesis-stress model accounts for how these interactions can become faulty. It has been proposed to describe behavior as a product of innate predispositions and environmental stress.

Diathesis-stress model states that a person is more likely to suffer an illness if they have a particular vulnerability (or diathesis) and are under a high level of stress.

Diathesis factors highly researched include individual psychological characteristics such as impulsivity and hostility, biological vulnerabilities (e.g., cardiovascular reactivity), and environmental characteristics (e.g., low socioeconomic status and an unstable childhood family environment).

Common motivators affecting behavior and influenced by biological and sociocultural forces are hunger, sex drive, and substance use.

Hunger, sex drive, and substance abuse

The brain (i.e., the hypothalamus's ventromedial and paraventricular nuclei), endocrine (i.e., leptin and insulin), and digestive systems regulate hunger motivation and behavioral eating.

Sociocultural factors regulating hunger motivation include appeal, availability, and time.

The brain, endocrine, and digestive systems regulate hunger motivation and eating

Biological factors involved in the regulation of sexual motivation include visual and olfactory senses, as well as the regulation of testosterone, estrogen, oxytocin, and vasopressin.

Sociocultural sex influences include cultural beliefs associated with sex, age, and emotions.

Biological factors of substance abuse include *genetics* and *limbic system biochemistry*.

Sociocultural factors of substance abuse include self-perception and esteem, emotion-regulation abilities and stress, and societal influence.

Biological factors influencing substance abuse include genetics and
biochemical reactions within the limbic system.

Stress

Nature of stress

Like emotion, the definition of stress is debated.

Stress is an acute threat to homeostasis (i.e., physiological balance). Stress is a negative or positive response to change.

Eustress is motivational positive stress (e.g., winning the lottery).

Distress refers to negative, unpleasant, and overwhelming stress experienced by an individual.

Distress causes anxiety and is usually experienced in response to an event that individuals believe they are unable to cope with.

Acute stress lasts for a brief period and involves the fear response.

Chronic stress persists over time and has been linked to numerous physical ailments.

Appraisal view of stress

Richard Lazarus developed the *appraisal view of stress*, which is divided into two stages, with stress as a combination of environmental stressors and a person's cognitive response.

Primary appraisal stage is the quick initial evaluation of the situation to assess the threats.

Appraisals from primary appraisals are that the situation is *irrelevant*, *positive*, or *threatening*. This primary appraisal state is adaptive because it only concerns the organism's survival.

Secondary appraisal stage is when a person evaluates their ability to adapt and cope.

Primary and secondary appraisal stages interact to form an *emotional response*.

Appraisal view of stress forms an emotional response

For example, if the situation is perceived as threatening during the primary appraisal stage, but individuals believe they have the resources to cope with the threat, their stress levels will be less than if they determine that a situation is threatening and believe that they do not have the necessary resources to cope with the threat.

Cognitive reappraisal refers to changing an emotional response by changing the thoughts associated with the stressor. It is used in many therapies, including cognitive behavioral therapy.

For example, an individual who fails a test may initially believe that this failure will threaten their plans (primary appraisal) and that they will not get a good grade (secondary appraisal). Reappraisal would view the test in the larger scheme of things and take a more neutral stance.

Types of stressors

Stressors are organized into *microstressors*, *personal stressors*, and *cataclysmic events*.

Microstressors are minor stressors encountered daily and include *ambient* chronic low-grade stressors (e.g., pollution and overcrowding). For example, spilling a drink, interacting with an irritating co-worker, and being stuck in traffic.

Microstressors refer to minor stressors encountered daily, such as traffic

Personal stressors refer to significant changes and milestones in a person's life. Personal stressors include moving, the birth of a child, losing a job, and sudden changes in finances.

Cataclysmic events (e.g., floods, earthquakes, hurricanes) and *catastrophes* (e.g., COVID-19, large-scale industrial explosions, terrorist attacks) are unexpected stressors occurring on a large scale and affect many people simultaneously.

Technostress, a recently identified form, is the discomfort caused by technology use. People experience technostress when they cannot adapt to technology.

Stress and psychological functions

In the early years of development, experiencing acute and chronic stress can be detrimental to an individual's mental health.

Exposure to personal stressors during childhood (e.g., abuse or marital conflict) is associated with personality disorders, school performance, anxiety, depression, and antisocial behavior.

Cataclysmic events during childhood are associated with depression and have been linked to the development of *post-traumatic stress disorder.*

Chronic childhood stress is associated with anxiety and depression.

During adulthood, stress is linked to the onset and maintenance of most psychopathologies. Stressful life events precede depressive episodes and the onset of anxiety disorders.

Research shows that stress is related to the onset of schizophrenia and relapses that may occur.

Stressful life events precede depressive episodes and the onset of anxiety disorders.

Exposure to a traumatic stressor often results in the development of post-traumatic stress disorder, which is characterized by nightmares, anxiety, and hypervigilance.

Substance abuse disorder is associated with chronic stress. Some models of addiction view substance abuse as a method of *coping with overwhelming distress.*

Interventions targeting *stress reduction* are successful in reducing relapses in individuals with substance abuse disorders.

Physiological response

Acute physiological responses to stressors include increased cortisol levels, adrenocorticotropic hormone (ACTH) levels, and heart rate as the body prepares for defense or to flee.

Overexposure to cortisol and other stress hormones may cause negative health effects.

Chronic stress is associated with negative health outcomes across a variety of diseases.

Chronic stress is associated with digestive problems, including irritable bowel syndrome, the worsening of ulcers, and *gastroesophageal reflux disease* (GERD).

Heart disease and *insomnia* have been linked to chronic stress.

Emotional response

Common emotional responses to stress include depression, anxiety, and anger.

How an individual interprets a stressor determines what emotions they experience.

People tend to experience depression in response to a stressor if they determine that they are unable to cope with it.

People experience anger in response to a stressor when they oppose it.

Fear and anxiety are experienced when a person determines that they will flee from the stressor.

Exhaustion often occurs following an acute stress response.

Behavioral response

People under chronic stress engage in unhelpful coping strategies to reduce their stress levels.

Unhealthy coping strategies include smoking, drinking, drug use, and binge eating, behaviors contributing to the physical effects of stress.

Self-injury is viewed as a negative response to stress under some theoretical models. In these models, individuals who engage in self-harm are theorized to have a lower distress tolerance.

Recent research has supported this idea by showing that individuals who engage in self-harm show higher physiological reactivity when performing a distressing task.

Stress reduction techniques

Techniques have been developed to help reduce and manage stress.

Diaphragmatic breathing involves inflating and deflating the abdomen rather than the chest. This is done on counts of five for each inhalation and exhalation. Diaphragmatic breathing reduces stress levels and is taught to people with panic disorder as part of a treatment plan.

Progressive muscle relaxation (PMR) systematically tenses and relaxes specific muscles to promote awareness of muscle tension and allows individuals engaging in PMR to practice reducing their muscle tension.

PMR improves sleep, increases energy, and lowers physiological stress indicators (e.g., salivary cortisol).

Exercise helps reduce stress. Studies suggest that exercise decreases fatigue, improves alertness, and aids sleep. Exercise relieves symptoms of anxiety and depression temporarily.

Regular exercise may help prevent the development of these disorders.

Holistic stress management

Holistic approaches to stress management often incorporate aspects of spirituality.

Spirituality gives lives context and can be found in religious and secular communities. It may reduce stress by providing a sense of meaning and purpose.

Spirituality enables individuals to give up control and acknowledge that much of life is outside of any one person's control.

Research has indicated meditation and mindfulness as powerful tools for combating stress.

During meditation and mindfulness, attention is focused on thoughts, emotions, physical sensations, external stimuli, or a specific phrase.

Mindfulness promotes non-judgmental awareness focused on the present, with breathing "anchoring" oneself in the present.

Mindfulness and meditation can reduce stress and increase positive emotions. They are often used in clinical settings with individuals who ruminate constantly or are excessively anxious.

Relationship matrix

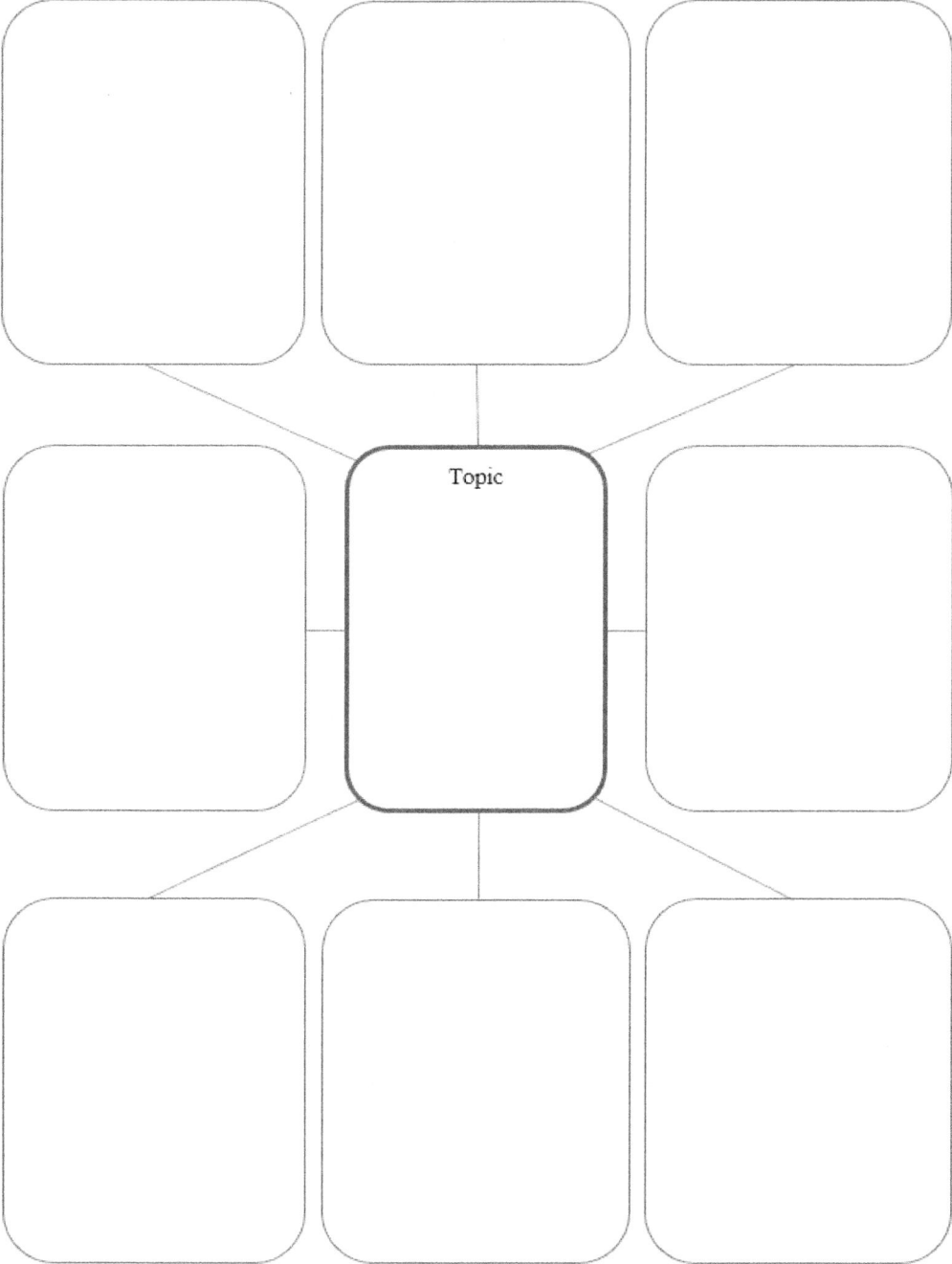

Topic

Notes for active learning

Notes for active learning

CHAPTER 7

Developmental Psychology

Developmental psychology studies behavior from conception to death and examines the processes contributing to behavioral changes throughout the lifespan.

Major areas of emphasis are prenatal development, motor development, socialization, cognitive development, adolescence, and adulthood.

Prenatal Development

Effects of nutrition, illness and socioeconomic factors

Proper nutrition is necessary to produce a healthy fetus. The lack of iron can cause the fetus to develop anemia, the lack of calcium can cause poor bone and teeth formation, and the lack of protein can cause a smaller fetus and developmental delay.

Exposure to environmental toxins in pregnancy has led to higher rates of miscarriage, sterility, and different congenital disabilities. These toxins include lead, mercury, and ethanol.

If a mother contracts a disease during gestation, the placenta cannot always filter out these pathogens. Babies can be born with ventral diseases transmitted by the mother.

Poverty has a negative influence on prenatal care and development.

Women of lower socioeconomic backgrounds tend to have children at a younger age, which is correlated with lower birth weights. Additionally, it is believed that these women do not have access to sufficient education and are less likely to be aware of the risks of smoking, consuming alcohol, and drug use during pregnancy.

Substance abuse

Maternal drug use occurs when drugs ingested during pregnancy are metabolized in the placenta and are ultimately transmitted to the fetus.

With the use of drugs or narcotics, there is a higher risk of congenital disabilities, low birth weight, and a higher rate of death or stillbirth.

Additionally, the chemicals within drugs can cause the newborn to be addicted as well.

Marijuana can stunt fetal growth rate and result in premature delivery.

Heroin can cause interrupted fetal development, stillbirth, numerous congenital disabilities, and miscarriages. Fetal abnormalities result in facial, head size, and gastrointestinal abnormalities.

Additionally, the risk of *sudden infant death syndrome* (SIDS) increases, and there can be dysfunction in the central nervous system as well as neurological dysfunction, such as tremors, sleep problems, and seizures.

Similarly, the use of cocaine puts the fetus at risk of being stillborn or premature. It can result in low birth weight, motor dysfunction, and overall damage to the central nervous system.

Alcohol use causes disruptions in fetal brain development, cell development, organization, and the maturation of the central nervous system. Additionally, alcohol can lead to organ defects in the heart and other major organs. The brain can be affected, leading to impaired learning.

Alcohol use during pregnancy increases the risk of the onset of behavioral problems, mental health problems, and facial abnormalities in newborns, as well as increasing the risk of miscarriage and stillbirth.

Fetal alcohol syndrome (FAS) is a developmental disorder caused by alcohol during pregnancy.

Children affected by fetal alcohol syndrome have a vast array of facial and cognitive defects.

During pregnancy, if an expectant mother smokes, the fetus is exposed to nicotine, tar, and carbon monoxide.

Nicotine causes blood flow to the fetus to decrease, as it constricts the blood vessels.

Carbon monoxide causes oxygen flow to the fetus to be reduced.

Decreased levels of blood and oxygen flow (e.g., nicotine and carbon monoxide) can result in stillbirth, low birth weight, and sometimes an ectopic pregnancy.

Additionally, there is an increased risk of SIDS, miscarriages, and premature birth.

Researchers have associated smoking during pregnancy and asthma in childhood.

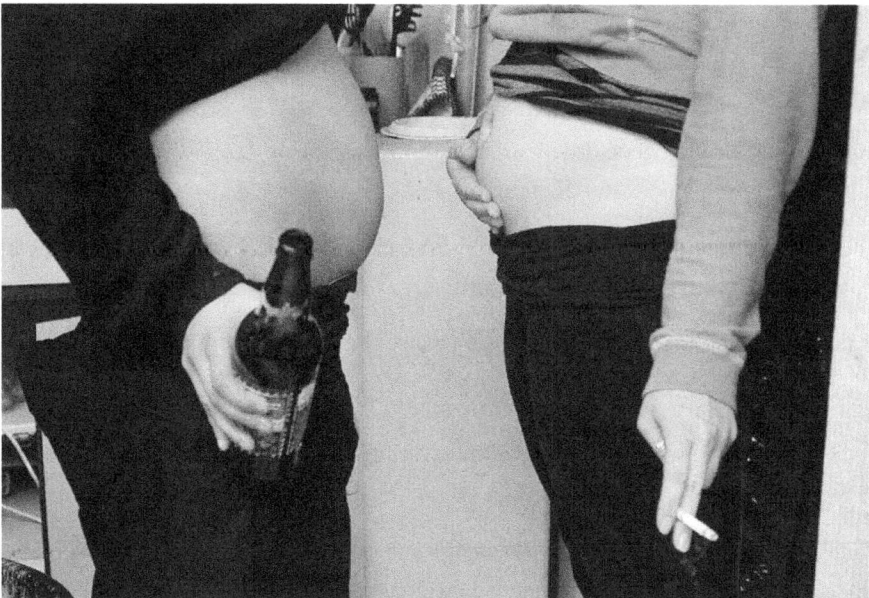

Smoking and drinking during pregnancy are linked to adverse effects on the fetus

Heredity–Environment Interaction

Nature *vs.* nurture

Nature refers to heredity (i.e., genetics), while *nurture* refers to environmental experiences during development. Some researchers propose that humans are *"pre-wired,"* while others propose that *life experiences and parenting* determine the course of human development.

Parenting styles' influence on development

Authoritarian parenting style uses strict standards to guide children's behavior; there is no discussion about their rationale, and punishment is used more than reinforcement. Children tend to be less trusting of others and are more withdrawn from their peers.

Permissive parenting style is characterized by parents who do not set clear guidelines for their children; the rules are constantly changed and are not usually enforced. Under this parenting style, it is easy for children to misbehave, and they tend to have emotional issues and problems with self-control and appear to be more independent.

Authoritative parenting style is when parents set consistent standards that are reasonable and explained, and the parents encourage their children's independence and praise them as often as they punish them. Their children are more socially capable and perform better academically.

Uninvolved parenting style is characterized by few demands, low responsiveness, and little communication. These parents fulfill their children's basic needs but are usually detached from their lives. In extreme cases, these parents may reject or neglect the needs of their children.

Motor development

Reflexes are innate, automatic responses to specific stimuli. There are some reflexes that humans are born with and are lost later in life.

Rooting reflex occurs when children are touched on the cheek, turn their heads, and seek to put the object in their mouth.

Sucking reflex is when an object is placed in the baby's mouth, and the baby sucks on it.

Grasping reflex occurs when a baby tries to grasp an object placed on their hand or foot.

Moro reflex is when startled babies fling out and retract limbs, becoming as small as possible.

Babinski reflex is when a baby's foot is stroked, and the baby spreads their toes.

Rolling over occurs at five-and-a-half-months.

Standing occurs at eight or nine months.

Walking occurs at 11-15 months, with slight environmental effects on motor development.

Maturation of cognitive abilities

Jean Piaget worked for Albert Binet, who created the first intelligence test. Piaget noticed that children of the same age gave similar answers to the test questions. His hypothesis proposed that children think in similar ways that differ from adults.

Theory of cognitive development is that children view the world through cognitive schemata. These are a set of cognitive rules that humans use to interpret the world.

For example, during *assimilation,* humans incorporate their experiences into their schemata. In contrast, humans tend to accommodate and change schemata to incorporate new information when it violates their schemata.

Four stages of cognitive development.

Sensorimotor stage of cognitive development is from birth to age two. Children explore the world with their *senses* and *reflexes* govern behavior until they develop their first cognitive schemata. A significant challenge is the development of *object permanence* or understanding that objects continue to exist even when they are out of the individual's sensory range.

Preoperational stage of cognitive development occurs from the ages of two to seven.

Object permanence prepares children to use symbols to represent real-world objects. This stage begins at the onset of language development when the first words are spoken.

Children are limited in thinking about the relationships between the characteristics of objects.

During this stage, individuals are egocentric and only see the world through their perspective.

Preoperational stage occurs from the ages of two to seven

Concrete operation occurs from eight to twelve. Children learn to think more logically about complex relationships between distinct characteristics of objects, and the concept of conservation is developed, as well as the realization that properties of objects remain the same even when their shapes change. Examples include volume, area, and numbers.

Formal operations occur from the age of twelve to adulthood. Individuals gain metacognition, which is the ability to think about thinking, and the ability for abstract reasoning begins to develop. An individual in this stage can start to form hypotheses.

Additionally, individuals can manipulate objects in their minds without physically seeing them and can contrast ideas in their minds without real-world correlates.

With every theory comes criticism. Piaget's critics argue that he underestimated children. For example, it has been found that many children go through stages much faster than others and enter them earlier than Piaget had thought. Also, it is argued that Piaget's test relied too heavily on the use of language and that his results were biased in favor of older children.

Information processing model of cognitive development is an alternative to Piaget's stage theory. Individuals' ability to memorize, interpret, and perceive gradually develops as they age, not in stages. This model explains the apparent cognitive differences that Piaget attributed to different cognitive stages.

Sex and gender's influences

Biopsychosocial theory focuses on the biological aspects of the nature and nurture interplay that produces gender roles.

Culture is vital for the roles associated with gender – and proposes that women have a larger corpus callosum, which affects how the brain hemispheres communicate.

Psychodynamic theory (also called *psychoanalytic theory*) proposes that personality is shaped by unconscious psychological processes, such as subconscious fears and wishes. The theory posits that childhood experiences are crucial in shaping adult personality.

Within psychodynamic lie *Oedipus* and *Electra complexes* (proposed by Freud and Jung, respectively) which state that during psychosexual development, children realize that they cannot overcome their same-sex parents for attention from the other parent.

Sigmund Freud and his mother

Social-cognitive theory focuses on the effects of society and an individual's thoughts about gender on role development.

Social psychologists look at how individuals react to children differently.

Cognitive psychologists focus on the internal interpretations made about gender-role-related messages as individuals receive these messages from the environment.

Gender schema theory proposes that messages about gender are internalized into cognitive rules about how each gender should behave.

Temperament and other social factors

Various researchers focusing on the role of nature in development hypothesize that every child is born with a set of characteristics, defined as *temperament,* by Thomas and Chess in 1977. These characteristics affect the response of the child's caregiver and mold the child's personality traits.

Three dimensions have been proposed to characterize temperament.

Negative emotionality is the first dimension of temperament, which includes irritability, negative mood, inflexibility, and high intensity as negative reactions.

Self-regulation is the second dimension of temperament, which includes persistence, non-distractibility, and emotional control.

Approach/withdrawal (or *inhibition, sociability*) is the third dimension of temperament, which includes new situations and people (or withdrawing from them).

The "easy" child is adaptable, playful, and responsive and gets much attention in the initial stages of development because interactions are pleasant and reinforcing.

The "difficult" child is fussy, has difficulty calming down, and has problems eating and sleeping; as a result, they provide little positive reinforcement to their caregivers.

The "slow to warm up" child is slow to adapt. Adults in contact with them are rewarded by positive behaviors usually found in the "easy child," but it takes longer to elicit this behavior.

Temperament is usually stable over time. However, recent research has suggested specific factors that affect temperament, including gender, children's participation in out-of-home care, and parental characteristics. Research shows that inhibited girls are more likely to change than inhibited boys, and children who receive outside childcare become less inhibited over time.

Over-controlling parents tend to have children who *remain inhibited* over time.

Notes for active learning

Behavioral Changes Throughout Life

Infancy

Psychological maturation is the stages humans pass after birth and during their lifespan.

Life course stages can be categorized as infancy, toddlerhood, early childhood, middle childhood, adolescence, adulthood, middle age, and old age.

Infancy is the first year of life. Newborns typically measure between fourteen and twenty inches at birth and weigh between five and a half to ten pounds. Infants spend much of their first year sleeping and can decipher distinct sound units in speech, eventually beginning to babble.

According to Piaget's theory of cognitive development, young infants are capable of simple reflexes (e.g., using their mouth to suck, closing their hand around an object that touches their palm, and following movement with their eyes).

At around six weeks of age, infants can imitate some actions using their bodies (e.g., waving their hands) and enter the phase of first habits and primary circular reactions.

By four months, infants have entered the secondary circular reactions phase, meaning they can grasp the desired object and repeat actions such as opening and closing a book.

Eight to twelve months, infants have increased coordinated hand and eye movements.

Toddlerhood

Toddlerhood refers to children from when they turn one to their third birthday. Increased mobility characterizes this stage, as walking typically occurs during the toddler years.

Children reach other critical developmental milestones during the toddler years, including physical growth, gross and fine motor skills development, and improved vision, hearing, speech, and social relationships.

Toddlerhood represents a part of the life cycle during which children begin to experience greater control over their movements (e.g., running and climbing during play), greater ability to draw, use utensils to feed themselves, see both near and far, and greater ability to communicate through hearing, speaking, and playing with other children.

Children take turns and engage in imaginary play at this age.

After age two, children typically experience a decreased need for naps, have an increased vocabulary, and often begin toilet training.

Toddlers may experience separation anxiety when separated from a caregiver.

Children frequently want to assert independence through temper tantrums or saying "No!"

Childhood and adolescence

Childhood is divided into *early childhood* and *middle childhood*.

Early childhood occurs before children enter school, so they are still in the play stage of their lives. It begins with toddlerhood and ends around age seven to eight. Children remain highly dependent on caregivers for emotional bonding.

Middle childhood begins when children enter first grade. Children become more independent and increase their peer friendship network.

Adolescence is the transition between childhood and adulthood. It is when teenagers go through puberty, leading to sexual maturity (i.e., primary, and secondary sex characteristics develop).

Primary sex characteristics include reproductive organs that grow and become functional.

Secondary sex characteristics include body hair, deepening of the voice (in boys), breast development, and the menstrual cycle (in girls). Females tend to develop faster than males.

Adolescents develop better processing speed, selective attention, memory, and metacognition.

Recent research suggests that more children are experiencing puberty before adolescence.

An adolescent is still considered a minor, yet adolescents strive for the increased independence that characterizes the adult years.

Adulthood

Adulthood cannot be defined purely by an individual experiencing puberty, so the boundary between adolescence and adulthood has no definite age. Instead, cultural, biological, individual, and familial beliefs and experiences vary.

Adulthood onset varies but occurs when a person experiences sexual maturity or has reached the age of majority.

In contrast to children and adolescents, adults are independent, self-reliant, and responsible for their actions and care.

Individuals may begin to establish a career and a family.

Middle-age stage is between thirty-five and sixty-five.

Old age is from sixty-five until death, when people may become physically and mentally frail and dependent on caregivers.

Physical and cognitive changes as people age

Development refers to age-related changes that occur over a person's lifespan.

Developmental theorists explore these changes and identify age-related milestones.

Developmental theories of identity formation focus on the evolution of distinct aspects of an individual's personality.

Theories of identity development include:

Freud's *psychosexual development theory*,

Erikson's *psychosocial development model*,

Vygotsky's *theory of sociocultural development*,

Kohlberg's *model of moral development*, and

present-day *theories of gender development*.

These theories typically focus on a specific development aspect, with sequential stages.

Developmental models have been criticized for drawing rigid boundaries between stages; identity development occurs gradually.

Continuity is when individuals develop steadily from birth to death.

Discontinuity is when development occurs in distinct steps with variable rates.

Stage theories are discontinuous theories of development.

Freud's psychosexual development model

Psychosexual development is a well-known theory of development proposed by Freud.

According to Freud, children become fixated on specific erogenous zones to decrease anxiety and satisfy their *libido* (or sexual drive).

Oral phase is the first stage of psychosexual development and lasts from birth to one year. The mouth is the focus of libidinal gratification, particularly in the form of breastfeeding.

Anal stage is the second stage of psychosexual development and lasts from one to three years of age and is characterized by *potty training*.

Phallic stage is the third stage of psychosexual development and lasts from three to six years of age. Genitalia is the erogenous zone for the child during this stage.

Children become aware of their bodies and the sexual differences between males and females.

Oedipus complex (Freud) emerges in boys during the phallic stage.

Electra complex (Carl Jung) emerges in girls during the phallic stage.

Latency stage is the fourth stage of psychosexual development and lasts from six until puberty. Sexual feelings are dormant, and there are no erogenous zones.

Genital stage is the final stage of psychosexual development, lasting from puberty until death. As with the phallic stage, the erogenous zone associated with this stage is the genital area.

Stage	Ages	Focus of Libido	Major Development	Fixation Examples
Oral	0 to 1	Mouth, tongue, lips	Weaning off of breastfeeding or formula	Smoking, overeating
Anal	1 to 3	Anus	Toilet training	Orderliness, messiness
Phallic	3 to 6	Genitals	Resolving Oedipus and Electra complexes	Deviancy, sexual dysfunction
Latency	6 to 12	None	Developing defense mechanisms	None
Genital	12+	Genitals	Reaching full sexual maturity	When stages are completed, a person is sexually mature and mentally healthy

Freud's stages of psychosexual development

Erikson's psychosocial development model

Erik Erikson was a Neo-Freudian who believed in the basics of Freud's theory but adapted it to fit his observations. According to Erickson, the psychosexual stage theory contains eight stages.

Psychologist Erik Erikson

Erickson thought that experiences with others profoundly influenced personality.

Erik Erikson developed an eight-stage model of development throughout the lifespan. Erikson's stage theory is the *psychosocial theory of development*.

Each stage is associated with virtue, psychosocial crisis, and existential questions.

First stage of the *psychosocial theory of development* is characterized by hope, which lasts from birth until age two. The psychosocial crisis is basic *trust vs. mistrust*. During this stage, infants question whether their caregivers can be trusted. The existential question during this stage is: "Can I trust the world?"

Erikson believed mistrust could develop during this stage if caregivers did not meet the child's basic needs or provide a secure environment. In this first stage, babies need to learn that they can trust their caregivers to fulfill their needs and that their requests are effective. Consequently, a sense of trust or mistrust remains throughout life.

Second stage of development, according to Erikson, is characterized by will and lasts from the ages of two to four. The existential question asked by the child is: "Is it okay to be me?" As this stage emerges, children gain control over their eliminative functions (potty training is an early effort at achieving autonomy).

Two conflicting forces during this stage are *autonomy vs. shame and doubt*. Caregivers who encourage their children to develop their interests allow them to gain a sense of autonomy.

Caregivers who restrict their children or are too demanding during this stage may instill a sense of shame and doubt in their children. In this stage, toddlers learn to control their temper tantrums. If they learn to control themselves and their environment, they will appropriately develop willpower and learn to control their bodies and emotional reactions in response to various social challenges.

Third stage is characterized by *initiative vs. guilt* conflict and occurs during preschool years. The existential question asked by the child during this stage is: "Is it okay for me to do, move, and act?" The value associated with this psychosocial stage is purpose.

During this stage, children develop the ability to plan and conduct behaviors. According to Erikson, if caregivers and teachers support a child's efforts, the child will develop initiative and independence. If trust and autonomy are achieved, natural curiosity about one's surroundings develops, and individuals often ask questions. If curiosity is encouraged, individuals feel comfortable expressing their constant curiosity.

Erikson theorized that if caregivers and teachers do not support a child's efforts during this stage, the child will develop guilt regarding his or her desires and will not express his or her sense of wonder.

Fourth stage in Erikson's model is *competence*. The conflict in this psychosocial stage concerns *industry vs. inferiority*. This stage lasts from five years old until the age of twelve. Children in this stage become aware of themselves as individuals and develop self-confidence.

According to Erikson, children praised for their efforts during this stage develop a sense of industry; children who are ridiculed develop a sense of inferiority about their capabilities and experience performance anxiety.

Fifth stage of psychosocial development is *identity vs. role confusion* conflict, which occurs between the ages of thirteen and nineteen, when the main social task is to discover what social identity individuals are most comfortable with. During this stage, adolescents are concerned about how they appear to others.

Existential question asked during this stage is: "Who am I, and what can I be?" Separate roles are tried out.

Identity crisis is when adolescents are not able to figure out a sense of self; they might have another identity crisis later in life.

Sixth stage is characterized by a conflict of *intimacy vs. isolation*, occurring during young adulthood and associated with the *virtue of love*. The existential question asked during this stage is: "Can I love?" or "Will I be loved or alone?"

Individuals in this stage gain intimacy through romantic relationships and marriage, or they may experience a sense of isolation when they cannot form these relationships. Erikson believes that individuals become isolated due to fear of rejection. Young adults resolve how to balance time and effort between work, relationships, and the self. The patterns chosen become relatively permanent.

Seventh stage is *generativity vs. stagnation,* characterized by care, occurring in middle adulthood. The existential question individuals ask in this stage is: "Can I make my life count?" According to Erikson, individuals who raise a family or contribute socially during this stage will experience a sense of generativity. A person who does not contribute to society is theorized to experience a sense of stagnation.

In this stage, individuals look critically at their life path. They try to ensure that their lives are going how they want; if not, they try to change it by controlling others or changing their identity. In a midlife crisis, individuals tend to see this as the last chance to achieve their goals.

Eighth (and final) *stage* is characterized by the conflict of *integrity vs. despair* and occurs from late adulthood until death. According to Erikson, individuals in this stage ask themselves the existential question, "Is it okay to have been me?" People in this stage look back on their life and accomplishments. If satisfied, they can stand out from their society and offer wisdom. If they are dissatisfied, they may sink into despair over lost opportunities.

Erikson's Stage Theory in its Final Version			
Age	**Conflict**	**Resolution or "Virtue"**	**Culmination**
Infancy (0-1 year)	Basic trust *vs.* mistrust	Hope	Appreciation of interdependence and relatedness
Early childhood (1-3 years)	Autonomy *vs.* shame	Will	Acceptance of the cycle of life, from integration to disintegration
Play age (3-6 years)	Initiative vs. guilt	Purpose	Humor; empathy; resilience
School age (6-12 years)	Industry *vs.* inferiority	Competence	Humility; acceptance of the course of one's life and unfulfilled hopes
Adolescence (12-19 years)	Identity *vs.* confusion	Fidelity	Sense of complexity of life; merging of sensory, logical, and aesthetic perception
Young adulthood (20-25 years)	Intimacy *vs.* isolation	Love	Intimacy; isolation from lack of relationships or fear of rejection
Middle adulthood (26-64 years)	Generativity *vs.* stagnation	Care	Caritas, caring for others, and agape, empathy and concern
Old age (65-death)	Integrity *vs.* despair	Wisdom	Existential identity; a sense of integrity strong enough to withstand physical disintegration.

Vygotsky's sociocultural theory of development

According to Russian psychologist Lev Vygotsky, individuals learn and develop through active interaction with their environment.

Vygotsky's theory of development is the *social development theory*, which focuses on the role of *social interaction* in cognitive development.

Vygotsky believed social learning was crucial to cognitive development; he proposed that social learning precedes an individual's development. Accordingly, the environment shapes an individual, particularly in how the individual will think and what they think about.

According to Vygotsky, infants have four mental functions developed by social interactions.

Elementary mental functions are 1) attention, 2) sensation, 3) perception, and 4) memory.

More Knowledgeable Other (MKO) was created by Vygotsky, which refers to a person who better understands a concept than the learner (e.g., adult *vs.* child).

A more knowledgeable other allows for a *zone of proximal development*, which refers to tasks that can be done when receiving help from a more knowledgeable other.

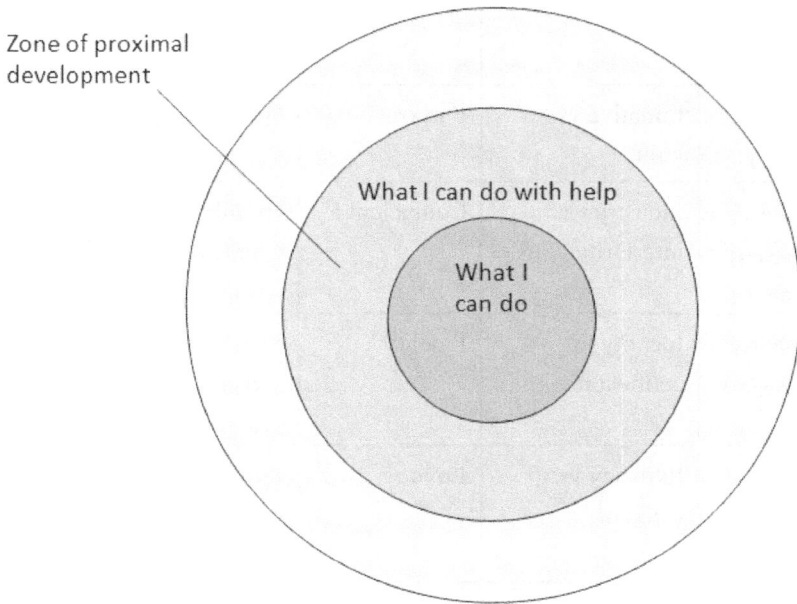

Piaget's stages of cognitive development

Jean Piaget, a Swiss psychologist, proposed that children think differently than adults and progress through *four stages of cognitive development.*

Piaget's model of the *four stages of cognitive development* is biologically based; as the child matures, they move on to the next developmental stage.

Piaget believed that children proceed through all four stages and that none can be skipped. He believed that children experience the stages in the same order, although they progress at different rates.

Sensorimotor stage is the first stage of *cognitive development* proposed by Piaget, occurring between birth and two years of age. During this stage, infants acquire knowledge about the world by manipulating their sensory experiences, and their intelligence is limited to basic motor and sensory information. An essential feature of this stage is learning *object permanence*.

Object permanence is the understanding that objects exist even when they cannot be seen.

For example, Piaget hid toys under a blanket while a child watched. He observed whether the child looked for the toy under the blanket. Piaget found that children develop object permanence at around eight months old.

Piaget found that children develop object permanence at around eight months –
the understanding that objects exist even when they cannot be observed.

Preoperational stage, according to Piaget, is the second stage of development. This stage lasts between the ages of two and seven. Children do not yet understand logic during this stage and cannot manipulate information mentally. It is characterized by engagement in pretend play.

Children in this stage are unable to take on the viewpoints of others and believe that others share the same viewpoints as them. This is known as *egocentrism*.

Piaget used a *three mountains task* to determine at what age children can take on the viewpoints of others. In this experiment, three model mountains were placed before a child. A doll was placed in various positions surrounding the mountains. Only at ages seven and eight were children able to identify the viewpoint of the doll as different from theirs.

Concrete operational stage is the third stage and occurs between the ages of seven and eleven. During this stage, children think rigidly and logically. Children acknowledge that others have different viewpoints. Hypothetical and abstract thinking have not yet been developed.

Formal operational stage is the fourth stage of cognitive development, starting around eleven and continuing throughout a person's development.

Children use hypothetical, abstract thinking, and develop the ability to use deductive and inductive reasoning. They develop the ability to think about thinking (or *metacognition*).

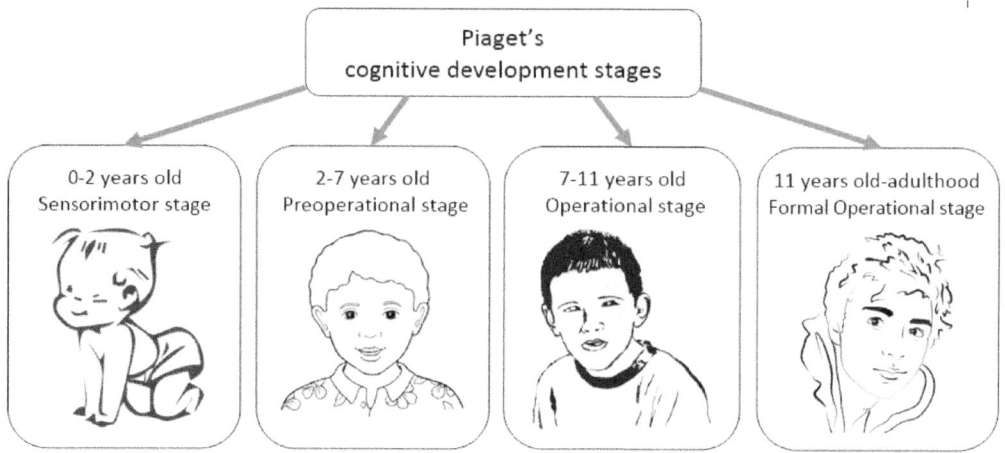

Paget's four stages of cognitive development

Moral Development

Kohlberg's stages of moral development

Lawrence Kohlberg was a psychologist who described how humans can reason about ethical situations that occur in life. Kohlberg proposed discussing moral dilemmas in schools to stimulate moral reasoning among children. He integrated moral dilemma discussion into the curricula of humanities and social studies classes.

Kohlberg found that moral discussion increases moral reasoning and works best if the individual is discussing with a person using more advanced reasoning (than them).

Kohlberg proposed a theory of *moral development consisting of six stages*.

First two stages are the *pre-conventional stages*.

> *Obedience and punishment orientation stage* is the first stage of moral development; individuals display moral behavior to *avoid punishment*.

> *Self-interest orientation* is the second stage where moral behavior occurs only when *beneficial*.

Conventional stage is the third and fourth stage of moral development.

> *Interpersonal accord* and *conformity* is the third stage of moral behavior due to *social norms*.

> *Authority-respecting* and *social order-maintaining* orientations are the fourth stage; concern for *obeying authority* and contributing to *social order*.

Post-conventional stage is the fifth and sixth stage of moral development.

> *Social contract orientation* is the fifth stage, when individuals view laws as social contracts and believe that laws should sometimes be changed to benefit the greatest number of people.

> *Universal ethical principles* are the sixth stage, when people use abstract reasoning to determine the validity of laws and make moral decisions.

Moral responses include pre-conventional, conventional, and post-conventional responses.

Heinz's dilemma is an example of Kohlberg's stages of moral development.

Heinz's dilemma is about a man whose wife is dying, and there is one costly treatment option for her that Heinz cannot afford. Heinz must make a moral choice about whether to steal a drug he cannot afford to save his wife's life.

Pre-conventional response stage, often experienced by young children, emphasizes making decisions that will avoid punishment. During this type of response, moral reasoning is limited to how the choice affects the decision-maker.

Conventional response looks at the moral choice through the eyes of others, and the decision is made based on how others will view the decision-maker after making the decision. The conventional response stage attempts to follow the conventional standards of right and wrong.

Post-conventional response involves moral reasoning. It examines the rights and values of each choice and allows the decision-maker to define the ethical principles. In this type of moral reasoning, the morality of societal rules is examined, not just unquestioningly accepted.

Carol Gilligan criticized Kohlberg's theories, arguing that his model was based exclusively on boys' responses. According to Gilligan's research, boys have an absolute view of morality, while girls focus on situational factors.

Research does not support Gilligan's theory of gender differences in moral development.

Relationship matrix

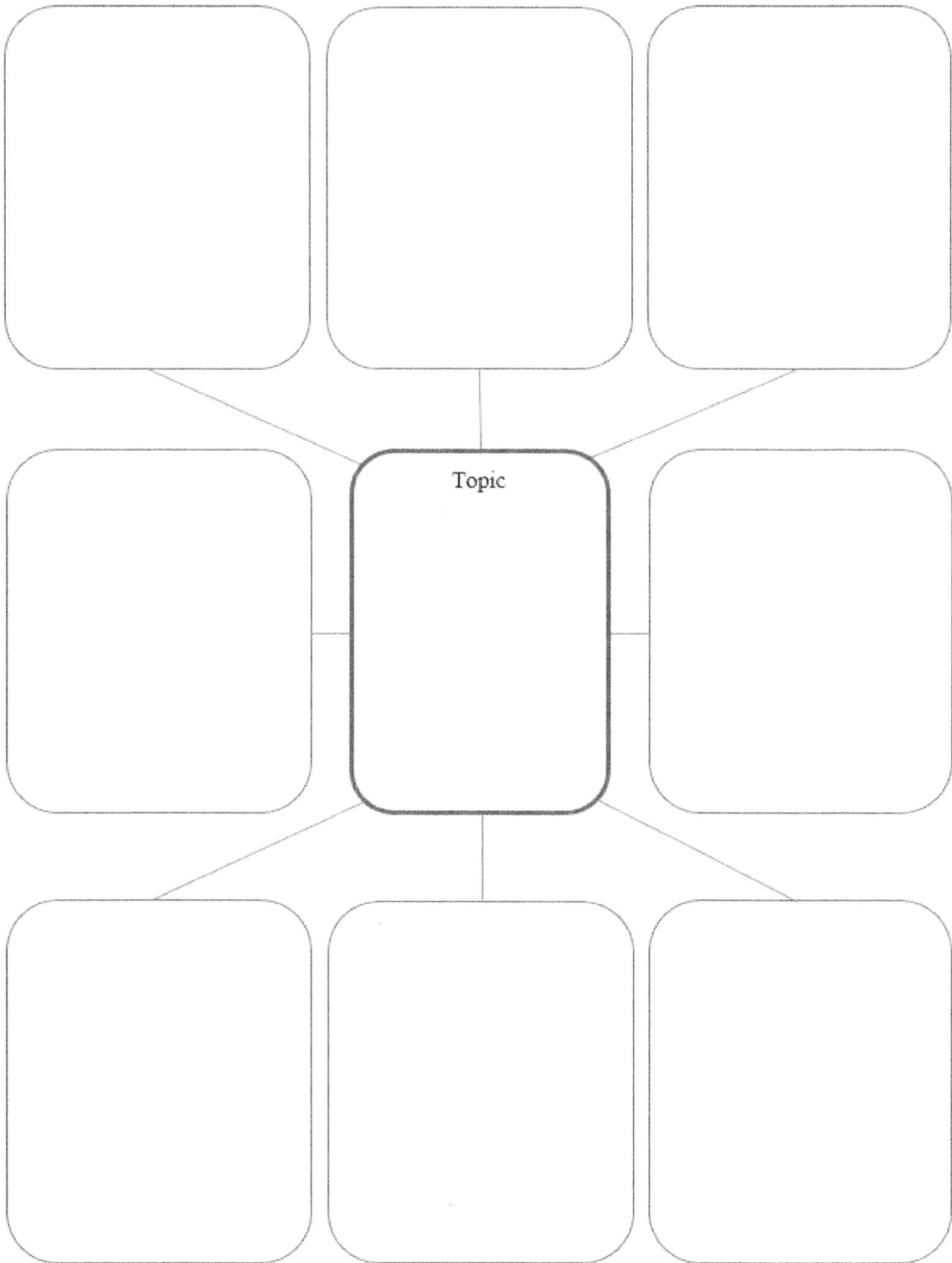

Notes for active learning

CHAPTER 8

Personality

Human development of enduring behavioral and personal characteristic patterns is explored through major theories (e.g., behavioral, humanistic, psychodynamic, social cognitive, and trait). Various associated personality assessment techniques are essential for insight.

Self refers to the thoughts and beliefs individuals have about themselves. The notion of self is complex and multifaceted; it includes gender, racial, and ethnic identities, and beliefs about an individual's ability to accomplish tasks and control different situations.

Self develops over time and is shaped by factors including society, culture, individuals and groups, and unique experiences. It emerges from how people view themselves and influences perception of others and interactions with them.

Personality

Theories of personality

Personality is individual characteristic patterns of thinking, behaving, and feeling.

The study of personality focuses on examining how the various parts of an individual become integrated and understanding the individual differences in personality traits.

Major personality theories attempt to understand, explain, or predict personality characteristics.

Most well-known theories attempting to understand the differences and commonalities among people include the psychoanalytic theory of personality and humanistic, trait, social, biological, and behaviorist theories.

Personality must be understood under each umbrella theory, as consensus is absent.

Psychoanalytic perspective

Freud's early exploration of the unconscious used hypnosis and free association techniques.

Freud believed that children passed through a series of psychosexual stages.

Freud mapped the psychosexual development stages, believing that personality develops during childhood and is highly influenced by unresolved, unconscious issues during early childhood.

Free association is the concept of being relaxed and relating to whatever comes to mind.

Psychoanalysis process reveals the mental dominoes of the patient's past.

Three components in Freud's personality structure interact: the id, superego, and ego.

> *Id* is the unconscious energy that drives a person to satisfy sexual and aggressive drives; it operates on the *pleasure principle*, demanding *immediate gratification*. Id focuses its libido, or sexual energy, on different erogenous zones.

> *Superego* is the aspect of personality representing internalized ideals based on the individual's standards of judgment or morals.

> *Ego* is the executive control system of the conscious mind, responsible for mediating the desires of the id and superego's desires, known as the *reality principle*.

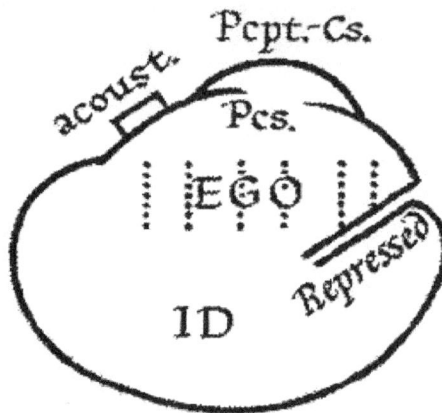

Freud's diagram of the ego and id

Psychosexual development stages

Oral stage is from birth to 18 months. The pleasure center is in the *mouth*, and activities persisting during this stage include sucking, biting, and chewing.

Anal stage is 18 to 36 months. Pleasure in this stage is focused on *bladder and bowel control*.

Phallic stage is 3 to 6 years. *Genitals* are the primary pleasure zone. During this stage, children cope with incestuous feelings; the *Oedipus* and *Electra complexes* form.

Latency stage (or *cooties stage*) is 6 to puberty when dormant sexual feelings form. Libido and sexuality are hidden in the unconscious, and children socialize with others their age and gender.

Genital stage (between puberty and death), in which there is a maturation of sexual interests.

Fixation is lingering pleasure-seeking energies persisting from earlier psychosexual stages.

Orally fixated people may need to chain smoke or constantly chew gum.

Anally fixated people can either be anal-expulsive or anal-retentive.

Defense mechanisms

Defense mechanisms are unconscious acts by the ego to redefine reality and reduce anxiety.

Seven types of *defense mechanisms*.

- *Repression* is banishing anxiety-driven thoughts deep into the unconscious. According to Freud, when people do not remember lusting after their parents.

- *Regression* is when a person faced with anxiety retreats to an infantile stage (or patterns of behavior) earlier in development. For example, thumb-sucking on the first day of school.

- *Reaction formation* is when the ego switches unacceptable impulses into the opposite. For example, being rude to someone they like romantically.

- *Projection* is disguising threatening personal impulses by attributing them to others. For example, they think their spouse intends to be disloyal when they are considering cheating on their spouse.

- *Rationalization* is self-justifying explanations instead of real, more threatening reasons to explain actions. For example, when someone does not get into their college of choice, they react by saying, "I did not want to go there anyway; it is too far from the mountains."

- *Displacement* shifts unacceptable impulses toward a safer outlet. For example, instead of yelling at an instructor, an individual may take his anger out by yelling at his girlfriend.

- *Sublimation* is re-channeling unacceptable impulses into acceptable or socially approved activities. For example, feelings of aggression (or violence) are channeled into aggressive sports play.

Unconscious mind

Methods of hypnosis or free association, as well as projective tests, are most commonly used to assess an individual's unconscious mind.

Projective tests are personality tests that provide ambiguous stimuli designed to trigger the projection of people's inner dynamics.

Thematic Appreciation Test (TAT) is a projective test for people to express feelings through stories they are asked to make up about a series of deliberately ambiguous scenes.

Rorschach inkblot test is a popularly used projective test. Ten inkblots are designed to identify people's feelings when asked to interpret what they see in the inkblots.

Neo-Freudians are psychologists who adopted and built upon Freud's theories; proponents include Alfred Adler, Karen Horney, and Carl Jung. Alfred Adler stated that childhood is vital to personality, yet he argued that the focus should be on social factors, not sexual ones.

Inferiority complex theory (Adler) proposes that human behavior is driven by efforts to conquer inferiority and feel superior.

Karen Horney theorized that childhood anxiety is related to feelings of helplessness and a dependent attachment. This triggers the constant yearning for love and security. She argued against Freud's *penis envy concept.*

Carl Jung put less emphasis on social factors and focused on the unconscious. He theorized that humans have a collective unconscious, a shared (or inherited) memory from human evolution.

Carl Jung, Swiss psychiatrist, and psychoanalyst

Humanistic perspective

Humanistic perspective proposes that people are *innately good*, determine their destinies through *free will*, and are motivated to *self-actualize* and reach their full potential.

According to this framework, *self-concept* and *self-esteem* have a crucial positive correlation.

Self-concept is a person's global feeling about the self.

Abraham Maslow and Carl Rogers were the founding fathers of *humanistic psychology*.

Maslow hypothesized a hierarchy of needs and suggested that *self-actualization* is at the top.

Carl Rogers' self-theory posed that people need *unconditional positive regard* to self-actualize.

Unconditional positive regard is the acceptance and support for a person regardless of what the person does or says.

Main criticism of humanistic theories is that they are *overly optimistic* and *lack objectivity*.

Determinism is the belief that what happens is dictated by what has happened in the past, a concept fully supported by psychoanalysts and behaviorists.

In contrast, determinism does not support the existence of free will.

Self-actualization — morality, creativity, spontaneity, problem solving, lack of prejudice, acceptance of facts

Esteem — self-esteem, confidence, achievement, respect of others, respect by others

Love/belonging — friendship, family, sexual intimacy

Safety — security of: body, employment, resources, morality, the family, health, property

Physiological — breathing, food, water, sex, sleep, homeostasis, excretion

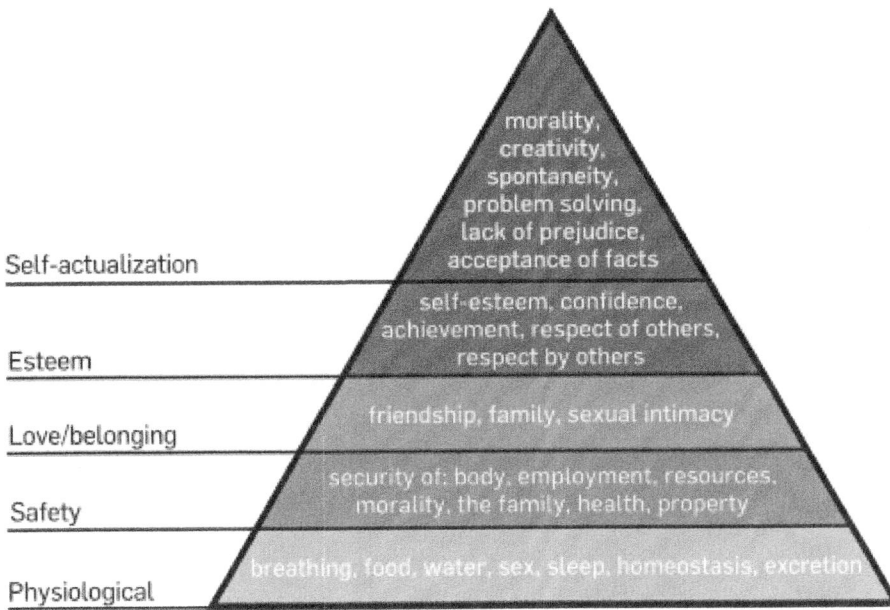

Maslow's hierarchy of needs

Trait perspective

Trait is a characteristic of behavior or a disposition to feel and act a certain way. According to this theory, three traits define an individual's personality.

Cardinal traits dominate an individual's life to the extent they become identified by them, as they shape and influence an individual's behavior.

Central traits are the foundation of personality and are represented by varying levels of specific individual characteristics. For example, intelligence or consideration are central traits.

Secondary traits are preferences or attitudes and tend to be expressed only in certain situations.

Big Five Personality Theory proposes that five broad dimensions describe personalities. According to this theory, traits are *stable* and *persist over time*.

Personality traits are at least partially attributed to genetics, apply cross-culturally, and predict other individual attributes.

Five-factor model (FFM) comprises openness, conscientiousness, extraversion, agreeableness, and neuroticism.

- *Openness* refers to being imaginative or practical, having various experiences or routines, and independent thinking or conforming.

- *Conscientiousness* refers to being organized or disorganized, careful or careless, and disciplined or impulsive.

- *Extraversion* is how sociable, fun-loving, and affectionate a person is.

- *Agreeableness* refers to being soft-hearted or ruthless, trusting or suspicious, and helpful or uncooperative.

- *Neuroticism* (or emotional stability) refers to being calm or anxious, secure or insecure, self-satisfied or self-pitying.

Extraversion measures how sociable, fun-loving, and affectionate a person is

Personality inventories are questionnaires aiming to gauge distinct aspects of personality. The NEO-FFI3 screener personality inventory measures the big five personality domains.

Minnesota Multiphasic Personality Inventory (MMPI) is the most widely used personality test. Although it was initially used to identify psychopathology, it is now used for screening purposes, making differential diagnoses, and aiding in treatment plan development.

Person-situation controversy focuses on whether traits are *stable* or *change over time*. Research studies have noted that traits change according to the situation.

Social cognitive perspective

Social cognitive theory emphasizes self-efficacy, observational learning, and interactions between contextual influence and cognitive processes. This perspective falls under the umbrella of behaviorism.

As introduced by Watson, behaviorism supports a direct and unidirectional pathway between stimulus and response, with human behavior seen as a simple reaction to external stimuli.

Social cognitive theory focuses on how individuals interact with their environment and how observing others influences behavior.

Reciprocal determinism describes the interpenetrative relationship between personality and social and environmental factors.

Social cognitive perspective states that different people choose different environments.

For example, the friends people frequently hang out with, the places they frequent, and people following their disposition often choose the music they listen to. Consequently, individuals are reciprocally influenced or shaped by environmental factors after choosing an environment.

Biological perspective

Hippocrates believed that personality was determined by the relative levels of the four humours.

The humours (or fluids) he described were blood, yellow bile, black bile, and phlegm.

Hippocrates was among the first to recognize the biological underpinnings of personality.

Heritability is a measure of the percentage of a trait inherited. Little evidence exists regarding the influence heritability has on specific personality traits.

Temperament is an emotional style and characteristic way of interacting with the world. Infants seem to differ immediately at birth due to their innate differences in temperament.

Temperament influences personality development.

Somatotype theory of personality is related to biology and was proposed by William Sheldon.

Somatotype theory of personality associates personality traits with three body types:

> *endomorphs* (or obese)
>
> *mesomorphs* (or muscular)
>
> *ectomorphs* (or thin)

Behaviorist perspective

Behaviorist theory states that personality is determined by an interaction between the individual and their learning experiences or surrounding environment.

Reinforcement contingencies promote and shape personality. Therefore, individuals can alter their personalities by changing the environment.

Behaviorist perspective, proposed by B. F. Skinner, refutes the belief that individuals must change their inner selves before they can experience a personality change.

Critics highlight its failure to recognize the importance of cognition in personality development.

Situational approach to explaining behavior

Personalities help create situations in which individuals then react.

For example, a counter-productive example of this would be to be unfriendly if someone believes the person is angry at them; in doing so, this individual creates or exacerbates the suspected behavior.

Situational approach theory follows the *stimulus-response-consequence model.*

Personal control is the sense individuals have of control over their environment rather than the control that their environment has over them.

External locus of control is the perception that chance (or outside forces) determine fate.

Internal locus of control is the perception that one controls one's fate.

Learned helplessness is hopelessness (or passive resignation) from repeated aversive events.

Attitudes

Outside actors

Generally, people believe they form opinions or attitudes about people, objects, and ideas.

However, psychologists have found that groups around us influence these attitudes more than most realize or are willing to admit.

Social psychologists have studied this phenomenon and recognize how vital *outside actors* are in forming our attitudes and opinions.

Components of attitudes

To understand how attitudes are influenced, attitudes must be defined.

Attitude is a set of beliefs (either favorable or unfavorable) toward a person, place, or object.

Attitudes have *cognitive, affective*, and *behavioral components* interacting to form attitudes.

> *Cognitive component* is what the person thinks about the topic. For example, "My boss always forgets what I tell him. He is a real jerk."

> *Affective component* of the attitude is the feeling or emotion associated with the attitude. For example, "Every time I see my boss, I feel angry."

> *Behavioral component* of the attitude is the action taken. For example, "I'm currently applying for other jobs within my company to get a different boss. I also try to avoid my boss as much as possible."

These components of the attitude result in an overall perspective toward the object or person.

Behavior influences attitudes

Attitudes and behavior are connected. In the above example, the attitude toward the boss is causing the individual to apply for new jobs and avoid the boss. However, what would happen if the individual spent more time with their boss? Might the attitude change?

After spending time with the boss, the person may discover that the boss is a single father and incredibly overworked and overwhelmed. Their attitude might change upon learning this because they understand why he forgets what they tell him. Thus, the attitude changed due to the behavior change (i.e., instead of avoiding their boss, they spent more time around him and learned something that made them feel differently about him). This is one example of how *behaviors may influence attitudes*.

However, there are other ways behavior influences attitudes.

One process is the *foot-in-the-door* phenomenon, named after door-to-door salespeople who believed that if they could get one foot in the door, the homeowner would be unable to turn them away. The foot-in-the-door phenomenon states that you should first ask for a simple request, and once this has been agreed to, you should follow up with a more substantial request.

For example, outside of the voting location, someone might ask a person to sign a petition so that a candidate may run for a particular office. Once you sign it, you may be asked to volunteer several hours to help this candidate's campaign.

Door-in-the-face technique is the opposite. With this technique, you start by asking for a substantial request, and when it is rejected, you follow up with a simple request that is likely to be accepted. For example, one might ask their neighbor to watch their 9-month-old baby for the weekend while they take a trip. When the neighbor says no, they may ask the neighbor to watch the baby for 2 hours while going to the grocery store. The idea is that the neighbor is so relieved about not being pressed to undertake a demanding task that they will help with a simpler one.

Role-playing is a process where behavior influences attitude. This was famously observed in Philip Zimbardo's *Stanford Prison Study*. In this study, a group of men were randomly assigned to be either correctional officers or prisoners in a mock prison set up by Dr. Zimbardo in the basement of a building at Stanford University. Local police arrested the "prisoners" and "booked" into the prison. The "guards" were given uniforms and free rein to run the prison.

After approximately one day, some of the "guards" began acting brutally toward the "prisoners." The study, which was supposed to last 2 weeks, was ended after only 6 days due to the sadistic behavior of the "guards" and the extreme distress of the "prisoners."

Stanford Prison Study is cited when discussing how role-playing affects attitudes. The participants in this study were average, emotionally stable, law-abiding American males, and it was due to the flip of a coin that one was assigned to be a prisoner or a guard. The result of playing these roles over a matter of days caused a severe shift in behavior in both the guards and prisoners. The guards' attitude was to perceive the prisoners as inferior, and the prisoners' attitude was to believe that they were inferior. Thus, the *role-playing* significantly influenced the attitude of the guards, prompting acts of sadism, and influenced the attitude of the prisoners, prompting submissiveness.

Self-presentation is another case where attitude can appear to change, though it usually does not. In this scenario, an individual will profess attitudes that match his or her actions to avoid feeling foolish. There is usually awareness that a discrepancy exists between the presented and true attitudes. However, contrary to the true attitude, the behavior is assumed to help one appear consistent.

Attitudes influence behavior

It is reasonable to assume that attitudes consistently predict behavior. Richard LaPierre demonstrated that this is not always true. In 1934, LaPierre drove the U.S. with a Chinese couple and stopped at over 250 restaurants and hotels. They were only refused service once.

Sometime later, LaPierre surveyed the owners of the restaurants and hotels about their attitudes toward Chinese people, explicitly asking if they would serve Chinese people in their business. Ninety-two percent stated that they would not serve Chinese people.

In this study, the attitude did not influence actual behavior. Most owners admitted to racial bias (i.e., attitude's cognitive and affective components). However, they did not act when confronted with serving the Chinese couple (i.e., the behavioral component of attitude).

Subsequent studies have focused on determining the circumstances when attitude predicts behavior. One of the biggest problems with attitudes predicting behaviors is that often, people are not honest about their attitudes, especially if there is a negative social consequence for holding a given attitude. For example, an individual may have a negative attitude toward a specific racial group; however, expressing this negative attitude may be socially unacceptable. Thus, the individual may try to hide their genuine attitude.

To minimize this, social psychologists have created the *bogus pipeline paradigm*, where a person is connected to wires and electrodes and told that the apparatus measures whether they are telling the truth. The wires and electrodes are not measuring anything. Still, this increases the probability that the subjects will be honest in their attitudes, making predicting behavior more accurate.

Bogus pipeline paradigm was created to simulate a lie detector

Asking about specific attitudes rather than general ones helps predict specific behavior. For example, if someone generally asks about a religious attitude, it is unlikely to predict whether they will attend church next weekend (a particular behavior). However, the attitude could predict the total number of religious behaviors over time (general behaviors). The more specificity with an attitude is identified, the higher the predictive value.

External factors (or conditions) impact whether attitudes affect behavior. One's attitude is more likely to affect behavior if no other external factors are involved. For example, an individual may not want to volunteer at a food bank because they believe people should find gainful employment if they want to eat. However, if that person's close friends volunteer at a food bank as a group, the individual may engage in the volunteering behavior. The external force of *peer pressure* influenced the behavior, not the attitude.

Desire to conform to a particular group's behavior is closely related. In one study, a group read about a proposed law to pay unemployment benefits. Half of the group was told it was a Democratic-backed proposal, while the other half were told it was a Republican one. Among those who were told it was Democratic-backed, those who identified as conservative said the proposal was too expensive, while liberals supported it.

However, among those who were told the proposal was Republican-backed, conservatives approved of the proposal, while liberals said the pay was not high enough. In this study, the participants demonstrated behavior (i.e., deciding whether to support the proposal) based on the political party of their preference and not the proposal's content itself. This is an example of how belonging to a group influences attitude and, thus, behavior.

Similar findings occur in the "real world" if two conditions are met. First, the individual must identify with the group. For example, someone with few ties to or no opinion on politics is unlikely to have a strong attitude about a politically charged topic.

The second condition is that the issue needs to be ambiguous. For example, people usually have strong feelings about abortion, but how much government assistance one should receive each month is more ambiguous.

Theory of reasoned action

Theory of reasoned action is a model used to predict behavior from attitude. Created by Icek Ajzen and Martin Fishbein, it purports three constructs:

> behavioral intention, attitude, and subjective norm.

Attitude and *subjective norms* combined determine *behavioral intention*.

Behavioral intention is the strength of the intention to perform a behavior. A person's behavior is determined by their attitude and how others perceive them for that behavior. Research has found that the most relevant application of this theory is in consumer behavior. The theory (and associated mathematical formula) predicts consumer behavior very well.

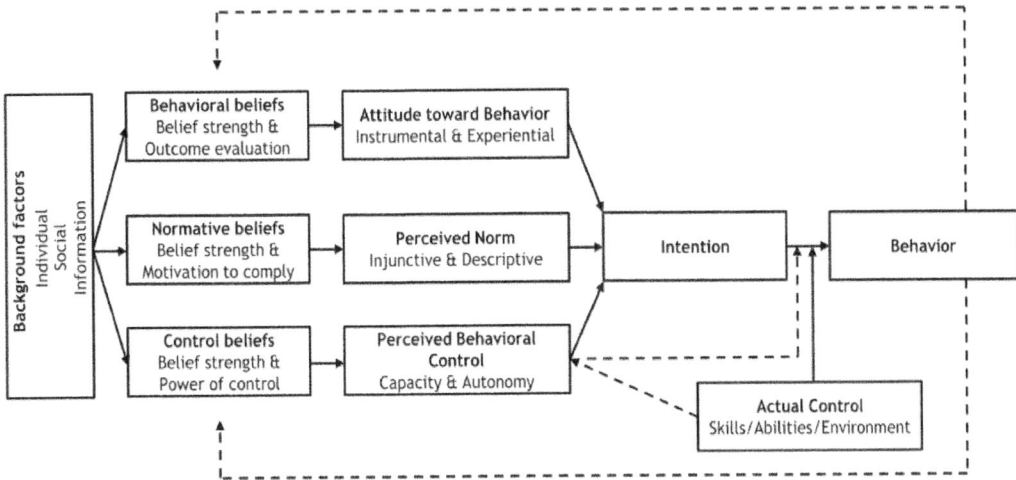

Reasoned action approach is a psychological model to explain and predict behavior

Not all attitudes are equal. The stronger the attitude is, the more likely it predicts behavior. Research has shown that individuals with a strong attitude have spent more time learning about the object of the attitude. This learning process serves to solidify the attitude and makes it not only difficult to change but a better predictor of behavior.

Individuals with firm attitudes are more likely to have experience with the object of the attitude. Again, these *experiences strengthen the attitude* and serve as a *stronger predictor* of behavior.

Cognitive dissonance theory

Cognitive dissonance theory is when attitudes, beliefs, and behaviors do not correspond. One can have two competing thoughts or beliefs, creating tension within that individual. Because this tension is uncomfortable, the individual will try to reduce it.

For example, a high school senior may want to attend Harvard. He may believe that Harvard is the only school worth attending if one is going to go to college and, therefore, spends his time studying and trying to get good grades. However, when he applied, he was rejected. Thus, there is tension between his goals and the reality of the situation. As a result, the high school senior may downplay how much he wanted to attend Harvard and proclaim that "there are better schools out there anyway." In this way, the high school senior *reduces the tension*.

Cognitive dissonance is when two thoughts compete (i.e., cognition) or are inconsistent (i.e., dissonance). Dissonance is uncomfortable, so the person attempts to lessen it.

Cognitive dissonance is essential to studying attitudes and behavior because changes in attitudes due to cognitive dissonance impact behavior.

For example, a child might want to purchase a gift for his mother. When he goes into the store to purchase the gift, he discovers he does not have enough money. However, he steals the gift, knowing this is what his mother wants.

The child thinks: "I stole the gift" and "stealing is wrong," conflicting, so dissonance occurs.

Resolving dissonance:

> 1) return the gift to the store and admit his wrongdoing or

> 2) think, "Stealing may be a bad thing sometimes, but when it is done to help someone, it is not that bad."

A change in cognition (2) reduces dissonance while allowing the behavior (i.e., stealing a gift).

Theories of Attitude and Behavior Change

Elaboration likelihood model

How attitudes form and change is not entirely understood.

However, research has led to the Elaboration Likelihood Model and Social Cognitive Theory.

Elaboration Likelihood Model is a theory of persuasion for attitude change.

It states that there are two persuasion routes: *central* and *peripheral.*

Central route (or *direct route*) involves individuals gathering information and using logic to form attitudes over time. If an attitude change occurs, it tends to resist change over time and predict later behavior.

Most people would like to believe that their attitudes derive from utilizing the central route; however, research has shown that the *peripheral route* forms many attitudes.

Peripheral route involves quick judgments based on positive or negative cues. Often, there is limited evidence and little time to research and logically think about the object of the attitude.

The peripheral route involves some vague impressions, emotions, and the characteristics of the message (as discussed below) when forming the attitude. One example of the peripheral route is the foot-in-the-door phenomenon.

Motivation and *ability* determine which route is taken.

Motivation is the desire to process messages, affected by relevance and existing attitudes.

Ability is the capability for critical evaluation and is influenced by distractions and familiarity.

```
                        ┌──────────────────────┐
                        │        Message        │
                        └──────────────────────┘
                                   │
                                   ▼
```

Message

Does the receiver have sufficient motivation?

Genuine interest, requirement and urgency can provide receivers with motivation.

Peripheral route attitude change for receiver

No

Yes

Yes

Does the receiver have the ability to process?

preoccupation, tiredness, stress and boredom can inhibit a receivers ability to process Whilst experience and prior knowledge can improve a receivers ability to process

No

Is the receiver using the peripheral route?

No

Yes

Yes

Receievers attitude remains unchanged

Attitude has undergone a positive shift?

Attitude has undergone a negaitve shift?

No

Yes

Yes

Has an impression been made on the receiver?

Yes +ve

Yes -ve

Central route attitude change for receiver

Central Route

Peripheral Route

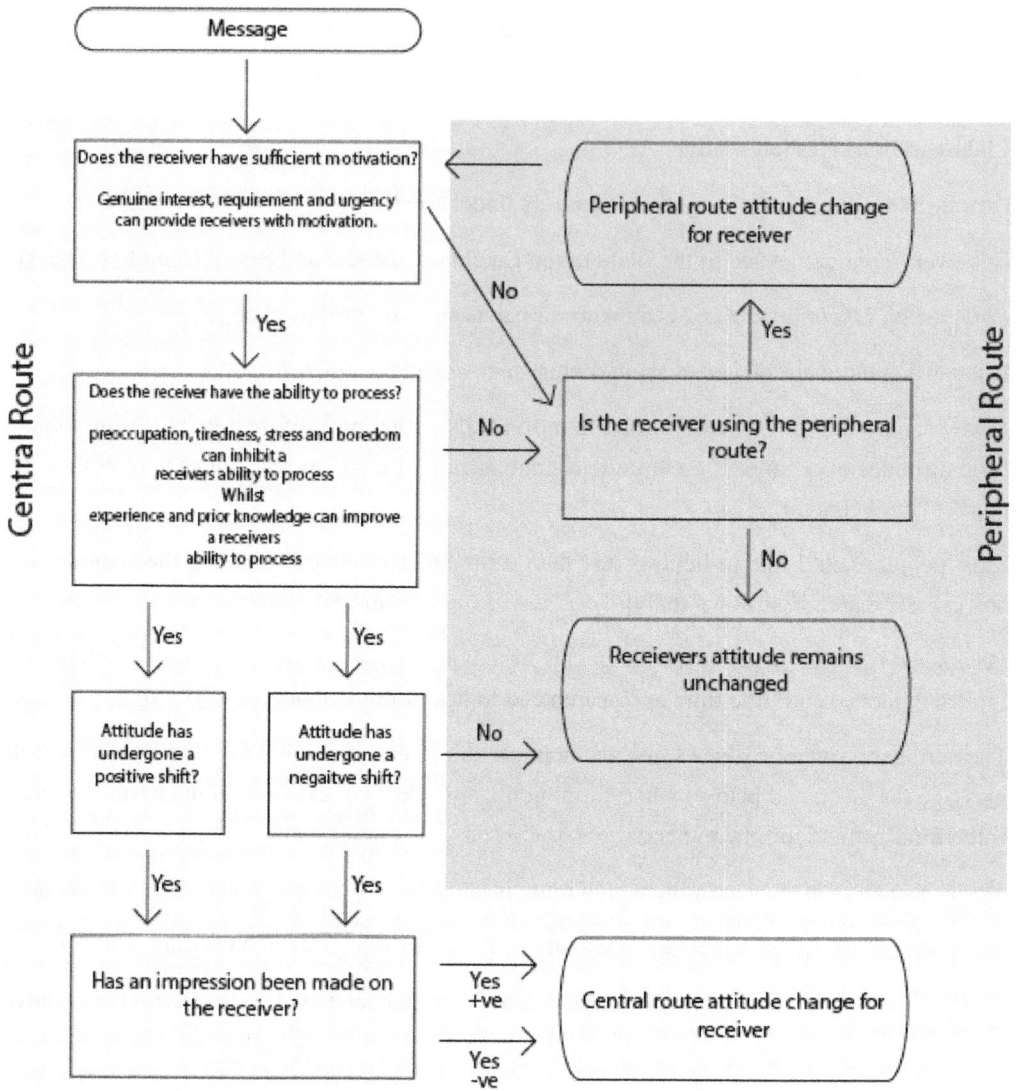

Elaboration Likelihood Model

Social cognitive theory

Albert Bandura developed *Social Cognitive Theory* and posits that an individual learns through observing others. Research shows that individuals learn behaviors and attitudes by observing others in the media, during social interactions, and experiences with external actors. In this way, humans do not have to evaluate the results of behaviors independently; they learn the consequences through observing others.

If an individual sees a desired consequence because of another having a particular attitude (or behavior), there is a likelihood that the individual will emulate that attitude (or behavior).

For example, suppose a celebrity goes on television and states that he or she lost much weight by eating food at a specific fast-food chain. In that case, someone watching this commercial may change their attitude toward that chain and now decide it is healthy eating.

Albert Bandura, psychologist

Factors that affect attitude change

Many factors affect attitude change and the ease at which people change their attitudes. One factor is the message source. Our willingness to change our attitude based on what someone says depends partially on the characteristics of that person (i.e., the communicator).

People are more likely to change their attitude with communicators who are more attractive and perceived as trustworthy or experts in a given topic.

Not only is the communicator influential, but so is the message content. Two-sided messages are when the communicator's message and the opposing viewpoint are presented. These are more effective than one-sided messages, where only the communicator's message is presented, assuming that the opposing side's viewpoint can be easily refuted. The characteristics of the target of the message also influence whether an attitude change will occur.

Even after the communicator has delivered the message, the characteristics of the target will determine if the message changes attitudes. Previous research has shown that less intelligent people are easier to persuade than more intelligent people.

Gender differences also seem to exist, but they are small. Women are more easily persuaded than men when these differences are found, especially with little background. However, men and women are equally likely to change their private attitudes.

Changing behavior changes attitude. In the *Stanford Prison Study*, the guards' attitudes began to shift, and they engaged in the brutal treatment of the prisoners. Likewise, after a few hours of "acting" like prisoners, the prisoners' attitudes began to shift, and they started to see the guards as powerful oppressors and themselves as inferior, bringing about a change in their behaviors (i.e., they became more submissive).

Individuals with similar attitudes often form groups; sometimes, these groups are formalized, and other times, they may be friends who share similar attitudes. Regardless, when members of the group discuss their attitudes with members of opposing groups, the original attitudes tend to become stronger and more solidified.

Group polarization is when discussion makes the attitudes of group members more pronounced.

Self-Concept, Self-Identity and Social Identity

Self-concept

Psychologists Carl Rogers and Abraham Maslow first identified *self-concept* and *self-identity*.

Self-concept and *self-identity* refer to beliefs people hold about *themselves* and their *abilities*.

Beliefs in three domains significantly influence a person's overall self-concept:

> *self-esteem*,
>
> *self-efficacy*, and
>
> *locus of control*.

Self-esteem

Self-esteem is the level of worth a person believes they possess.

High self-esteem people see themselves as valuable and are accepting of themselves. They are typically *confident* and *optimistic* about the future.

Low self-esteem persons view themselves negatively. They tend to be *highly self-critical* and *sensitive to criticisms* from others. They typically have *low self-confidence* and are *pessimistic*.

Self-efficacy

Self-efficacy refers to one's belief in their ability to reach a goal. It concerns the level of competence a person believes they possess for a particular task.

For example, someone who believes they can quit smoking possesses high self-efficacy, while someone who believes they will never be able to quit possesses low self-efficacy.

Research shows that the level of self-efficacy a person has about a given task influences both their level of success on that task and the likelihood that they will start the task.

High self-efficacy people are more likely to take risks than those with low self-efficacy and can recover more quickly from setbacks.

Low self-efficacy people avoid challenging tasks and lose confidence in their abilities when faced with a setback.

Locus of control

Locus of control is a person's beliefs about how much they can control events affecting them.

Individuals with an *internal locus of control* feel they can control many of the events affecting them. They are more likely to *take responsibility for their actions* and circumstances than those with an external locus of control.

Individuals with an *external locus of control* blame outside forces (e.g., luck or chance) for their circumstances. This often leads to feeling hopeless when faced with challenges.

Locus of control lies on a *continuum*; most people fall between an internal and external locus.

Locus of control has become more internal with *age* and varies by *culture*.

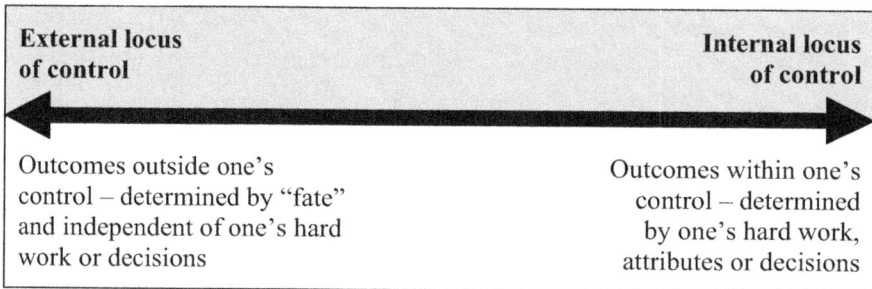

External locus of control	Internal locus of control
Outcomes outside one's control – determined by "fate" and independent of one's hard work or decisions	Outcomes within one's control – determined by one's hard work, attributes or decisions

Social identities and ethnicity

Social identity refers to their psychological relationship to particular social categories. It is primarily based on groups that an individual belongs to.

Research suggests that a person's social identity is influenced by race or ethnicity, gender, age, sexual orientation, and class, factors interacting to form a person's self-identity.

Intersectionality is when an individual simultaneously belongs to two or more social groups.

Ethnicity refers to distinctions based on national origin and culture, including language, relation, and place of origin. A person's racial and ethnic background can influence how they perceive themselves. Racial and ethnic identities are passed on from earlier generations.

Ethnic identity is believed to develop during adolescence. Jean Phinney proposed a model for adolescent ethnic identity development that breaks up this process into three stages.

In the first stage of ethnic identity development, an adolescent's ethnic identity is unexamined. Many theorists believe that adolescents from a dominant culture stay in this stage and do not form a sense of ethnic identity.

During the second stage, *moratorium*, adolescents search for the meaning of their ethnicity.

In the third stage of ethnic identity development, adolescents feel secure about their sense of ethnic identity; their identity becomes an integral part of their self-identity.

Racial identity

Race refers to physical distinctions (e.g., skin color and eye shape) and a social construction.

Psychologist William Cross proposed a model for *racial identity development*, particularly Black identity development, which comprises four identity statuses.

Pre-encounter is the first stage of *racial identity development* when individuals are unaware of their race and the effects their race has on others.

Encounter stage is when a person has an encounter that leads to examining their racial identity.

Immersion stage follows the encounter stage, where individuals explore their racial identity, through interaction with individuals of the same race.

Internalization and commitment are the final stages of racial identity development when individuals have formed a secure sense of racial identity and can form positive relationships with individuals who share their racial identity and those who do not.

Gender and sexual orientation

Gender is a social category that refers to attitudes and behaviors a culture associates with a particular biological sex.

Gender identity refers to a person's subjective experience of their gender, typically as male or female. When an individual's gender identity and biological sex are incongruent, they may identify as transsexual or transgender.

Sexual orientation is a person's sexual identity about the *gender to which they are attracted*.

Sexual orientation includes *heterosexuality*, *homosexuality*, *bisexuality*, and *asexuality*.

Stigma may be associated with homosexuality, bisexuality, and asexuality.

Sexual identity is how individuals think of themselves regarding who they are sexually attracted to and may or may not align with sexual orientation. Contemporary models of sexual identity acknowledged its formation occurs in both sexual minorities and majorities.

Age identity

Age identity refers to a person's inner experiences of age and aging.

Research on age identity has found that older individuals tend not to feel old. Researchers have suggested that this is due to self-continuity and self-enhancement.

Self-continuity is the desire to remain the same over time.

Self-enhancement refers to maintaining a positive self-image.

In the United States, people with *older identities* report *lower life satisfaction* levels.

Societies often associate aging with decline; older individuals may wish to identify as younger. Thus, age and age identity differences are less pronounced in Asian cultures, where age is less associated with decline.

Older individuals tend not to feel old due to self-continuity and self-enhancement

Social class identities

Social class refers to social divisions in which individuals are classified by *wealth*, *education*, and *occupation*.

Social classes are typically *lower*, *middle*, and *upper class*. Social class has wide-ranging effects and may become a part of a person's identity.

Individuals from the upper class are typically able to send their children to better schools, while those from the lower class may believe that getting a good education is beyond the means of their class.

Being in a lower social class also has *negative health consequences*. Lower-class people often receive poorer quality healthcare than the upper classes.

Influence of Social Factors on Identity Development

Gender development

Gender is a social construct that forms over time.

Gender identity development begins at an early age, between the ages of three and six.

Some theories of gender development break the formation of gender into three stages.

First stage of gender development is when toddlers learn about the socialized traits of gender.

Second stage of gender development is when gender consolidates and becomes rigid, typically between the ages of five and seven.

Third stage is when socially defined gender roles become relaxed for the individual.

Sandra Bem developed *gender schema theory* as a cognitive theory for gender development.

Gender schemas are sets of gender-related beliefs an individual holds that influence behavior. Bem proposed these schemas form by children's observing males and females within society.

Bem proposes that gender identity is formed primarily from being *sex-typed* at an early age. *Sex-typed* refers to the acquisition of sex-appropriate preferences and behaviors.

Social-learning theory approach to *gender development* focuses on the role of parents and caregivers in an individual's acquisition of gender identity. Walter Mischel proposed that parents reward their children for engaging in gender-appropriate behavior.

For example, a boy might be praised for being interested in fixing cars, and a young girl might be praised for wearing a dress.

Influence of individuals

Imitation is a form of social behavior that refers to copying another person's behaviors.

Imitation occurs even in young infants, suggesting that people have an innate ability to imitate others. One area of research within this field concerns mirror neurons.

Mirror neurons are neurons that are activated when an individual engages in a task and when an individual observes another person engaging in the same task.

Mirror neurons may be responsible for the propensity to imitate others.

Expectations of others influence identity formation. Individuals within a family or group tend to take on a specific role. The influence of this role formation is closely related to social norms; we adapt to the expectations of others.

Roles in one setting (e.g., family) can carry over into another (e.g., peer group). Individuals can internalize these roles and view them as parts of themselves. For example, a girl who takes on a mothering role to her brother may act in a nurturing manner within her friend group and subsequently view herself as a nurturer.

Looking-glass self is a social psychological concept that a person's identity grows out of the perceptions of others. Accordingly, people form their self-identity by combining how others view them.

Three components of the *looking-glass theory*:

> 1) imagine how they appear to others.

> 2) imagine others' judgments about how they appear.

> 3) develop a sense of self through the judgments of others.

Looking-glass self states that a person's identity grows out of the perceptions of others, imagining how others view and judge them.

Reference groups

Social groups are collections of people who share similarities and interact with one another.

Social groups can function as powerful influencers of behaviors.

Reference groups are groups that the individual uses to compare themselves to.

Three reference groups:

*Aspirational reference group*s have people that an individual wishes to be more like.

Associative reference groups have individuals with similar interests to themselves.

Dissociative reference groups (or *out-groups*) have unfavorable individuals to whom the person does not want to belong.

People typically adopt the social norms of aspirational and associative reference groups while actively disdaining the norms of dissociative reference groups.

Primary and secondary groups

Social groups are divided into *primary* and *secondary groups*.

Primary groups are groups in which individuals intimately interact with one another.

Primary groups typically exert a great deal of emphasis. They commonly include families, fraternities, sororities, classmates, and friends.

Secondary groups are groups individuals belong to but do not interact with often.

Relationships within a secondary group are typically brief. They do not exert as much influence on the individuals belonging to them as primary groups.

Influence of culture and socialization on identity formation

How people view themselves is heavily influenced by their childhood culture and socialization. This occurs through the social roles that individuals learn through socialization. When individuals internalize these roles, they become a part of their identity.

Individuals form their identities by comparing themselves to others they interact with.

People compare themselves to the *ideals and expectations* of their culture. Individuals who do not meet these cultural expectations may develop poor self-esteem.

Culture has been found to influence the *locus of control* of individuals.

For example, individuals from the United States typically have a more *internal locus of control* than individuals from Japan.

In the U.S., African Americans tend to have a more *external locus of control* than whites.

Notes for active learning

Self-Presentation and Interacting with Others

Expressing and detecting emotion

Individuals vary in how they express their emotions and detect the emotions of others. Researchers are increasingly concerned with the factors that influence these processes.

Emotional intelligence is the ability to express one's emotions and detect the emotions of others.

People with *high emotional intelligence* have social support and avoid interpersonal conflicts.

Individuals with high emotional intelligence are *less likely* to abuse drugs and alcohol.

Gender and *culture* have been found to shape how individuals express and detect emotions.

Gender in the expression and detection of emotion

Researchers have found differences between how men and women express and detect emotions. Women can typically read verbal and visual emotional reactions better than men.

Women *experience emotions* more intensely than men and are likelier to *display emotions*.

Women are more likely to experience disgust, shame, and guilt, while men are more likely to experience anger.

Men are typically able to tolerate *distressing emotions* more than women.

Research has found that *women score higher* on emotional intelligence tests than men.

However, men with high emotional intelligence are typically more successful than men with low emotional intelligence.

There is much debate on why these sex differences exist.

Some researchers point to *biological factors* (e.g., hormone levels) for these differences.

Some theorize that *cultural stereotypes and socialization* are responsible for gender differences. For example, the parents of a young boy might express disapproval when he cries, while a young girl's parents might comfort her.

A combination of biological factors and socialization likely contribute to gender differences.

Role of culture in the expression and detection of emotion

While emotions are universal, how emotions are perceived and regulated differs across cultures. Research by Paul Ekman has found that cultures share the same facial expressions of emotions.

These expressions, however, occur at different frequencies depending on the culture.

Display rules are the cultural expectations of the expression of emotions.

Norms dictate which emotions are acceptable for people to display in the presence of others.

Display rules differ across cultures; for example, individuals in the Utku Eskimo population rarely express anger and face ostracism when they do.

In the U.S., expressing emotions is encouraged; repressing emotions is considered insincere.

For example, Americans prefer excited smiles over calm smiles. In contrast, Japanese culture discourages the expression of emotions; suppressing emotions is viewed as mature.

Impression management

Impression management is engaging in behaviors to influence the perception of others. It can be conscious or subconscious.

Common strategies in impression management include *flattery*, *ingratiation*, and *intimidation*.

Impression management contributes to an individual's social identity, which refers to how individuals are regarded in social situations. It is goal-directed, meaning that the individual engaging in impression management wants the person they are interacting with to perceive something in a specific way.

Individuals often engage in impression management to increase their self-esteem. Thus, they may highlight their accomplishments and positives while downplaying their failures.

People may change their behavior to adapt to the person they are interacting with.

For example, an individual might put on their "*best self*" when interacting with their boss but joke around with a coworker.

Impression management is used for self-presentation and when an individual wants something or someone else to be perceived in a certain way.

For example, a person might tell his parents good things about his significant other while leaving out information that puts his significant other in a negative light.

Front stage *vs.* backstage self

Dramaturgy is a sociological perspective on social interactions proposed by Erving Goffman.

Dramaturgy uses theater as a metaphor for presenting oneself in social situations; thus, how an individual presents himself is considered their "performance." This approach emphasizes the *context* in which social behavior occurs.

According to Goffman, people's actions are influenced by those around them.

Erving Goffman, Canadian-American sociologist and writer

Goffman identified three stages in which people "perform."

Front stage is when the individual knows they are being observed and behaves according to the audience's expectations.

Backstage is when performers are present, but their usual audience is not. Thus, performers can act "out of character" but still act to fit in with their fellow performers.

Off-stage is the place where individuals are not involved in any performance.

For example, a server is front stage when waiting tables and interacting with customers, backstage in the kitchen with fellow servers, and off-stage driving to work.

Verbal and nonverbal communication

Interpersonal communication involves both verbal and nonverbal communication. Verbal communication is explicit communication, whereas nonverbal communication is implicit communication. Nonverbal communication includes body movements, posture, eye contact, and facial expressions. Verbal and nonverbal communication interact to form a complete idea. Therefore, isolating nonverbal communication and analyzing individual gestures is not typically helpful.

Posture includes *open* and *closed postures*.

Open posture is a body position that conveys openness, typically sitting or standing with arms and legs uncrossed.

Closed posture conveys disinterest or discomfort with arms and legs crossed.

Mirroring is an important aspect of posture. Individuals who mirror another reflect body movements and position. Mirroring indicates interest in the other person.

Researchers typically categorize nonverbal communication by the functions that they serve.

Emblems are gestures that can be roughly translated into words. For example, a handshake can be roughly translated into a greeting.

Illustrators serve to emphasize spoken language. For example, an individual might point somewhere while giving directions to someone.

Affect displays are gestures that show the other person how someone feels. For example, someone feeling sad might frown to let the person they are talking to know how they feel.

Regulators are social gestures used to give another person feedback during a conversation. For example, someone might nod to indicate they are listening and encourage the speaker to continue talking.

Adaptors are gestures that satisfy a physical need (e.g., adjusting a leg after it falls asleep).

Relationship matrix

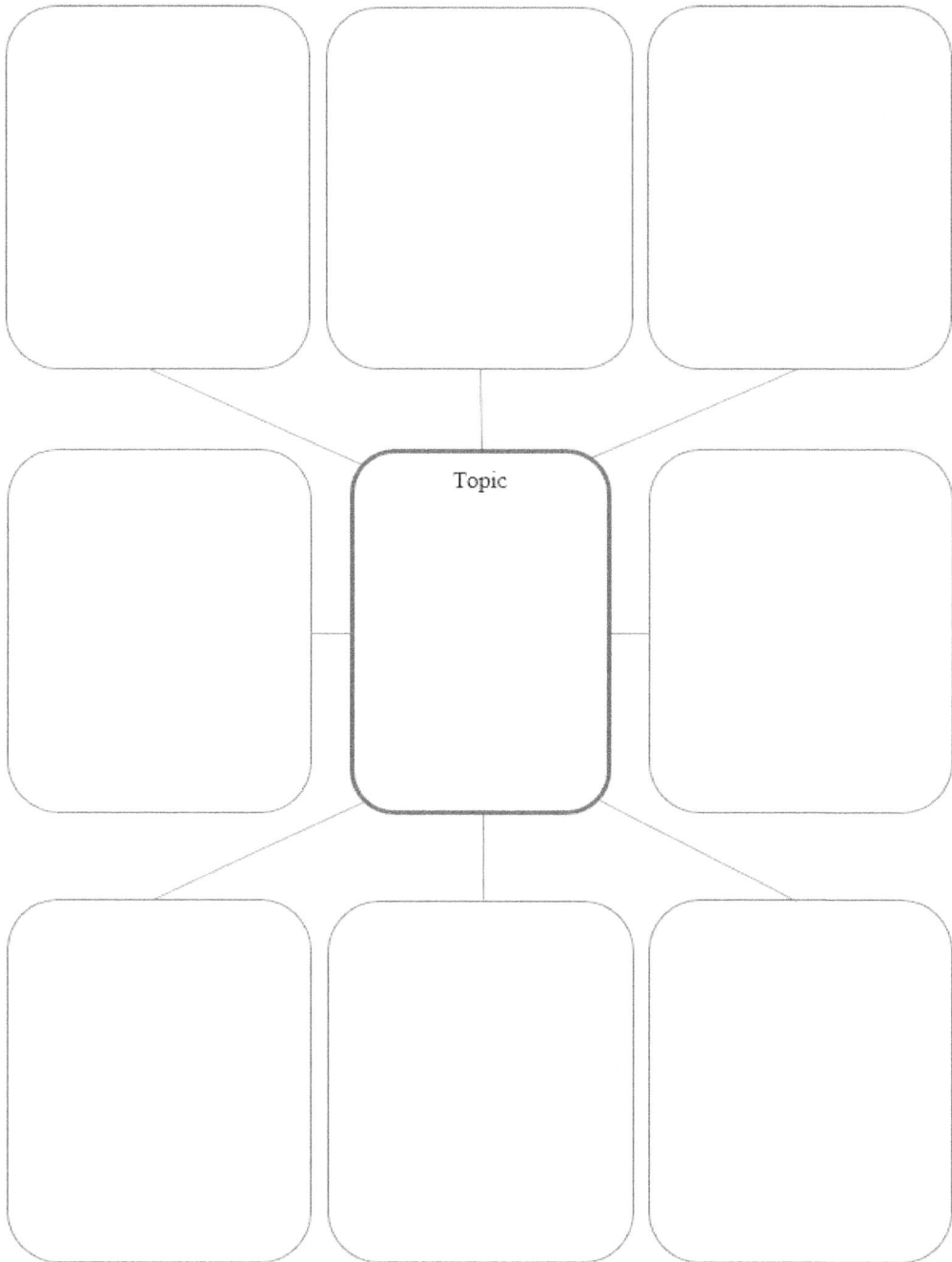

Topic

Notes for active learning

CHAPTER 9

Intelligence & Testing

Understanding intelligence and assessing individual differences in intelligence or personality is a crucial psychology competency.

Intelligence and personality test construction and fair use issues are crucial. How an assessment is constructed and thoroughly mastering the concepts of standardization, reliability, and validity are critically important.

These concepts can be challenging to grasp. Doing so requires familiarity with the historical roots of intelligence testing and consideration regarding the associated ethical issues, particularly the test result uses.

Intelligence

Intelligence theories

Intelligence is conceptualized as the ability to reason (or think rationally), use resources to solve problems, and capacity to understand the world.

Much ongoing debate exists about what comprises intelligence and the best way to measure it. The following are accepted theories of intelligence and difficulties in measuring it.

Historical and contemporary theories of intelligence

Sir Francis Galton is an important figure in modern intelligence testing. He hypothesized that intelligence is quantifiable and normally distributed. He proposed that a score could be assigned to intelligence, where most people would fall in the average range, and the individual's score would increase or decrease according to their variation from the average.

In the early 20th century, Charles Spearman developed a theory of general intelligence. Spearman was interested in examining correlations among the many measures of intelligence.

Spearman applied a statistical technique (i.e., factor analysis), which revealed that the different measures of intelligence were measuring the same construct. He hypothesized that revealing one construct was evidence of general intelligence.

General intelligence, or "g," is the basic, underlying trait responsible for all cognitive tasks, including learning, reasoning, and solving problems. Many studies have been conducted on "g," which correlates with income, success in long-term relationships, and psychological well-being.

However, other research has shown that people vary widely in their ability to socialize, be artistic, and be physically active. These abilities are not well explained by "g."

Charles Spearman, an English psychologist

Primary Mental Abilities

In 1938, L. L. Thurstone utilized Spearman's techniques to examine general intelligence scores, finding seven different constructs that he named *Primary Mental Abilities*, which he believed more accurately described intelligence.

Thurstone asserted that seven constructs (or factors) were independent, and people possessed them to varying degrees.

Primary Mental Abilities identified seven factors:

1) *Verbal comprehension* – define and understand words

2) *Verbal fluency* – produce words rapidly

3) *Number or arithmetic ability* – solve arithmetic problems

4) *Memory* – memorize and recall

5) *Perception* – note differences and similarities among objects

6) *Inductive reasoning* – find rules

7) *Spatial visualization* – visualize relationships.

Testing his theory, Thurstone found that his factors correlated.

Additional data caused him to conclude that each factor comprises a *general factor* that all factors share and an *independent factor* that makes *each factor unique*.

Fluid and crystallized intelligence

Raymond Cattell and John Horn developed their theory of intelligence in 1966. Cattell and Horn proposed two types of intelligence: *fluid intelligence* and *crystallized intelligence*.

Fluid intelligence allows abstract reasoning, helps adapt to new situations, and solves problems without previous knowledge.

Cattell and Horn propose that fluid intelligence is the biological aspect of intelligence.

Crystalized intelligence consists of knowledge (i.e., information, skills, and strategies) acquired through experience; it is skill expansion throughout life. This type of intelligence is considered the most stable because it relies on experience and knowledge, not innate ability.

Raymond Cattell, psychologist

However, both types of intelligence are considered necessary for everyday life.

For example, when trying to stay within budget at the grocery store, a person uses *fluid intelligence* to devise a strategy for prioritizing what needs to be purchased and *crystallized intelligence* to calculate the cost of groceries as they are being placed into the shopping cart.

Fluid and crystallized intelligence increases through mid-adulthood.

However, around ages 30-40, fluid intelligence begins to decline while crystallized intelligence continues to expand.

Individuals can lose some abilities but not others from head injury, stroke, or brain damage. For example, a person who experienced a stroke may lose the ability to produce speech but other aspects of intelligence (e.g., the ability to comprehend speech and understand what is being said), depending on where the damage is in the brain.

Because of cases like this, more modern theories of intelligence continue to emphasize the belief that *multiple abilities comprise* the construct of intelligence. For example, the *triarchic theory of intelligence* supports this construct.

Triarchic theory of intelligence

Triarchic theory of intelligence, created by Robert Sternberg, hypothesized that intelligence consists of *creative*, analytical, and *practical domains*.

>*creative intelligence* is the ability to solve problems in a new way;

>*analytical intelligence* is the problem-solving, mathematical, and verbal types of intelligence (and most closely resembles "g");

>*practical intelligence* is the ability to solve real-world problems (e.g., those that arise in work and family situations).

Sternberg hypothesized that these three domains are separate constructs; he acknowledged that they overlap and interface in day-to-day functioning.

Multiple Intelligence Theory

Like Sternberg, Howard Gardner created a theory of intelligence encompassing domains.

However, Gardner's theory outlines nine intelligence domains (or spheres).

Multiple Intelligences Theory identifies spheres of intelligence for the ability to:

1) *Musical* – sense rhythm, tones, and sound

2) *Bodily-kinesthetic* – use the body effectively

3) *Logical/mathematical* – reason and calculate

4) *Linguistic* use words effectively

5) *Spatial* – make spatial judgments and visualization in the mind

6) *Interpersonal* – understand and interact with others

7) *Intrapersonal* – understand one's self

8) *Naturalist* – nurture and relate information to one's surroundings

9) *Existential* – conceptualizing the larger questions about human existence.

Naturalist and *existential* were not in Gardner's original theory; he added them ten years later. Gardner acknowledges that many more *intelligence spheres* may have yet to be identified.

Gardner asserts that domains are *independent* (rather than overlapping and collective).

Gardner's theory accounts for losing some intelligence (e.g., brain injury) but retaining others.

Gardner created his theory without research. Subsequent research to evaluate the theory found that the nine intelligences correlate with "g."

Rather than supporting many separate spheres of intelligence, research findings support a single, underlying intelligence, as Spearman had theorized.

Howard Gardner, American developmental psychologist

Stanford-Binet Intelligence Scale

How intelligence is measured creates debate about what intelligence encompasses and how to measure it. In 1904, the French government commissioned Alfred Binet and Theodore Simon to create a method to identify students needing alternative education.

Binet and Simon reasoned that performance on specific tasks is expected to improve with chronological (or physical) age; performance on these tasks could distinguish more intelligent people from less intelligent ones (those needing alternative education) within an age group.

Binet and Simon created a series of tasks to represent children's abilities at given ages and "*mental age*," which was the child's score on the tasks on which children were tested.

A marked gap between the child's chronological age and the tested mental age indicated a need for alternative education. These children could then receive additional assistance to bolster their mental age to match their chronological age.

In 1908, H.H. Goddard brought the Binet-Simon test to the United States after it was translated into English. In 1913, the United States Public Health Service began administering the Binet-Simon test to immigrants.

Several groups did not do well, but instead of examining the test and identifying why these groups might not do well, these immigrants were labeled "feebleminded." Lewis Terman at Stanford University modified the Binet-Simon test to identify high-achieving adults.

Binet-Simon Intelligence Scale from 1908 asks children to identify prettier faces

Terman's *Stanford-Binet Intelligence Scale* was published in 1916.

The scale, as used by the Public Health Service and Termon, was criticized for focusing too much on verbal abilities. It is now believed that many immigrants did not do well on the Binet-Simon test because it was administered in English, and many immigrants did not speak English.

Thus, their scores were more indicative of their abilities in English than their intelligence.

Stanford-Binet Intelligence Scale now balances measures of verbal and other abilities. It consists of several tasks that vary according to the age of the individual being tested and is thought to measure overall innate (general) intelligence.

For example, a 4-year-old should be able to define simple words (e.g., "ball") and discriminate between shapes. A 12-year-old should be able to do everything younger children can do, define more complex words (e.g., "muzzle"), and repeat five digits in reverse order.

Stanford-Binet Intelligence Scale measures sub-domains of intelligence, including:

> fluid reasoning (i.e., ability to problem-solve),
>
> basic knowledge (i.e., knowledge acquired through education),
>
> quantitative reasoning (i.e., ability to think mathematically),
>
> visual-spatial processing (i.e., ability to see patterns and relationships in visual stimuli)
>
> working memory (i.e., storing and processing information in memory temporarily).

Stanford-Binet Intelligence Scale: a 4-year-old child should be able to define simple words (e.g., ball) and discriminate between different shapes.

Even so, the Stanford-Binet Intelligence Scale continues to be criticized for relying too much on verbal measures.

Thus, the argument against this test is that it measures only verbal abilities, not intelligence itself (assuming that intelligence is more than just verbal abilities).

Wechsler Intelligence Scale

David Wechsler, labeled "feebleminded" at 9 years of age when his family immigrated to the U.S. from Romania, developed the primary competitor to the Stanford-Binet Intelligence Scale.

Wechsler created this intelligence scale because he believed the Stanford-Binet Intelligence Scale focused too much on verbal abilities. Wechsler sought to find a way to measure both verbal and nonverbal abilities.

Wechsler Intelligence Scale consists of the:

> Wechsler Preschool and Primary Scale of Intelligence (WPPSI; for children aged 2 years, 6 months to 7 years, 7 months);

> Wechsler Intelligence Scale for Children (WISC; for children aged 6 years to 16 years, 11 months); and

> *Wechsler Adult Intelligence Scale* (WAIS; for people aged 16 to 90 years, 11 months).

These scales measure intelligence regarding *verbal abilities* (i.e., *General Ability Index*) and *nonverbal abilities* (i.e., *Cognitive Proficiency Index*).

Verbal abilities include stating similarities between objects, defining words, and demonstrating general knowledge.

Nonverbal abilities include spatial perception, abstract problem-solving, and spatial reasoning.

For example, a test subject may be asked to examine a pattern of shapes and predict the next shape in the sequence. This ability does not require verbal abilities, only nonverbal reasoning abilities. Thus, individuals can demonstrate intelligence even if their verbal ability is poor.

Information-Processing Approach to Intelligence

While most people think of intelligence as the ability to problem-solve and demonstrate knowledge, other theories of intelligence emphasize the speed at which the problem is solved.

Francis Galton hypothesized that synaptic efficiency (i.e., how quickly information is processed) accounts for why one individual is more intelligent than another.

Correlations exist between *intelligence* and *inspection time* (time to perceive a stimulus), *reaction time*, and *evoked potentials* (i.e., brain wave response upon perceiving a stimulus).

Information-Processing Approach to Intelligence emphasizes how material is stored in memory and then used to solve problems. The processes used to solve a problem are examined instead of the structure or content of intelligence.

It emphasizes the belief that the time it takes an individual to solve a problem (i.e., the speed at which it is processed) is a more accurate reflection of his or her overall intelligence.

This approach draws a parallel between the human mind and a computer; both are information processors, and the important things to study are the processes between the stimuli (in the environment) and the responses made to them.

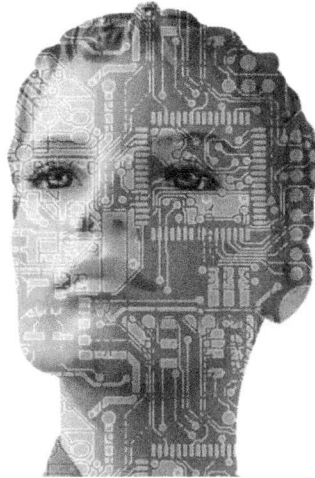

Information-Processing Approach to intelligence focuses on how material is stored in memory and used to solve problems.

Raven Progressive Matrices

In the 1930s, John Raven recognized that intelligence tests might be biased against certain groups. He argued that intelligence tests should not be bound to a particular language or culture and sought to develop a culture-free test.

Raven developed the *Raven's Progressive Matrices*, where individuals are asked to examine a pattern in shapes and colors and then determine which shape or color completes the pattern.

Raven argued that because the individual was looking at shapes and colors, no verbal abilities were needed, and therefore, the test was a more culturally fair IQ test.

Raven was not the last to hypothesize about intelligence and the influences of culture. It has been frequently cited that some IQ tests consist of items that discriminate against minority groups.

It is hypothesized that because minority groups have different experiences than the dominant culture, they cannot do as well on these IQ tests.

There have been many attempts since Raven to create IQ test items that examine experiences common to cultures and do not require language. However, this is difficult to do because an individual's unique experiences, attitudes, and values impact their answers.

Research detects differences in intelligence between members of racial and ethnic groups.

The debate remains: are observed differences in intelligence among ethnic and racial groups due to intelligence tests that are culturally unfair (or culture-free), due to differences in their environment, or in innate ability?

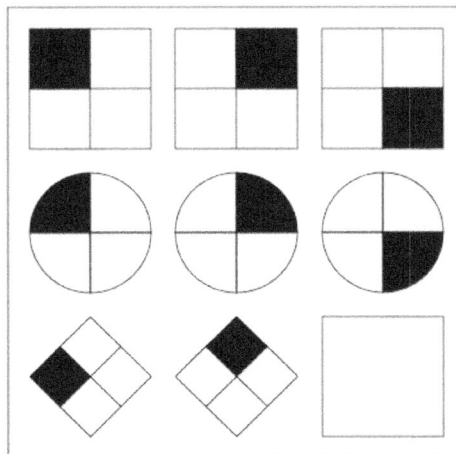

Raven's Progressive Matrices

Recently, research has focused on intelligence in Africa, Asia, and other non-Western cultures.

Ideas about intelligence (e.g., what intelligence is comprised of and how to measure intelligence) are conceptualized differently in non-Western cultures.

For example, in Western cultures, people tend to see intelligence as a way to engage in debate and put people in categories. However, people in non-Western cultures see intelligence as a way to recognize complexity among individuals and to play their social roles successfully.

Researchers believe that differences in views of intelligence between Western and non-Western cultures are related to differences in the basic cognitive processes of the distinct cultures.

Some researchers say the focus of research should be on developing new intelligence tests sensitive to cultures' unique aspects of intelligence and values. It is argued that intelligence can be accurately assessed based on cultural values and differences in viewpoints on what intelligence is.

Raven Progressive Matrices was designed to be a culture-free test. However, subsequent research has shown that even this test is culturally loaded. It is argued that even if a test is not a verbal test, nonverbal intelligence is still based on cultural constructs.

In Western societies, where formalized education and media technologies (e.g., television and video games) are typical, individuals have an advantage in visual tests.

Translating a Western intelligence test into a different language will not remedy this problem. Intelligence tests need to be explicitly created for a culture.

Heredity and environmental influences

Speed of mental processing depends on neurological efficiency and maturation, controlled by genetic factors. Children who possess genetic defects, such as Down Syndrome, tend to have lower IQs than non-affected children.

However, convincing evidence comes from twin and adoption studies. Many researchers have utilized monozygotic (identical) and dizygotic (fraternal) twins to investigate the impact of heredity on IQ.

Monozygotic twins are initially one fertilized egg that separates and is genetically identical.

Dizygotic twins come from two separate fertilized eggs and share about 50% of their genetic makeup (like siblings). If identical twins have similar genetic composition, heredity significantly impacts intelligence and cognitive development.

Most twins tend to be raised by the same parent in the same home, sharing similar environments and genetic makeup. However, sometimes twins are raised separately but still have similar IQs. These twins are more similar than fraternal twins raised in the same home.

Another way to portray this finding is through adoption studies. Researchers have found that while children's IQ scores are more highly related to the scores of their biological parents, their environment tends to be more closely aligned with their adopted parents.

In a group of people who placed their newborns up for adoption, the parents with the highest IQ had children who also had the highest IQ despite their being raised by other people.

IQ correlations between adopted children and their biological parents become more robust, and correlations between children and their adoptive parents become weaker with age, especially during adolescence.

These studies cannot completely distinguish the impact of heredity and the environment. The environment also makes an appreciable difference (discussed below).

Research with identical and fraternal twins investigates the impacts of heredity on IQ.

Research indicates that the environment has a significant impact on cognitive development. Evidence is found in twin studies and adoption studies. Studies of the effects of nutrition, toxic substances, home environment, early intervention, and formal schooling provide additional support for the influence of the environment. A steady increase in performance on intelligence tests over the past decades (i.e., *Flynn Effect*) may be attributable to environmental factors.

Severe malnutrition during the early years causes neurological development deterioration and eventually impacts intelligence and cognitive development. Improper nutrition levels negatively affect attention, memory, abstract reasoning, and general school achievement.

Toxic substances (or *teratogens*) in prenatal or postnatal environments affect neurological development. These toxic substances include alcohol, drugs, radiation, or lead-based paint.

Fetal Alcohol Syndrome affects children when a pregnant mother consumes alcohol, resulting in poor motor coordination, delayed language, and overall cognitive delays.

Adoptive parents tend to be financially stable and educated and provide a stimulating environment compared to their biological parents. In a stimulating household, parents interact with their children frequently, have learning and reading materials readily available, encourage the development of skills, and communicate with complex language. These factors are attributed to higher cognitive development and, in turn, higher IQ.

When the same parents raise two biologically different children about the same age, their IQs are usually more similar than expected by chance. This suggests that this similarity results from environmental influences.

The effect of going to school initiates small increases in IQ. Children who attend school at an early age regularly have higher IQ scores than children who do not attend school. If children start school later than normal, their IQs are usually five points lower for every year of delay.

The school has a great benefit for intellectual growth. The famous psychologist Vygotsky noted that school provides a systemic means through which children can obtain many concepts and perspectives that previous generations have developed, which the child can then use to perform day-to-day activities and solve problems.

Flynn Effect is the slow, steady increase in performances on IQ tests. This trend is observed in children's performance on traditional Piagetian tasks.

These improvements cannot be caused by heredity because the same gene pool is passed along from one generation to the next, suggesting that the cause must be environmental. Better nutrition, smaller family sizes, higher quality home environments, better schooling, and more enriching and informative stimulation are all possibilities.

Intellectual abilities

Many argue that quantifying intelligence correctly is impossible, and IQ tests only test knowledge and abilities. While it is true that a person can learn to improve their IQ score, this can only occur if correct responses are taught to the person, which is highly unethical.

Research shows that our IQ score remains consistent with age.

Some argue that modern IQ tests are prejudiced against certain ethnicities and cultures and tend to result in higher scores for other groups. Where this leaves us, however, is uncertain.

As of today, IQ tests are the best psychometric tool to quantify intelligence.

Intelligence Quotient (IQ) score considers the individual's chronological and mental age (as measured by an intelligence test).

Average IQ is 100, with 95 percent of the population having an IQ score between 70 and 130.

Individuals with scores below 70 have an intellectual disability, and those with a score above 130 are intellectually gifted.

Individuals with an IQ score below 70 are outside the norm for intellectual ability.

Intellectual disability refers to a person's level of cognitive ability or impairment presenting below the average level of intellectual functioning. People with intellectual disabilities are limited to two or more adaptive skill areas.

Intellectual developmental disorder is when individuals score below 70 and have difficulties with adaptive functioning, such as conceptual skills (e.g., ability to use money, ability to keep track of time), social skills (e.g., gullibility, naiveté), or practical skills (e.g., ability to engage in personal care, ability to provide own transportation).

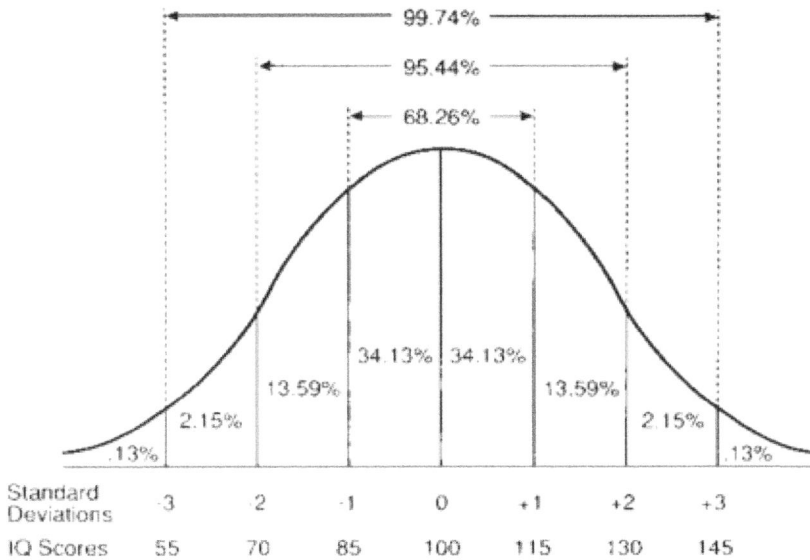

Standard Deviations	-3	-2	-1	0	+1	+2	+3
IQ Scores	55	70	85	100	115	130	145

Distribution of IQ scores follows a normal distribution curve

Intellectual developmental disorder affects 3-5% of the U.S. population, and causes include fetal alcohol syndrome, trisomy 21 (i.e., Down syndrome), head injuries, and meningitis. This category is divided into mild, moderate, severe, and profound, depending on IQ scores.

Mild intellectual disability has an IQ of 50-70 and academic skills at the 3rd to 6th-grade levels.

Moderate intellectual disability has an IQ of 35-49 and skills at or below the 2nd-grade level.

Severe intellectual disability is represented by an IQ score of 20-34, with little ability to communicate and requiring direct supervision. The need for additional daily help characterizes severe intellectual disability. In the U.S., many programs are in place to assist such individuals.

Profound intellectual disability is represented by an IQ score below 20, with little or no speech skills and requiring constant supervision and care. A family history of intellectual disabilities is common in affected individuals. The integration of intellectually challenged individuals into a normal academic setting is one treatment option.

On the other end of the spectrum, intellectually gifted individuals have an IQ higher than 130 and represent 2-4% of the population. Many individuals in this category are talented in one area but average in others. Also frequently seen are significant discrepancies between verbal and nonverbal abilities.

Unlike Intellectual Developmental Disorder, programs for the gifted are rare. When they are in place, they are designed to provide a more enriching environment that allows the individual's talents to grow and flourish.

Test Design

Psychological testing

Psychological testing has five purposes:

> classification (i.e., diagnosis),
>
> prediction (e.g., behavior in a setting),
>
> description (e.g., a person's strengths and weaknesses),
>
> choice of treatment, and
>
> monitoring a person over time (e.g., if a treatment is effective).

Psychometrics focuses on theory and techniques for measuring psychological traits and abilities. It attempts to create assessments that objectively measure personality, attitudes, intelligence, mood, and abilities.

Items on tests designed to measure constructs are carefully evaluated to ensure they measure the trait they intend to measure. Standardization, norms, reliability, and validity are essential when designing a test.

Standardization and norms

Standardization is a critical aspect of the test. Because so many variables can affect how someone responds to psychological testing, the test must be given exactly as intended. Without this, it cannot be ensured that the construct the test intends to measure is what is being measured.

For example, if an anger test is given in a sweltering room, it is unclear if the responses measure the general level of anger or irritation with the temperature.

Standardization in test administration helps eliminate conscious or unconscious biases. For example, without standardization in test administration, a researcher may give subtle hints about how they want the test results to turn out. This may not be done intentionally but may still influence the test taker.

By ensuring the test is standardized, scores can be compared across groups who may have been given the test at various times. In addition to ensuring the tests are administered uniformly, they must be scored uniformly. If tests were scored haphazardly, the scores would not be able to be interpreted accurately and would not be able to be compared across individuals.

Norms are comparison scores that allow individuals to be compared or evaluated relative to a standard or typical score. Norms are created for a test by administering the test to hundreds of people and then calculating a mean and standard deviation.

Mean is the average of all scores, and the standard deviation is the variability around the mean.

Standard deviation can be conceptualized as the average distance from the mean. For example, most intelligence tests have an average score of 100 and a standard deviation of 15. (See *Meaning of scores and the normal curve* below for more details.)

When the score an individual obtained is known, that score can be compared with the norms for the test and allow the researcher to make general statements about that individual.

For example, if someone obtains a score of 102 on an intelligence test, this score is close to average. Without norms, a test score only has meaning if ranked with other test scores.

Reliability and validity

Reliability and *validity* are necessary for assessing a construct.

Reliability answers, "Does this test consistently measure what it says it measures?" There are several types of reliability, including *test-retest* and *inter-observer reliability*.

Test-retest reliability examines whether a test produces the same results consistently over time.

For example, if an individual completes a test of intelligence in January and then again in June, the second score is expected to be about the same since intelligence is thought of as a construct that does not change over time. If both scores are similar, the test has good test-retest reliability.

Inter-observer (or inter-rater) reliability is the similarity in which observers rate a behavior.

For example, if the test is a rating scale for aggressive behaviors in children, two investigators trained in administering the rating should score behaviors of the same child similarly if the scale has good inter-observer reliability.

Validity answers, "Does this test measure what it says it measures?"

For example, if a test says it measures depression, does it measure symptoms of depression, or is it measuring anxiety, psychosis, or something else?

A researcher might purport that they measure intelligence by measuring the length of the ring finger on the right hand. The length of this finger is not expected to change in an adult so it could be measured repeatedly with the same results. Thus, the measurement has *reliability*.

However, is it valid? Does the length of the ring finger on the right hand have anything to do with intelligence? This question is getting at validity. The measurement is invalid because the length of the ring finger on the right hand has nothing to do with intelligence.

Reliability may be present, but not validity. For example, a test may purport to measure anxiety. This test may be given over time and produce consistent results in individuals taking it (i.e., it has reliability).

Unless the measure correlates with other measures of anxiety, it is uncertain as a measure for anxiety. It may be consistently measuring another construct, such as depression.

Standardized tests require validity and reliability

Reliability is necessary but *not sufficient* for validity.

Reliability and validity are critical when constructing and evaluating tests.

Types of tests

Clinical psychology has been focused on testing; even today, psychological testing is done primarily by a clinical psychologist. Tests provide one dimension of an individual; a clinical interview provides another. There are many psychological tests to assess various characteristics, depending on what type of information is sought.

Psychological tests can be categorized differently. Some tests are completed individually, and others in groups. Knowing how the test is administered before it is given is essential.

Since standardization is an integral aspect of testing, giving a test meant to be administered individually to a group violates standardization, and thus, the results would be unreliable.

Tests can be performance-based (i.e., the person does something) or verbally based (i.e., the person uses language to convey something). Several tests looking for deficits after a brain injury are performance-based, while tests exploring different personality traits tend to be more verbal.

Psychological tests are *structured* (i.e., objective) or *unstructured* (i.e., projective).

Structured tests have clear items directed towards what is being measured. The individual has limited responses, and the scoring method tends to be simple.

Unstructured tests have test items that are ambiguous by design. These items are ambiguous because they measure how the individual interprets and answers the questions. These types of tests tend to be more difficult to score because they have an infinite number of response options.

Finally, tests can be categorized based on the content area they attempt to measure.

Personality tests attempt to measure traits that an individual possesses. Because it is generally believed that personality is stable over time, it is expected that personality measures remain stable over time and across tests, assuming the tests measure the same personality traits.

Neuropsychological tests examine brain functioning, such as processing speed, language, memory, thinking patterns, and executive functions.

Psychology tests can focus on the effects and symptoms of disorders. These tests assess how a person is feeling and functioning based on their emotional well-being.

Meaning of scores and the normal curve

Test scores have no meaning without context, something to compare them to. Recall that norms give a comparison group for test scores so that statements can be made about the score obtained.

If a test is given to a large group and the scores are plotted on a graph, the scores will form a normal curve (or *normal distribution*).

Normal curve is symmetrical and bell-shaped; the right half mirrors the left (*see figure below*).

Mean (or *average*) of all the scores is in the middle of the curve.

Standard deviation (i.e., the average variability around the mean) can be calculated.

Normal curve means 68% of people score one standard deviation below (34% of people) or one standard deviation above (34% of people) the mean.

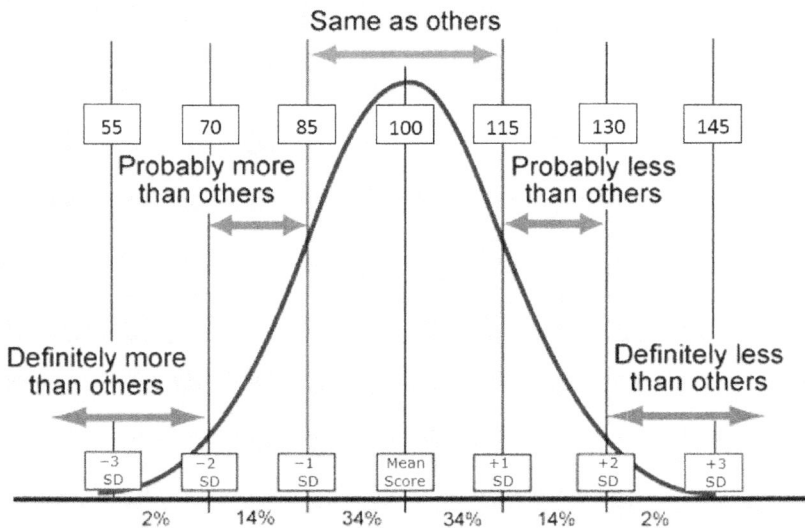

Normalized distribution of IQ with a mean of 100 and standard deviation of 15

For example, the mean of intelligence tests is 100, and the standard deviation is 15. Based on these scores and the normal distribution rules, 68% of people will obtain scores between 85 (i.e., 100 minus 15) and 115 (i.e., 100 plus 15).

Scores two standard deviations above and below the mean capture 95% of the test-takers (i.e., 48% of the test-takers scores will be below the mean, and 48% will be above the mean).

95% of the people who take an intelligence test will obtain a score between 70 and 130.

Scores with one standard deviation (or greater) above or below the mean are of interest because they indicate that the individual's score is outside the expected range.

What this means depends on the test; however, for intelligence tests, someone with an IQ score of 70 or below (i.e., three standard deviations below the mean) may meet the criteria for Intellectual Developmental Disability. In contrast, someone with an IQ score above 130 (i.e., three standard deviations above the mean) may be considered intellectually gifted.

Ethics and standards in testing

American Psychological Association (APA) Code of Ethics outlines principles that govern the practice of psychology, including testing.

Psychologists must have competence in the area they intend to practice and know the limits of their expertise. In the realm of testing, a psychologist does not utilize a test they are not trained in administering, scoring, and interpreting.

Psychologists must determine when psychological testing may and may not be useful. For example, when a psychologist can diagnose based on a clinical interview, testing may not be appropriate. Further, the psychologist must know if a test is appropriate for a particular individual (regarding culture, language, etc.).

Psychologists must recognize when testing is being misused and attempt to correct this.

In addition to the general principles from the APA Code of Ethics applied to psychological testing, there are also specific standards.

Professional relationships should be established before conducting any psychological testing. For example, a psychologist would never score and interpret a psychological test without first meeting the individual.

Psychologists must ensure that the tests are used appropriately and that the tests being used are developed considering scientific procedures, including reliability and validity. Only up-to-date tests ensure that the correct norms are used for interpreting tests.

Psychologists understand that tests have limitations, and it is important to consider them when scoring and interpreting tests. After scoring and interpreting tests, explanations of the results should be given to the tested individual in a way that he/she can understand.

Relationship matrix

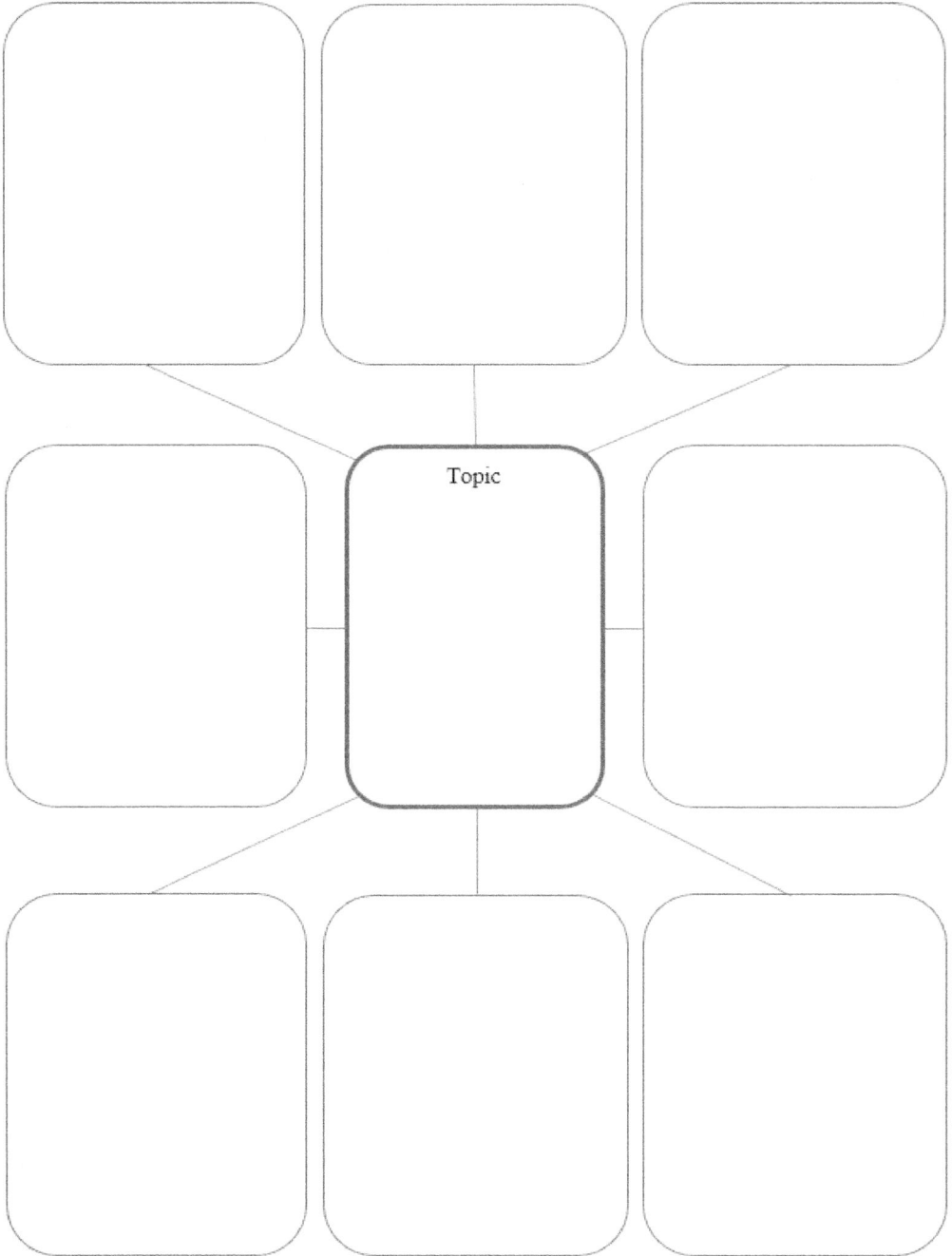

Topic

Notes for active learning

Notes for active learning

CHAPTER 10

Psychological Disorders

Psychological disorders have various etiologies and can be characterized by a wide range of symptoms. Psychologists utilize formal conventions to establish the diagnosis and assess the severity in order to devise the appropriate empirically-based treatment.

Psychology professionals need to be competent in distinguishing various approaches for differing mental illnesses; these can include behavioral, biological, cognitive, humanistic, and psychodynamic approaches.

Towards these ends, a foundational definition of abnormal behavior is important, and stereotypes can complicate diagnosis. In an environment of inadequate societal understanding of psychological disorders, the controversy surrounding labeling has emerged.

Understanding Psychological Disorders

Psychological disorders

Psychological disorders are a challenging subject to understand, given the complexity of determining what separates a "*healthy*" mind from an "*unhealthy*" one. The word "*abnormality*" is used frequently in this research topic, which gives the impression of something being *wrong* with an individual.

However, abnormality can be viewed oppositely. For example, a genius like Albert Einstein is *abnormal* instead of *normal* because his intelligence surpassed most people's.

Abnormality is behavior different than what the general population considers "healthy" or "appropriate." Classifying Einstein as "disordered" would be difficult due to his intelligence. Researchers in the field have determined several definitions of abnormality to help elucidate the differences between normal and abnormal behavior.

Definitions of abnormality

Abnormal behavior can be defined in several ways, which include *statistical infrequency*, *norm violation*, and *personal suffering*. Before clinicians diagnose, they often consider whether a person's behavior, cognition, or emotions deviate from the norm. It is imperative to consider these different spectrums, as each definition of abnormality has merits and flaws.

Statistical infrequency suggests that behavior that deviates from what is expected (or what most people do, think, or feel) is abnormal. While this provides some insight into the behavior of someone anxious (i.e., constantly seeking reassurance), it fails to account for the fact that some highly desirable traits are outside the spectrum of normal behavior.

For example, Olympians have *abnormal* athletic ability.

A genius IQ is *abnormal*, as are groups with minority opinions outside the typical spectrum.

The problem with using statistics alone to classify "outliers" as *abnormal* is that it neglects that the individual's traits could be positive. Researchers avoid this way of defining abnormality.

Instead, psychologists and other experts in the field say that abnormality *must* involve behavior that negatively or pervasively impacts one's life – whether it is socially, at work, at home, or in a relationship.

Personal suffering/distress is a required criterion for most psychiatric disorders. This means there must be some impairment in an individual's functioning (i.e., not attending school, failure to complete assignments at work, inability to have a good relationship with peers or family members, confusion with managing personal finances or medications, etc.).

In addition, many individuals use personal suffering to determine whether they should seek treatment for their symptoms. Most people are likely to experience distress, such as the loss of a family member or the diagnosis of a disability. This does not mean they are abnormal; instead, they are experiencing an acute stressor.

Some individuals who exhibit abnormal behavior may not experience distress; For example, someone experiencing mania or antisocial personality disorder.

Personal suffering and distress underly many psychiatric disorders

Norm violation can be used to measure whether a behavior, thought, or cognition is abnormal. It suggests that since cultural rules and norms dictate appropriate behaviors if someone violates social norms, their behavior is abnormal. Thus, if behavior is bizarre or unusual enough, it would be considered abnormal.

For example, someone who constantly fails to maintain eye contact or respond in social situations violates social behavior norms. One major flaw with this definition is that social norms vary by culture; what is acceptable in one culture may be unacceptable in another.

The 4 Ds suggest that abnormal behavior can be conceptualized in the context of whether the behavior is deviant, dysfunctional, distressing, or dangerous.

It is essential to consider whether behavior is dangerous. Some abnormal behavior is illegal. Laws have been enacted to both protect and punish those who have psychological disorders.

For example, mentally ill patients are protected by the law from having their medical and psychiatric information revealed to *anybody* other than their therapist, as this could affect their employment or expose personal details. This is "doctor-patient confidentiality," which applies to mental health and other medical conditions.

Conversely, an example of punishment would be how the judicial system does not simply write off mentally ill people from the consequences of their actions if they understand right from wrong. "Pleading insanity" is not well understood. For example, if a serial killer "gets away" with an "insanity plea," they can be held indefinitely at a psychiatric institution and never be granted access back into society.

Biomedical *vs.* biopsychosocial approaches

Professionals in the field of psychology have divided themselves into two critical categories: treatment and conceptualizing mental illness. Here is a brief explanation of each.

Biomedical therapy hypothesizes that the cause of the disorder is some chemical imbalance in the brain, which must be modified. Psychiatry is directly involved in this form of treatment.

Psychotropics (e.g., antidepressants and benzodiazepines) are prescribed to alter the brain's abnormal functioning, thereby allowing the person to function in society. This alone is a strictly short-term treatment. To stop taking the drug means returning to abnormal behavior.

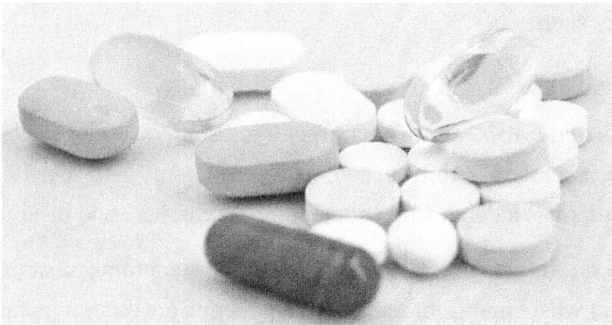

Medications (antidepressants, benzodiazepines) can alter the brain's abnormal functioning

Biopsychosocial therapy is an amalgamated approach to treat mental disorders:

Bio(logical) – the health professional may first examine one's physical state – are they maintaining a healthy lifestyle? Do their genetics have a role in the abnormality?

Psycho(logical) – to obtain insight into what is happening in the mind. How emotional are they? Do they have beliefs about themselves or others, causing them to behave abnormally?

Social – the professional assesses the people in the individual's life. Did they grow up in an abusive environment? Were they the popular kid in elementary school, or were they unfortunately isolated from making real connections with others?

Treatment may be considered more effective due to the increased focus on getting to the "root" of issues, but it can fail because of the amount of effort and time required to "cure" the issue.

Classifying psychological disorders

Diagnostic and Statistical Manual of Mental Disorders, Fifth Edition (DSM-5) was created for populations, including inpatient, outpatient, and community mental health settings.

DSM-5 has three main parts:

> diagnostic classification
>
> diagnostic criteria sets
>
> descriptive text

Diagnostic classification lists all official mental disorders so clinicians can review the symptoms that their patient exhibits and compare them with existing disorders. Each psychological disorder has a diagnostic code, aiding researchers and insurance companies.

Diagnostic criteria set for a disorder indicate how many symptoms must be present, which are absent, duration, and what conditions exclude the patient from receiving a particular diagnosis.

Descriptive text informs clinicians about each disorder subtype (or specifier). It provides information for diagnoses, such as what other disorders should be considered (or excluded).

Controversy exists regarding the usefulness of providing diagnostic labels.

Labels often lead people to experience self-fulfilling prophecies or discrimination.

Labels are required for insurance companies to bill for services and for researchers to understand how treatments work, how to improve outcomes, and what the prevalence rate of different disorders is.

Rosenhan's experiment investigated the validity of psychiatric diagnoses. In this study, eight healthy subjects feigned hallucinations to be admitted to psychiatric hospitals in different states. After admission, the patients acted normally and informed healthcare providers that they no longer were experiencing hallucinations.

Despite being healthy and no longer "having hallucinations," all participants were diagnosed with a mental illness and given antipsychotics as a condition of release. The findings highlight challenges for psychiatric facilities in distinguishing *normal* from *abnormal*.

Rates of psychological disorders

The exact rate of psychological disorders varies by country and by the disorder. In the U.S., about one in every five people suffers from a mental health condition at some point in their life.

Some disorders (e.g., anxiety and depression) are more common than others.

Rare disorders include dissociative identity disorder, selective mutism, and factitious disorders.

Prevalence rates for varying psychological disorders can be found in the DSM-5.

In the United States, about one in every five people suffers from a mental health condition at some point in their life.

Notes for active learning

Types of Psychological Disorders

Categorizing disorders

DSM-5 categorizes disorders into groupings based on shared symptoms or shared presentations.

These groupings include neurodevelopmental disorders, schizophrenia spectrum and other psychotic disorders, bipolar and related disorders, depressive disorders, anxiety disorders, obsessive-compulsive and related disorders, trauma and stressor-related disorders, dissociative disorders, somatic symptom and related disorders, feeding and eating disorders, elimination disorders, sleep-wake disorders, sexual dysfunctions, gender dysphoria, disruptive, impulse-control and conduct disorders, substance-related and addictive disorders, neurocognitive disorders, personality disorders, paraphilic disorders, other mental disorders, medication-induced movement disorders and other adverse effects of medication and other conditions that may be the focus of clinical attention.

Some broad categories, such as depressive and anxiety disorders, occur more commonly.

DSM-5 categories

DSM-5 includes twelve unique disorders, such as *anxiety disorders*.

Twelve disorders include separation anxiety disorder, selective mutism, specific phobia, social anxiety disorder (social phobia), panic disorder, panic attack specifier, agoraphobia, generalized anxiety disorder, substance/medication-induced anxiety disorder, anxiety disorder due to another medical condition, specified anxiety disorder, and unspecified anxiety disorder.

The hallmark of these anxiety disorders is excessive fear or anxiety to aversive stimuli.

The *fight-or-flight* response is often seen across each anxiety disorder. A person's automatic response is to fight or flee when faced with a feared stimulus.

For example, if someone is walking through the woods and encounters a bear, they experience elevated levels of anxiety. In this situation, most people would run away or fight the bear.

While anxiety disorders have common elements, they can be differentiated by examining the circumstances (i.e., settings and situations) that produce fear or avoidant response.

Research indicates a high symptom overlap among anxiety disorders, and most individuals diagnosed with an anxiety disorder will have at least one other comorbid anxiety disorder.

Before a diagnosis can be made for each disorder, it is imperative to verify that the symptoms cause significant distress in one or more areas of functioning (i.e., school, work, home, etc.) and that another mental health or physical disorder does not better explain the symptoms.

Separation anxiety

Separation anxiety disorder is most common in children but occurs in adults. It is characterized by excessive fear upon actual or anticipated separation from a parent or other caregiver. The fear must be inappropriate for the person's age.

Children and adults with separation concerns may worry that something terrible will happen to their caregivers when they are separated or that something bad may happen to them during the separation. This may include being in an accident, getting kidnapped, or becoming sick.

As a result, there is often a behavioral pattern in which the individual constantly refuses to leave home due to their worries about being separated from the caregiver. There is also a reluctance to go places alone unless accompanied by a caregiver.

Separation anxiety disorder in children is characterized by excessive fear of actual or anticipated separation from a parent or other caregiver.

For example, children may refuse to go to school or a friend's house unless a parent goes with them. They may need a caregiver to fall asleep or experience frequent nightmares about being separated from their caregiver.

These individuals may complain of various physical symptoms during separation (e.g., upset stomach, headache). Only three of the symptoms need to exist for a diagnosis of separation anxiety disorder. Also, the excessive fear must have been persistent for at least four weeks for children or six months for adults.

Selective mutism

Selective mutism is a pattern of refraining from speech in some settings despite the ability to speak in other settings. This behavior of not speaking in some situations (e.g., school) negatively impacts achievement or social development. A child who is shy or does not talk sometimes is different from a child with selective mutism.

DSM-5 indicates that the pattern of not speaking in one or more settings must have been going on for at least one month (excluding the first month of school). Furthermore, if a child is unfamiliar with the language spoken, they cannot be diagnosed with selective mutism. Selective mutism can be confused with other childhood communication disorders (e.g., autism).

Selective mutism is a pattern of refraining from speech in some settings despite ability

Typically, children with selective mutism refuse to speak in school (or social situations) despite being overly talkative at home. They may refuse to answer questions in class, initiate conversations, or respond to peers. Children may not speak around their extended family. They may be comfortable pointing, writing, or using alternative methods of communication.

This rare disorder can impede children's academic and social skill development. For example, it is difficult for teachers to evaluate whether the child meets reading milestones if the child refuses to speak.

Specific phobia

Specific phobia is the most common psychological disorder. Often, individuals with specific phobias meet the criteria for more than one specific phobia. Phobias may include a variety of fears, such as a specific animal (e.g., dog) or a specific situation, such as flying or seeing blood.

Children commonly express their excessive fear of an object or situation by crying, freezing, or having a temper tantrum. Adults can also meet the criteria for a specific phobia if they display excessive fear of a particular object or situation.

However, excessive fear is not the only criterion for a specific phobia. Also, the feared stimuli must often produce immediate fear or anxiety (not just occasionally); the person tries to avoid the stimuli or experiences it only with extreme distress, and the experienced fear/anxiety is unrealistic compared to the actual danger posed.

For example, an adult may refuse to drive over a bridge due to an excessive fear of the bridge collapsing. They may require someone else to drive over the bridge or refuse to go over it. Most people can drive over bridges every day without collapsing, so this would be an unrealistic fear compared to the actual danger of driving over a bridge.

In specific phobias, the core fear is a persistent concern (lasting for six months or more), not a temporary fear of something. Many phobias develop in childhood, including animals (e.g., snakes, spiders), costumed characters, injections, heights, bodies of water, etc.

Social anxiety disorder

Social anxiety disorder is the excessive and unreasonable fear some individuals experience in social situations where they may be judged or scrutinized by other people. There are numerous types of feared social situations.

Typical examples are eating in front of others in a restaurant or cafeteria, presenting in front of an audience, meeting people, or sometimes simply conversing with a boss or coworker. This disorder occurs in children and adults. However, for children, anxiety must be present with peer interactions, not only when interacting with adults.

Regardless of age, there is a fear that others will negatively judge or evaluate the individual.

For example, an individual may worry that they will trip and embarrass themselves or say something that might offend other people. Social situations must often produce anxiety (not just occasionally), and the individuals must be actively avoiding social situations or experiencing them with great distress.

Excessive fear must be disproportional to the danger of the situation, last for six months, and be unrelated to other medical or mental health conditions.

Performance anxiety is diagnosed if the individual worries about performing in public.

Panic disorders

Panic disorder is when repeated, intense surges of fear or discomfort subside within minutes.

During the intense fear, at least four of the following physical symptoms must occur: pounding heart, sweating, shaking, feeling short of breath, experiencing feelings of choking, having chest discomfort, abdominal discomfort, feeling faint, feeling very cold or hot, feeling numbness or tingling in parts of the body, feeling like things are not real, feeling out of control or fearing that one is dying.

Furthermore, the first attack must be followed by at least one month of continual worry about having another panic attack or behavior changes, such as avoidance of the place of the previous attack or unfamiliar places to prevent more attacks. The symptoms of panic disorder can mimic physical disorders, such as hyperthyroidism, so it is essential to have a physical examination to rule out other causes for the symptoms endorsed before a diagnosis of panic disorder.

Panic disorder specifier is the diagnosis of panic attacks without a diagnosis of panic disorder. Panic attacks may occur within any of the other anxiety disorders as well as non-anxiety disorders, such as depression and post-traumatic stress disorder. It occurs when repeated, intense surges of fear of discomfort subside within minutes.

During the intense fear, at least four of the following physical symptoms must occur: pounding heart, sweating, shaking, feeling short of breath, experiencing feelings of choking, having discomfort or pain in the chest, abdominal discomfort, feeling dizzy or faint, feeling very cold or hot, feeling numbness or tingling in parts of the body, feeling like things are not real, feeling out of control or fearing that one is dying. Unlike panic disorder, there does not have to be a month where there are behavioral or cognitive changes due to the first attack.

Agoraphobia is when an individual demonstrates extreme fear or anxiety in at least two situations: using public transportation like buses or trains, going to open spaces like a shopping mall or parking lot, being in enclosed places such as a store or movie theater, waiting in line or standing in a large group of people, or being alone outside of the person's home.

Furthermore, the fear or avoidance of these situations must be due to concerns about being unable to get away or get help if panic symptoms occur. These situations must produce anxiety most of the time and must be actively avoided or experienced only with great distress. The fear must be unrealistic compared to the actual danger and must have lasted at least six months.

Generalized anxiety disorder

Generalized anxiety disorder is challenging to diagnose because it occurs when an individual worries about several areas, which may overlap with other anxiety disorders (i.e., *social anxiety disorder*). Areas of worry may include school or work performance, finances, peer or family relationships, the health of the individual or family members, current events, or other domains.

The worry must be excessive and occur most days for at least six months. Furthermore, some of the following symptoms must be present (one symptom for children and at least three for adults): feeling restless or on edge, getting tired easily, having trouble focusing on things, feeling irritable, having muscle tension, or having difficulties sleeping.

Most importantly, the individual may struggle to control their worries. As with other anxiety disorders, it is essential to rule out mental and physical disorders before making this diagnosis.

Substance/medication-induced anxiety disorder is when the anxiety can be attributed to intoxication or withdrawal from some substance or to the use of medication.

Anxiety disorder due to another medical condition is anxiety caused by another medical condition, as determined by a physical exam or laboratory findings.

Other specified anxiety disorders can be used when there is evidence of anxiety symptoms that do not meet the full diagnostic criteria of another anxiety disorder. For example, a person may have much anxiety but not endorse enough of the required symptoms to be diagnosed with a disorder such as panic attacks.

Alternatively, instead of endorsing enough symptoms, a person may not endorse one of the required criteria of a disorder. For example, they may endorse every other symptom of generalized anxiety disorder except that they do not worry more days than not, thereby ruling out the generalized anxiety disorder diagnosis.

Several disorders that exist in other cultures (such as wind attacks and attacks of nerves) may mimic anxiety symptoms but not meet the full criteria of other anxiety disorders. In those instances, clinicians may diagnose the other specified anxiety disorder.

Unspecified anxiety disorder is most often used by clinicians when there is not enough information to determine the exact anxiety disorder, for example, in emergencies or before completing an intake assessment. However, clinicians may use this diagnosis when there are symptoms that mimic an anxiety disorder but do not meet the full criteria for any specific anxiety disorder.

Obsessive-compulsive disorder

Obsessive–compulsive disorder (OCD) is when an individual experiences either obsessions or compulsions. Frequently, people experience both obsessions and compulsions.

Obsession is a recurring thought, urge, or mental picture that is unwanted and causes distress.

For example, a person with a contamination fear might think their hands have germs on them. The person will try to alleviate this by frequent hand washing, which would be considered a compulsion if the individual felt compelled to wash his hands to counter the obsession.

OCD manifests in a contamination fear that might have a recurring concern for germs.

Compulsions help alleviate a person's anxiety or prevent an unwanted event (or situation), even though the unwanted outcome will not occur regardless of the behavior. For example, a child may fear being kidnapped unless he lines up his toys from largest to smallest.

OCD can be challenging to diagnose in children since they may not have insight into what is causing the behavior.

Regardless of whether a child or adult is experiencing obsessions or compulsions, additional criteria must be met to meet the OCD diagnostic criteria. The person must dedicate much time to the endorsed obsessions or compulsions, and the behaviors or thoughts must interfere with daily functioning. Medical and mental health conditions must be ruled out before diagnosis.

Individuals have varying levels of insight into whether the feared beliefs might or might not come true. As such, clinicians may specify whether the individual has good, fair, poor, or no insight into their disorder.

Body dysmorphic disorder is when a person is preoccupied with at least one perceived flaw in their body. These flaws are only minimally noticeable to others or are not apparent at all. For example, a person may spend hours staring in the mirror at a spot on their skin. The individual may feel compelled to engage in repetitive behaviors related to the perceived flaw (e.g., grooming, picking their skin), and it causes them great distress. Other disorders, such as the weight concerns seen in eating disorders, should be ruled out before assigning this diagnosis.

Hoarding disorder is when a person excessively collects material possessions, which accumulate. Furthermore, the person feels that the material items must be saved and experiences great distress if they let go of them. As such, living areas often become cluttered and potentially unusable. Family members or other supporters may need to maintain the cluttered areas.

In extreme cases, authorities may become involved if the living area becomes a hazard. Keeping items must cause significant distress and interfere with daily functioning, including living in a safe environment. Clinicians may specify the patient's level of insight related to their hoarding.

Trichotillomania (hair-pulling disorder) occurs when an individual repeatedly pulls or plucks their hair, and the hair loss is noticeable. The person must have tried to stop pulling their hair, and this behavior must cause elevated levels of distress and interfere with daily functioning.

Excoriation (skin-picking) disorder occurs when the repeated behavior of picking at one's skin leads to lesions on the skin. The person must be unable to stop the skin-picking behavior, which must cause distress and interfere with daily functioning.

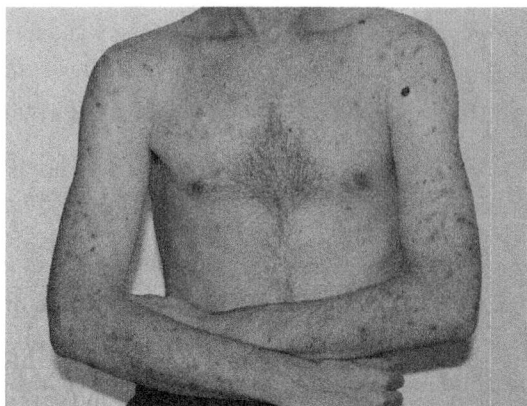

Excoriation (skin-picking) disorder

Substance/medication-induced obsessive-compulsive and related disorders may be diagnosed if there is evidence from a medical examination or lab result that indicates that an obsession, compulsion, skin picking, or hair pulling has occurred soon after starting or stopping the use of a medication or substance.

Obsessive-compulsive and related disorders due to a medical condition may be diagnosed when an obsession, compulsion, hair-pulling, or skin-picking behavior is attributed to another medical condition. A physical examination or lab result must prove this.

Other specified obsessive-compulsive and related disorders mimic OCD but do not meet the criteria for other OCD disorders. For example, a person may display body dysmorphic-like behaviors but have an actual flaw readily apparent to others.

Unspecified obsessive-compulsive and related disorders are when symptoms of OCD cause distress and impairment in functioning yet do not meet the full criteria for another disorder.

Trauma and stressor-related disorders

Reactive attachment disorder occurs in children who are emotionally distant from their adult caregivers. When they become distressed, they do not seek out their caregivers for comfort and rarely respond to caregivers' attempts to offer comfort when they are upset. At least two of the following criteria must be met: they rarely respond socially or emotionally to other individuals, have minimal positive gestures (i.e., smiling), and become irritable, sad, or fearful for no reason.

Furthermore, one or more of the following must also be true: the child must have experienced neglect or emotional deprivation at some point in his or her life, stable attachments could not form due to frequent changes in primary caregivers, or the child was brought up in a setting that inhibited attachment (i.e., an orphanage).

This pattern of insufficient attachment must first have appeared before the child's fifth birthday, and the child must be at least nine months of age. It is important to rule out other medical and mental health conditions, particularly autism, given the overlap in lack of social responsiveness.

Disinhibited social engagement disorder is diagnosed in children who meet at least two criteria when interacting with new adults: reluctance or refusal to approach new adults, treating a new adult as if they are very familiar with them, failure to look back toward their known caregiver (the child might even tend to venture away) or going off with a new adult without hesitation.

These behaviors must not be limited to impulsive behaviors like those in children with ADHD. Instead, there must be social deficits, which must be due to some neglect or deprivation. This often occurs due to abuse, being raised in a non-traditional setting such as an orphanage or being moved around to different foster care homes. A child must have a developmental age of at least nine months, and the symptoms must have been present for at least one year.

Post-traumatic stress disorder

Post-traumatic stress disorder (PTSD) can be diagnosed in any individual who is at least six years of age, although the exact criteria needed for diagnosis vary depending on age.

PTSD refers to a condition that occurs when a person is in a situation where the threat of bodily harm or even death is present (e.g., the threat of rape, abuse, car accident, fighting, terrorist attack, or war experiences).

This may have happened to the person, or the person may have witnessed this event happen to someone else. For example, someone who escaped the terrorist attacks on 9/11 or even those who witnessed the attacks, or the aftermath may qualify for a diagnosis of PTSD.

To determine whether the individual has PTSD, they must have repeated and unwanted memories of the event, upsetting dreams about the violent event, "flashbacks" where the person feels as if the event is happening again, or distress when hearing some cue that reminds them of the violent event (e.g., hearing screams, sirens).

The person attempts to avoid these distressing memories or flashbacks, including behavioral avoidance of people, places, topics, or other things that remind them of the violent event.

PTSD patients must have *at least two* of the following:

- experience worsening mood (or thoughts) related to the event, including the inability to recall important details of the traumatic event;
- have negative beliefs about oneself;
- blaming oneself or others (who bear no responsibility) for the event;
- have a constant negative emotional state (such as anger or horror);
- reduced interest in becoming involved in activities of interest;
- feel detached from others;
- be unable to feel positive emotions.

People must change how they become aware and respond to things associated with the original event, such as reckless behavior, being overly aware of surroundings, exaggerated responses to non-threatening stimuli, trouble concentrating or sleeping, and irritable or angry outbursts.

The criteria must have existed for at least one month, and these changes must cause distress and impairment nearly every day.

Service dogs provide aid to military veterans with PTSD

Trauma disorders

Acute stress disorder is similar to PTSD, except for the timeline and severity of the stressor. It is diagnosed three days to one month after the event. After one month, the diagnosis would change to PTSD. It involves exposure to a traumatic event in which death or physical harm to oneself or another was likely. They must meet at least nine specific symptoms, including intrusive symptoms, negative mood, dissociative symptoms, behavioral avoidance, and changes in arousal due to the event.

Adjustment disorder occurs when any stressor provokes either emotional or behavioral changes in an individual within three months of experiencing the stressor. These changes must be out of proportion with the actual danger posed by the stressor and must cause impairment in daily functioning. Mental and physical disorders must be ruled out, including the possibility that the person is grieving normally for the person they lost. Once the stressor is removed, the symptoms must be remitted within six months.

For example, PTSD includes the possibility that bodily harm or injury may occur. However, the stressor referred to as an adjustment disorder may be less severe but equally upsetting. For example, the person may have lost their job, gotten divorced, or lost custody of a child.

Other specified trauma and stressor-related disorders can be used as a diagnosis when symptoms mimic hallmarks of trauma or stressor-related disorder yet do not meet the full criteria for another disorder. This may occur due to not meeting the time criteria or having a presentation that may be culturally different.

Unspecified trauma and stressor-related disorders are often diagnosed when the clinician does not have enough information to determine which traumatic or related disorder applies.

For example, in a crisis like an emergency room, the clinician may not yet have enough information to determine whether the patient meets the full criteria for another disorder. Thus, the clinician may choose to give this diagnosis if symptoms of a traumatic disorder are present.

Somatic symptoms and related disorders

Somatic symptom disorder can be diagnosed when at least one physical symptom is distressing and causes excessive disruption in daily functioning due to maladaptive thoughts, feelings, or behavioral responses due to the physical symptom.

For example, the person may have elevated levels of worry or spend excessive time thinking about their physical symptoms. The person must have had at least one somatic symptom (it could be different symptoms) for at least six months.

Illness anxiety disorder occurs when individuals become convinced that they have, or will have, become seriously ill. Unlike somatic symptom disorder, symptoms are rarely present or only mildly present, yet the person is still convinced that they will develop an illness. The person becomes easily worried about their health and, as a result, engages in excessive health-checking behaviors or avoids checking for fear of what they or will find.

For example, someone may avoid medical appointments or check for signs of disease. The worry about illness must have existed for at least six months, and other disorders must be ruled out. Clinicians may specify if the individual displays *care-seeking* or *care-avoidant behaviors*.

Conversion disorder (functional neurological symptom disorder) is a condition in which a person has symptoms of being blind or paralyzed (or has altered motor or sensory skills), which another medical or mental health condition cannot explain. This condition may occur with seizures, weakness or paralysis, atypical movements, sensory loss, etc. The episodes may be acute if they last less than six months and persistent if they last longer than six months.

Psychological factors affecting other medical conditions are when psychological factors negatively impact a medical symptom or condition in at least one of the following ways: development, worsening, or delayed recovery from the disorder due to psychological causes, psychological factors inhibiting adequate treatment (i.e., the person refuses to take their medication), health risks or psychological factors that influence the cause or maintenance of the disorder need to be addressed. The clinician may indicate whether the condition is mild, moderate, severe, or extreme. In extreme cases, the patient may not report symptoms of a major health risk, such as heart attack or seizure symptoms.

Factitious disorder can be imposed on the individual themself or another. Individuals with this disorder falsify information about symptoms of either a medical or mental health condition. The person indicates that they or another is ill or injured. Deceptive behavior continues when rewards are removed. Delusional disorder and psychotic disorder must be ruled out. Clinicians may specify whether this is a single or recurrent episode.

Other specified somatic symptoms and related disorders may be diagnosed when symptoms that mimic those seen in somatic symptoms and related disorders are evident yet do not meet the criteria for another disorder. For example, this may occur during a brief somatic symptom disorder or illness anxiety that lasts less than six months.

Unspecified somatic symptoms and related disorders are when symptoms of a somatic disorder are present, but the clinician chooses not to specify which disorder. This most often occurs when there is insufficient information to make this determination, such as in a hospital setting.

Bipolar and related disorders

Bipolar I disorder is the classic bipolar disorder, in which a person experiences a manic episode. They must have had at least one manic episode, usually a period of increased activity and productivity. Ideas of grandiosity, distractibility, and excessive talkativeness characterize these. Hypomanic or depressive episodes may occur before or after the manic episode.

Bipolar II disorder differs from Bipolar I disorder because it requires that the person has experienced at least one episode of *major depression* and at least *one hypomanic episode.*

Cyclothymic disorder can be diagnosed in both children and adults when both hypomanic and depressive experiences have occurred (for at least two years for adults and one year for children). While these episodes occur, they do not meet the full criteria for hypomania, mania, or major depressive disorder.

Substance/medication-induced bipolar and related disorders can be used when symptoms mimic bipolar I, bipolar II, or cyclothymic disorders but can be attributed to the use of a substance or medication. A physical examination or laboratory testing must evidence this.

Bipolar and related disorders due to another medical condition are used when the elevated or irritable mood symptoms that mimic bipolar disorders are due to another medical condition, as evidenced by a physical examination or laboratory testing.

Other specified bipolar and related disorders are diagnosed when symptoms mimic the symptoms of bipolar and related disorders but do not meet the full criteria. This could occur due to the short duration of the illness or not meeting enough of the criteria to qualify for a hypomanic, manic, or depressive episode.

Unspecified bipolar and related disorders are most often used in emergencies when symptoms of a bipolar or related disorder are apparent. However, insufficient information is available to determine which disorder best matches the individual's symptoms.

Depressive disorders

Disruptive mood dysregulation disorder is a new addition to the DSM-5. It was added to address growing concerns that children were being diagnosed with too many disorders, all of which had a component of dysregulation of mood.

These children often display irritability and have episodes in which they cannot control their behavior. They display severe temper or verbal outbursts and may even become physically aggressive for unknown reasons. These outbursts must happen about three times per week and be inappropriate for the child's age.

In between these outbursts, the child must display an angry or irritable mood most of the time. The symptoms must have occurred for at least three but not more than twelve months and must occur in multiple settings (for example, at school and home).

The child must be between six and eighteen, and the symptoms must have been apparent in the child's history before his or her tenth birthday. The disorder may mimic bipolar disorder, oppositional defiant disorder, ADHD, and other childhood disorders. Children with these symptoms are often later diagnosed with either a depressive disorder or an anxiety disorder.

Major depressive disorder describes episodes of sadness lasting at least two weeks and involves observable changes in mood, thoughts, and other bodily functions such as sleep and weight.

At least five of the following symptoms must be present for most of the two weeks: feeling sad most of the day, a loss of interest in previously enjoyed activities, weight loss or weight gain, sleeping more or less than usual, speaking a lot more slowly or quickly than normal, feeling fatigued most of the day, experiencing feelings of worthlessness or guilt, having difficulty concentrating or making decisions or frequently thinking about death or dying.

These symptoms must interfere with daily functioning and must cause distress. Clinicians may specify whether the episode is mild, moderate, or severe. Only one episode is needed to make the diagnosis; however, clinicians must ensure that the level of sadness exceeds that usually seen during typical bereavement.

Persistent depressive disorder (dysthymia) is a more enduring pattern of sadness than major depressive disorder, as it must last for at least one to two years instead of only two weeks. The sadness must last one year for children and two years for adults. During this time, two of the following symptoms are evident: eating more or less than usual, sleeping more or less, feeling easily tired or tired often, not feeling worthwhile, having difficulty concentrating or being indecisive, or feeling like "things are never going to work out." Clinicians may specify whether the disorder is mild, moderate, or severe and whether the patient had an early or late onset.

Major depressive disorder describes an episode of sadness for two weeks and involves observable changes in mood, thoughts, and other bodily functions such as sleep and weight.

Premenstrual dysphoric disorder

Premenstrual dysphoric disorder is a condition in which women become extremely sad before the onset of their period; the symptoms improve a few days after the period begins.

At least five symptoms characteristic of a major depressive disorder must be evident (e.g., changes in weight and sleeping patterns).

At least one of the following symptoms must exist: extreme mood changes (such as feeling sad quickly), feeling irritable or angry, feeling depressed, hopeless, or bad about oneself, or feeling anxious or on edge.

Furthermore, at least one of the following symptoms must appear: no interest in previously enjoyable activities, trouble concentrating, feeling tired easily, changes in eating patterns, sleeping, feeling overwhelmed, or feeling bloated or tender in areas of the body.

Symptoms must cause distress and interfere with the woman's ability to perform school, work, or home life tasks.

Substance/medication-induced depressive disorder occurs when an individual experiences a chronic low mood or lack of interest in activities that they previously enjoyed and when there is evidence that these changes are due to the use or withdrawal from a substance or medication. Substances that can cause these symptoms are alcohol, opioids, and cocaine.

Depressive disorder due to another medical condition is when the depressed mood that a person exhibits results from a medical condition, as evidenced by a medical examination or laboratory finding. Adjustment disorders should be ruled out. Distress interferes with daily functioning.

Other specified depressive disorders refer to varied presentations of depressive disorders in which the symptoms do not qualify for another depressive disorder.

For example, *brief recurrent depression* and *short-duration depressive episodes*, in which the symptoms of depression last for less than 13 days, ruling out the major depressive disorder.

This category may be used if the minimum number of depression symptoms is not met, yet the individual experiences sadness and at least one other symptom of a major depressive episode that causes distress and has been occurring for at least two weeks.

Unspecified depressive disorder may be diagnosed when an individual has symptoms that mimic depression and cause distress and impairment. However, the individual does not meet the full diagnostic criteria for any of the previous depressive disorders. This most often occurs in an emergency room when a clinician is uncertain or does not have enough information about the patient's symptoms.

Schizophrenia spectrum

Schizotypal (personality) disorder is on the schizophrenia spectrum.

Delusional disorder is when there has been at least one month during which an individual has experienced delusions without psychotic symptoms, and daily functioning is not impaired.

Delusion types include:

erotomanic (i.e., a false belief that another is in love with them),

grandiose (i.e., a belief in unrecognized exceptional talent or brilliant insight),

jealous (i.e., a belief that that spouse or lover is disloyal),

persecutory (i.e., a belief that someone is conspiring, harassing, or spying on them),

somatic (i.e., delusions about feelings in the body),

mixed (i.e., no identifiable delusion theme) and

unspecified (prominent delusion is unable to be determined or multiple types).

Clinicians may specify whether the delusion contains bizarre content and whether it is the first episode of delusional thinking.

Brief psychotic disorder must occur for more than one day but not longer than one month. During this period, a person must experience delusions, hallucinations, or disorganized speech. Major depressive disorder, or bipolar disorder, must be ruled out before diagnosis.

Clinicians may specify whether there is a marked stressor, meaning an event that would be stressful to anyone in that situation. Clinicians may specify whether the psychotic symptoms occurred during pregnancy or within the first four weeks after giving birth.

Schizophrenia must last for at least six months, during which there must be at least one month where symptoms are in the active phase (delusions, hallucinations, disorganized speech, behavior that is catatonic or disorganized, or negative symptoms such as avolition). The symptoms must significantly impact at least one area of functioning.

Schizophreniform disorder is similar to schizophrenia except that it has a shorter duration, less than six months, during which symptoms occur. It differs from schizophrenia in that there is no requirement that the person's daily functioning level has declined.

To meet the criteria for schizophreniform disorder, an individual must display at least two of the following symptoms for one month: delusions, hallucinations, disorganization during speech processes, behavior that is disorganized or catatonic, or negative symptoms such as decreased emotional expressions. Depressive and bipolar disorders must be ruled out.

Schizoaffective disorder is when there is a mood problem, and the active-phase symptoms of schizophrenia co-occur (i.e., disorganized speech, negative symptoms, etc.).

Additionally, these symptoms were preceded by hallucinations or delusions, lasting for at least two weeks without the presence of mood symptoms. Clinicians may specify whether the specific symptoms are best described as bipolar or depressive and whether catatonia is present.

Psychotic disorders

Substance/medication-induced psychotic disorder occurs when the psychotic symptoms that an individual exhibits are the result of drug abuse, medication use, or toxin, and the symptoms remain after exposure to the medication or substance has stopped. There must be evidence from a physical examination or laboratory tests indicating that a substance (or medication) has caused the psychotic symptoms. Medications and substances that may cause psychotic symptoms include alcohol, inhalants, amphetamines, and cocaine.

Psychotic disorder due to another medical condition occurs when the psychotic symptoms that an individual experiences are the result of another medical condition, as evidenced by a physical examination or laboratory results.

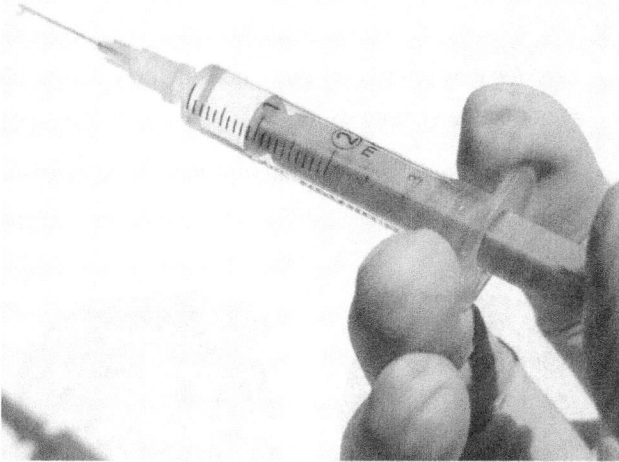

Substance/medication-induced psychotic disorder occurs when the psychotic symptoms that an individual exhibits are the result of drug abuse, medication use, or toxin.

Catatonia associated with another mental disorder can be diagnosed with at least three of the following symptoms: stupor, copying another's movements, copying another's speech, facial grimacing, stereotypic behaviors, odd mannerisms, posturing, not responding or following directions, not speaking, waxy flexibility or catalepsy.

Catatonic disorder due to another medical condition is when a person meets three criteria for catatonia. However, the catatonic state is due to another medical condition, as evidenced by a physical examination or lab result.

Unspecified catatonia may be diagnosed when symptoms that mimic catatonia are present and cause distress and impairment but do not meet the full criteria for another diagnosis. Additionally, it can be used if the underlying medical or mental health disorder causing it is unclear or if there is not enough information to make a more accurate diagnosis.

Other specified schizophrenia spectrum and other psychotic disorders can be used to describe symptoms that are characteristic of schizophrenia and related disorders yet do not meet the full criteria for another disorder. This may occur with repeated auditory hallucinations, delusions that overlap with mood episodes, and other unique cases.

Unspecified schizophrenia spectrum and other psychotic disorders are often diagnosed when there is not enough information to determine the specific disorder that matches the patient's symptoms. There is evidence of symptoms that fall on the schizophrenia spectrum. However, the clinician may be uncertain or not have enough information to make a more accurate diagnosis, such as when seen in an emergency room.

Dissociative disorder

Dissociative identity disorder is when two or more personalities exist with repeated episodes of amnesia. Others may notice the symptoms, or the individual may notice them.

Individuals have gaps or holes in their memory and may have trouble recalling personal information about typical events. Seizure disorders, personality disorders, PTSD, and bipolar and major depressive disorders must be ruled out.

Dissociative identity disorder occurs when two or more different personalities exist, and there are repeated episodes of amnesia.

Dissociative amnesia is when people cannot recall information about themselves, such as their name, where they live, or where they were born. Often, people cannot recall some traumatic event or some of the details surrounding the event.

Depending on the individual, the type of amnesia may differ; it can be localized, selective, or generalized. PTSD and neurocognitive disorders must be ruled out.

Depersonalization/derealization disorder occurs when there are repeated episodes of depersonalization or derealization. During the experiences, the person is aware of reality.

Other specified dissociative disorders may be applied when symptoms of a dissociative disorder are present, but they do not meet full criteria for one of the disorders. This may occur, for example, when there is an identity disturbance due to outside coercive forces, as can sometimes be seen in prisoners of war.

Unspecified dissociative disorder is when there is evidence of a dissociative disorder but not enough information to determine which disorder. Most often, it occurs in emergency rooms.

Personality disorders

Personality disorders are divided into three clusters:

> *Cluster A* (*odd, eccentric* cluster: *paranoid, schizoid,* and *schizotypal personality disorder*),

> *Cluster B* (*dramatic, emotional, erratic* cluster: *antisocial, borderline, histrionic,* and *narcissistic personality disorder*)

> *Cluster C* (*anxious, fearful* cluster: *avoidant, dependent,* and *obsessive-compulsive personality disorder*).

Paranoid personality disorder involves a persistent distrust or suspicion of other people.

Four of the following symptoms must be evident, beginning before early adulthood:

- worries that others are going to harm, exploit, or deceive them;

- excessively worried about the trustworthiness or loyalty of peers;

- hesitant to confide in others because they will use the information to harm them;

- interpreting benign remarks as demeaning or threatening;

- holding grudges;

- believing that others are attacking their character and responding with anger;

- persistent suspicions about spouse or lover being unfaithful.

Schizoid personality disorder is a consistent pattern of behaviors, beginning before early adulthood, with restricted emotional expression and detachment from social relationships that occurs in more than one setting.

Individuals must experience at least four of the following symptoms:

- no desire for or enjoyment of interpersonal relationships;

- preference for solitary activities;

- little or no interest in sexual activities;

- experiencing no pleasure in activities;

- paucity of close relationships;

- indifference to praise and critiques from other people;

- detachment or flat affect.

Schizotypal personality disorder is a repeated pattern of social and interpersonal difficulties, including discomfort with close relationships. It is marked by thought or perceptual changes and eccentric behavior beginning in early adulthood.

Symptoms must be present in more than one setting, and five of the following must be met:

- endorsement of ideas of reference (i.e., daily experiences are destiny);
- eccentric beliefs;
- strange perceptual experiences;
- oddities in thinking or speech;
- paranoia;
- inappropriate or restricted affect;
- odd behavior or appearance;
- few close friends;
- social anxiety that does not remit even after becoming familiar with a person.

Antisocial personality disorder is a consistent pattern in which an individual flagrantly disregards the rights of others. The individual must be at least 18 years old, and the behavior must begin before their fifteenth birthday.

Three of the following criteria must be met:

- disregard for social norms, which results in arrests;
- repeated lying or deceit;
- impulsive behaviors;
- violence or aggressiveness toward others;
- lack of caring for one's safety and the safety of others;
- irresponsibility in areas of work and financial obligations;
- not feeling bad when one's actions are hurtful to others.

Borderline personality disorder manifests chronic instability in self-image, close relationships, and affect. Typically marked by impulsive behaviors, and begins by early adulthood.

Five of the following behaviors must be present:

- fear of real or imagined abandonment;
- interpersonal relationships that alter between idealization and hate;
- disturbance in self-image;

- impulsivity in two or more areas that are self-damaging (i.e., excessive spending, risky sex, reckless driving, binge eating);

- repeated suicidal gestures, threats, or self-harm;

- instability in moods;

- feeling "empty" most of the time;

- difficulty controlling anger or temporary paranoid ideation.

Histrionic personality disorder is a chronic pattern of excessive attention-seeking and emotional behaviors that begins before early adulthood.

Five of the following symptoms must be present:

- discomfort in situations where they are not the center of attention;

- inappropriate sexual or provocative behavior;

- changing and shallow emotional expression;

- using physical appearance to gain attention;

- speaking in an impressionistic manner or speech that lacks specificity;

- dramatic or exaggerated speech;

- impressionable by others or believing relationships are closer than they are.

Narcissistic personality disorder is a pattern of behavior in which a person displays grandiose ideas, wants admiration, and cannot empathize with others.

Pattern by early adulthood and meets five of the following with other conditions ruled out:

- exaggeration of one's achievements or talents;

- often thinking about achieving unlimited wealth, power, success, or love;

- belief in being "special" and associating with "special" (famous) people;

- needing much admiration;

- a sense of entitlement, arrogance;

- using others to achieve goals;

- unable to empathize with others;

- jealousy of others.

Avoidant personality disorder is a repeated pattern of social inhibition, feeling hypersensitive or inadequate, which occurs in more than one context and begins before early adulthood.

Four of the following criteria with other conditions ruled out:

- avoidance of interpersonal contact, even in the work setting, due to fear of criticism or rejection;

- lack of involvement with others unless they are sure they will be liked;

- hesitation in intimate relationships because of fear or shame;

- worry about being criticized or rejected when around other people;

- feeling inadequate in new situations, which leads to social concerns;

- believing oneself to be inept or inferior to others;

- reluctant to take personal risks or to become involved in novel activities because of fear of embarrassment.

Dependent personality disorder is a repeated pattern where the person has an excessive need to be cared for by others due to fear of separation.

Behaviors must begin by early adulthood and meet at least five of the following criteria:

- trouble making everyday life decisions without advice from others;

- letting other people take responsibility for major areas of one's life;

- having difficulty expressing disagreement;

- lacking the self-confidence to do things on their own;

- going to great extremes to get support from other people;

- feeling uncomfortable when alone;

- needing a relationship as a source of care;

- frantically seeking a replacement relationship after one ends;

- excessive fears about caring for themselves alone.

Obsessive-compulsive disorder (OCD) is a repeated pattern of behavior that overemphasizes neatness, perfection, and control over mental and personal issues. People with OCD have limited flexibility and openness.

Symptoms must begin by early adulthood and include at least four or more of the following:

- excessive worry about details, rules, organization, schedules, or order;

- perfectionism that interferes with finishing assignments;

- spending excessive time on work and being "productive" instead of doing recreational activities or spending time with friends;

- caring too much about morality, ethics, and values;

- difficulty letting go of worthless objects without sentimental meaning;

- having a hard time delegating tasks to others;

- spending very little money on oneself and others;

- being stubborn or rigid.

Personality change due to another medical condition is an established change from a person's previous personality pattern. There must be evidence from a physical examination or laboratory finding that indicates that such a change is due to another medical condition. Other medical and mental health conditions must be ruled out, and the symptoms must cause significant distress in one or more areas of functioning.

Clinicians may specify several subtypes, including being *paranoid*, *aggressive*, or *apathetic*.

Other specified personality disorders may be used to designate symptoms that mimic those of a personality disorder and cause distress, or impairment yet do not meet the full diagnostic criteria of another mental health disorder.

Unspecified personality disorder is diagnosed when symptoms of a personality disorder are present, yet it is unclear which personality disorder best matches the patient's symptoms. It may be used if there is insufficient information to determine a more specific diagnosis.

Eating disorders

Pica occurs when food without nutrients (or nonfood items) is consistently eaten for at least one month. For example, a child may repeatedly eat a small toy, coin, or pencil tip. The items eaten must be items that are not typically eaten in that individual's culture and may only be diagnosed in the context of another mental health disorder (i.e., autism spectrum) if the behavior is severe enough to merit treatment.

1,440 items were found in the stomach of a patient with pica

Rumination disorder occurs when food is repeatedly spat up for at least one month. This may include re-chewing, re-swallowing, or spitting out chewed-up food. The repeated spitting of food may not be due to another medical disorder (i.e., acid reflux), and it must not occur only during another eating disorder. If symptoms co-occur with another mental health disorder (e.g., autism), they must be severe enough to merit clinical attention.

Avoidant/restrictive food intake disorder is a repeated pattern of eating in which certain foods are avoided based on a lack of interest in food, the food's appearance or taste, or concern about the negative consequences of eating the food. As a result, the individual fails to maintain adequate nutritional needs as evidenced by at least one of the following: weight loss or failure to achieve weight gain in children, nutritional deficiency, the need to be fed through tubes or nutritional supplements, and interference with daily functioning. Food must be available and culturally appropriate.

Anorexia nervosa occurs when an individual restricts their food intake due to a desire to lose weight. As a result, a significantly low body weight, based on Body Mass Index (BMI), is reached. The person fears gaining weight and demonstrates behaviors interfering with weight gain. Furthermore, there is a *distortion* in how the individual perceives their weight or shape.

The two subtypes are the restricting type, in which food is not eaten or eaten in minimal quantities, and binge-eating/purging, in which repeated episodes of eating substantial amounts of food followed by some method to purge the food (e.g., vomiting, laxative use).

The condition may be mild, moderate, severe, or extreme based on the individual's BMI.

Anorexia nervosa is when a person restricts their food intake due to a desire to lose weight.

Bulimia nervosa occurs when there are repeated episodes of binge eating, in which more food than most people would eat is consumed, and the person may feel out of control when they are eating. The individual engages in compensatory behaviors to compensate for the quantity of food eaten, such as vomiting or fasting to avoid gaining weight.

The eating and compensatory behaviors must occur for at least three months, approximately once per week. The person with bulimia overvalues their shape and weight.

Bulimia nervosa is repeated episodes of binge eating and the individual engages in compensatory behaviors, such as vomiting or fasting, to avoid weight gain.

Binge-eating disorder involves repeated episodes of eating more than most individuals would eat at one time or an individual feeling out of control while eating. During the eating episodes, at least three of the following criteria must be met: eating more quickly than normal, feeling ill or full, eating even when not physically hungry, eating alone due to being embarrassed about the quantity of food being consumed, or feeling disgusted, guilty, or depressed after eating.

There is distress, with no compensatory behaviors present. The disorder may be mild, moderate, severe, or excessive, depending on the number of weekly binges.

Other specified feeding or eating disorders describe atypical presentations of eating disorders, including atypical anorexia (an individual's weight is within the normal limits despite weight loss), binge eating, or bulimia of low frequency or limited in-time or night-eating syndrome.

Unspecified feeding or eating disorder may be used to describe a disorder where symptoms of an eating disorder are present yet do not meet the full criteria for the disorder. It may be used if insufficient information is available to diagnose accurately.

Neurodevelopmental disorders

Intellectual disability (intellectual developmental disability) is marked by gaps in general cognitive abilities, such as reasoning, planning, abstract thinking, or solving problems. It may include trouble with academic learning or learning from one's experiences.

As a result, there are deficits in adaptive functioning, and the individual has trouble with typical tasks associated with daily life (e.g., school, peer relationships, communication, and self-care).

Global development delay occurs when individuals do not meet their expected developmental milestones compared with peers of the same age. This disorder suggests that several areas of cognitive abilities are impacted, and as a result, these individuals cannot be assessed using IQ tests. This may occur due to head trauma or a congenital disability.

Unspecified intellectual disability (intellectual developmental disability) may be used for children over the age of 5 who are unable to be assessed due to physical or sensory issues. This disorder requires that children be reassessed after a reasonable amount of time.

Language disorder connotes chronic difficulties with learning or using language due to a lack of understanding or ability to produce language. Criteria must be met: reduced vocabulary, inability to use a wide variety of sentence structures, and having trouble using vocabulary or connecting sentences. Language level must be significantly below same-age peers.

Speech sound disorder is characterized by problems making sounds or not being able to make sounds. As a result, everyday communication is limited.

Childhood-onset fluency disorder (stuttering) affects the normal flow and timing of speech and is considered abnormal, given the child's age and language abilities. These symptoms persist for a long time and occur with at least one of the following: repeating sounds or syllables, prolonged sounds of consonants and vowels, pauses when saying a word, blocking, substituting words that are difficult to pronounce for words easier to pronounce, physical tension when saying a word or whole word repetitions. Typically, this condition produces anxiety about having to speak and usually emerges in young childhood.

Social (pragmatic) communication disorder connotes difficulty using verbal and nonverbal communication in social settings. This may include greeting people, sharing information, changing the communication to match the needs of the listener, trouble following rules when conversing with other individuals, and inability to make inferences from what is being said. This often begins in early childhood.

Unspecified communication disorder may be diagnosed when symptoms of a communication disorder are present, but more information is needed to determine the exact diagnosis.

Autism spectrum disorder represents chronic impairments in social realms across different contexts. These may include a lack of communication, not looking, not responding, or lack of non-verbal cues. Children display restricted or repetitive movements (e.g., hand flapping, repeating words, or arranging toys in the same way). These symptoms must begin in early childhood and cause significant impairment.

Attention deficit hyperactivity disorder (ADHD) may occur in both children and adults. A chronic pattern of trouble paying attention or impulsivity is present to the extent that it impairs the person's ability to perform daily tasks. Symptoms of inattention may include failure to follow directions or listen, trouble organizing tasks, or forgetting materials needed for school or work. Symptoms of impulsivity include fidgeting, getting up frequently, staying quiet, and waiting for one's turn.

Other specified attention deficit hyperactivity disorder may be used when symptoms of ADHD are present, but the full criteria of ADHD are not met.

Unspecified attention deficit hyperactivity disorder may be used when symptoms of ADHD are present, but there is not enough information to make a more accurate diagnosis.

Specific learning disability refers to problems either learning or applying different academic skills. At least one of the following symptoms must be present for at least six months: slow reading, trouble understanding what has been read, trouble spelling, difficulty expressing oneself in writing, or trouble mastering math skills. The deficits must be significantly below those of same-age peers, and other disorders must be ruled out.

Developmental coordination disorder is a problem in acquiring and using motor skills. As a result, movement may be slowed or look clumsy.

Stereotypic movement disorder occurs when individuals exhibit repeated purposeless behaviors like hand flapping, rocking back and forth, or banging their heads. These repeated motions cause problems with peers, family, school, or home life.

Tic disorders are marked by motor or vocal tics that occur repeatedly. A tic is a sudden, repetitive, non-rhythmic movement (or vocalization) of discrete muscle groups. They may be unnoticeable to the observer (e.g., abdominal tensing, toe crunching). Eye blinking and throat clearings are typical motor and phonic tics, respectively.

1 in 100 people may experience some tic disorder, usually before puberty; tic disorders are more common among males than females. *Tourette syndrome* is a severe tic disorder, and researchers link it to genetic susceptibility.

Other specified and unspecified tic disorders are when symptoms of a tic disorder are present but do not meet the full criteria for a tic disorder.

Other specified neurodevelopmental disorders are when symptoms of a neurodevelopmental disorder are present, but the symptoms do not meet the full criteria.

Unspecified neurodevelopmental disorders mimic other neurodevelopmental disorders, but not enough information is available to make a diagnosis.

Notes for active learning

Biological Bases of Nervous System Disorders

Schizophrenia

Despite evidence for a biological basis of schizophrenia, the mechanisms underlying this disease remain unclear.

Current conceptualization might comprise multiple versions of the disorder; the "disorder" might be better conceptualized as a "syndrome" with multiple etiologies and outcomes.

Neuroanatomical studies evidence enlarged ventricles (especially third and lateral ventricles) and enlarged *cortical sulci* in many patients with schizophrenia.

Researchers have observed a subtle reduction in brain volume of about 3%, primarily in the gray matter versus the white matter of the brain, particularly in the front-temporal regions.

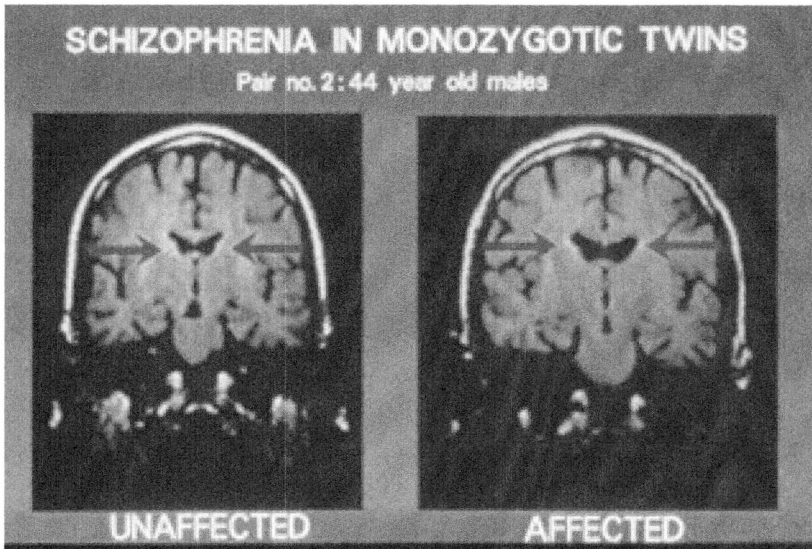

Enlarged lateral ventricles in schizophrenia

Dopamine hypothesis of schizophrenia was a theory of neurochemical underpinnings. The first version of this theory was derived from an early finding in 1950, which noted that the drug chlorpromazine alleviated symptoms in schizophrenic patients.

The theory has undergone multiple revisions, with the latest version stating that the disease's symptoms result from increased activity in the dopaminergic system, specifically dopamine type 2 receptors (D2).

Later findings have provided further support for this hypothesis, as many effective anti-psychotic medications block dopamine brain receptors, and their potency is correlated to the strength of binding to D2 receptors in the brain.

Moreover, the administration of drugs that increase dopamine can elicit symptoms that resemble the symptoms of schizophrenia. Post-mortem studies have found increased D2 receptors in the basal ganglia and the limbic system.

However, there are multiple limitations to the dopamine hypothesis of schizophrenia. One issue is that clozapine, one of the drugs effectively used to treat schizophrenia, has a low affinity for D2 receptors. Moreover, it is unlikely that dopaminergic dysfunction is the sole cause of schizophrenia; antipsychotics bring dopamine levels up to normal quickly but need to be taken for a while before alleviating symptoms. Current pharmacological treatment also fails to alleviate symptoms in all patients.

Other hypotheses conceptualize schizophrenia as caused during early neural development perinatally or intra-uterine. Another theory conceptualizes schizophrenia as progredient neurodegeneration and a result of abnormal or excessive synaptic pruning.

Depression

Search for the biological basis of depression has been guided by knowledge about mechanisms of effective anti-depressive drug treatment.

Monoamine hypothesis is the prominent theory about depression, hypothesizing that the emergence of depression is linked to underactivity at serotonergic and noradrenergic synapses. It has been supported by studies showing that the brains of depressed patients show increased amounts of serotonergic and noradrenergic synapses. These findings point to up-regulatory mechanisms to compensate for monoamine deficiency.

The monoamine hypothesis has limitations. First, it is unlikely that serotonin system dysfunction is the sole cause of depression, as antidepressants usually bring serotonin levels up to normal quickly. However, it often takes at least two to four weeks for depressive symptoms to improve significantly. Moreover, some effective antidepressants, such as *Tianeptine* and *Opipramol*, do not act through the monoamine system.

Consistent with the monoamine hypothesis, a longitudinal study examining the genetic basis of the disorder uncovered a moderating effect of the serotonin transporter (5-HTT) gene on susceptibility to depression after stressful life events. This finding is consistent with the *diathesis-stress model* of depression, which proposes that depression is a result of both an innate vulnerability to depression (e.g., comprising genes, prenatal development) and later life events.

An individual then develops depression if they have both vulnerability and the experience of certain stressful life events. This model is supported by findings that depression seems especially likely to follow stressful life events, but even more so for people with one or two short alleles of the 5-HTT gene. Serotonin may help to regulate other neurotransmitter systems, and decreased serotonin interferes with this regulation. Different facets of depression may be emergent properties of this dysregulation.

Alzheimer's disease

Studies examining the biological basis of Alzheimer's disease have identified specific structural pathology characterized by neuritic plaques and neurofibrillary tangles. The mechanisms, however, remain unclear.

Recent studies suggest that ACT and ApoE4 proteins are related to fibrous clumps. Neurochemical abnormalities were also suggested, with a decrease in the enzyme choline acetyltransferase, suggesting a deficit in a specific neurotransmitter. Another theory points to a loss of subcortical neurons; however, signs of brain atrophy may or may not be present.

Parkinson's disease

Primary symptoms of Parkinson's disease have been associated with the degeneration of the *substantia nigra*, a part of the brain that controls motor functioning.

Substantia nigra is deep within the brain stem, and its neurons project via the *nigrostriatal pathway* to the *striatum*. Striatum controls movements and balance, as well as walking.

Primary neurotransmitter in the substantia nigra is *dopamine*, which is responsible for relaying messages between the striatum and substantia nigra.

Substantia nigra cellular deterioration corresponds with a decreased production of *dopamine*.

Decreased levels of dopamine interfere with *controlled motor function*.

Decreased levels of dopamine adversely affect the neurotransmitter *acetylcholine*.

Motor function of the striatum depends on the balance between dopamine and acetylcholine; a disrupted balance between neurotransmitters may contribute to disease progression.

Notes for active learning

Treatment of Psychological Disorders

Treatment approaches

While differing treatments exist to address mental disorders, treatments share commonalities.

Treatments include a patient, a therapist trained to assist the patient, and the development of a patient-therapist relationship.

Theories used to treat clients have some hypotheses about the cause of the patient's symptoms.

Psychodynamic

Psychodynamic mode of treatment was made famous by Sigmund Freud. Freud attempted to understand the conflict between the id, the ego, and the superego through psychoanalysis.

Freud and his followers used *free association* to help people get to the root of their problems. This process involves patients lying on a couch and saying whatever comes to mind without filtering their thoughts.

The goal is to help individuals gain insight into their unconscious to see how those conflicts transfer to daily life. Psychodynamic therapy has often been criticized for the length of time needed to treat patients; it is often several years.

Humanistic

Humanistic psychologists believe that patients' ailments stem from how they interpret occurrences or situations. As such, they believe that patients can choose to control their actions and decisions. In this therapy, therapists promote a patient's natural growth by enhancing their awareness, expression, and acceptance of their feelings.

Unlike psychodynamic therapy, humanistic therapists strive to promote an individual's insight into present situations, not childhood conflicts. Humanistic psychologists emphasize the importance of *acceptance* during the therapist-patient relationship.

Therapist and patient develop a patient-therapist relationship

Behavioral

Behavioral therapists believe that maladaptive thoughts and behaviors are learned behaviors that can be changed by learning new adaptive behaviors. John Watson, Ivan Pavlov, and B.F. Skinner suggested using classical conditioning, operant conditioning, and observational learning to change human behavior.

The therapeutic relationship must be developed to be productive. Therapists must listen closely to the behaviors and thoughts to be targeted for change. The behavioral therapist acts as a teacher by assigning homework, offering home-based learning opportunities, and helping the client take some defined action to address the problem.

Behaviorists use techniques to change behavior, including systematic desensitization, modeling, positive reinforcement, extinction, aversion therapy, and punishment.

Cognitive

Cognitive therapy posits that negative feelings stem from how people think and feel about themselves and the world around them. Therefore, they try to change their client's maladaptive thought processes. For example, an individual may have a negative cognition such as "no one likes me." This leads to avoiding people and, thus, to sadness.

Clients are taught that these three constructs — cognition, behavior, and feelings — are linked and that making a change in one often leads to changes in the other two. It is often easiest for clients to change their behavior to influence their feelings and thoughts.

Biological

Biological therapy most often involves the use of psychopharmacology to treat symptoms. That means that medication is given to the client to counteract the imbalances that may be occurring in his or her brain.

However, biological therapy can use more drastic treatments, such as electroconvulsive therapy, psychosurgery, and prefrontal lobotomy.

Stem cell therapy for regenerating CNS neurons

National Institutes of Health (NIH) researchers have been investigating regenerative mechanisms of the central nervous system.

Recently, stem cells (i.e., undifferentiated cells like those in a developing embryo) in the adult brain have been discovered to give rise to new neurons and neural support cells. This implies that some parts of the adult human brain can generate new neurons. They found that the new neurons arise from "neural stem cells" in the fetal and adult brains.

Moreover, researchers found that neural stem cells could generate many cell types in the brain. This can include neurons, oligodendrocytes, and astrocytes (important neural-support cells). These findings have raised hopes that it may be possible to repair central nervous system damage by restoring lost functions through cell-replacement therapy.

Researchers are investigating two ways to make use of this discovery. Differentiated cells can be grown in a laboratory dish or implanted into a patient. Also, growth hormones and other trophic factors support a patient's stem cells and endogenous repair mechanisms.

Community and preventative approaches

Community approaches aim to screen and treat large populations for mental health disorders. They focus on providing psychoeducation regarding mental illness to community members.

Preventative approaches to mental health are similar to yearly physical examinations. The goal is to prevent mental health problems by helping people learn how to manage stress, increase social support, and recognize mental health disorder symptoms.

Coping skills are effective in reducing mental health disorders.

Community and preventative approaches are cost-effective solutions to mental health issues.

Cultural and ethnic contexts influence the choice and acceptance of treatment.

For example, in the Latino culture, machismo is prevalent. As a result, if the male head of the household does not agree to seek treatment for a family member, it may be challenging to convince other family members of the need for mental health treatment.

Some cultures consider it stigmatizing to seek mental health care.

High treatment costs, distance, and time may cause some to terminate treatment prematurely.

Modes of therapy

Treatment can occur on an inpatient or outpatient basis.

Inpatients are treated in a hospital or residential setting admitted voluntarily or involuntarily.

Inpatient admission occurs when symptoms are so severe that the patient is either a threat to themselves or others. Depending on state laws and the patient's symptoms, inpatient stays range from days to years.

Often, psychotropic drugs are used to assist patients in achieving stability.

Outpatients are treated with psychotherapy or medication while living in a community setting. Depending on the severity level, they may visit a psychiatrist or psychologist, usually one to three times per week. Group therapy may be used for additional support.

Individual therapy occurs when a patient meets with only one therapist alone.

Group therapy is conducted with several unrelated patients.

A group leader or therapist encourages positive interactions among members of the group.

Group themes depend on patients, but groups usually have people with similar issues.

For example, alcoholism, depression, anxiety, or personality disorders are discussion themes.

Group therapy enables therapists to gain insight into how clients interact with others. It offers patients a support system, enabling them to see that others share similar problems, thereby reducing their isolation.

Patients learn from and help each other boost self-confidence.

Family and couples therapy uses one couple or members of the family.

Family systems theory suggests that the identified patient (i.e., displaying symptoms) reflects family functioning problems.

Goal of family therapy is to *create balance* within the family.

Group therapy helps patients remove isolation and gain support from others

Relationship matrix

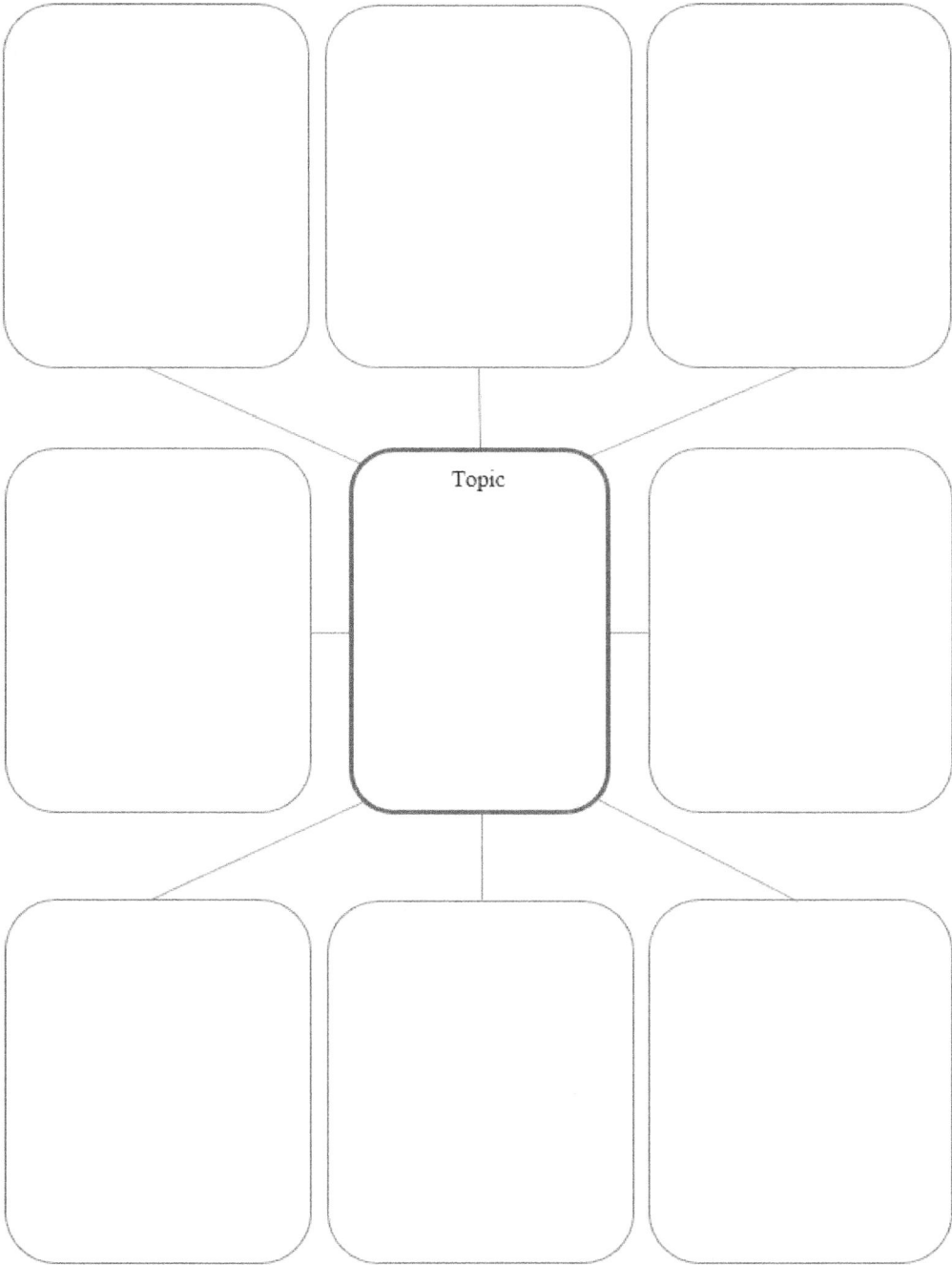

Topic

Notes for active learning

CHAPTER 11

Research Methods

Psychology is an empirical discipline since knowledge is developed through conducting empirical research. Psychologists may use experimental and correlational research, surveys, observations and case studies. The phenomenon being investigated determines the research method to be used. Each method brings advantages and disadvantages and has the potential to contribute to the understanding of psychological phenomena. Reasonable conclusions are derived through proper and quality research design, which establishes validity. The resulting data provides the grounds for theory development, which can be used in the treatment of mental and behavioral problems. Regardless of the chosen research method, professional psychologists must adhere to ethical guidelines that govern research design.

Social Science Research

Purposes of social science research

Social science research attempts to make sense of human behaviors and patterns.

Research isolates, defines, and explains the relationship between critical variables to understand and predict the underlying nature of reality.

Social science research observes and analyzes human and animal behavior.

Social science (e.g., psychology, sociology, and anthropology) is objective and uses research, observations, data collection, analysis, and conclusions.

Evaluation research guides social sciences and public policy by identifying specific and measurable relationships. It measures program effects against goals, outcomes, or criteria for decision-making and improves outcomes.

Policy analysis identifies actions (or inactions), causes, and consequences by studying:

> *proposals* (specified means for achieving goals),
>
> *programs* (authorized means for achieving goals),
>
> *decisions* (specified actions taken to implement programs), and
>
> *effects* (measurable impacts).

Results are categorized into *subgroups* (or *themes*), which help researchers interpret findings.

Theory and concepts

Theory-before-research model proposes that theory must occur *before* empirical research.

Research-before-theory model proposes that empirical research must occur *before* theory.

Theories are logical explanations for interrelated patterns, concepts, relationships, or events, explaining the relationship between variables (i.e., objects, concepts, or characteristics).

Theory organizes concepts, frames research, guides interpretations, and fosters decision-making. It addresses the *why* by defining parameters that measure and filter inputs people use to process complex phenomena.

Concepts are abstractions representing objects, properties, or features with a:

> *symbolic element* (i.e., word, term, or symbol) and
>
> *definitional element.*

For example, the concept of delinquency communicates the idea of a young person engaged in crime, truancy, or problems with parents and adults.

Concepts are abstractions:

> 1) assigned numerical values encompass *quantitative research* and

> 2) sensitizing ideas encompass *qualitative research*.

Propositions are statements about relationships between concepts.

Quantitative (*nomothetic approach*) and qualitative methods (*idiographic approach*) are used to generate and evaluate hypotheses (e.g., human behavior and cognition).

Paradigms and relationships

Paradigms are theoretical and methodological beliefs for evaluation. They organize reality into structures, frameworks, and perspectives.

Operationalization defines concepts by describing how they will be measured.

Operational definitions are conceptual meanings and criteria for measuring the empirical existence of a concept.

Objectivity is value neutrality (or dispassionate approach) to the subject.

Hypothesis specifies the proposed relationship between variables.

Deduction involves moving from a level of generalized theory to a specific hypothesis.

Cognitive reality consists of thoughts within a person's mind.

Induction involves inferring a whole group based on knowing about some cases.

Methodological fanaticism (*methodological narcissism*) is when methods overlook substance.

Knowledge is what people create symbolically to represent reality.

Sensory reality consists of substances and experiences of the external world.

Empathy is the willingness to put oneself in the role of another.

Research Methods Overview

Empirical research

Research methods answer questions about human cognition, behaviors, and emotions.

Researchers develop a hypothesis and use the research objective (i.e., question posed) to inform the research design.

Empirical research collects data by *observation and experience* (as opposed to theoretical).

Choosing the proper design is essential to valid and productive research.

Investigators must understand the design's *strengths*, *weaknesses*, and *purpose*.

Three research designs in social sciences:

> 1) *controlled experiments* (including *clinical trials*)
>
> 2) *correlational studies*
>
> 3) *survey research*

Each of these research designs has its advantages and limitations, and it is not uncommon in the field to use a mixed research design when testing complex hypotheses and developing theories.

Skilled researchers first develop their hypothesis and then let their question dictate and inform the most appropriate research design, depending on the goal of the question.

Research design terms

Null hypotheses state hypotheses of no difference based on independent variables.

Methodology is the collection of accurate facts.; it concerns *what is*.

Cross-sectional designs study one group and refer to a representative sample of this group.

Longitudinal studies focus on a group over time, and studies *change over time*.

Time-series designs involve measuring a single variable at successive points in time.

Pretest is an observation before treatment, and a *posttest* is a measurement after treatment.

Single-masked studies are when participants are unaware of the experiment.

Double-masked experiments are when investigators are unaware of the treatment and control group identities.

Experimental mortality is the expected loss (or *attrition*) of subjects during a study.

History is specific events occurring during the study and may have produced the results.

323

Maturation is biological or psychological changes unrelated to the experimental variable.

Multiple-treatment interference is when more than one predictor (i.e., treatment or independent variable) is used on the same subjects; the outcome may result from a specific combination of independent variables that can be uncovered only by more sophisticated research designs.

Reactivity (i.e., awareness of being studied) produces atypical behavior by subjects. Thus, an awareness of being studied, rather than the experimental treatment (i.e., *independent variable*), may become a factor in the outcome.

Replication is the repetition of experiments or studies utilizing the same methodology.

Replicability produces comparable results in replicating experiments; results should be the same when measured at separate times.

Statistical regression is the tendency of groups with extraordinarily high or low scores to *regress* (i.e., move toward) the mean (or average) on second testing.

Selection bias is when the researcher chooses *non-equivalent groups* for comparison, negatively impacting the ability to infer findings beyond the group studied.

Non-representative selection of groups invalidates attempts to generalize to larger populations.

Selection-maturation interaction is when factors other than the predictor variable are responsible for the results.

Single-subject designs are quantitative case studies using longitudinal (i.e., over time) dependent variable measurement on a single subject (or case).

Testing bias (or *pretest bias*) is knowledge introduced to respondents from pretesting; on a second test, they are no longer naïve regarding the subject and may use sensitivities, information, and attitudes garnered from the pretest.

Testing effect is when pretests eliminate naiveté of respondents to variables and alter awareness (or sensitivity), complicating the ability to generalize responses to a larger population.

Verification confirms the accuracy of findings (or *certitude in conclusions*) by observations.

Research Strategy and Design

Study designs

Research design is a study's plan and includes the investigations of who, what, where, when, why, and how.

Research designs control *invalidity* or resolve *causality problems*.

Investigators do not report a *control group* unless they for a *controlled experiment*.

Comparison groups (or *non-equivalence comparison groups*) have no random assignment. A variable may be manipulated but *without* random assignment. For example, studying the 10th-grade curriculum uses classes that cannot be assembled, so the investigator finds two comparable classes to study. Thus, *randomization* is an issue with inherent differences between the academic abilities of early risers (for 8:30 am class) versus late risers (for 1:00 pm class) and the representation of majors *vs.* non-majors.

Observational research studies are *qualitative* or *qualitative*. Methods include using observed data and recorded cases, ethnographic, and ethnological studies.

For example, a case study uses extensive notes based on client observations and interviews.

> *Advantages of experiments* include controlling factors that affect internal validity; the researcher controls for *causal factors* that invalidate findings. Researchers control the stimulus, environment, treatment time, and degree of subject exposure.

> *Disadvantages of experiments* include controls imposed by the researcher for *internal rival causal factors* that may create *atypical conditions*, impeding the ability to extrapolate to larger populations.

Replication in natural settings is complex since obtaining conditions with similar variable manipulation is difficult.

Investigators must answer how these differences are related and justify that the two groups are comparable.

Case study methods are in-depth, qualitative studies of illustrative cases. It includes oral and life historical recounts of events by participants.

Research design types

Experimental design includes:

>   *controlled experiments vs. quasi-experiments vs. non-experiments.*

Research design types:

1)   *controlled experiments* (e.g., clinical trials)
2)   *correlational research* (or non-experimental)
3)   *quasi-experiments*

Research design considers:

>   *random assignment*
>
>   *manipulation of variables*
>
>   *controlling extraneous factors*

To design a study, investigators build from previous studies, explaining the merits of the proposed study.

Formulate *testable hypotheses* and *define concepts and variables.*

Methodological problem is isolating interventions' effects from *confounding causes* by identifying the intervention's effect through a controlled statistical design.

Confounding factors are not considered by statistical controls but by direct comparisons (e.g., intervention effects).

Confounding variables are minimized by evaluating the treatment and control groups similarly (e.g., both measured during the summer or during the winter, but not differently), eliminating time as a variable (a *confounding variable*).

Qualitative research

Qualitative and *quantitative* methods are used, but the data obtained differs.

Qualitative research requires a broad spectrum of observational methods, including exploratory statistics, structured interviews, and participant observation, to gather rich information unattainable by classical experimentation.

For example, if a researcher wants to measure students' level of satisfaction with their teachers, they may ask open-ended questions like *"What do you like and dislike about Mr. Patel's teaching style?"* Responses will include many descriptive words offering insight and feedback. Information analysis can be used to increase student retention and satisfaction, inform teachers about strengths and weaknesses, and be used in promotion decisions.

Quantitative research

Quantitative research uses numbers to describe data.

For example, a researcher might be interested in how long adolescents watch television daily. Thus, they might ask a local high school: "*How many hours per day do you watch television?*"

Instead of providing students with an open-ended question, they provide the following options: 1 hour, 2 hours, 3 hours, 4 hours, or 5 or more hours per day. Students select one response, and researchers quantify each student's television viewing habits.

Quantitative research provides numbers that can be analyzed. For example, investigators might study demographic information (e.g., age, number of family members or pets).

Notes for active learning

Controlled Experiments

Establishing cause and effect

Controlled experiments are preferred for empirical research.

Controlled experiments are the only research design using *random assignment* to treatment and *control groups* where an *independent variable* is manipulated to observe outcomes (*dependent variable*).

Controlled experiments establish a *cause-and-effect* relationship between two variables.

For example, a social scientist wants to study whether playing violent video games causes aggression in children. The investigator studies whether video games (*independent variable*) cause aggression (*dependent variable*) in children. The independent variable (e.g., video games) is manipulated in the treatment and control groups, and the outcome (i.e., dependent variable) is measured to evaluate cause and effect.

Investigators chose two video games (*Hitman* and *Call of Duty*) and recruited children ages ten through twelve to participate in the study, and eighty children signed up. As each signed up, they were randomly assigned to a category: A) *Hitman*, B) *Call of Duty*, or C) Control group (children playing a non-violent video game Tetris).

After playing three hours of *Hitman*, *Call of Duty*, or *Tetris*, the investigator measured each child using the *Video Aggression in Children Inventory*, rating aggression on a scale of 1-5. The researcher obtains child and parent-report data regarding the number of violent acts (e.g., hitting, kicking, biting, or intentionally causing pain to another) the child engages in throughout the week after playing the video games.

Controlled experiment includes the Wolfer and Visintainer study (1975), which examined the effects of systematic preparation and support on children scheduled for minor inpatient surgery.

Alternative hypothesis was that such preparation would reduce the amount of psychological upset and increase the amount of cooperation among three young patients. Eighty children were selected and randomly assigned to the treatment or control group.

During their hospitalization, the *treatment group* received the *intervention* (i.e., independent variable), and the *control group* received the *placebo*.

Measures (i.e., dependent variable) included heart rates before and after blood tests, ease of fluid intake, and self-report anxiety measures.

The study demonstrated that systematic preparation and support reduced these kids' difficulties of being in the hospital.

Variables in experimental design include the following:

      independent (or treatment),

      dependent (outcomes), and

      confounding (unstudied) *variables*.

Researchers can control (*independent*) variables and examine outcomes (*dependent variable*).

Independent variable is the attribute manipulated.

Controlled experiments methods

Variables are operationalized concepts that change in response to other factors.

Random assignment is when each subject has an equal probability of selection for treatment or control groups.

Controlled experiments test subjects *similarly* and use a *double-masked* design. Imposing experimental controls is easier with laboratory studies.

Controlled experiments

      1) *variables* are *manipulated* and *monitored* (i.e., subject to change)

      2) *random assignment* of participants into experimental or control groups.

Experimental (or *treatment*) group receives the treatment (*independent variable)*, and the control group does *not*.

Independent variable is manipulated to examine its *influence on the dependent variable*.

Independent variable is the *predictor variable* that causes (or precedes) the dependent variable.

Dependent variables are outcome variables.

Dependent variables are measured, and the experimenter does not control it.

Dependent variable evaluates if treatment (*independent variable*) has a statistically significant (not chance) effect.

Control group compares the outcomes (i.e., *dependent variable*) due to the *independent variable* (treatment).

For example, clinical trials evaluate the efficacy of a treatment by using carefully designed studies. Clinical trials randomly assign the treatment (*independent variable*) and control (or *placebo*) groups. They are *double-masked* experiments with neither patients nor clinicians knowing which patient receives the treatment or placebo (control).

Experimental design included:

> *Control group* to determine if outcomes (i.e., dependent variable) were due to treatment (i.e., independent variable) or other factors. Controls provided a comparison.

> *Independent variable* was the presence (or absence) of the stimulus (e.g., treatment).

> *Dependent variables* are outcomes (e.g., heart rates, fluid intake).

> *Random assignment* balances the participants between the control and treatment groups.

> For example, if *friendly* children were placed in the treatment group, investigators would not know whether they were less anxious and cooperative (i.e., dependent variable) because of the treatment (i.e., independent variable) or because they were *friendly*. (another variable).

Clinical research

Clinical research determines the effectiveness and safety of treatments or medications. The proposed treatment, whether to prevent a disease or treat a disorder, must be effective.

Clinical research differs from clinical practice because treatments are not yet established. It permits investigators to compare novel modalities for *efficacy* (i.e., effectiveness) and *safety*.

Clinical research is frequently conducted in medical schools or large hospitals.

Non-experimental studies have neither *random assignment* of subjects nor the ability to *manipulate variables*.

Experimental design limitations

Experimental design enables researchers to evaluate *cause-and-effect* between variables.

Experiments provide precision and a controlled environment but may lack *ecological validity*.

Ecological validity is how realistically the experiment represents human behavior.

Ethical limitations (e.g., physical violence or trauma) restrict research methods.

Furthermore, if laboratory manipulations generalize to real-world situations, it is unknown.

Each research design has advantages and limitations, so a *mixed research design* (qualitative and quantitative methods) is used when testing complex hypotheses or developing theories.

Quasi-experimental design

Quasi-experimental design has *one element missing* (i.e., random selection and assignment).

Quasi-experiments *do not* use random assignment but *manipulate variables.*

For example, quasi-experiments include studies of violence inside prisons; human behavior is studied in natural settings, providing *ecological validity* but less *internal validity.*

Quasi-experimental designs match (i.e., groups without randomization for equivalence) comparison groups on how similar the groups are to the treatment group on crucial variables.

Quasi-experiments require distinguishing what is experimental and what is non-experimental.

Quasi-experiments study naturally formed groups or use pre-existing groups.

For pre-existing groups not naturally formed, the variable manipulated between the groups is the independent variable (e.g., intervention). Except for *no random assignment*, study design is like *controlled experiments.*

For naturally formed groups, the variable under study is a subject variable.

Without random assignment, therefore, no causal statements can be made based on the results.

Quasi-experimental designs:

> *Comparison groups* (or *non-equivalence comparison groups*)
> *without* random assignment.
>
> *Variable manipulated*

For example, studying the 10th-grade curriculum uses classes that cannot be assembled, so the investigator finds two comparable classes to study. Thus, *randomization* is an issue with inherent differences in the academic abilities of early risers (8:30 am class) versus late risers (1:00 pm class), representing majors *vs.* non-majors. Investigators must answer how these differences (e.g., study groups) are related and justify that the two groups are comparable.

Correlational studies

Correlational research examines *covariation* (i.e., the relationship between independent and dependent variables) with empirical data.

Correlation research is *observational research,* as investigators *do not* manipulate variables.

Correlation research variables are *not manipulated* but merely correlated. Non-experiments (or *correlational research*) have no:

> 1) randomization or
>
> 2) manipulation of variables.

For example, controlled experiments studying violent video games are impractical; surveys and questionnaires are appropriate. Elicited data collected and answers correlated.

Reciprocal causation is prone with correlational research and mitigated with longitudinal *vs.* cross-section studies.

Correlational studies examine the association between two variables that cannot be controlled experimentally; variables are *not manipulated*, loosely describing relationships, and asserting behavior (or events).

Correlational studies use *random selection,* but variables are *not* manipulated.

Correlational research is *unrelated* to cause-and-effect conclusions. It is *not causal*, and no statements concerning *cause and effect* are valid because the:

1) *direction of the cause* is unknown, and

2) *unknown variables* may be involved (i.e., an unknown variable may affect the variables studied).

Correlation studies describe relationships and provide data to make predictions and examine (or create) hypotheses for further studies.

Correlational design cannot be used to determine causality (i.e., *cause and effect*) and can only provide insight into the magnitude and types of existing relationships.

For example, an unstudied variable may cause an observed relationship since not all variables can be controlled.

Causal relationships (i.e., *cause and effect*) are *not* established by correlational design because the *independent variable* (or *treatment*) is *not* controlled.

For example, a correlational study evaluates the association between morning caffeine intake and reported higher levels of focus in college students. Since each student's caffeine intake is not controlled, only an association (or tentative relationship) between alertness and caffeine intake is proposed, *not* a cause-and-effect relation.

Another example of correlation research is when an investigator wants to determine if people's weight is related to height. They use a correlational design because they cannot randomly assign people their weight. One hundred participants were randomly selected and asked to report weight and height. Data (e.g., self-reporting results) are examined, and a *systematic relationship* is found between two variables: people who weigh more tend to be taller.

Correlational research is often exploratory to *identify variables* for controlled experiments.

For example, initial studies on smoking tracked the number of cigarettes smoked. Data was collected on smoking (i.e., independent variable) and lung disease (i.e., dependent variable) without controlling other factors (e.g., number of daily cigarettes). Smoking research examined *covariation* (not *cause and effect*) of smoking and lung disease.

333

For example, low levels of norepinephrine are associated with increased levels of clinical depression. The two variables *covary* (i.e., a relationship exists), but investigators *cannot* conclude a causal relationship (i.e., causation).

It is unknown whether a depletion in norepinephrine neurotransmitters causes depression or depression causes a depletion in neurotransmitters. Subsequently, other investigators determined that the number of postsynaptic neuron receptors increases in depression, which may be responsible for the relationship between neurotransmitter levels and depression.

Cause-and-effect statements *cannot* be based on *correlational research*.

Survey research

Survey methods are used in social science research.

Survey research uses *self-report questionnaires* or *interviews* to assess beliefs, feelings, values, and attitudes.

Likert Scale asks respondents to rate answers on a 5-point scale (from 1 to 5), with 1 being the weakest and 5 being the strongest agreement (or disagreement) with the statement prompt.

Survey research methods include a true *vs.* false response paradigm.

Survey research includes *focus groups* and *qualitative interviews*, where open-ended questions elicit information from the participants about a specific topic.

For example, the U.S. Census, which occurs every ten years and describes the demographics of the entire American population, is survey research. The government asks about age, family size, employment, and residence. This data helps policymakers allocate funding and resources.

Another example is a clinical psychologist who wants to know how many immigrants have PTSD (post-traumatic stress disorder). Since many countries have underdeveloped mental health care systems, she developed a questionnaire for newly arrived immigrants about PTSD symptoms. The questionnaire asks whether they experienced traumatic events, have flashbacks, etc. She determines whether their symptoms meet PTSD based on established criteria.

Questionnaires and interviews

Surveys involve questionnaires or interviews and are often classified as observational research.

Verbal surveys are *interviews* and *written surveys* are *questionnaires*.

Survey questions must be short and straightforward, without skips or open-ended questions.

Participant reactivity can be minimized by social desirability scales (i.e., "Do you always?").

Interviews can be structured or unstructured and allow for probing.

Descriptive survey research may use *statistical probability* to assess sampling error.

Analytic survey research explores *cause-and-effect* questions like experimental research.

Investigators utilize research design before the fact to remove the effects of *rival causal factors*. Survey researchers try to remove these rival factors after the fact using *statistical analysis*.

Survey research includes *errors* in the interpretation of findings. In most instances, surveys record either expressed attitude or claimed behavior, seldom the behavior itself.

Survey research answers questions to address problems, establishes baselines against which comparisons can be made, analyzes trends across time, and describes what exists, in what amount, and in what context.

Independent and dependent variables define the study's scope but cannot be explicitly controlled by the researcher.

Before conducting the survey, the researcher must predict and identify expected relationships among variables. The survey is constructed to evaluate the hypothesis by observations.

Three distinguishing characteristics of survey research.

1) Quantitatively describes aspects of a population, examining relationships among variables.

2) Data is collected from people and is, therefore, subjective.

3) Uses a selected portion of the population with findings generalized to the population.

Surveys suffer from "*no responses*" and "*refusals*" to respond.

Survey number must allow for no response and unusable, illegible, and incomplete responses.

Too many *unusable responses introduce bias*.

Strengths and limitations of survey research

Survey research allows social scientists to collect descriptive information inexpensively.

Survey designs provide data from many people. However, this may cause sampling errors, such as *oversampling* of a particular subpopulation (e.g., age, income, religion, ethnicity), distorting (or skewing) the results.

Questions may be misunderstood, and participants may guess the answer.

Participants' *response bias* (specific answers) may influence the results.

People may rush and answer questions without reading the choices or entire questions.

For example, a participant consistently picks the middle option, regardless of the question.

Surveys can elicit information about attitudes challenging to measure with observations.

In contrast to survey research, a survey is a data collection tool for social science research.

Surveys gather information about many people's characteristics, actions, or opinions and assess needs, evaluate demand, and examine impact. They are well suited for demographic data describing the sample's composition.

Statistics

Descriptive statistics

Statistics may seem intimidating initially, but descriptive statistics are straightforward.

Descriptive statistics are:

> 1) *central tendency*
>
> 2) *measures of variability*
>
> 3) *correlation coefficients*

Statistical power

Statistical power is the probability that the researcher *rejects the null hypothesis* when the alternate hypothesis is true.

Statistical power is determined, in part, by *effect size* and *sample size*.

Effect size is a determinant of statistical power evaluating *the overall importance of a result*.

Surveys use a sample of participants within the population; each random sample has a *mean* and *variance*.

Effect size is the extent to which the distributions of means for the *null and alternate* hypotheses *do not* overlap.

The greater the difference in the distributions of means, the *higher the power*.

Distribution of means is the distribution of *possible population means*, given *null hypothesis*.

> *Sample distribution* (representing the alternate hypothesis) is compared to the *distribution of means* (representing the null hypothesis) to determine whether the *sample distribution* differs significantly from the null hypothesis.

As the sample size increases, the distribution of means becomes narrower, and variance decreases, thereby reducing overlap between the null and alternative hypothesis distributions and increasing power.

Correlation coefficients

Correlation coefficient is *co-relationship strength* between variables; *not* implying causation.

Correlation coefficients measure the *relationship between variables*, ranging from +1.0 to –1.0.

Correlation of +1.0 or –1.0 is the strongest correlation, but rare.

Positive correlation means that the variables both increase or decrease together.

Negative correlation means that one variable decrease while the other increases.

+ and – signs indicate a *positive* (related) or *negative correlation* (inversely related).

Numeric value (i.e., magnitude) is the *strength* (i.e., predictability) of the correlation.

Strong correlations predict the strength of the relationship (i.e., correlation).

Weak correlation (+0.03) might result from people's height *vs*. IQ, unrelated variables.

Stronger correlation (+0.83) for the relationship between variables.

Central tendency

Central tendency uses the mean, the median, and the mode to describe the scores most representative of the entire group of numbers.

For example, four friends are asked how long they studied for a statistics exam; their responses in hours are 1, 3, 3, 5.

Median (or *midpoint*) values assigned to each item are taken as its score or weight.

Weighted values at intervals along the scale are retained for the final scale administered to respondents.

Means and medians are represented with line graphs, bar graphs, or histograms, depending on purpose and measurement scale.

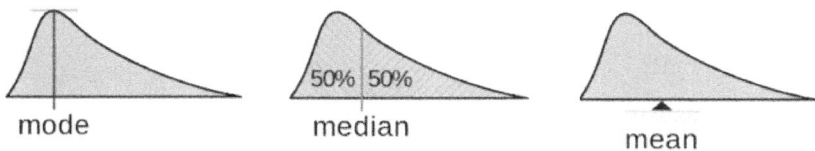

mode   median   mean

Mode

Mode is used for nominal and ordinal interval/ratio.

 Most common category or score value.

 Can have multiple modes (bimodal, trimodal, etc.).

 Not necessarily reflective of "*central*" in the distribution of a quantitative variable.

Mode is the score in the distribution that occurs most frequently. For example (1, 3, 3, 5), 3 occurs most frequently. Thus, 3 is the mode.

Distributions can have one or more modes. For example, everyone in class was asked what their favorite color was, and the results were 10 blue, 10 green, 9 pink, 8 orange, 5 red. The data is a bimodal distribution because both blue and green occur most often.

Mode reports data collected using a *nominal scale* (i.e., favorite restaurants, college majors).

Median

Median is used for ordinal and interval/ratio (espesially if skewed); the middlemost score.

Median finds the midpoint of scores and divides the group into two equal-size groups.

Median is the score in the middle of the distribution, equally divided, so 50% of subjects scored at or below the median.

> Odd number of scores; the median is the middlemost.

> Even number of scores, halfway between two in the middle.

Odd number samples are arranged in ascending order (e.g., 1, 3, 3, 5). For example, 3 is the median because 2 values (i.e., 1 and 2) are below it, and 2 (i.e., 4 and 5) are above it.

Even number samples are arranged in ascending order (i.e., 1, 3, 3, 5), identify the middle two numbers and divide by 2. For example, $1 + 3 + 3 + 5$; use $(3 + 3/2 = 3)$. Thus, 3 is the median.

Median offers several *advantages over the mean* and is preferable for *ordinal scale data*.

> Not necessarily "*central*" in a distribution of quantitative variables.

Median should be used if the distribution has an extreme or *skewed score* because the *mean is susceptible to disproportional scores*. For example, 5 people report their income, and one is a billionaire; their income is an extreme score that *skews* (or *slants*) the data.

However, the median will identify the group's middle number, so an *outlier* (i.e., statistically different value) does not distort the descriptive statistic.

Mean

Arithmetic mean is used for interval/ratio and requires interval data (or at least equal-appearing ordinal scores)

Mean may be distorted by skewed distributions. Cutting extremes produces trimmed mean.

Sum of arithmetic means is the arithmetic mean of a sum. For example, SAT scores (verbal + quantitative). Permits linear transformation.

Geometric mean – used for data of ratios, proportionate growth, and percentage change.

Lessens the impact of positive skewness.

Geometric mean of ratios is the *ratio of geometric means*.

Mean of a group of numbers is the mathematical *average*.

Mean (denoted *M*) is calculated by summing scores in the distribution and dividing by the total number of scores. For example, add $1 + 3 + 3 + 5 = 12$. Then, 12 is divided by 4 since the sample has four numbers. ($12 / 4 = 3$), mean is 3.

Mean has characteristics that should be noted. Since the mean includes all scores in a distribution, changing one number changes the mean.

If a constant value is added (or subtracted) from each score, the same value must be added (or subtracted) from the mean. Similarly, the mean changes by multiplying (or dividing) scores by a constant.

These rules are helpful to change the units of measurement (e.g., hours into minutes).

Variability

Measures of variability include *range*, *interquartile range*, and *standard deviation*.

Measures of variability describe how close (or far apart) scores are in distribution. If scores in a data set were the same, there would be *no variability*.

It is uncommon to have no differences in research data. Some phenomena have little variability (e.g., the number of hands each person has), while others vary greatly (i.e., response time in answering test questions).

Variability describes differences in distribution and explains the degree to which a score is representative of the sample.

Range

Range is the difference between the highest and lowest values in the data set. For example, if someone asked everyone in a room to report their ages, they would identify the lowest value (e.g., youngest) and the highest value (e.g., oldest person) as the range.

Range describes the spread of scores in a distribution; it does not account for middle values. For example, a room chose to poll at a birthday party for a grandmother turning 100. Her niece is one and the youngest. The range is $100 - 1 = 99$; there is no information on the average age of people present.

Range uses the two extreme scores (youngest and oldest) and ignores others; this is problematic for outliers in a distribution and does not accurately describe the variability.

Range is *unreliable* for measuring *variability* since it uses two extreme values.

Interquartile range

Interquartile range, unlike range, ignores extreme scores and focuses on numerical values covered by the middle 50% of the distribution.

For example,

> Data for the number of jeans each participant owns: 1, 2, 3, 4, 5, 6, 7, 8.

> Identify the boundary at which 25% of the scores fall below to locate the *interquartile range* and *label Q1* (or *quartile 1*). A line is drawn between the 2 and the 3.

> Identify the boundary at which 25% of the numbers fall above, *labeled Q3* (or *quartile 3*). The line is drawn in between 6 and 7.

> Thus, the middle 50% would be between 3 and 6.

Calculate the interquartile range by drawing a *histogram* (graph).

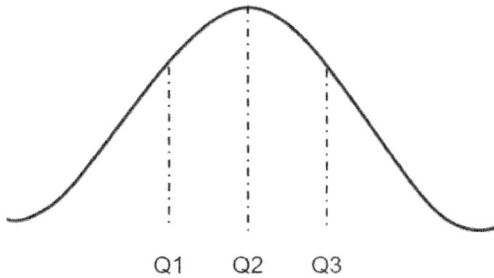

Q1   Q2   Q3

Quartile range where Q1 has 25% below, Q2 is median and Q3 has 25% above

Standard deviation

Standard deviation (SD) is a measure of *variability* (or *dispersion*), showing the variation from the "*average*" (or mean).

Standard deviation informs investigators how far the data points are from the mean.

Low standard deviations indicate that the data points are close to the mean.

High standard deviations indicate that the data are spread over a broad range of values.

Standard deviation of a statistical population (or complete population), data set, or probability distribution is the *square root of the variance*:

$$\sigma = \sqrt{\frac{(x_1 - \mu)^2 + (x_2 - \mu)^2 + \cdots + (x_N - \mu)^2}{N}}$$

where σ is the standard deviation, $x_1, x_2, \ldots, x_N$ are values from a finite data set, μ is mean, and N is the number of values in the data set.

Sample standard deviation is used when the data is obtained by random sampling from some parent population, and the denominator is reduced by one:

$$s = \sqrt{\frac{\sum_{i=1}^{N}(x_i - \bar{x})^2}{N-1}}$$

where s is the sample standard deviation, $\{x_1, x_2, ..., x_N\}$ are the observed values of the sample, x is the mean value of observations, and N is the number of observations in the sample.

Standard deviation has the *same units* as the data points.

For example, the average height of adult males in the US is about 70 inches, with a standard deviation of 3 inches.

One standard deviation: most men (about 68%, assuming a normal distribution) have a height within 3 inches of the mean or between 67 and 73 inches (i.e., one standard deviation above and below the mean).

Two standard deviations: most men (about 95%) have a height within 6 inches of the mean or between 64 and 76 inches (i.e., two standard deviations above and below the mean).

Three standard deviations account for 99% of the sample, assuming a normal distribution (bell-shaped curve).

Zero standard deviation means all men would be 70 inches tall.

If the standard deviation were as large as 10 inches, then men would have much more variable heights, with a typical range of about 60 to 80 inches within one standard deviation.

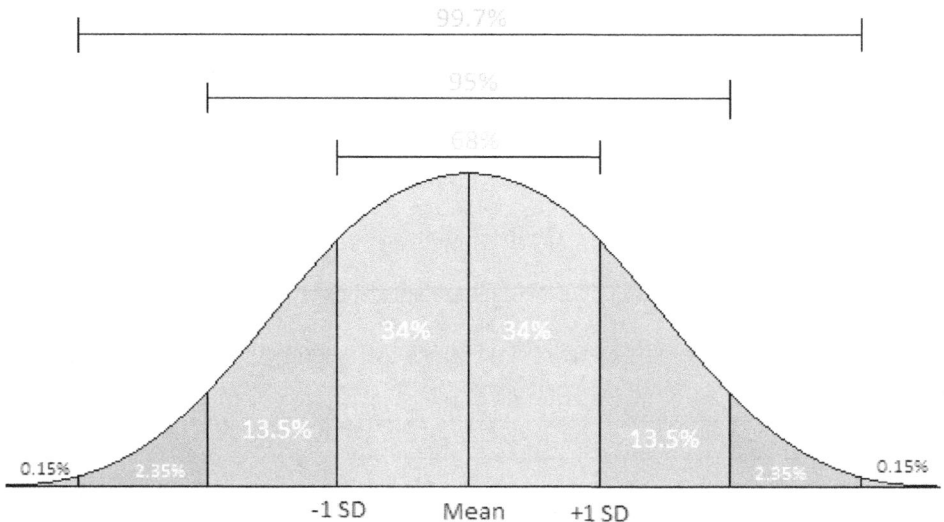

Bell-shaped curve for standard deviation (SD) of normal distribution curve
with 1 SD at 68%, 2 SD 95% and 3 SD at 99.7%

Statistically significant differences

Inferential statistical information from the sample is generalized to the populations.

Samples (i.e., a limited number of subjects) are used to investigate questions since it is impractical (i.e., too costly or time-consuming) to include the entire population.

For example, to evaluate the efficacy of an anxiety medication, investigators select a sample from the population, administer the *independent variable* (i.e., medication) to the treatment group, and *simulate* the treatment (i.e., placebo) with the control group.

Data is generated and analyzed to determine whether the groups have a *statistically significant difference* (unrelated to random change) between the *dependent variables* (i.e., effects).

> *Statistically significant difference* is when the *independent variable* has influenced the treatment group compared to the control group.

Statistically significant differences are evaluated by probability using *z-score* statistics.

z-score around 0 (or *population mean*) is representative of the population.

Extreme scores (e.g., +2.00 or –2.00) are statistically different (not due to chance).

Therefore, the *null hypothesis* (i.e., no expected difference) is *rejected*, and the *alternative hypothesis* (there is a difference) is *accepted.*

Notes for active learning

Visual Representation of Data

Graphing

Data visualization is essential for social scientists to present, analyze, and share information to make data more accessible and understandable.

Data visualization is the *graphical representation* of information and data.

Visual elements like charts, graphs, and maps are data visualization tools that provide an accessible way to identify and understand trends, outliers, and patterns in data.

Visual elements present data to non-technical audiences without confusion.

Data visualization techniques are essential to analyze massive amounts of information for *data-driven decisions*.

Advantages of data visualization are sharing information and visualizing relationships.

Disadvantages of data visualization include biased or inaccurate information; correlation does not mean causation, and the core messages can be obscured.

Charts

Charts represent data in a *graph*, *diagram*, or *tabular format*, with data displayed along two axes as a *graph, diagram*, or *map*.

Familiar charts include *scatterplots*, *bar charts*, *line graphs*, and *pie charts*.

These chart types, or a combination, address questions for relational data.

Charts draw points using cartesian coordinates (e.g., X, Y, Z) based on dimensions and measures.

Dimensions (e.g., categories, dates) and measures (e.g., deaths, temperature) are analyzed.

Measures are then rendered with coordinates to create a visualization.

Some visualizations favor displaying many dimensions (e.g., ordered bar charts), while others support few with clarity (e.g., pie charts).

Each chart type has its strengths and weaknesses.

Aesthetic conventions combine form and function to affect the perception of the data.

Scatter plots

Scatter plots represent the relationship between *two variables*.

Three scatter plots:

> *Positive correlation*

> *Negative correlation*

> *Null correlation*

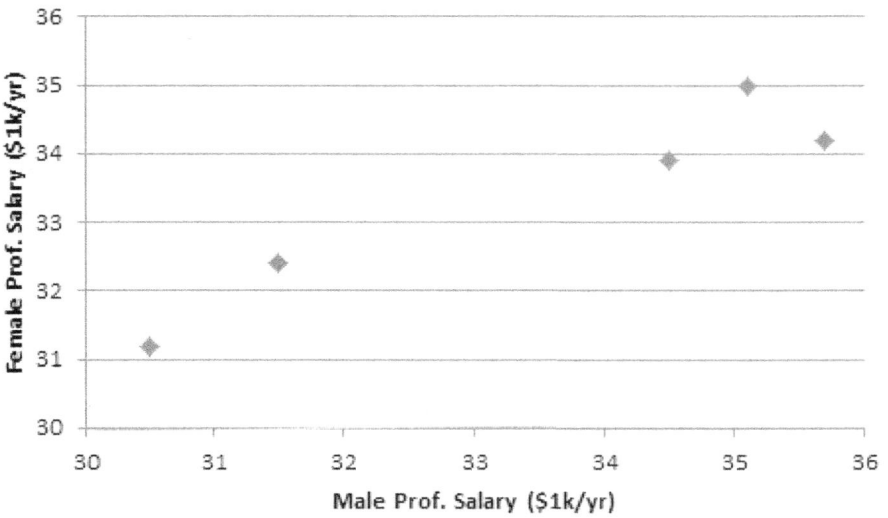

Scatter plot showing a strong positive correlation

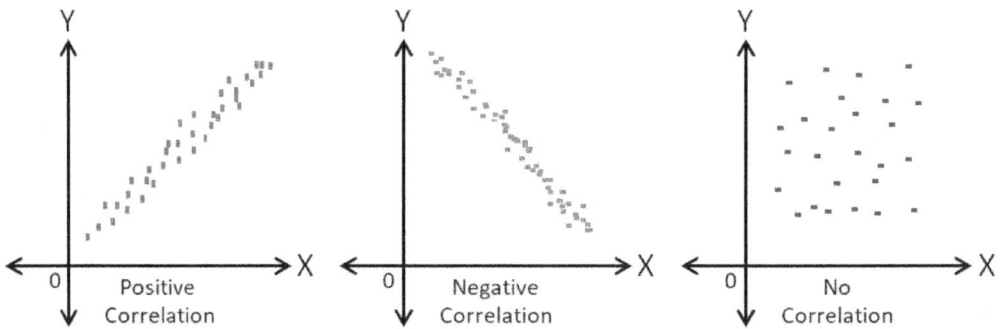

Scatter plots and correlation examples

Tables and graphs

Table: a set of figures displayed in rows and columns.

Graph: a diagram of points, lines, segments, curves, or areas representing variables in comparison, usually along two axes at a right angle.

Geospatial: a visualization in map form using shapes and colors to show relationships between pieces of data and specific locations. These visualizations focus on the relationship between data and its physical location to create insight. Any positional data works for spatial analysis. Scale makes geospatial visualizations unique is the scale.

Geospatial visualizations primarily use maps, highlighting the physical connection between data points.

Geospatial maps are susceptible to common pitfalls that may introduce errors:

> *Scaling* - changes in the size of the map can affect how the viewer interprets the data.

> *Auto-correlation* may create an association between data points *appearing* close on a map, even for unrelated data.

Infographics combine visuals (e.g., charts or diagrams) and words to represent data.

Dashboards collect visualized data displayed in one place to analyze and present data.

Area maps are geospatial visualizations with specific values set over a map of a country, state, county, or other geographic location.

Choropleths and *isopleths* are common types of *area maps*.

Bar charts

Bar charts represent numerical value comparisons (e.g., integers, percentages), with the bar's length representing each variable's value. For example, bar charts show variations in categories scaling width or height across simple, spaced bars or rectangles.

Bar charts have quantitative measures vertically, on the y-axis, or horizontally, on the x-axis. The style depends on the data and the questions the visualization addresses.

Qualitative dimension is plotted against the *quantitative measure*.

Bar charts typically have a baseline of zero. If another starting point is used, the axis should be clearly labeled to avoid misleading the viewer.

Bar charts have many variations. For example, stacked bar charts, side-by-side bar charts, clustered bar charts, and diverging bar charts.

Labels and legends help the viewer determine the details included in these charts.

Bar charts show a comparison of subcategory values. For example, bar charts may plot what a small business spends by expense type or how many different items each department sells across a consistent interval of time.

For example, bar charts can show the effectiveness of strategies to achieve a goal. Partition five strategies applied to the same subcategories, then compare the results for each method.

Stacked bar charts show extra detail within the overall measure.

For example, an office supplies store uses colored blocks in a bar representing revenue to represent sales opportunities. Blue blocks represent the contribution from office furniture, while green blocks represent electronics.

Bar charts show measures over a specific (discrete) length of time, while other chart types can show a continuous amount of time.

Well-designed bar charts:

> start at zero
>
> have labeled axes
>
> legend is consistent and defined
>
> image does not have too many bars

Poorly designed bar charts have bars with different widths, too many bars with subcategories, and unlabeled axes.

Box and whisker plots

Box-and-whisker plots (or *box plots*) show ranges (the box) across a set measure (the bar).

Box and whisker plots show the distribution of data points across a selected measure. These charts display ranges within the variables measured and include outliers, the median, the mode, and where most of the data points lie in the "box."

Box and whisker plot visuals compare the distribution of many variables against each other.

Box and whisker plots portray data distribution, outliers, and the median.

Box within the chart displays where around 50% of the data points fall and summarizes a data set in five categories.

Category with the greatest value is the *maximum* and likely falls far outside the box.

Category with the lowest value is the *minimum* and likely falls outside the box on the opposite side as the *maximum*.

Box itself contains the lower quartile, the upper quartile, and the median in the center.

Median separates the higher half from the lower half of a data sample, a population, or a probability distribution. The median is "the middle" value in a set of numbers based on a *count of values* rather than based on a *numeric value*.

Box and whisker plot sections help viewers see where the median falls within the distribution.

Lower quartile is the 25th percentile, while the *upper quartile* is the 75th percentile.

Whiskers are lines extending from each side of the box.

Range (the box) is the boundary for outliers.

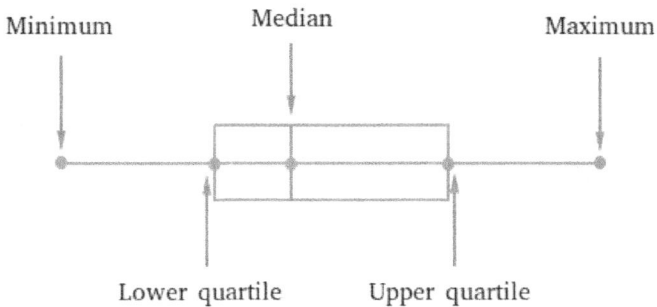

Box and whisker plot with median, lower, and upper quartiles, and minimum and maximum values

Gantt chart depicts timelines and tasks and is typically used in *project management*.

Heat map is a geospatial visualization displaying specific data values in distinct colors.

Highlight table uses color to categorize data, allowing viewers to read it easily and intuitively.

Histogram is a bar chart splitting continuous measures into vertical lines per distribution.

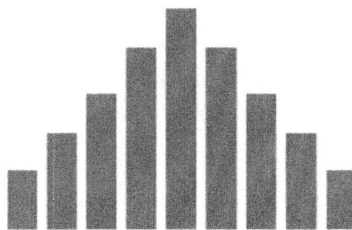

Histogram with heights indicating relative values for separate categories

Pie charts

Pie chart is circular with triangular segments that show data as a percentage of a whole.

Pie charts organize and show data as a percentage of a whole using a circle to represent the whole and slices to represent categories.

Pie charts help users compare dimensions' relationships (e.g., products, individuals, countries) within a specific context. Usually, the chart splits numerical data (measure) into percentages of the total. Slices represent proportions.

Pie charts show relationships of parts to the whole and should have a limited number of categories. They draw attention to values if one section of the whole is overrepresented (or underrepresented) and are less valuable when comparing exact numbers.

Well-designed bar charts have 2 to 5 categories, one more prominent than the others.

Poorly designed pie charts have too many categories, similar values for the chosen dimensions, do not represent a uniform whole (or percentages do not add to 100), and there are negative values (or complex fractions) for reported values.

Each pie slice should be labeled with the correct number (or percentage) attached to the slice.

Slices should be ordered by size (e.g., biggest to smallest) to make slice comparisons evident.

Limit legends and external references as they make it harder to focus on the dimensions. A 3-dimensional pie chart is much harder to analyze.

Labels should be attached to the slices whenever possible.

Consider a different chart type for more than *five slices*; use a legend, list, or table for context.

Do not complicate the visual display; complicating the chart with graphics can overwhelm it.

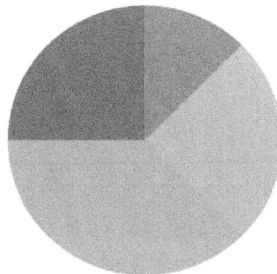

Pie graphs are valuable for comparisons among five or fewer categories

Graphing distributions

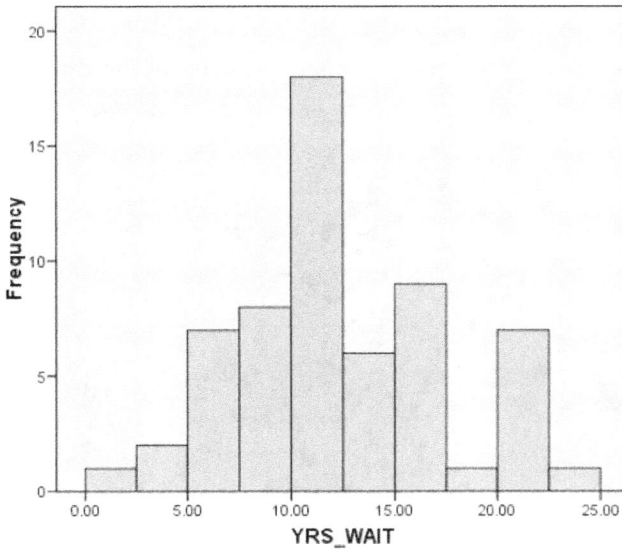

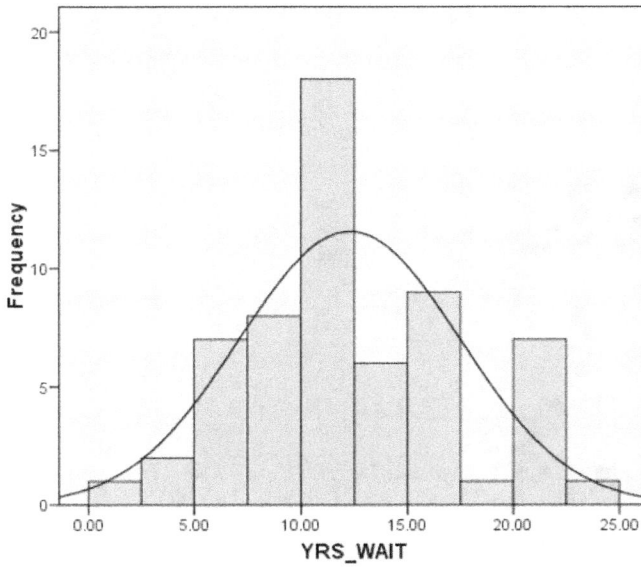

Histogram showing distribution, with standard curve overlayed on the bottom graph

Graphing selective variable

Data selected to graph can influence the viewer's perception.

Plotting specific data can influence the observer's interpretation of the data. For example, highlighting specific regions by reporting *the highest or lowest kidney cancer rates.*

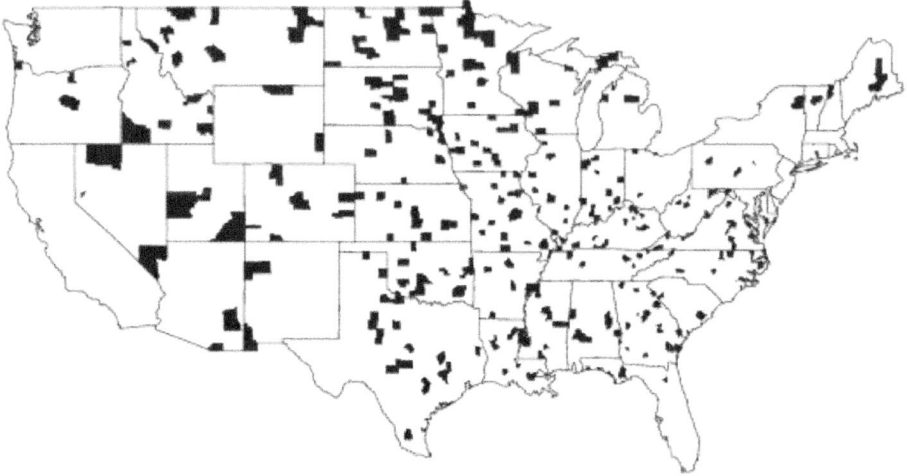

Highest kidney cancer death rates

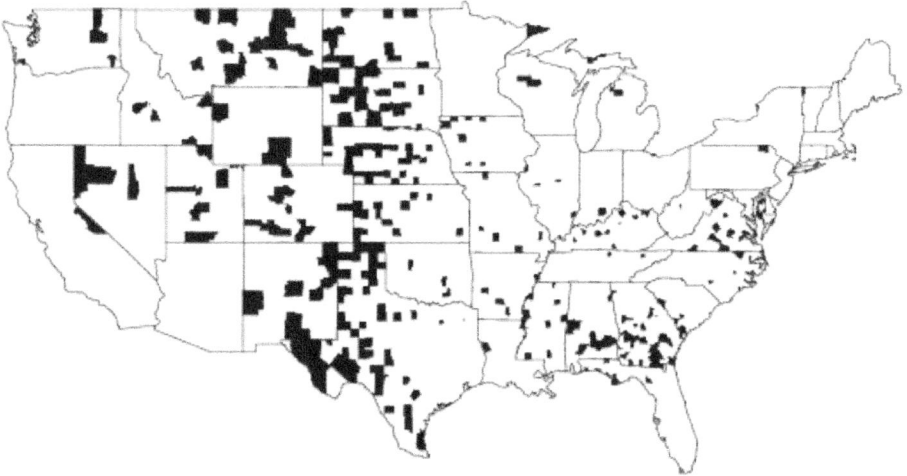

Lowest kidney cancer death rates

Ethics in Research

Principles of ethics

Ethics rely on values and morals, as opposed to facts, so it can be challenging to differentiate right from wrong.

Ethical *vs.* unethical behavior is often within a gray area.

General Principles require researchers to respect and protect people's civil and human rights.

Historically, guidelines became necessary after the unfair treatment of humans was discovered. Humans have been subjected to dangerous medical and psychological research without their consent. For example, during World War II, the Nazis forced prisoners to undergo cruel experiments.

Social science (e.g., psychological, or sociological) research ethics include:

1) *Ethical treatment* of humans and animals participating in research studies.

2) *Accurate and fair research conduct* and *reporting of findings*.

Ethics guidelines and practices help investigators distinguish ethical *vs.* unethical research. Principal instigators must train and oversee research teams to maintain high ethical standards.

Federal Department of Health and Human Services (DHHS) issues guidelines for ethical research. State and municipal boards may promulgate regulations for human research.

Ethical guidelines are issued by professional organizations, government, and institutional review boards (IRB). Professional organizations promulgate detailed documents describing an investigator's role in protecting the welfare of human and animal subjects.

Academic and clinical investigators take specific training required by *institutional review boards* (IRB) at universities or hospitals. Ethics and Institutional Review Boards are committees that oversee human research. Institutional Review Boards (IRBs) oversee research projects so investigators neither physically nor emotionally injure research subjects.

Academic and clinical research is guided through IRBs, which often consist of at least five members, including one community member with a non-scientific interest.

IRBs require research proposals to include a method description, whether human or animal subjects will be involved, informed consent, and debriefing information. IRBs request copies of literature or forms used (e.g., questionnaires, survey questions, and participant info).

During debriefing, participants are allowed to ask questions about the information, nature, and results

Researchers must obtain approval for the research before commencing human studies and agree to conduct their research study without changing the approved protocol. Investigators must not change approved methods without obtaining approval to ensure research oversight and that the researcher cannot decide what is ethical.

Expedited reviews are read and determined by the designated IRB committee member rather than the full committee. Studies entitled to expedited review are evaluations of educational institutions examining organizational effectiveness, instructional techniques, curricula, or classroom management strategies.

Ethical issues in research

Ethical issues inform and constrain social science research studies, including:

> *informed consent*
>
> *respect for privacy*
>
> *confidential data*
>
> *research team training*
>
> *accurate results reporting*

Honor commitments to respondents and respect reciprocity.

Reciprocity involves a mutual trust and obligation between the researcher and subjects.

Risk-benefit assessment considers maximal benefits balanced with minimal harm and used for the subject's protection; potential benefits must exceed hazards to respondents; some risks are justified if the knowledge gained exceeds the potential harm.

Paramount is avoiding procedures that harm participants. Researchers should not conduct studies that may harm subjects, particularly if the potential harm has not been explained and without informed consent.

Objectivity and professional integrity are required when performing and reporting research. The researcher should attempt to maintain a value-free, po0litically indifferent approach to the subject matter.

Confidentiality and privacy of respondents must be protected. Researchers should avoid deliberate misrepresentations of their identity when entering the private realm of subjects' lives, which otherwise would be barred to the researcher.

Confidentiality removes elements that might indicate a subject's identity from research records.

Anonymity means that the subjects remain nameless.

Data collection and storage require *confidentiality* and *precautions* when storing sensitive data (e.g., de-identifying information if stolen). Researchers may use codes instead of names to decrease the likelihood of identification.

Power differential exists between participants and researchers, with this disparity pronounced for underrepresented groups, such as non-native speakers, children, and minorities.

Informed and implied consent

General Principles require informed consent from research participants. Researchers must inform prospective participants about the research's purpose, length, and procedures.

Qualitative relationships differ from quantitative approaches as most conventional procedures for *informed consent* and *protection of human subjects* amount to little more than ritual.

Researchers must inform participants of the right to refuse participation, decline any portion of the study, or withdraw after it begins. Participants receive contact information for questions about their involvement or rights.

Researchers must disclose factors that may influence a participant's willingness to be in the study (e.g., medical procedure, loss of confidentiality, uncomfortable questions).

Informed consent is the *knowing and willing* agreement (i.e., free choice) to participate, absent fraud, deceit, duress, unfair inducement, or manipulation. Subjects must be made aware of the study's intentions.

Informed consent includes *potential benefits and risks* given to research participants. It must be written to make the procedures understandable, and participants' questions should be addressed.

Informed consent must be obtained *before* beginning research unless the study uses only observation in public places or archival data, avoiding identifying or harming individuals.

Implied consent may be indicated, for example, when a subject signs a completed questionnaire.

Active consent is the *formal written permission* by an informed parent or legal guardian that allows a child to participate in a research project.

Active consent requires *informed consent, which is* too stringent for many qualitative research.

Passive consent assumes parental permission is granted if parents do not return a refusal form after being informed about the study's purpose. The moral question is whether passive procedures inform parents about the research or provide sufficient opportunities to refuse participation.

Researchers must obtain informed consent from prospective participants

Deception in research

Deception is an issue in research and should be avoided if another research design is available.

If a non-deceptive procedure is unavailable, deception is allowed only if significant value is to be gained from the study.

For deception, researchers must inform participants and permit them to withdraw their data.

Deception is not allowed if physical pain or elevated levels of emotional distress are possible.

Compensation to participants for time and travel is permitted, but excessive financial inducements are avoided.

Researchers must debrief research participants, and participants must be allowed to ask about the study's information, nature, and results. Researchers should correct the participant's confusion regarding their role or the study's aims.

If investigators become aware that research has harmed someone unforeseeably, they must minimize the harm and report the unforeseen harm to a governing board (e.g., IRB).

Ethics violations

Lucifer effect transforms human character and causes good people to engage in evil actions.

Fraud occurs when researchers purposely fabricate or misrepresent their findings.

Plagiarism is fraud in which a writer presents the ideas or work of someone else as their own.

Scientific misconduct includes negligence, deception, cover-ups of misconduct, reprisals against whistleblowers, malicious allegations of misconduct, and due process violations in addressing misconduct.

Misbehavior includes sexual or other harassment, misuse of funds, gross professional negligence, tampering with the experiments of others, and violation of government research regulations.

Researchers must remain objective and '*value-free*' in approaching and reporting their findings.

Guiding ethical principles

Belmont Report has three principles:

   1) *Respect for persons* requires autonomy and protection.

   2) *Beneficence research* must not harm subjects.

   3) *Justice* requires benefits and burdens to be distributed equitably.

Shield laws constitute prosecutorial immunity as state-guaranteed confidentiality for researchers if subpoenaed.

Research areas excluded from review:

   Information obtained is recorded so the participants cannot be identified.

   Disclosure of the participant's responses outside the research cannot reasonably identify the subject.

   The study and results do not place the participant at risk of criminal or civil liability, nor will they damage their financial standing, employability, or reputation.

Research conducted on preexisting data, documents, records, pathological specimens, or diagnostic specimens publicly available or investigator records if subjects cannot be identified.

Ethical concerns

Voluntary participation may conflict with the methodological principle of representativeness.

In 1958, Gold proposed the typology of a researcher's four roles as a *field researcher*:

> Complete participant
>
> Participant as observer
>
> Observer as participant
>
> Complete observer

Qualitative research may have the relationship between researcher and subject ongoing and evolving.

Ethical relativists propose that they have a scientific right to study any group, whether it is interested in being studied or not, provided this researcher furthers scientific understandings.

Ethical absolutists propose that researchers have no right to invade people's privacy for scientific research and that deliberate deception regarding the researcher's intentions can harm subjects.

Ethics shape which treatment conditions are used, administration frequency, and duration.

Ethical experimenters rely on a randomized experiment only if the relative effectiveness of treatments is unknown; one of the treatments may be a control.

Ethical compromise

Ethical compromise includes:

> Simple dose-response experiment with strong and weak treatments compared.
>
> Deployment of treatment so that
>
> > 1) everyone gets the treatment at some point, and
> >
> > 2) treatment is delayed randomly for some recipients to form a temporary control group.
>
> Recognizing that a no-treatment control does not exist in many settings and, in some cases, should not.
>
> Consider the need and supply for effective treatment.

People confuse the idea of the random allocation of eligible individuals from a specified eligible sample to alternative treatments with a random selection of ineligible individuals from a sample within an undefined target population.

Assign randomly to treatments those who are marginally needy or deserving (i.e., a continuum of need or merit).

Alter eligibility requirements to meet standards of human ethics and evidence in experiments, recognizing that subsets of eligible individuals might be randomized even if the primary target population cannot.

Avoid ethically objectionable imbalances in the characteristics of individuals assigned to different treatments; people are randomly assigned to treatments in randomized trials.

Individual Privacy and Confidentiality of Research Records

> *Privacy* is an attribute of the individual.

> *Confidentiality* is an attribute of records.

Research acquires information to understand the effectiveness of programs, notably in randomized experiments.

Relationship matrix

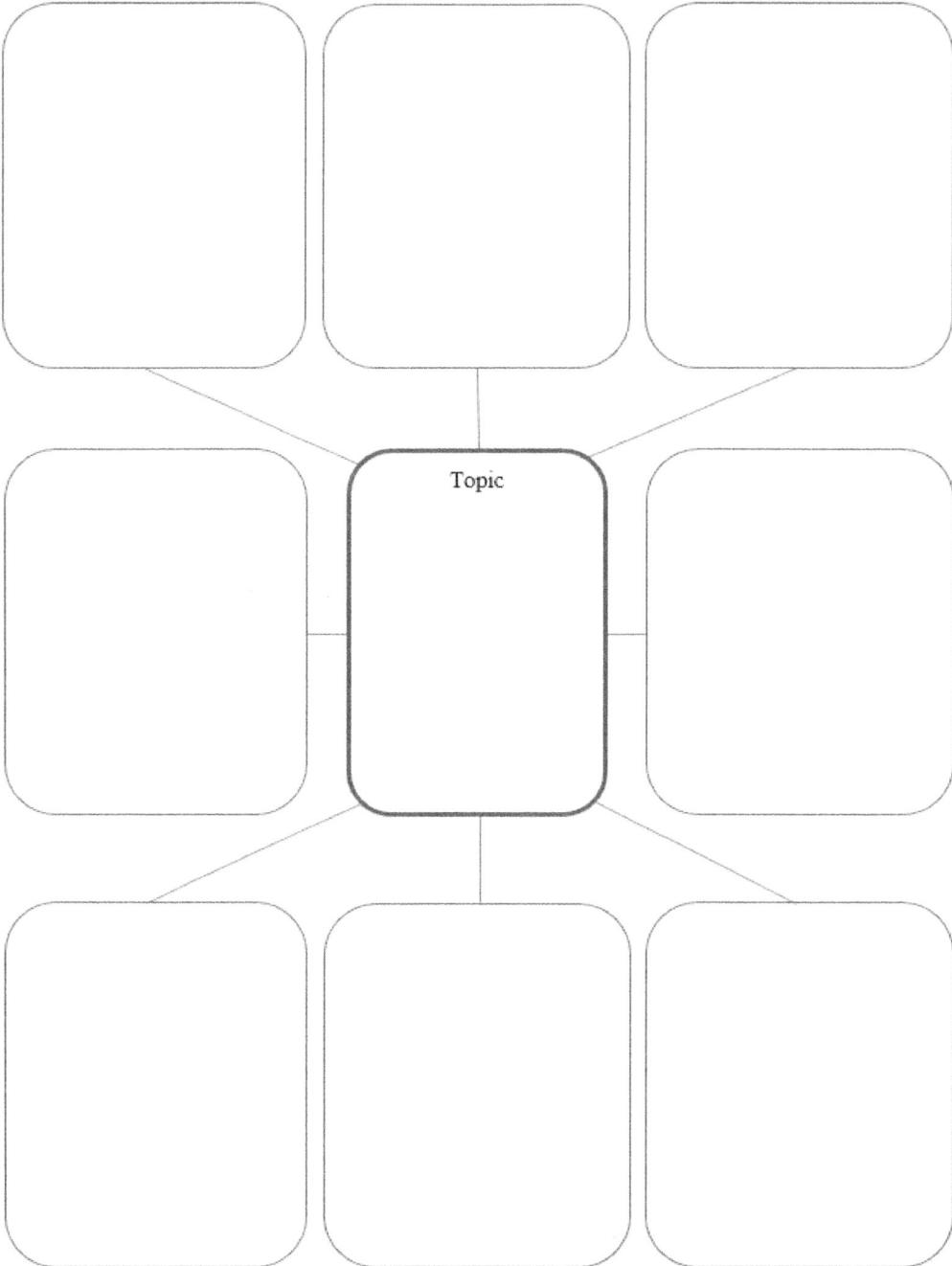

Topic

Notes for active learning

Notes for active learning

Appendix

Notable Psychologists by Field

History and Approaches

Mary Whiton Calkins – first female president of the APA, she earned her Ph.D. at Harvard University under William James.

Charles Darwin – evolutionary psychologist

Dorothea Dix – American activist for the more humane treatment of and provision for poverty-stricken mentally ill people, creation of American mental hospitals.

Sigmund Freud – psychoanalytic perspective

G. Stanley Hall – first psychology lab in America at Johns Hopkins University in 1883; 1st President of the APA

William James – first psychology textbook

Ivan Pavlov – classical conditioning; associative learning; stimulus-stimulus.

Jean Piaget (*4 Stages of Cognitive Development*) – cognitive development

Carl Rogers – self-theory; client-centered therapy, active listening, and unconditional positive regard

B.F. Skinner (*Skinner Box*) – operant conditioning

Margaret Floy Washburn – first female Ph.D. in psychology.

John B. Watson – behaviorism; Little Albert

Wilhelm Wundt – first psychology laboratory at the *Institute for Experimental Psychology* at the University of Leipzig, Germany in 1879.

Biological Bases of Behavior

Paul Broca – speech production area in the frontal lobe

Charles Darwin – natural selection, survival of the fittest

Michael Gazzaniga – split-brain research; understanding of functional lateralization in the brain; how the cerebral hemispheres communicate.

Alexander Luria – studied the relationship between language, thought, and cortical functions; his work resulted in the field of neuropsychology.

Roger Sperry – surgery designed to treat people with epilepsy by severing the corpus callosum; contributed to understanding the lateralization of brain function.

Carl Wernicke – speech comprehension area in the temporal lobe.

Sensation and Perception

Gustav Fechner – absolute threshold

David Hubel (*with Wiesel*) – discovered feature detectors in the visual system.

Ernst Weber – law to detect just noticeable difference (JND); change must be proportional to the stimulus' magnitude.

Torsten Wiesel (*with Hubel*) – discovered feature detectors in the visual system.

Learning

Albert Bandura (*Social Learning Theory*) – *Bobo Doll* experiment, imitation in learning.

John Garcia (*The Garcia Effect*) – conditioned taste aversion.

Ivan Pavlov – classical conditioning; associative leaning; stimulus-stimulus.

Robert Rescorla (*Contingency Theory*) – a stimulus must provide the subject information about the likelihood that certain events will occur.

B.F. Skinner (*Skinner Box*) – operant conditioning; positive and negative reinforcement and punishment.

Edward Thorndike (*Law of Effect*) – instrumental conditioning

Edward Tolman (*Latent Learning*) – rats in mazes

John B. Watson (*Behaviorism*) – "Little Albert"

Cognition

Noam Chomsky – Language Acquisition Device (LAD)

Hermann Ebbinghaus – studied memory with nonsense syllables; retention and forgetting curves.

Wolfgang Kohler – insight from chimps.

Elizabeth Loftus – eyewitness testimony, misinformation effect, false memories.

George A. Miller – STM's "Magic Number" = 7 ± 2

George Sperling (*Iconic Memory*) – sensory memory sub-type with cued recall tasks.

Benjamin Whorf (*Whorf's Linguistic Determinism Hypothesis*) – language determines thought.

Consciousness

William James – stream of consciousness.

Sigmund Freud – unconscious motives, wishes, and urges.

Ernest Hilgard – the role of hypnotism in human behavior and response.

Motivation and Emotion

William James (*James-Lange Theory of Emotion*) – bodily reaction comes first; the emotion comes quickly follows.

Alfred Kinsey – controversial research on sexual motivation in the 1940s and 50s.

Abraham Maslow (*Hierarchy of Needs*) – strives for self-actualization.

David Matsumoto – study of facial expressions and emotions; first training tool to improve the ability to read micro-expressions; studied spontaneous facial expressions in blind individuals; discovered that many facial expressions are innate and not visually learned.

Stanley Schachter (*with Singer*) – 2-Factor Theory of Emotion, arousal, and cognitive label.

Hans Selye (*General Adaptation Syndrome*; GAS) – alarm, resistance, exhaustion.

Developmental Psychology

Mary Ainsworth – secure *vs.* insecure attachment.

Albert Bandura (*Social Learning Theory*) – *Bobo Doll* experiment, imitation in learning.

Diana Baumrind – types of parenting styles: authoritarian, permissive, authoritative.

Erik Erikson – 8 Stages of Psychosocial Development.

Sigmund Freud – 5 Stages of Psychosexual Development

Carol Gilligan – criticized Kohlberg's work, which studied privileged white men and boys; she felt this caused a bias against women.

Harry Harlow – wire mother monkey studies, contact comfort.

Lawrence Kohlberg (*Levels of Moral Development*) – pre-conventional, conventional, and post-conventional.

Konrad Lorenz – imprinting in animals.

Jean Piaget (*4 Stages of Cognitive Development*) – cognitive development

Lev Vygotsky (*Zone of proximal development*; ZPD) – the range of tasks a child can complete independently; studied inner speech in language development.

Personality

Alfred Adler – inferiority complex, sibling rivalry.

Albert Bandura (*Social Learning Theory*) – personality development is affected by observational learning and modeling, Bobo Doll experiment.

Paul Costa and Robert McCrae (*Big Five Trait Theory*) – CANOE: conscientiousness, agreeableness, neuroticism, openness to experience, and extraversion.

Sigmund Freud – unconscious, childhood experiences, 5 stages of sexual development.

Carl Jung – collective unconscious, archetypes.

Abraham Maslow (*Hierarchy of Needs*) – strive for self-actualization.

Carl Rogers (*Self Theory*) – real *vs.* ideal self; sees people as basically good.

Martin Seligman – positive psychology

Intelligence and Testing

Alfred Binet – first intelligence test.

Francis Galton (*Psychometrics*) – developed the ideas of correlation, standard deviation, and regression toward the mean.

Howard Gardner   *Theory of Eight Multiple Intelligences*

Charles Spearman (*2-Factor Theory of Intelligence*) – "g" factor (general intelligence), an inherited intellectual ability that influences all-around performance; "s" factor (specific abilities), which accounts for differences between scores on different tasks.

Robert Sternberg (*Triarchic Theory of Intelligence*) – creative, analytical, practical.

Louis Terman (*of Stanford University*) – altered Binet's IQ test, calling it the Stanford-Binet.

David Wechsler (*Wechsler Scales*; WIAS, WISC) –the most widely used intelligence test.

Psychological Disorders

Albert Ellis – founder of cognitive-behavioral therapies.

Sigmund Freud – psychoanalysis, dream analysis, free association.

Mary Cover Jones – counterconditioning of fears.

Carl Rogers – client-centered therapy, active listening, unconditional positive regard.

B.F. Skinner (*Behavior Modification, Token Economies*) – behavioral therapies using the principles of operant conditioning.

Joseph Wolpe (1973) – developed the exposure therapy technique of flooding.

Social Psychology

Solomon Asch – studies conformity using lines.

Leon Festinger – *Cognitive Dissonance Theory*

Fritz Heider (*Attribution Theory*) – how people explain (i.e., make attributions) behavior; behavior is attributed to a *disposition* (internal) or a *situation* (external).

Stanley Milgram – obedience studies; "teacher" and "learner" shock experiment.

Philip Zimbardo (*Stanford Prison Study*) – the power of power when roles become a reality.

Notes for active learning

Important Researchers in Psychology (in alphabetical order)

Alfred Adler (1870-1937) was an Austrian physician and psychotherapist. He is known for his work establishing the school of individual psychology and his development of personality theory. He is noted for his attentive focus on the inferiority complex, an element in personality development with an isolating effect. Adler collaborated with Sigmund Freud to promote the emergent psychoanalytic movement.

Mary Ainsworth (1913-1999) was an American-Canadian developmental psychologist who developed *attachment theory*. Ainsworth devised a situation design to study the emotional attachment of infants to their caregivers. In these experiments, a child would play in a room for twenty-four minutes while caregivers and strangers entered and exited. Children were observed based on the amount of exploration they engaged in, their reactions to the departure and return of their caregiver, and their level of stranger anxiety. Children were categorized based on behavior as secure, anxious-avoidant, or anxious-ambivalent/resistant.

Elliot Aronson (born 1932) is an American psychologist known for his *jigsaw classroom*. In this classroom model, classmates are divided into small groups to work on a task. These groups include a mix of races and academic abilities. This model's use positively affected performance, self-esteem, and racial attitudes.

Solomon Asch (1907-1996) was a Polish-American social psychologist. Asch was a Berlin School of Experimental Psychology member and emphasized the role of the "whole" in his research. Asch researched conformity. He found that group pressure can change the opinions of individuals.

Albert Bandura (1925-2021) was a Canadian-American psychologist. He is known for developing social *learning theory* and his Bobo doll experiment. In this experiment, Bandura found that children who had seen an adult playing aggressively with a Bobo doll were more likely to play aggressively with the same doll than children who had seen an adult playing gently with the doll.

Philip Bard (1898-1977) was an American physiologist primarily known for his work on the nervous system. He was particularly interested in the role of the vestibular system in emotions. In conjunction with Walter Cannon, Bard developed the *Cannon-Bard theory* of emotions, which posits that emotions occur independently of physiological changes.

Diana Baumrind (1927-2018) was an American clinical and developmental psychologist known for categorizing parenting styles as authoritarian, permissive, and authoritative and for her criticism of the use of deception in psychological research.

Aaron T. Beck (1921-2021) was an American professor of psychiatry and the founder of cognitive therapy. Additionally, Beck has developed theories relevant to clinical depression and created anxiety self-reporting measures.

Alfred Binet (1857-1911) was a French psychologist and inventor of the first intelligence test (the Binet-Simon Scale). His intelligence test was intended to gauge children's cognitive abilities at various ages using thirty tasks of increasing difficulty. The number of tasks completed corresponded to child's mental age.

Pierre Bourdieu (1930-2002) was a French sociologist, anthropologist, and philosopher known for social stratification based on aesthetic taste. Bourdieu theorized that social classes pass their aesthetic preferences to the younger generation. These passed-down aesthetic dispositions are intended to distance oneself from other social groups.

John Bowlby (1907-1990) was a British psychologist, psychiatrist, and psychoanalyst known for his childhood development and attachment theories. Bowlby's work emphasized the importance of having a warm and nurturing mother or mother figure. He theorized that children and infants who had the presence of a warm caregiver in their lives would develop a secure base from which to learn and explore. He called this *secure attachment*.

Paul Broca (1824-1880) was a French anatomist, anthropologist, physician, and surgeon known for his work on the human brain's frontal lobe. His research revealed that the presence of lesions on the cortex of patients typically corresponds to the diagnosis of aphasia, providing the first anatomical proof of the brain's localization of function.

Mary Whiton Calkins (1863-1930) was an American philosopher and psychologist known for researching dream content and its general reproduction of persons, places, and events recently experienced by sense perception but rarely directly connected with what is deemed of utmost importance in the dreamer's real life. Calkins is known for her work on memory and self-psychology, where she advocated practicing introspection on one's mental experience.

Walter Bradford Cannon (1871-1945) was an American physiologist. He identified the *fight-or-flight* response, a term first coined to describe animals' physical responses to threats and expanded to include humans. Additionally, he developed the *Cannon-Bard theory* with Philip Bard.

Noam Chomsky (born 1928) is an American cognitive scientist, historian, linguist, logician, (analytical) philosopher, political activist, and social critic. He contributed to developing a new cognitivist framework for studying language and the mind, creating *universal grammar theory*, *generative grammar theory*, Chomsky hierarchy, and the minimalist program.

Charles Cooley (1864-1929) was an American sociologist known for his concepts of the looking-glass self, primary and secondary groups. According to his *looking-glass self-theory*, individuals' identities are formed through the perceptions that others have of them. Cooley identified primary groups as closely-knit groups that exert tremendous influence on their members, with secondary groups being less influential and more temporary social groups.

Paul Costa, Jr. (born 1949) is an American psychologist who developed the *Revised NEO Personality Inventory*, a 240-item measure of extraversion, agreeableness, conscientiousness, neuroticism, and openness to experience (collectively, the *Five-Factor Model*). He worked with Robert McCrae in developing six subordinate dimensions for the Five-Factor Model's partitions.

William E. Cross, Jr. (born 1940) is a psychologist and theorist known for studies on ethnic and racial identity development, particularly his *Nigrescence model*. This model proposes five stages people of color go through when forming their racial identity. First is the *pre-encounter stage* when the individual is unaware of their race. Second is the *encounter stage*, when individuals have experiences that make them conscious of their race. Third is the *immersion/emersion stage,* when individuals strongly identify with their racial identity and disparage the dominant racial culture. Fourth is the *internalization stage* when individuals stop disparaging the dominant racial culture and establish relationships with whites. Fifth is the *internalization or commitment stage* when individuals advocate for the concerns of people of color and have a positive sense of their racial identity.

Charles Darwin (1809-1882) was an English naturalist and geologist. Darwin proposed the *theory of evolution* that claims all of Earth's species (both current and extinct) are connected, over time, to shared common ancestors. The branching pattern of species from these common ancestors is the product of natural selection, the condition by which only the most successful members of a species are the ones to survive and successfully reproduce, passing on their phenotype.

Dorothea Lynde Dix (1802-1887) was an American activist for the more humane treatment and provision for poverty-stricken mentally ill people. The United States' first mental asylums were created due to her vigorous and successful lobbying of state legislatures and Congress, actions inspired by her abhorrence of the mentally ill being largely confined in cruel, makeshift fashion around the country.

Hermann Ebbinghaus (1850-1909) was a German psychologist whose renowned pioneering study of memory led to the discovery of the forgetting curve, the learning curve, and the spacing effect. He is credited with having drafted and standardized the first research report.

Albert Ellis (1913-2007) was an American psychologist famous for his 1955 development of Rational Emotive Behavior Therapy (REBT) and for guiding psychotherapy's cognitive revolutionary paradigm shift. This shift emphasized enabling people to understand their self-defeating behavior through rational analysis and cognitive reconstruction processes, allowing the development of more rational constructs to supersede core irrational beliefs.

Erik Erikson (1902-1994) was a German-American psychologist known for his theory of psychosocial development (*Erikson's stages of psychosocial development*). He proposed eight stages of development characterized by a psychological conflict between the favorable and unfavorable. Stages are trust *vs.* mistrust, autonomy *vs.* shame and doubt, initiative *vs.* guilt, industry *vs.* inferiority, identity *vs.* role confusion, intimacy *vs.* isolation, generativity *vs.* stagnation, and ego integrity *vs.* despair.

Gustav Fechner (1801-1887) was a German philosopher, physicist, and experimental psychologist who inspired subsequent scientists and philosophers in experimental psychology and the founding of psychophysics. Gustav is renowned for noticing that psychological sensations and the physical intensity of a stimulus had a non-linear relationship. Collaborating with Ernst Heinrich Weber, this became the *Weber-Fechner law*.

Leon Festinger (1919-1989) was an American social psychologist known for *cognitive dissonance* and *social comparison theory*. Festinger's research on cognitive dissonance revealed that inconsistency is psychologically uncomfortable, and individuals experiencing dissonance will try to reduce it by changing their behaviors or cognitions. Social comparison theory proposes that humans evaluate their opinions by comparing them to those close to them.

Sigmund Freud (1856-1939) was an Austrian neurologist known for psychoanalysis and psychosexual development theories. Freud conceptualized and articulated critical mental mind functions with the id, ego, and superego. Freud proposed that a libido (or energy) drives human behavior. Freud argued that libido is expressed differently depending on a person's psychosexual development. The five stages are the oral, anal, phallic, latent, and genital stages.

Francis Galton (1822-1911) was an English anthropologist, explorer, geneticist, geographer, inventor, meteorologist, polymath, progressive, proto-geneticist, psychologist, psychometrician, sociologist, and statistician. Academically, he articulated statistical correlation and advocated recognizing the regression toward the mean phenomenon. This statistical phenomenon holds that if a first measurement's variable is extreme, a second measurement will place it closer to the average. Reciprocally, if the second measurement's variable is extreme, its first measurement will tend to have been closer to the average.

John Garcia (1917-2012) was an American cartoonist, educator, farmer, and psychologist famous for taste aversion research. His work discovered the survival mechanism nature of conditioned taste aversion, a response intended to allow an organism to recognize poisonous foods to be avoided.

Howard Gardner (born 1943) is an American developmental psychologist acclaimed for his *theory of multiple intelligences,* a claim that intelligence can be differentiated into nine categories: musical-rhythmic and harmonic, visual-spatial, verbal-linguistic, logical-mathematical, bodily-kinesthetic, interpersonal, intrapersonal, naturalistic, and existential.

Michael Gazzaniga (born 1939) is an American psychologist and cognitive neuroscientist. He pioneered studies on split-brained patients' learning and understanding abilities. Specifically, he studied how people with this rare condition function, with attention given to which half controls bodily functions.

Carol Gilligan (born 1936) is an American ethicist, feminist, and psychologist academically praised for her endeavors on ethical communities and relationships. She is renowned for collaboration with–and male-oriented criticism of–Lawrence Kohlberg and his stages of moral development. Gilligan advocates the recognition of two moral voices: the masculine (logical and individualistic) and the feminine (interpersonal and utilitarian).

Erving Goffman (1922-1982) was an American sociologist known for studying symbolic interaction and dramaturgical analysis. According to Goffman, people's behavior varies based on the "stage" they are currently in. *Front stage* refers to the parts of our lives where we engage with people and put on a performance tailored for them. *Backstage* refers to times when we do not need to put on a show and can act like ourselves. Goffman developed impression management; a set of strategies people use to portray themselves to others in a certain way.

G. Stanley Hall (1846-1924) was an American psychologist and educator researching childhood development and evolutionary theory. Hall is famous for his interest in debunking psychic mediums by conducting rigorous psychological and physiological tests. On childhood development, Hall was interested in discovering the effects adolescence has on education (educational psychology) and the inheritance of behavior.

Harry Harlow (1905-1981) was an American psychologist researching caregiving and compassion in social and cognitive development. He conducted maternal separation, dependency needs, and social isolation experiments on rhesus monkeys. While his research successfully developed critical insights, its sometimes-cruel methods inspired the emergent animal liberation movement.

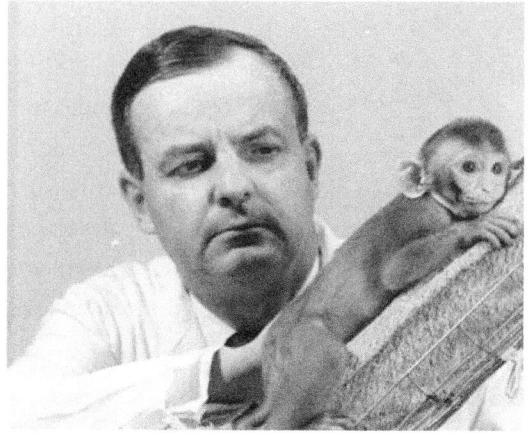

Ernest Hilgard (1904-2001) was an American psychologist famous for his hypnosis research. Specifically, Hilgard was interested in the applicability of hypnosis to control pain. Controversially, Hilgard promoted the idea of the "hidden observer," an entity that was a part of human consciousness created during hypnosis that allows the subject to be aware of physical sensations but not to feel or experience them directly (such as suffering).

David Hubel (1926-2013) was a Canadian neurophysiologist who researched the structure and function of the visual cortex (a portion of the brain responsible for processing visual information) and shared the Nobel Prize with *Torsen Nils Wiesel* in 1981. In one of their famous experiments, Hubel and Wiesel surgically inserted a microelectrode into the primary visual cortex of a domestic cat. By projecting light and dark patterns on a screen in front of the animal and observing neuron behavior, they observed how simple stimulus features provide the basis for visual systems to construct complex representations.

William James (1842-1910) was an American psychologist and philosopher. He is the "father of American psychology" for his contributions to the field. James founded functional psychology, a school that considers thoughts and behaviors as adaptive responses to the environment.

Mary Cover Jones (1897-1987) was an American psychologist who helped pioneer behavior therapy. She developed desensitization techniques to cure phobias, notably through her "Little Peter" experiment, in which she treated a three-year-old boy's irrational fear of white rabbits (and any objects approximating one in appearance) by direct conditioning (through which a positive stimulus comes to be associated with the phobia trigger).

Carl Jung (1875-1961) was a Swiss psychiatrist, psychotherapist, and founder of analytical psychology (of which the central concept is individuation, the process of integrating opposites while maintaining their relative autonomy). He is famous for creating the psychological concepts of the archetype, the collective unconscious, the complex, extraversion, and introversion. His work has had a broad, lasting effect on anthropology, archaeology, literature, philosophy, psychiatry, and religious studies.

Alfred Kinsey (1894-1956) was an American biologist, entomologist, sexologist, and zoologist known for his contributions to the field of sexology. In 1948, he published *The Kinsey Reports on Human Sexual Behavior*, two widely cited volumes discussing sexual behaviors. Kinsey gathered information through face-to-face interviews, believing they were the best way to get accurate data. Kinsey developed a heterosexual/homosexual rating scale, a measure still sometimes used today.

Lawrence Kohlberg (1927-1987) was an American psychologist and educator. Kohlberg is best known for his theory on the stages of moral development. According to Kohlberg, individuals go through six stages of moral development. In the earlier stages, individuals engage in moral behaviors by doing what will allow them to avoid punishment and receive benefits. As they develop to later stages, individuals engage in moral behavior out of a sense of universal ethical principles.

Wolfgang Köhler (1887-1967) was a German-American psychologist critical in creating Gestalt psychology (a holistic attitude toward psychology). He played an essential role in the study of problem-solving and introspection. His quote embodies his professional perspective, "The whole is different from the sum of its parts" (often misquoted as "greater than").

Carl Lange (1834-1900) was a Danish physician known for his work *On Emotions: A Psycho-Physiological Study*, which gave rise to the *James-Lange theory* of emotion. This theory states that emotions result from physiological responses to stimuli.

Elizabeth Loftus (born 1944) is an American cognitive psychologist and human memory expert known for her work on the misinformation effect, eyewitness memory, false memories, and recovered memories.

Konrad Lorenz (1903-1989) was an Austrian ethologist, ornithologist, and zoologist. He studied birds, which revealed the *imprinting principle* (newborn nidifugous birds' bonding with the first moving object they see) and the *innate releasing mechanism* (a fixed action pattern by which certain external sensory stimuli result in instinctive behavior). Collaborating with biologist Nikolaas Tinbergen, Lorenz helped establish ethology as a biology sub-discipline.

Abraham Maslow (1908-1970) was an American psychologist known for his *Hierarchy of Needs* diagram. This model states that individuals must fulfill their most pressing needs before moving on to higher needs. According to Maslow, physiological needs are the most pressing, followed by safety, belonging, esteem, and self-actualization. Maslow studied "peak experiences." Self-actualized individuals would experience profound moments of happiness, termed *peak experiences*.

Robert R. McCrae (born 1949) is an American personality psychologist best known for his cross-age and cross-culture study of personality stability. Further, he proposed that personality is a biological trait, and his findings showed that upon age 30, the Five-Factor Theory's traits of agreeableness and conscientiousness tend to increase while neuroticism and extroversion decline. A curve shape peaking near age 19 marks openness to experience.

Robert Michels (1876-1936) was a German sociologist and student of Max Weber. He is known for his theories that contributed to *elite theory*. Michels proposed the *iron law of oligarchy*, a political theory claiming that rule by an elite is inevitable within any democratic organization.

Stanley Milgram (1933-1984) was an American social psychologist and educator known for obedience research. In his famous experiment, volunteer participants were told they were partaking in a study examining memory. Participants were instructed to administer shocks to Milgram's confederate (pretend volunteers) whenever they answered questions incorrectly. The confederate was not receiving shocks. Whenever participants seemed disturbed by the confederate's "pain" and wanted to stop, the experimenter provided strong verbal encouragement to continue. Milgram found that 65% of participants would persist until they had administered the final "shock" of 450 volts. Milgram concluded that most individuals lack the cognitive resources to resist authority.

George Armitage Miller (1920-2012) was an American psychologist best remembered as one of the founding minds behind psycholinguistics and cognitive science. Miller is credited with discoveries on human short-term memory capacity limitations.

Ivan Pavlov (1849-1936) was a Russian physiologist renowned for breakthrough discoveries in *classical conditioning*. His famous experiment, inspired by observing dogs salivate before the food is given, first demonstrated the relationship between environmental stimuli and behavioral responses. From this experiment came the term *"conditioned reflex,"* an innate response resulting from a previously neutral stimulus that, over time, had been inculcated (where, before, a potent stimulus was required).

Jean Piaget (1896-1980) was a Swiss psychologist known for his theory of cognitive development. Piaget identified four stages of cognitive development: a sensorimotor stage, a preoperational stage, a concrete operational stage, and a formal operational stage. He proposed that the cognitive processes of children are inherently different from those of adults.

Robert A. Rescorla (born 1940) is an American psychologist whose research is primarily concerned with cognitive processes and classical conditioning. He is famous for his involvement in developing the Rescorla-Wagner Model of conditioning with Allan R. Wagner, which has deeply enriched knowledge of the learning processes.

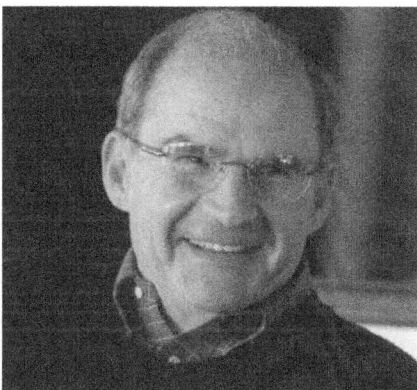

George Ritzer (born 1940) is an American sociologist known for "McDonaldization." Ritzer identified four dimensions of McDonald's that have influenced society; efficiency, calculability, predictability, and control.

Carl Rogers (1902-1987) was an American psychologist. He helped establish the humanistic approach and psychotherapy research. Roger called his humanistic approach *person-centered therapy* (PCT), which aims to allow clients to develop a sense of self and become perceptive about how their attitudes, feelings, and behavior are being negatively affected.

Julian Rotter (1916-2014) was an American psychologist. Rotter developed the *locus of control* concept and *social learning theory*. He identified that some individuals believe they can control events affecting them, and some believe outside forces cause them. Those who believe they can control events affecting them have an *internal locus of control*. In contrast, those who do not believe they have any control over them have an *external locus of control*.

Stanley Schachter (1922-1997) was an American psychologist known for developing the Schachter-Singer model of emotion. This model proposes that emotions result from physiological arousal and the cognitive label assigned to this reaction.

Hans Selye (1907-1982) was an Austrian-Canadian endocrinologist known for his work on stress and the stress response. He coined the term "stress" and found that the physical stress response was the same for positive and negative stressors.

Muzafer Sherif (1906-1988) was a Turkish-American psychologist and founder of modern social psychology. He is known for his *social judgment theory* and *realistic conflict theory*. *Social judgment theory* is a framework for studying human judgment that proposes that people weigh innovative ideas at the instant of perception. They then categorize these ideas based on their preferred position, the alternatives, and the level of ego involvement with issues. *Realistic conflict theory* proposes that deviance and hostility result from competition over resources.

B. F. Skinner (1904-1990) was an American behaviorist, psychologist, inventor, social philosopher, and innovator of radical behaviorism. Skinner developed the principle of reinforcement and the term *operant conditioning*.

Charles Spearman (1863-1945) was an English statistician and psychologist known for promoting factor analysis, developing Spearman's rank correlation coefficient, and researching models for human intelligence.

Roger Wolcott Sperry (1913-1994) was an American neurobiologist and neuropsychologist. His early research focused on efforts to rearrange motor and sensory nerves. Later and more famously, he researched with Torsten Wiesel on the split-brain condition. This led to the discovery that cutting the corpus callosum portion of the brain prevents epileptic seizures from migrating from one hemisphere of the brain to the other.

Robert Sternberg (born 1949) is an American psychologist and psychometrician. He developed the *triarchic theory of intelligence,* and his work related to creativity, love and hate, thinking styles, and wisdom. His triarchic theory of intelligence consists of a componential, experiential, and practical part.

Lewis Terman (1877-1956) was an American psychologist noted for his early commitment to the emergent educational psychology movement. He is known for his study of intelligence, including his Stanford-Binet IQ test revision and development of the Genetic Studies of Genius.

Edward Thorndike (1874-1949) was an American psychologist known for developing connectionism and inspiring the emergence of educational psychology. He influenced *reinforcement theory* and *behavior analysis* through his *law of effect* principle, which holds that "responses that produce a satisfying effect in a particular situation become more likely to occur again in that situation, and responses that produce a discomforting effect become less likely to occur again in that situation."

Edward C. Tolman (1886-1959) was an American behaviorist and psychologist renowned for founding purposive behaviorism and promoting Hugh Blodgett's concept of latent learning. His best-remembered experiments involved rats placed in mazes to prove that animals can learn facts that they can use flexibly (instead of simply acquiring automatic responses triggered by environmental stimuli).

Lev Vygotsky (1896-1934) was a Russian-Jewish psychologist renowned for cognitive development, emphasizing the importance of sociocultural factors. Vygotsky developed the concept of a zone of proximal development. According to Vygotsky, individuals best learn tasks they cannot do independently but can complete with guidance.

Margaret Floy Washburn (1871-1939) was an American psychologist whose research focused on animal behavior and cognition. She developed the *motor theory of speech perception* and legitimized the study of mental events (the unseen), believing that they are just as important as behavioral events (the seen).

John B. Watson (1878-1958) was an American psychologist known for establishing behaviorism, which intended to shift analysis emphasis from the internal mental state of people to their external behavior because it promotes an objective method. He studied emotions, language, speech, and memory. In his controversial "Little Albert" experiment, Watson conditioned a child who was initially unafraid of a white rat to demonstrate fear of the animal by clanging a metal rod whenever the creature was presented. Eventually, no accompanying loud noise was needed to induce fear.

Ernst Heinrich Weber (1795-1878) was a German physician best remembered for helping establish experimental psychology. His research primarily centered on sensation and touch. Some of his more praised contributions include just-noticeable difference, Weber's Law, *experimental wave theory*, hydrodynamics, the two-point threshold technique, and Weber's illusion.

Max Weber (1864-1920) was a German sociologist and a founder of sociology. He is known for his thesis on the Protestant ethic and his model of bureaucracy. Weber identified six characteristics of an ideal bureaucracy and believed that bureaucracies were the ideal model for government agencies.

David Wechsler (1896-1981) was an American psychologist renowned for his research on intelligence and his development of intelligence scales (e.g., the Wechsler Adult Intelligence Scale (WAIS) and the Wechsler Intelligence Scale for Children (WISC)).

Carl Wernicke (1848-1905) was a German anatomist, physician, and psychiatrist that researched aphasia. This work revealed areas of the brain besides Broca's area where damage can affect speech and language.

Torsten Nils Wiesel (born 1924) is a Swedish neurophysiologist. He is known for his contribution to the study of sensory processing and his collaborations with David Hubel on ocular dominance columns. They were awarded the Nobel Prize in 1981 for their research.

Joseph Wolpe (1915-1997) was a South African psychiatrist. He is known for being a critical advocate for behavior therapy and his innovative approach to treating soldiers experiencing post-traumatic stress disorder (PTSD). Seeing few successful treatment outcomes were using the then-predominant approach of administrating drugs to encourage discussion of traumatizing events, Wolpe developed his alternative Reciprocal Inhibition techniques.

Wilhelm Wundt (1832-1920) was a German philosopher, physician, physiologist, and professor. Regarded as one of modern psychology's founding figures, Wundt established the first laboratory dedicated to psychological research. Subjects he studied included the nature of religious beliefs, mental disorders, abnormal behavior, brain damage, and the three areas of mental functioning (thoughts, perception, and feelings).

Philip Zimbardo (born 1933) is an American psychologist and professor known for his Stanford "prison" experiment. In this experiment, 24 students declared sane were randomly assigned to the roles of prisoner or guard. The guards were not given instructions on how to treat the prisoners. After only six days, the experiment was stopped due to the guards' cruel behavior. Zimbardo concluded that situational influences could make people act in cruel ways.

Annotated Glossary of Psychology Terms

The study of psychology spreads across disciplines and helps understand aspects of the mind related to health, human development, sports, media, law, and even industry. Psychology terms are a learning resource for studying the different concepts included in psychology.

A

A-B-A design (*experimental design*) – participants first experience the baseline condition (A), then the experimental treatment (B), and then return to the baseline (A).

Abience – an urge to withdraw or avoid a situation or an object.

Abductive reasoning – showing a connection between unrelated facts and using intuitive (without conscious reasoning) thinking. Induction and deduction are the states that succeed.

Ablation – surgical removal of brain tissue, aids identification of brain localization.

Abnormal – behaviors and mental illnesses that are unusual and atypical.

Abnormal behavior – atypical and regarded by society as deviant or maladaptive. *Diagnostic and Statistical Manua*l (DSM) requires an individual to suffer or have maladaptive functioning for behavior to be classified as abnormal.

Abnormal psychology – an empirical study that describes, explains, and predicts abnormal behavior; concerned with unusual and atypical behavior. It is a broad subject covering depression, obsession, compulsion, and sexual deviation. Addresses disorders, deviations, or abnormal behavior.

Abnormality – a behavioral attribute reflecting deviation of the mind from its normal state or typical behavior; subjective concept may be reflected in different forms.

Abreaction (*psychoanalytical*) – reliving an experience to purge its emotional baggage.

Absent-mindedness – 1. a low level of attention (*blanking* or *zoning out*), 2. intense attention to a single object of focus (*hyperfocus*) that makes a person oblivious to events around them, or 3. unwarranted distraction of attention from the object of focus by irrelevant thoughts or environmental events.

Absolute poverty – a life-threatening deprivation of resources; living on, or just above, the margin of survival (i.e., not having enough money to afford the necessities of life).

Absolute refractory period – neuron is dormant immediately after an action potential; no additional stimulation can prompt an all-or-none response until repolarization.

Absolute threshold – the minimum energy required for a sensory experience. The minimum amount of physical energy needed to produce a reliable sensory experience is operationally defined as the stimulus level at which a sensory signal is detected half the time.

　　　　　　　　　　　　　　　　397

Abstinence syndrome (or *withdrawal*) – physically painful and unpleasant symptoms (e.g., vomiting, shaking, headaches, convulsions) suffered by a physically dependent drug user as the drug wears off.

Abstract – existing only in mind; separated from embodiment; "abstractions 'truth' and 'justice.'"

Abstraction – retaining relevant information required for generalizing it. In the process of abstraction, the original information is extracted or summarized to form a reduced resultant content.

Aboulia – in this state, the subject cannot make decisions or take the initiative.

Abuse – treating oneself with harm; subjected to abuse could be a person, substance, idea, item, or vocabulary. Child abuse, elder abuse, animal abuse, and drug abuse are examples.

Acceptance and commitment therapy (*cognitive-behavioral therapy*) – increasing psychological flexibility as a psychological intervention based on observational, experimental, and experiential information collection methods.

Accessibility – in long-term memory, remembering and forgetting depend on effective retrieval; without the proper cues, information in long-term memory may not be accessible.

Accommodation (*Piaget's theory of cognitive development*) – changing schemas when added information cannot be assimilated. Accepting information, ideas, and experiences alters existing schemas or thoughts. Restructuring cognitive structures so that new information can fit into them more easily works in tandem with assimilation.

Accommodation (*vision*) – the process by which the shape of an eye's lens adjusts to focus light from objects nearby or far away.

Accreditation – a process to certify authority, competency, or credibility.

Acetylcholine – neurotransmitter for muscle movement, attention, memory, and emotion.

Acetylcholine – a brain neurotransmitter crucial for regulating memory (loss of acetylcholine has been implicated in Alzheimer's disease*)* and in the peripheral nervous system, where it activates the actions of muscles.

Achievement motivation – the inclination to persevere with complex or demanding tasks.

Achievement motive – an impulse to master challenges; striving for a standard of excellence.

Achievement test – measures skills and knowledge that people have already learned.

Acquired immune deficiency syndrome (AIDS) – a deadly disease caused by the *human immunodeficiency virus* (HIV), weakening immunity and lowering resilience to infection.

Acquisition (*classical conditioning*) – the stage in a classical conditioning experiment during which the conditioned stimulus first elicits the conditioned response.

Acrostic – a phrase in which each word begins with a letter acting as a memory cue.

ACT-R (*Adaptive Control of Thought-Rational*) – a cognitive architecture developed at Carnegie Mellon University, defines the mind's perceptual and irreducible operations to complete a task.

Acting out – an action performed by impulsive behavior rather than constructively responding. Such actions are anti-social, and the person might end up causing harm to themself or others.

Action potential – nerve impulse traveling the axon and triggers the release of neurotransmitters into a synapse, a short-lived change in electric charge inside a neuron.

Action research – aimed at improving problem-solving. It is an introspective process that emphasizes improving the practices, strategies, and knowledge of the group or system's environment. For action research to be fruitful, combined efforts of people striving towards a common goal are required.

Action science (1974) – focuses on practical solutions to problems by generating knowledge. Chris Argyris developed it with Robert Putnam, Donald Schon, and Diana McLain Smith.

Action slips – absent-mindedness when a person performs an unintended action caused by not paying attention to what is happening.

Activation-synthesis theory – neurons in the brain activate randomly during REM sleep.

Active intellect – the formal aspect of the mind or intellect; it is used in philosophical studies and aligns with the theory of hylomorphism. Aristotle first cited the idea of active intellect in the book *De Anima*.

Active learning – instruction models emphasizing encouraging the learners to take responsibility for learning. The concept of active learning originated and developed from discovery learning.

Active listening – a feature of patient-centered therapy involving empathetic listening, by which the therapist echoes, restates, and clarifies what the patient says.

Activity theory – individuals prefer to remain active and productive in later life, even resisting disengagement from society. Contrast social disengagement theory. Engagement and interaction with the environment result in the creation of tools, which are the real-world manifestation of their mental processes. These tools make mental processes communicable and accessible to people.

Actor *vs.* observer biases – the tendency for 1. actors to explain their behavior in situational terms and 2. observers to explain the behavior of others in dispositional (person) terms.

Actualization (*Abraham Maslow*) – realizing one's potential. According to Maslow, actualization is the final stage of psychological development after all basic and mental needs are fulfilled. Kurt Goldstein (1878-1965), an organismic theorist, introduced psychology theories.

Actualizing tendency (*Rogers's theory*) – an innate drive reflecting the desire to grow, develop, and enhance capacities.

Acute stress – a transient state of tension-arousal with typical onset and offset patterns.

Adaptation – 1. an organism evolves by natural selection (1859) to enhance fitness. 2. adapting life to medicine or being forced to change habits without medicine. *For example, sedatives to manage a stressful life.*

Adaptation – an inherited characteristic increase in a population because it provides a survival or reproductive advantage.

Adaptive behaviors – actions that increase reproductive success, adjusting to new situations. Often used to substitute disruptive behavior with constructive or positive behavior.

Adaptive Control of Thought-Rational (ACT-R) – a cognitive architecture developed at Carnegie Mellon University, defines the mind's perceptual and irreducible operations to complete a task.

Additive strategy – listing the attributes of each decision element, weighing them according to importance, adding them, and determining which is most appealing based on results.

Addiction – excessive psychological dependence on a thing.; physical dependence associated with adverse effects, such as social functioning. *For example, a person could be addicted to drugs, money, work, gambling, eating, nicotine, or video games.*

Adience (*psychology*) – an urge to accept or approach a situation or an object.

Adjustment – balancing conflicting needs, a behavioral attribute found in humans and animals; overcoming obstacles the environment presents to fulfill personal needs.

Adjustment disorder – when an individual cannot make the necessary adjustments to fulfill the needs and overcome stress-related problems.

Adler, Alfred (1870-1937) – Austrian physician and psychologist, initially influenced by Freud, and later developed his theory of personality and psychotherapy through "individual psychology." Adler strongly believed in treating each patient holistically as a "whole person," his ideas have been applied to psychology, including cognitive behavioral therapy and holistic psychology.

Adolescent psychology – interests and issues about adolescents are addressed in the discipline of adolescent psychology. The emotional issues faced in adolescence, i.e., during the transitional stage between childhood and adulthood, are studied under this science.

Adoption – proceeding with creating a parent-child relationship.

Adoption studies – researchers examine trait similarities between adopted children and their biological and adoptive parents to determine whether that trait might be inherited. Demonstrate the influence of genetics (as opposed to the environment) by comparing the correlations between adopted children and their biological parents or adoptive parents on a measurable trait. *For example, intelligence.*

Adorno, Theodor (1903-1969) – German-born psychologist who researched authoritarian personality traits with the Fascism Scale (F-Scale) was a philosopher, sociologist, and composer. Defined the authoritarian personality (i.e., intolerance of ambiguity, prejudiced attitudes, and conformity to authority, emphasizing childhood experiences and internalization) and the subsequent development of the F-scale (a measurement of the authoritarian personality).

Adrenal cortex – the outer part of the adrenal glands, which secretes corticosteroids.

Adrenal glands – endocrine glands just above the kidneys, essential in arousal and stress. The *cortex* (outer layer) secretes corticosteroids, and the *medulla* (inner core) secretes epinephrine(adrenaline) and norepinephrine(noradrenaline).

Adrenal medulla – the inner part of the adrenal glands secretes catecholamines.

Adrenocorticotropic hormone (ACTH) – released by the anterior pituitary during stressful situations and triggers the release of corticosteroid hormones from the adrenal cortex. Corticosteroids produce effects on the stress response.

Advanced Placement Psychology (*AP Psychology*) – a course for high school students interested in studying psychology administered by the College Board (USA).

Advertising – seeks to influence consumer attitudes and behavior through persuasive techniques. *For example, the use of fear appeals.*

Affect – emotion or mood (e.g., sadness); feelings or experiences associated with emotion. Within abnormal psychology, patients may display distinct affect disturbance (e.g., blunted, flat, or inappropriate affect). In other contexts, the act of displaying or exhibiting emotions through gestures or facial expressions.

Affect display – the exhibition of emotions through gestures, facial expressions, or vocalizations (laughing, crying), essential for interpersonal communication.

Affectional bond (*John Bowlby*) – the attachment between two individuals, displayed through their behavior. *For example, mother and child.* Bowlby named the behavior, and it evolved between the 1940s and 1970s.

Affectional orientation – defines feeling or emotion that directs a person to fall in love with another. It is a broad term that includes many other emotions, including sexual orientation.

Affectionless psychopathy (*John Bowlby*) – when a person displays little remorse or guilt for their unfavorable actions.

Affective disorder (or *mood disorder*) – the disturbances in a person's mood grouped under a common; replaces *mood disorder* since it explains external reflection of expressions caused by underlying emotional disturbances. Mood disorders, however, reflect a person's mental or emotional state precisely.

Affective flattening (or *blunted affect*) – a condition in which a person does not exhibit emotional reactivity. *For example, behaviors include hypervigilance, recurring nightmares, and stress avoidance.*

Affective forecasting (*cognitive biases*) – one's emotional state of the future. Systematic errors in thought processes cause suffering from affective forecasting.

Affective science (*scientific study of emotions***)** – the neurological and physiological aspects of mood, decision-making, emotionally driven behavior, self-regulation, and attention are studied. The subjects or components studied are recognition of emotion, emotional experience, and emotion elicitation.

Afferent nerves – the communication of the senses experienced by the body is conveyed to the central nervous system by afferent neurons for processing. Bundles of neurons carry signals from muscles and sense organs to the central nervous system (CNS).

Affiliation – the desire of people to associate with others.

Afterburn (Eric Berne, *the father of transactional analysis*) – past events influence an individual's mental state and daily activities.

Afterimage – a color perceived after another color is removed; an optical illusion when an individual sees the image after it has been removed from sight. The afterimage of a light bulb is a typical example observed in day-to-day life. The persistence of vision is related to afterimage since a rapid portrayal of pictures in a series causes an illusion of a continuous motion picture.

Age regression – a technique of many therapies, including hypnotherapy. The therapy aims to find information about the personality that is challenging to access. An individual tries to access memory, taking them to an earlier phase of life.

Age of viability – when a fetus may survive outside the mother if born prematurely.

Ageism stereotyping and discrimination against the elderly, similar to racism and sexism in its use of negative stereotypes.

Agency – the belief that humans are free to make decisions and control their lives.

Agency theory (*Milgram*, 1963) – people obey orders against their conscience. Experimental theory by Milgram demonstrates that a person acts in an *Agentic State* (devoid of free will) or an *Autonomous State* (based on one's thoughts and inclinations). *For example, when people envision themselves as agents of another, they will obey that person's orders, feeling free of individual responsibility.*

Agentic state – when a person acts on another's behalf without free will. Opposite to *Autonomous State.*

Aggression – behavior intending harm or pain to another; reflected in mental, verbal, and physical forms. Assertiveness is often confused with *aggression.*

Aging – the accumulation of change; changes are psychological, physiological, and social. In psychology, aging results in the expansion of knowledge and wisdom.

Agitated depression – a state of mind with symptoms of depression and mania simultaneously. A person might display impulsiveness, irritability, guilt, anxiety, fatigue, agitation, paranoia, or panic.

Agitation – the excitement of emotions; extreme agitation is *psychomotor agitation.*

Agnosia – inability to recognize objects by the senses; it is the state when an individual cannot identify or recognize persons, objects, shapes, sounds, or smells. It is a neurological disorder that results from damage to the occipitotemporal border, a part of the ventral stream. The condition is, however, not associated with memory loss or any impairment of sensory organs.

Agonists – chemicals mimic the action of a neurotransmitter.

Agoraphobia – anxiety disorder in which a person feels anxiety about experiencing panic attacks in public and, therefore, avoids public situations. A disorder involving anxiety about situations from which escape would be difficult or embarrassing or where there might be no help if a panic attack occurred.

Agreeableness (*Big Five Personality Trait*) – personality trait of appeasing and agreeing.

AIDS (*acquired immune deficiency syndrome*) – caused by the *human immunodeficiency virus* (HIV) virus, damaging immunity, and weakening the body's ability to fight infection.

Aims (*research*) – the general investigative purpose of the study.

Akathisia – when an individual cannot remain motionless; a manifestation of side effects of medicines (e.g., phenothiazines, butyrophenones, thioxanthene) or Parkinson's.

Alarm reaction – see *general adaptation syndrome.*

Alcohol amnestic disorder (or *Korsakoff's syndrome*) – amnesiac common in chronic alcoholics, a deficiency of thiamine (vitamin B_1) with symptoms including retrograde amnesia, anterograde amnesia, confabulation, apathy, and lack of insight.

Alcoholism (or *dipsomania*) – physical dependency on alcohol; a disorder in which a person resorts to compulsive alcohol consumption and loses the ability to recognize its adverse effects. Side effects of alcoholism include stress and degeneration of emotional health.

Alexia – an acquired form of dyslexia; the person loses the ability to read.

Alexithymia – when a person faces problems in dealing with emotions. The person loses their ability to understand and convey emotions.

Alienation – the disintegration of perceptual and cognitive powers of the mind.

Alienist (or *psychiatrist*) – certified to treat mental disorders and has received proper training for diagnostic evaluation and psychotherapy.

Algorithm – a step-by-step procedure providing the correct answer for a problem.

All-or-none law – the magnitude of the action potential is unaffected by increased stimulation intensity beyond the threshold level. Neurons generate an action potential only if stimulation reaches a minimum threshold.

Allophilia (*positive attitudes*) – liking or love felt for people despite being from different races, religions, nationalities, classes, and genders. An antonym for negative prejudices, racism, classicism, speciesism, ageism, and phallocentrism.

Alogia (*poverty of speech*) – a condition in which a person cannot speak fluently. It is one of the symptoms observed in people with schizophrenia. The inability to speak fluently makes it challenging to treat alogia.

Alpha bias – theories and research assuming fundamental and enduring differences between men and women. Beta bias theories and research have traditionally ignored or minimized differences between men and women.

Alpha waves – the average brain wave pattern (between eight to thirteen cycles per second) while in a relaxed, wakeful, or meditative state.

Altered states of awareness – differ from ordinary waking awareness; examples include meditation, sleep, drug-induced states, and psychosis.

Altered state of consciousness (*Charles Tart*, 1969) – the state of mind that has undergone a temporary change and deviates from everyday consciousness. *For example, it is induced by hypnosis, meditation, sleep, or a mental disorder such as Major Depressive Disorder. Beta waves designate altered brain activity during this phase.*

Alternate-forms reliability – a test producing the same results when different versions are administered to the same group.

Alternative hypothesis – a testable statement of the study's expected result, specifying the independent variable's effect upon the dependent variable, based on the researcher's knowledge from observations, related studies, and previous investigations.

Altruism – an act of goodwill towards another, either selflessly or with the expectation of a return of the favor. The quality of unselfish concern for the welfare of others. Prosocial behaviors a person carries out without considering safety or interests.

Altruism (animal) – engaging in altruistic behavior when, by so doing, it increases the survival chances of another animal while decreasing its own.

Altruism (human) – involves costs and benefits to the recipient. Unlike animal altruism, there is often evidence of 'kindly intent' on the part of the altruist.

Alzheimer's disease – a degenerative brain disorder with gradual memory loss, deteriorating cognitive skills, increasing disorientation, and reduced intellectual ability. Memory loss associated with difficulty remembering facts learned recently is linked to the deterioration of acetylcholine pathways in the brain. The patient becomes irritable and aggressive in advanced stages and faces mood swings.

Amacrine cells – integrate information across the retina rather than sending signals toward the brain. Amacrine cells link bipolar cells to other bipolar cells and ganglion cells to other ganglion cells.

Ambiguity – a perceptual object with more than one interpretation.

Ambiguous figure – a stimulus perceived in multiple ways.

Ambiguous language – can be understood in several ways.

Ambivalence – a state of mind in which a person has mixed emotions or conflicting feelings towards a thing or person. A person in this mental state experiences emotions or thoughts of positive and negative valence. *For example, expressions such as 'sitting on the fence' and 'cold feet' describe the condition or state of ambivalence.*

Ambivalent – uncertain or unable to decide about what course to follow.

Ambiversion – a balanced disposition intermediate between extroversion and introversion.

American Psychological Association (APA) – the largest professional organization of psychologists in the United States, with over 140,000 scientists, educators, clinicians, consultants, and students.

American Sign Language – manual-visual language system that uses gestures for the hearing-impaired.

Amnesia – memory loss due to brain damage or psychological trauma. The causes of memory loss could range from trauma and brain injury to the use of sedative drugs. Psychological factors like defense mechanisms are the functional cause. One example is hysterical post-traumatic amnesia. Amnesia commonly observed in middle-aged people is spontaneous. *Anterograde amnesia* is the inability to learn and remember new information after brain damage; retrograde amnesia is the loss of memories before brain damage.

Amok (Filipino, *mad with rage*) – commonly used in the context of 'running amok' or violent or wild behavior. A person who runs amok (out of control) tends to injure or kill others.

Amphetamine delusional disorder – results from excessive use of amphetamines; its primary symptom, extreme paranoid delusions, can make it appear symptomatically identical to paranoid schizophrenia.

Amplitude – the height of a wave.

Amygdala – a part of the brain's limbic system that regulates aggression and emotions, particularly fear. An almond-shaped neural anterior temporal lobe structure of the cerebrum, connected with the hypothalamus and hippocampus, and the cingulate gyrus as part of the limbic system, is vital in motivation and emotional behavior.

Anal personality (*Freud's theory of psychosexual development*) – an adult who has remained 'fixated' during the anal stage and displays an anally retentive personality, characterized by obsessive cleanliness, stinginess, and aggressiveness because of excessive or insufficient gratification of id impulses during the anal stage. The person is focused on meticulous neatness, suspicion, and reserve, said to be formed in early childhood by fixation during the anal stage of development (usually because of toilet training).

Anal-retentive – a personality in which a person is obsessed with extra importance placed on details.

Anally retentive (*commonly abbreviated anal*) – a person with diligence that obsession becomes an annoyance to others and can be detrimental to the person.

Anal stage (*Freud's Stages of Psychosexual Development*) – follows the Oral Stage (birth until the first year) and up to age 3. A preoccupation with oral satisfaction, such as feeding, is superseded by satisfaction from defecation. The child faces ego, id, and super-ego conflicts during this phase. This phase of life is associated with toilet training. Successful completion of this stage depends on the interaction of parents with the children. Disruption at this stage can lead to anal fixation with anally retentive personalities showing signs of obsessive orderliness, while anally expulsive types may be messy or disorganized later.

Anal stage (*Freud's theory of psychosexual development*) – the second stage, from 15 months to 3 years. A child's leading source of pleasure is the anus.

Analogy (*cognition*) – transferring information from the source (or analog subject) to the target subject; a linguistic expression for information transference. Necessary for problem-solving, perception, decision-making, memory, explanation, emotion, and communication.

Analysand (or *psychoanalysis*) – a patient of psychoanalysis; studies human psychological behavior and functioning. Investigating the mind to treat psychological illnesses and as a set of systematized theories of human behavior.

Analytical psychology (*Jungian psychology*) – apprehension and integration of the underlying motivations and deep forces of human behavior is the prime objective of practicing analytical psychology. Emphasizes the interplay between oppositional forces within the psyche and how these internal conflicts affect personality development. Studying the accumulative phenomenology and significance of folklore, dreams, and mythology helps achieve the objective.

Analytical psychodrama – uses three activities or concepts (i.e., role-playing, observation of mental activities, and use of transfer for treatment.

Analysis of variance (ANOVA) (or *covariation principle*) – individuals attribute behavior to a causal factor if it existed while the behavior occurred but not when it did not occur.

Anchoring – the mind's tendency to use just one piece of information for decisions.

Anchoring heuristic – an insufficient adjustment up or down from an original starting value when judging the probable value of some event or outcome.

Androcentrism – the tendency of some theories to interpret women based on an understanding of men. See *alpha/beta bias*.

Androgens – hormones related to masculinity; the most important is testosterone.

Androgynous – having male and female characteristics; partly male and partly female.

Androgyny – gender role identity where an individual has male and female (personality) characteristics.

Anger – the state of being very annoyed.

Anger management – therapy encourages looking at anger differently, often involving relaxation to prevent anger. Teaches individuals how to apply self-control to reduce anger against others.

Anhedonia – when a person cannot derive pleasure from day-to-day activities like exercise, eating, or social interaction.

Animal cognition – capabilities of non-human animals; researchers trace the development of cognitive capabilities across species and continuity from nonhumans to humans.

Animal language – 1. attempts to teach nonhuman animals to speak or 2. studies of animal language in their natural environment.

Animal research – using non-human animals in empirical research based on greater control, objectivity, and similar genetic makeup. However, using non-human animals has raised many ethical and moral questions.

Anima (*Jungian archetype*) – the inner self in touch with the unconscious. It represents qualities considered idealized feminine attributes, such as compassion and sensitivity, and repressed in males. Conversely, *animus* in females represents masculine qualities.

Animal psychology – focused on the behavior of animals.

Animism – the belief that inanimate objects are alive and have life-like qualities such as feelings and intentions. Animism is characteristic of the child's egocentric reasoning – if the child has feelings and intentions, then so must all other things. A child may get angry and smack their bicycle because it 'made them get hurt.' Animism is characteristic in children in Piaget's second stage of intellectual development, the *pre-operational stage*.

Animus – see *Anima*.

Anonymity – a state within a crowd where each person loses their sense of individuality.

Anorexia nervosa (literally, *nervous loss of appetite*) – an eating disorder in which an individual weighs less than 85% of their expected weight and has a negative body image or fear of gaining weight. The person suffers from the fear of gaining weight. Characterized by the pursuit of extreme thinness and weight loss; refusal to maintain a body weight in the typical range, intense fear about gaining weight, and highly distorted body image.

ANS (*autonomic nervous system*) – part of the nervous system that maintains normal physiological functioning. ANS has two subdivisions: 1. sympathetic division, whose activity mobilizes energy resources and prepares the body for action, and 2. parasympathetic division, which conserves body energy resources and restores inner calm. Division of peripheral nervous system (PNS) connected to the heart, blood vessels, glands, and smooth muscles.

Antagonist – a substance hindering the activity of a biomolecule by reducing the amount available; chemicals blocking the action of biomolecules (e.g., neurotransmitter).

Antagonistic – opposition in physiological action.

Antecedent control (*behavioral*) – intervention occurs before the behavior arises. Antecedent procedures include education, attitude change, and inducing or preventing behaviors by controlling the triggers that cause them.

Anterior pituitary (or *master gland*) – the front portion of the pituitary, a small gland in the brain. Hormones secreted by the anterior pituitary influence growth, sexual development, skin pigmentation, thyroid, and adrenocortical function.

Anterograde amnesia – the inability to learn and remember information after brain damage; an inability to remember events after a brain injury or traumatic event.

Anthropomorphism – assigning human feelings and emotions to non-human animals.

Antianxiety drug – a central nervous system (CNS) depressant with the primary behavioral effect of anxiety reduction.

Anticipatory coping – efforts made before a potentially stressful event to overcome, reduce, or tolerate the imbalance between perceived demands and available resources.

Anticipatory socialization – learning how to perform a role one does not yet occupy.

Anti-conformity – behavior carried out to oppose the group's norms.

Antidepressants – a drug to treat clinical depression, primarily by enhancing the activity of the neurotransmitter serotonin.

Anti-inflammatory medication – reduces inflammation (i.e., the body's response to injury, irritation, or infection).

Anti-psychiatry – opposing classifying people with abnormal behavior or thoughts as mentally ill.

Antipsychotic drug – tranquilizer to treat psychotic conditions for a calming effect; treats psychotic symptoms, such as disordered thoughts, delusions, or hallucinations.

Antisocial personality behavior (or *psychopath*) – individuals lacking regard for others, are impulsive, and behave in a socially unacceptable manner; characterized by a lack of conscience and respect for other people's rights, feelings, and needs, beginning by age fifteen. Behavior that harms or offends another lacks consideration for others and a lack of judgment. *For example, a person might cause damage to the property of others. Such behavior is the manifestation of anti-social personality disorder.*

Anticathexis – the energy an individual derives from the superego controls the ego.

Anticipation – an emotion that involves pleasure or anxiety regarding an unexpected event. Depending on the event, emotions could be positive or associated with irritation. Per the psycho-evolutionary theory of Robert Plutchik, anticipation is one of eight basic emotions.

Antilocution (*talking behind someone's back*) – verbal remarks used against a person or community without addressing the target directly. Gordon Allport defined antilocution in his 1954 book *Nature of Prejudice*; it has far-reaching effects, causing the behavior to become prejudiced.

Antipathy – a strong feeling of dislike or aversion. The opposite of sympathy. Sometimes, a person exhibits antipathy without any apparent reason fitting a cause-and-effect explanation. The cause for a person exhibiting antipathy could be an experience of the past.

Anxiety – an intense emotional response caused by preconscious recognition that a repressed conflict is about to emerge into consciousness. It is a psychological state characterized by emotional, cognitive, behavioral, and somatic components. An unpleasant feeling associated with fear, uneasiness, stress, or worry; a vague unpleasant emotion in anticipation of a misfortune; a negative emotional state characterized by high physiological arousal, nervousness, or fear.

Anxiety disorders – the most common of adult mental disorders, characterized by severe anxiety, feelings of tension, and intense apprehension without apparent reason. An umbrella term for anxieties and fears included in psychiatry at the end of the 19th century. *Phobias* are common anxiety disorders.

APA (*American Psychological Association*) – the largest professional organization of psychologists in the United States, with over 140,000 scientists, educators, clinicians, consultants, and students.

Apathy – when a person suppresses their emotions like motivation, excitement, concern, and passion; exhibiting sluggishness and lacking interest in social, emotional, or physical life.

Aphanisis – the state in which a person loses sexual desire.

Aphasia – language impairment due to brain injury or lesions; it is a disorder in which language modality is impaired. In this acquired language disorder, the person cannot understand or produce written or spoken language.

Aphonia – an inability to produce normal speech sounds.

Apparent motion – an illusion when stationary lights going on and off in succession are perceived as a single moving light; the simplest apparent motion is the *phi phenomenon*.

Apperception – when an individual assimilates and transforms a new experience using the residuum of past experiences. Thus, it is the process of understanding the new experience with the help of prior experiences.

Application – using psychological knowledge in an applied or practical setting.

Applied behavior analysis – applying experimental behavioral principles to improve socially significant behavior.

Applied psychology – psychological principles to practical problems (e.g., education, industry, marketing). Using knowledge from psychological theories, studies, and experiments to help people overcome mental issues and other areas of life.

Appraisal (*psychology*) – judgment about whether a potentially stressful situation is threatening, challenging, or harmful; evaluating an environmental challenge to determine whether resources are available for dealing with it.

Approach-approach conflict –arises between two desirable alternatives.

Approach-avoidance conflict – when a situation has both positive and negative features. Such conflicts result from an emotional state of mind and *ambivalence*, causing stress.

Aptitude tests – measure a person's aptitude, knowledge, and skills; predict people's future ability to acquire skills or knowledge. Responses to sets of questions measure these attributes; used in education, psychology, counseling, and the military.

Archetype (*Jungian psychology*) – images or thoughts with the same meaning for all humans; patterns or frameworks within the collective unconscious organize experiences, providing the basis of many fantasies, myths, and symbols. Model concepts in the collective unconscious manifest as characters in cultural artifacts (e.g., paintings, myths, folk lures). Archetypes include the *Great Mother*, the *Trickster*, and the *Wise Old Man.*

Arousal – the body's level of alertness and activation as reflected in specific physiological responses such as heart rate or muscle tension.

Arteria cerebelli – an artery that supplies oxygenated blood to the cerebellum.

Arteria communicans – any of three brain arteries that comprise the *circle of Willis.*

Artificial creativity – the objective of artificial or computational creativity is to simulate, model, or replicate creativity using a computer. The purpose is to create a computer capable of human-level creativity, formulating an algorithmic perspective on human creative behavior and creating tools that help to enhance human creativity.

Artificial intelligence (AI) – in computer science, the attempt to build machines that can function intelligently and use such machines to evaluate understanding of human intelligence.

Asch, Solomon (1907-1996) – Polish psychologist studied human conformity in groups.

Asch effect – see *conformity* (majority influence).

Ascribed status – a social position that a person is born into.

Asian psychology – the ethnic psychological concepts related to an Asian setting are studied.

Asperger syndrome – difficulties in social interaction with repetitive and restricted behavior patterns as symptoms.

Assertiveness – a personality trait characterized by communicating without being afraid to speak one's mind. Assertive people defend their boundaries without being aggressive or passive.

Assimilation (*Piaget's theory of cognitive development*) – 1. fitting the latest information into existing schemas; broadening an existing schema to include added information. 2. bringing ethnic and racial diversity into a shared cultural fold, making them more alike or more like the dominant ethnic or racial group (i.e., melting pot).

Association – involves linking two concepts. *For example, drink-driving advertisements encourage the association of drink-driving with car accidents.*

Associationism – a theory that interconnection is the basic principle of mental activity.

Association areas – parts of the cortex that receive input from multiple sensory systems.

Association cortex – parts of the cerebral cortex where high-level brain processes occur.

Association theory – interconnection is the basic principle of mental activity.

Assumption – something taken for granted as being true.

Atherosclerosis – hardening of arteries because of cholesterol deposits.

Atkinson and Shiffrin's model of memory (or *multi-store model of memory*, 1968) – memory with three sequential stages: 1. short-term memory, 2. long-term memory (7+/- 2 "chunks" of information), and 3) sensory memory.

Atomism – a theory of reducing mental phenomena to simple elements (e.g., sensations and feelings) that form complex ideas by association.

Attachment disorders – the close bond between babies and caregivers; an inability to develop an attachment bond with the 'primary caregiving figures' during stages of childhood. This mood-related disorder results in problematic expectations and behavior in social life.

Attachment styles – include secure attachment, anxious-ambivalent attachment, and avoidant attachment.

Attachment theory (*John Bowlby's Attachment Theory*) – a bond formed in the initial stages of development between an infant and caregiver (e.g., a parent); a two-way bond between two individuals (humans or some animals), in which each individual gains a sense of security from the other. Behavior shows proximity to one another and results from the activity of several behavioral systems. Bowlby emphasized the importance of such attachments and claimed that the quality of such bonds has effects later in life. The study of human relationships from psychological, ethological, and evolutionary perspectives. Developmental psychology emphasizes forming a secure attachment between the infant and primary caregivers.

Attention (*cognition*) – focuses on a single aspect while ignoring the others, selectively focusing on stimulus elements, typically those deemed most significant.

Attention deficit disorder (ADD) – a neurological condition often evident from childhood. *ADD may cause restlessness, disorganization, hyperactivity, distractibility, and mood swings.*

Attention-deficit hyperactivity disorder (ADHD) – common in children with hyperactivity and attention problems. 3-5% of children are affected globally.

Attention span – when a person focuses on something without getting distracted.

Attentional processing (or *controlled processing*) – a conscious mental operation, relatively slow and easily interrupted; requires attention; often difficult to perform more than one controlled process at a time.

Attenuator model of attention (*Ann Treisman*, 1964) – instead of selecting one channel and blocking the others, the filtering mechanism (a) selects one channel and passes it on for semantic analysis and (b) allows the unattended channels through for processing but in weakened (attenuated) form.

Attitudes – the learned, relatively stable tendency to respond to people, concepts, and events evaluatively. Evaluations people make about objects, ideas, events, or others. Attitude is associated with positive or negative views that a person has about places, events, or other people altogether. Denotes the degree of like or dislike an individual exhibits for a thing; a personal belief of an evaluative nature, such as good or bad, likable or not likable, influences reactions toward people or things.

Attractiveness – the quality of arousing interest.

Attribution – judgments about the causes of outcomes.

Attribution (of causality) – the causes of behavior according to a set of cognitive rules. As a result of these strategies, behavior caused by stable characteristics results from situational influences.

Attribution theory (*social psychology*) – a social-cognitive approach describing how social perceivers use information to generate causal explanations. Inferences people make about the causes of events and behavior; how an individual describes or explains the cause of events, behavior, and behaviors of others associated with the events. The study of how people try to explain their behavior and those around them; explain causes of behavior as dispositional (personality) factors or situational factors.

Attributional bias (*cognitive bias*) – affects decision-making as to what or who is responsible for a cause of events. An example is self-serving bias, in which people attribute good and worthy behaviors to personality factors (I gave my mother flowers because I am kind) and harmful or unworthy behaviors to situational factors (I shouted at my mother because I have a headache). Common faults in attributing causes to behavior, such as mistakes being made, and the causes of behavior being misunderstood.

Atypical antipsychotic drugs – a class of drugs effective for treating negative and positive symptoms of schizophrenia. They target the neurotransmitters serotonin and dopamine.

Atypical depression – a disorder characterized by mood reactivity. A person with this disorder experiences an improved mood in response to positive events.

Atypical psychology – see *Abnormal Psychology.*

Audience design – shaping a message depending on the audience for which it is intended.

Audience effects – the impact that a passive audience has on the performance of the task taken up by a person; how performance on a task can be affected by others watching – either improve performance (*social facilitation*) or reduce performance (*social inhibition*).

Auditory adaptation – repeated sounds appear less loud over time. With habituation to sound, the apparent loudness decreases.

Auditory cortex – the area of the temporal lobes that connects the auditory nerve fibers and interprets nerve impulses in a form perceived as sound.

Auditory fatigue – intense sound exposure causes a persistent reduction in apparent loudness.

Auditory nerve – carries impulses from the cochlea of the ear to the brain's cochlear nucleus.

Autassassinophilia – a person engages in life-threatening situations for sexual arousal.

Authenticity (*psychology and philosophy*) – denotes the degree of truth one holds towards their spirit, personality, or character.

Authoritarian personality (*Theodor Adorno*, 1950) – strongly associated with prejudiced attitudes, where the person is intolerant of ambiguity or uncertainty, submissive to those in authority, and dismissive or arrogant towards those perceived to be of lower social status. Traits include authoritarian submission, conventionalism, authoritarian aggression, superstition, power, stereotypy, destructiveness, toughness, projectivity, cynicism, and exaggerated concern with sexuality. Authoritarian personality types may be influenced by harsh treatment in the early developmental years, resulting in empathy with authority.

Authoritarianism (*political philosophy*) – believing power should be concentrated in a limited group of persons or for a dictatorship, often a singular person. Authoritarians require complete obedience from subjects prone to arbitrary behavior, such as punishments, and may be resistant to those who question the source of their authority.

Autism – a disorder characterized by impaired communication and social interaction. Repetitive and restricted behavior are symptoms in people with this disorder.

Autism Diagnostic Observation Schedule – the standardized protocol to assess communicative and social behavior associated with autism.

Autistic disorder – a developmental disorder whereby children are unresponsive, avoid contact with others, and demonstrate a lack of language and communication skills. Autism is a pervasive developmental disorder.

Autodidacticism – a substitute for self-directed learning or self-education.

Autoeroticism – sexual stimulation in the absence of any external stimulus.

Autokinetic effect – an optical illusion experienced when a person in a dark room sees a stationary spot of light appearing to move.

413

Automatic behavior – the spontaneous production of motor or verbal behavior without the person being conscious. Individuals with schizophrenia, epilepsy, psychogenic fugue, and narcolepsy exhibit such behavior.

Automatic processing – does not require attention; often performed with other tasks without interference. A rapid mental operation that does not involve conscious awareness and often improves with practice. For example, the *Stroop effect*.

Automatic thoughts – self-defeating judgments people make about themselves; the model constructed by the mind to deal with the world and achieve objectives and goals.

Autonomic conditioning (or *learned operant control of autonomic responses*) – the conditioning of changes in autonomic (involuntary) responses (e.g., heart rate or blood pressure) using operant reinforcement.

Autonomic nervous system (ANS) – part of the nervous system that maintains normal physiological functioning; a subdivision of the peripheral nervous system controls the body's involuntary motor responses by connecting the sensory receptors to the *central nervous system* (CNS) and the CNS to smooth muscle, cardiac muscle, and glands. Part of the peripheral nervous system (PNS) is connected to the heart, blood vessels, glands, and smooth muscles. ANS has two subdivisions: 1. sympathetic division, whose activity mobilizes energy resources and prepares the body for action, and 2. parasympathetic division, which conserves body energy resources and restores inner calm.

Autonomous state – actions based on thoughts and inclinations; opposed to *Agentic State*.

Availability – in memory, the principle that remembering is determined by whether the information exists in long-term memory; forgetting implies that the information is destroyed.

Availability heuristic – a rule-of-thumb strategy in which people estimate probability based on how quickly they remember relevant instances, a cognitive shortcut, when an individual tries to predict the frequency of an event or the proportion in a population.

Aversion therapy (*behavior modification*) – a stimulus evokes an unpleasant response paired with a stimulus that evokes a maladaptive behavior when a stimulus is provided to the patient while simultaneously being exposed to discomfort. Aversion therapy conditions the patient's mind so that the stimulus is associated with the discomfort caused. The treatment is used to stop specific undesirable behavior. *For example, to rid a patient of an undesirable habit (e.g., smoking) by pairing the habit with unpleasant (aversive) consequences.*

Aversive – an unpleasant stimulus or event; the unpleasant stimuli used to induce behavioral changes through punishment. Using aversive helps curb undesirable behavior.

Aversive conditioning (*behavior modification*) – induces an aversive response to stimuli associated with existing undesirable behaviors.

Avoidance-avoidance conflict – arises if a choice is between two undesirable alternatives.

Avoidance learning – consequences modify the form and occurrence of a behavior.

Avoidant personality disorder – involving social withdrawal, low self-esteem, and extreme sensitivity to being evaluated negatively; when a person exhibits characteristics like social inhibition, sensitivity to negative evaluation, and feeling of inadequacy. Patients tend to avoid social interaction.

Avolition – when a person lacks the desire, motivation, or drive to pursue a meaningful goal. Patients with schizophrenia commonly exhibit this symptom, one of the four crucial symptoms of the disorder.

Awareness (*biological psychology*) – the ability or state in which a person can feel, perceive, or is conscious about the sensory patterns, objects, or events around them. Awareness comprises a human's or an animal's perception and cognitive reaction to a condition or event. Awareness does not necessarily imply understanding, just an ability to be conscious of, feel, or perceive.

Axon – an elongated nerve fiber with *all-or-none* depolarization extending from a neuron's *cell body* (soma) to the axon terminus; provides the signal pathway for a nerve impulse.

B

Babbling – producing sounds that resemble many different languages.

Backward conditioning (*classical conditioning*) – the conditioned stimulus is presented after the unconditioned stimulus.

Backward conditioning – when a conditioned stimulus follows the unconditioned stimulus.

Baddeley & Hitch (*Working Memory Model*, 1974) – a theory of memory consisting of a central executive, articulatory-phonological loop, and visuospatial sketchpad.

Baddeley, Alan (*Working Memory Model*, 1974) – British psychologist worked on memory.

Balance theory (*Heider*, 1946) – whereby people are motivated to seek balance in their attitudes toward themselves and others. "Sentiment" or liking relations may be balanced or unbalanced according to the overall valence of effect between people.

Bandura, Albert (1925-2021) – Canadian developmental psychologist focuses on Social Learning Theory; a proponent of behaviorism using observational learning (or modeling) in the *Bobo doll* experiments (1961-63). His work includes self-efficacy, aggression, and personality theory.

Bar chart – displays nominal data and average scores in a graph. There are gaps between bars plotted on the graph.

Barnes Akathisia scale – a rating scale to assess the severity of drug-induced akathisia.

Barnes Maze (1979) – measures memory and spatial learning in psychological laboratory experiments.

Basal ganglion – any of several subcortical grey matters at the base of each cerebral hemisphere that regulate voluntary movement.

Basal metabolic rate (BMR) – the resting rate at which energy (*calories*) are consumed.

Baseline – a datum of comparison to measure against the effects of a *manipulated* variable (i.e., independent variable).

Basic anxiety (*Karen Horney's psychodynamic theory*) – an intense sense of isolation and helplessness is the primary source of human motivation.

Basic level – categorization retrieved from memory most quickly and efficiently.

Basic trust (*vs. mistrust*) – **a** sense of security towards a parent/caregiver and the world around them that develops in an infant after being given loving and responsive care.

Basilar membrane – the inner ear's cochlea running along the length of the cochlea, when set into motion, stimulates hair cells that produce the neural effects of auditory stimulation.

Beck's Cognitive triad (*Aaron Beck*, 1967) – negative thoughts about self, the world, and the future. People with depression exhibit such negative emotions or feelings.

Behavior – actions that an organism exhibits concerning the surroundings or environment; the aggregate of the responses made by an organism.

Behavior analysis – focuses on the environmental determinants of learning and behavior.

Behavior change – the transformation or modification in a person's behavior.

Behavior genetics – the study of behavior and personality differences among people.

Behavior modification – the systematic use of learning principles to increase the frequency of desired behaviors or decrease the frequency of problem behaviors. A general label for attempts to change behavior using appropriate and timely reinforcement. Techniques to improve behavior, often using conditioning; implementing change techniques demonstrated empirically.

Behavior therapy (*psychotherapy*) – treats anxiety disorders, depression, and phobias; aims to change behavior using systematic desensitization, behavior modification, or aversion therapy. Treatments involve complex conversations between therapists and patients aimed at directly influencing maladaptive behaviors through learning principles.

Behavioral communication – studies day-to-day behavior in communication.

Behavioral confirmation – how people behave to elicit from others specific expected reactions and then use those reactions to confirm their beliefs.

Behavioral data – observational reports about behavior and the conditions under which the behavior occurs or changes.

Behavioral imprinting (or *imprinting*) – phase-sensitive learning during which an individual learns rapidly independent of behavioral consequences, occurring at the stage of life when the person learns the characteristics of some stimuli.

Behavioral measures – overt actions and reactions observed, exclusive of self-reported behavior.

Behavioral model of abnormality – maladaptive learned responses to the environment that more adaptive behaviors can replace.

Behavioral psychology – emphasizes the learning of behavior and objective recording. The thinking, feeling, and actions an individual performs are forms of behavior.

Behavioral rehearsal – procedures to establish and strengthen essential skills, social-skills training programs, requiring the client to mentally rehearse a desirable behavior sequence.

Behavioral science –explores the activities of organisms and the interactions between them.

Behaviorism – a scientific approach that limits the study of psychology to measurable or observable behavior. An approach to psychology that emphasizes observable, measurable behavior, focusing on external (as opposed to cognitive) behavior. Concentrates on overt (*observable*) behavior rather than covert (*unobservable*) mental processing acquired by learning, and the environment's role is crucial in development.

Behaviorist perspective – primarily concerned with objectively recorded observable behavior and the relationships of observable behavior to environmental stimuli.

Behavioristic psychology – an approach emphasizing observable, measurable behavior.

Belief – a proposition held to be true.

Belief-bias effect – prior knowledge, attitudes, or values distort reasoning by influencing the person to accept invalid arguments.

Belief perseverance – rejecting evidence that refutes one's beliefs.

Belongingness – the needs of humans when they feel connected to or accepted by social groups, family, and peers.

Beneficence – the quality of being kind, helpful, or generous.

Benzodiazepines (*tranquilizers*) – a class of anti-anxiety drugs.

Bereavement (or *grief*) – the feelings a person exhibits upon losing something or someone.

Berkowitz, Leonard (1926-2016) – specialized in aggression, instrumental and emotional aggression, the frustration-aggression hypothesis, and intergroup hostility.

Bestiality – the practice of sex between animals and humans.

Beta bias – theories and research have traditionally ignored or minimized differences between men and women. Alpha bias assumes theories and research with real and enduring differences between men and women.

Beta rhythm (or *beta activity*) – when a person is alert and responsive, beta activity is depicted by irregular, low-amplitude waves on an EEG.

Beta waves – brain waves when a person is awake and alert.

Bateson, Gregory (1904-1980) – proposed the *double bind* theory of faulty communication patterns within families of patients of schizophrenia.

Between-subjects design (research design) – participants are randomly assigned to experimental or control conditions.

Bias – a source of error resulting in systematic distortion of results by a variable not in the hypothesis.

Bias disorder – an individual inclined towards violence and believes that war is the ultimate solution to problems.

Biased sampling – some subjects are not representative of the population from which it was taken and thus are likely to over-represent one group (e.g., by gender, working class)

Bibliomania – collecting books excessively might damage health and social relations.

Bicameralism – a hypothesis that the human brain is in a state of a bicameral mind. *The bicameral mind operates so that one part of the brain gives orders while the other listens.*

Big Five Personality Traits – common areas of personality: 1. *Openness to Experience*, 2. *Conscientiousness*, 3. *Extraversion*, 4. *Agreeableness*, and 5. *Neuroticism*.

Binge eating – a disorder in which an individual consumes excessive food rapidly. The person feels ashamed about over-eating and might suffer from depression. *Bulimia nervosa sometimes occurs without the compensatory behavior to eliminate the excess calories.*

Binocular cues – depth perception cues that require both eyes.

Binomial sign test (*non-parametric inferential statistical test*) – with nominal data, the research repeats measurements (or matched pairs). It seeks a difference in the effect each level of the independent variable has on the dependent variable.

Biochemical – chemical processes for biological function.

Biofeedback – a self-regulatory technique by which an individual acquires voluntary control over nonconscious biological processes (e.g., heart rate, muscle tension).

Biological approach – genetic and biochemical influences on mood and behavior.

Biological constraints on learning – limitations on an organism's capacity to learn caused by the inherited sensory, response, or cognitive capabilities of members of a given species.

Biological perspective – identifying causes of behavior that focus on the functioning of the genes, the brain, the nervous system, and the endocrine system.

Biological psychology – the study of relationships between the physiological systems in the body and behavior; applied in studying behavior and mental processes.

Biological rhythm – occurs with regularity. Infradian rhythms occur less than once a day (e.g., human menstrual cycle), circadian rhythms repeat themselves every 24 hours (e.g., sleep/waking cycle), and ultradian rhythms occur more than once a day (e.g., stages of sleep during one night).

Biological therapies (*biochemical* or *somatic therapies*) – treating mental disorders with physical or chemical methods. Treatments for psychological disorders that alter brain functioning with chemical or physical interventions (e.g., drug therapy, surgery, or electroconvulsive therapy.

Biomedical approach to abnormality – emphasizes the role of physiological processes (i.e., genetic, and biochemical factors) in causing mental disorders and treating disorders.

Biomedical therapies –directly altering biological functioning through medication, electric shocks, or surgery.

Biopsychosocial model of illness – interaction among biological, psychological, and sociocultural factors. A model of health and illness are determined by multiple factors, including social, cultural, psychological, and biological, which can thus have multiple effects.

Bipolar cells – nerve cells in the visual system that combine impulses from many receptors and transmit the results to ganglion cells.

Bipolar disorder (or *manic-depressive disorder*) – alternating between periods of depression and mania; a mood disorder characterized by extremes of mania and depression. A person suffers from elevated mood and depression since an individual is subject to extreme conditions such as mania (elevated mood) and depression.

Blocking – a phenomenon in which an organism does not learn a new stimulus that signals an unconditioned stimulus because the new stimulus is presented simultaneously with a stimulus already effective as a signal.

Blood-brain barrier – a membrane that lets some substances from the blood into the brain but excludes others.

Blunted affect (or *affective flattening*) – a person does not exhibit emotional reactivity. Hypervigilance, recurring nightmares, and avoidance of stress characterize it.

Bobo doll (*Albert Bandura*, 1961) – an inflatable toy for studying aggression imitation.

Body image – the subjective experience of the appearance of one's body.

Body language (or *non-verbal communication*) – indications about mood or frame of mind by facial expression, how they are standing or sitting, etc.

Borderline personality disorder – impulsive behavior, unstable relationships, emotions, and self-image.

Boomerang generation – young adults who return to their parents' homes after living independently or never leaving.

Bowlby, John (1907-1990) – British developmental psychologist with *attachment theory*. Focused on attachment bonds between a caregiver and child and how the strength or deprivation of the bond affects the child's cognitive, social, and emotional development. Epitomized in Bowlby's *maternal deprivation hypothesis*.

Bonding – the process whereby the young of a species form a bond with their parent. Parents bond with offspring and safeguard them from abuse or abandonment.

Bottom-up approach (*offender profiling*) – starts from the available evidence from the crimes committed by an offender (the 'bottom') and attempts to look for connections and links between them to indicate the criminal's characteristics.

Bottom-up processing – information (*stimulus*) determined solely by aspects of the stimulus. Perceptual analyses are based on sensory data in the environment; results of analyses are passed upward, forming more abstract representations.

BPS – abbreviation of *British Psychological Society*.

Brain – the main organ in the nervous system; a portion of the central nervous system lies within the skull and controls various behaviors. The brain is the centerpiece of the nervous system, consisting of three interconnected layers: the *central core*, *limbic system*, and *cerebral cortex*. Areas of the brain perform distinct functions.

Brain cell – a nerve cell in the brain.

Brain disorder – any abnormality in the brain from impaired functioning or thinking.

Brain stem – the region at the top of the spinal cord regulating the body's basic processes, composed of three primary structures: the medulla, pons, and midbrain (includes part of the hypothalamus).

Brain ventricles – cavities in the brain that contain a clear, colorless cerebrospinal fluid that acts as a buffer against damage caused by blows to the head.

Brainwashing – behavior modification through the internalization of ideas or an ideology.

Brain wave (*neurophysiology*) – rapid voltage fluctuations between parts of the cerebral cortex detectable with an electroencephalograph.

Breuer, Josef (1842-1925) – Austrian physician with the patient Anna O, whose case history influenced the theories of his protege, Sigmund Freud. Breuer co-authored *Studies on Hysteria* (1895) with Freud.

Brief – a description given to participants to indicate what is expected during a study and its general purpose so that they can give informed consent to participate, stating their right to withdraw at any time.

Brightness – the dimension of color space that captures the intensity of light.

British Crime Survey – a regular, extensive, face-to-face survey of adults living in private households in England and Wales. Its primary purpose is to monitor trends in crime, but it also covers a range of other topics, such as attitudes to crime.

Broca, Pierre Paul (1824-1880) – French physician and anatomist named Broca's area.

Broca's aphasia – disturbance of speech production while language comprehension remains intact. Occurs because of damage to Broca's area.

Broca's area – in the brain's left frontal lobe involved speech production; the inferior prefrontal cortex of the brain's left hemisphere, hypothesized by Broca as the center of speech production, was named for Paul Broca, 1824-1880.

Brown & Kulik (*Flashbulb Memories*, 1977) – recollections from noteworthy events.

Buffers (*social influence research*) – any aspect of a situation that protects people from confronting the consequences of their actions.

Bulimia nervosa – secret binge eating followed by vomiting, misuse of laxatives, diuretics, and excessive exercise. A disorder involving binge eating followed by compensatory behaviors such as vomiting, fasting, excessive exercise, or using laxatives, diuretics, and other medications to control body weight. *For example, voluntary, rapid losing weight.*

Bureaucratic authority (or *rational-legal authority*) – power legitimized by legally enacted rules and regulations (e.g., the majority rules, the chain of command).

Bureaucracy – an organizational model based on rational thought that seeks to accomplish tasks in a specialized and efficient manner (large businesses, governments, schools, etc.).

Bystander behavior (or *bystander apathy*) – witnesses in an emergency tend to ignore it when in the company of others.

Bystander effect – the tendency of people to be less likely to offer help to someone who needs it if others are present.

Bystander intervention – the act of assisting strangers in an emergency.

421

C

Cabin fever – a claustrophobic reaction resulting from an individual being isolated for a prolonged period in a situation with little to do.

Calculation – when one or more inputs are converted into more than one result.

Cannon-Bard theory of emotion – the experience of emotion happens at the same time physiological arousal happens; any action preceded is a related emotion at first. The actions could be perspiration, muscular tension, or other physical manifestations.

Capacity – quantifies the amount of information that can be held in memory. For example, short-term memory has a limited capacity of 7 +/- 2 items.

Capacity model of divided attention (or *resource allocation model of divided attention*) – proposes a pool of processing resources allocated according to the task's demands and environmental factors.

Cardiovascular system – consists of the heart and the blood vessels; a system for distributing oxygen and nutrients to the organs in the body. Heart rate, blood pressure, and local blood volume are three measures of cardiovascular activity common in research by psychophysiologists.

Case study (*research method*) – a detailed description of a single individual typically provides information on the person's history and interprets behavior.

Cassandra phenomenon (or *Cassandra metaphor*) – a state of mind in which valid concerns or warnings are disbelieved.

Castration anxiety – boys suffering during the Oedipus complex that their rivalrous father may castrate them for desiring their mother.

CAT (computed axial tomography) scans – non-invasive, multiple imaging procedures for creating brain images.

Catalepsy – a nervous condition causing muscles to be rigid, and posture fixed with loss of pain sensitivity; sudden paralysis of muscles by laughter, anger, or strong emotions; a hallmark of narcolepsy. A rare disease (5 out of 10,000 people) resulting in the loss of muscle tone. People with narcolepsy are prone to this problem, often triggered by emotions and associated with *Excessive Daytime Sleepiness* (EDS).

Catatonia (or *catatonic excitement*) – a syndrome associated with motoric and psychic disturbances such as post-traumatic stress disorder, bipolar disorder, depression, etc. It could be related to autoimmune disorders and infections such as encephalitis. Catatonic stupor and Catatonic schizophrenia are variations.

Catatonic schizophrenia – a person displays motor abnormalities, for instance, changing between a state of complete immobility to energized excitement.

Catatonic type (*schizophrenia subtype*) – unnatural movement patterns such as rigid, unmoving posture or continual, purposeless movements, or unnatural speech patterns such as the absence of speech or parroting other's speech.

Catecholamines – hormones released by the adrenal medulla in response to stress.

Categorization – recognizing, differentiating, and understanding objects and ideas; a shortcut for processing information. A category is a set of items with one feature in common. In interpersonal perception, categories such as young-old and male-female are used.

Catharsis – a purging of emotional tensions: release of usually repressed emotion in psychodynamic psychology; releasing tension when repressed thoughts or memories move into a patient's conscious mind. *For example, crying to release sadness.*

Cathexis – an individual invests or spends emotional or mental energy on an idea, object, or person.

Cause and effect – establishing that the independent variable has had an apparent effect on the dependent variable.

Central core – includes the thalamus, pons, cerebellum, reticular formation, and medulla. The central core regulates essential processes such as breathing, pulse, arousal, movement, balance, sleep, and the early stages of processing sensory information.

Central nervous system (CNS) – the brain and spinal cord nerve pathways.

Central tendency – a single value representing a set of numbers by indicating the typical value. Three measures of central tendency are the mean, median, and mode.

Centration – a thought pattern typical during the beginning of the preoperational stage of cognitive development; characterized by the child's inability to take more than one perceptual factor into account simultaneously. Children center on one aspect of a problem and overlook other perceptual factors.

Cerebellar artery – an artery that supplies the cerebellum.

Cerebellar hemisphere – either of two lateral lobes of the cerebellum.

Cerebellum (Latin, *little brain*) – two small hemispheres beneath the cortical hemispheres at the back of the vertebrate brain. A part of the hindbrain that controls balance and coordination of movement.

Cerebral cortex – an area of the brain resembling a folded sheet of grey tissue that covers the rest of the brain. It directs the brain's higher cognitive and emotional functions. It has two almost symmetrical cerebral hemispheres with four lobes. Areas within these lobes regulate conscious experiences, such as emotion, perception, thought, planning, and unconscious cognitive and emotional processes. The cerebral cortex includes the *frontal, occipital, parietal*, and *temporal lobes.*

Cerebral dominance – the tendency for one brain hemisphere to be superior for functions.

Cerebral hemispheres – two half spheres comprised of the cortex and underlying structures, a significant portion of the brain.

Cerebral peduncle – a bundle of myelinated neurons joining parts of the brain.

Cerebrospinal fluid (CSF) – a clear liquid produced in the ventricles of the brain; cushions and nourishes the brain and spinal column.

Cerebrum – anterior part of the brain consisting of two hemispheres; the largest part of the brain involved in abstract thought and learning.

Chaos theory – a branch of mathematics dealing with non-linear functions applied to modeling such as weather and stock markets; non-linear systems are not predictable because minimal changes in initial conditions can result in radical differences later.

Charisma – a personal attractiveness or interest that enables you to influence others.

Checklist – a simple list of behaviors being recorded. A single tally is recorded on every behavior on the list. Observation ends with a record of the occurrences of each behavior investigated.

Child-directed speech – speech with an exaggerated and high-pitched intonation that adults adopt when speaking to infants and young children.

Child psychology (*developmental psychology*) – studies children's social and mental development.

Child rearing styles – parenting styles classified according to the extent parents are demanding of their child or responsive to the child's needs, including authoritative and authoritarian parenting.

Chi-squared (x^2) test of association (*nonparametric inferential statistics*) – with nominal data, seeks an association between the independent and dependent variables.

Chromosomes – proteins and double helix strands of DNA that contain genes; thread-like genetic structures composed of double-stranded DNA and histone proteins containing the genes. In humans, there are twenty-three pairs of chromosomes.

Chromosome abnormalities – typically when a chromosome is missing or with an extra chromosome. *For example, Downs syndrome is a trisomy for chromosome 21.*

Chronic schizophrenia – people with schizophrenia who show no significant improvement after therapy or treatment over an extended period.

Chronic stress – a continuous state of tension arousal in which an individual perceives demands as more significant than the inner and outer resources available for dealing with them.

Chunk – the primary measure of short-term memory capacity, representing a meaningful unit, such as random letters, numbers, or words.

Chunking – combining individual information, letters, or numbers into a meaningful process of taking single information items and recoding them by similarity or other organizing principles.

Cilia – hair cells embedded in the ear's basilar membrane.

Cingulotomy – a surgical procedure that involves the destruction of part of the frontal lobes. It is sometimes done to treat severe disorders that do not respond to other treatments.

Circadian rhythms – biological cycles occur every twenty-four hours; an internal body clock determines a 24-hour cycle. *For example, the sleep-wake cycle.*

Circannual rhythm – a biological cycle occurring once each year. *For example, birds' annual migrations.*

Circle of Willis – a ring of arteries at the base of the brain.

Civil religion – a quasi-religious loyalty binding individuals in a secular society and a sense of solidarity (e.g., patriotism, socialism, or any social or political movement or program that people strongly feel about).

Class system – a stratification supposedly based on individual merit or distinction but often includes structures of inequality like inheritance, sexism, racism, and ethnocentrism.

Classical Adlerian psychology – helps patients overcome insecurities by developing a deep connectedness. The psychotherapist indulges in a dialog with the patient and corrects their mistaken attitudes, feelings, and behavior regarding themself and the world.

Classical conditioning *(Pavlovian conditioning* or *respondent conditioning)* – learning in which a subject responds to a neutral stimulus as they would to another stimulus by learning to associate the two stimuli. When a neutral stimulus is repeatedly paired with an unconditioned stimulus (UCS) that naturally produces an unconditioned response (UCR), after several trials, the neutral stimulus is now a conditioned stimulus (CS) and thus produces a conditioned response (CR).

Claustrophobia – an intense fear of confined spaces (e.g., elevators).

Client – used by clinicians who think of psychological disorders as problems in living, not as mental illnesses, to describe those being treated.

Client-centered therapy *(Carl Rogers)* – a humanistic approach in which the person seeking treatment, not the therapist, directs the therapy process. Emphasizes the healthy psychological growth of the individual based on the assumption that all people share the basic tendency of human nature toward self-actualization.

Clinical ecology – a field of psychology that relates disorders such as anxiety and depression to environmental irritants and sources of trauma.

Clinical interview – a flexible research method that uses open-ended questions to obtain much information from a participant.

Clinical psychologist – an individual who has earned a doctorate in psychology and trained in assessing and treating psychological problems.

Clinical psychology – focuses on assessing and treating abnormal or maladaptive behavior; applications to understand, prevent, and relieve dysfunction or distress psychologically based. Personal development and subjective well-being are promoted through this therapy.

Clinical social worker – a mental health professional whose specialized training prepares them to consider the social context of people's problems.

Clinician – a practitioner who interacts directly with patients.

Closed questions – questions that have set answers for participants to choose from.

Closure – 1. Gestalt therapy for the emotional experience of moving on from past trauma. 2. tendency to interpret familiar, incomplete forms as complete by filling in gaps. A perceptual organizing process leads people to see incomplete figures complete.

CNS – see *central nervous system.*

Coan, James (1997) – *Lost in the Mall* technique is a method of implanting false memories of an event that never occurred. The technique was popularized by an experiment in which James Coan provided family members with reminiscing stories. He told his brother that he was lost in a shopping mall as a child - it was invented, but when questioned, the brother believed it had happened to him. *Lost in the Mall* technique demonstrates the effect of retroactive interference on memories.

Cochlea – the primary organ of hearing; a fluid-filled coiled tube located in the inner ear.

Cochlear – relating to the cochlea of the ear.

Cocktail party effect – a person's ability to concentrate on just one conversation with others around them. The way a person engages in (attending to) one conversation will nevertheless hear their name if it is mentioned in a nearby conversation.

Codes of practice (*ethics*) – produced by psychological organizations such as the BPS and the APA, containing advice on research and practice.

Cognition – processing of information by reasoning, thoughts, attitudes, and memories. The psychological result of perception and reasoning.

Cognitive – information storage and retrieval, which can be utilized flexibly in behavior; thinking that involves mental activities such as understanding, problem-solving, decision-making, and creativity. In humans, cognition relates to mental operations (i.e., thought processes). *For example, reasoning, calculation, and planning.*

Cognitive ability – perceiving, knowing, conceptualizing, judging, and reasoning.

Cognitive appraisal – how physiological arousal is interpreted for circumstances in the setting in which it is experienced; the recognition and evaluation of a stressor to assess the demand, the size of the threat, the resources available for dealing with it, and appropriate coping strategies.

Cognitive appraisal theory of emotion (*Lazarus*, 1966) – the experience of emotion is the combined effect of physiological arousal and cognitive appraisal, how an ambiguous inner state of arousal will be labeled. Emotional experience depends on how a person appraises or evaluates the events.

Cognitive approach (*Ulric Neisser's book Cognitive Psychology*, 1967) – emphasizes the significance of cognitive processes, such as thoughts, as an influence on their behavior.

Cognitive behavioral programs – modifying behavior by changing attitudes and thoughts.

Cognitive behavior modification – the therapeutic approach combines a cognitive emphasis on thoughts and attitudes influencing motivations and response with behavioral emphasis on changing performance through modification of reinforcement contingencies.

Cognitive behavioral therapies – patients identify their negative, irrational thoughts and replace them with more positive, rational ways of thinking.

Cognitive development – the growth of cognitive (thinking) abilities; the development of thinking capacity. This may be studied by examining changes in the form and structure of children's thinking as they age or by looking at individual differences in the power of children's thinking as measured. For example, IQ tests.

Cognitive dissonance (*Festinger's theory*) – a state of tension created when there are conflicts between an individual's behavior and beliefs or between two beliefs; an unpleasant state of tension arises when a person has related cognitions that conflict.

Cognitive interview – a police investigation technique to elicit accurate information from eyewitnesses.

Cognitive labeling theory (*Schachter and Singer's theory*) – the combination of physiological arousal and cognitive appraisal that leads to the experience of emotion.

Cognitive map (*Tolman*) – the mental representation of learned relationships among stimuli.

Cognitive model of abnormality – the view that stresses the role of cognitive problems (such as illogical thought processes) in abnormal functioning.

Cognitive neo-association theory (*Berkowitz's theory*) – thoughts, memories, and behavior may be triggered by affective states or priming.

Cognitive neuroscience – a hybrid discipline identifying the biological bases of cognitive processes by combining techniques for studying cognitive processes with measures of physiological processes.

Cognitive operation – the performance of some composite thinking and reasoning activity.

Cognitive pathology – researchers selectively ignore simplifying assumptions and other limitations, which are part of the foundations of their theories and methods.

Cognitive perspective –stresses human thought and processes of knowing, such as attending, thinking, remembering, expecting, solving problems, fantasizing, and consciousness.

Cognitive processes – higher mental processes, such as perception, memory, language, problem-solving, and abstract thinking. The performance of some composite cognitive activity; aspects of mental 'behavior' that focus on acquiring, storing, retrieving, and using knowledge. For example, in memory and perception.

Cognitive psychology – emphasizes internal mental processes and focuses on acquiring, storing, retrieving, and using knowledge. Studies higher mental processes such as attention, language use, memory, perception, problem-solving, and thinking.

Cognitive restructuring (*Ellis's rational-emotive therapy*) – modifying faulty beliefs and the negative emotions they produce to develop realistic beliefs and self-acceptance.

Cognitive schema – a mental model of some aspect of the world.

Cognitive science – studying human intelligence and symbol processing for cognition.

Cognitive therapy (*rational-emotive therapy* or *cognitive behavioral therapy*) – identifying and changing maladaptive thinking patterns that can result in negative emotions and dysfunctional behavior; focusing on the role of faulty beliefs and thought patterns in abnormal behavior; it encourages testing beliefs via behavioral strategies.

Cohabitation – two unrelated people are not married but live together, often in sexual relationships.

Cohort – individuals with a common characteristic (e.g., classmates, birth year, generation).

Collective unconscious (*Carl Jung*) – part of minds containing universal memories of shared human past; a biologically based portion of the unconscious that reflects universal themes and ideas, not an individual experience. A collection of memories and ideas that everyone inherits, regardless of the culture or period into which they were born. The collective unconscious contains archetypes that may surface in dreams and myths independently across societies.

Collectivism – emphasizes a person's connections and obligations to a social group (e.g., family, tribe). When applied to a culture, it typically contrasts with individualism.

Collectivist society – a high level of mutual interdependence between individuals.

Collectivistic cultures – valuing group loyalty, preferring the group to individual decisions, and where the needs of the group outweigh the concerns of the individual.

Colonialism – the process by which some nations enrich themselves through political and economic control of other countries (e.g., European colonists in the Americas or Africa in the 18th and 19th centuries).

Color blindness – a hereditary condition with people unable to distinguish between colors.

Color processing (or *color vision*) – detecting chromatic colors (or hues) such as yellow, green, and blue. Two theories have been proposed trichromatic and opponent-process – but no complete explanation exists.

Comfortable Interpersonal Distance Scale – a measurement of a person's personal space.

Commitment – the intent to continue a meaningful relationship even with difficulties.

Comorbidity – experiencing more than one disorder simultaneously.

Communicating artery – any of three arteries in the brain that make up the *circle of Willis*.

Community environmental design – differs from urban renewal because these projects allow the current residents to have an input in the redesign of the area.

Community mental health movement – advocates treating people with psychological problems in their communities, providing outpatient treatment for psychological disorders.

Compassionate love – warmth, trust, and tolerance with whom one is romantically involved; the emotional state that combines affection and attachment characterized by mutual concern for each other; less intense than romantic love.

Comparative psychology – concerned with the behavior of animals.

Compatibilism – a theory that free will and determinism can coexist.

Compensation (*Alfred Adler*) – striving to rid normal feelings of inferiority; activities intended to produce a feeling of superiority over others to overcome feelings of inferiority.

Competitive altruism (or *costly signaling theory*) – a concept that individuals will make immense public sacrifices if they believe there is a long-term personal benefit.

Complementarity – construct when two valid models are not reconcilable.

Complementary colors – colors opposite each other on the color circle; when additively mixed, they create the sensation of white light.

Complexity (*of light*) – the range of wavelengths in light.

Compliance – social influence whereby an individual seeks to influence another to comply with a demand; a behavior change consistent with a communication source's direct requests.

Complementarity – a relation between two opposite states or principles that exhaust the possibilities together.

Componential intelligence – the ability assessed by intelligence tests.

Compulsions – repetitive behaviors that help to prevent or relieve anxiety; irresistible.

Computerized axial tomograms (CAT) – non-invasive, multiple imaging procedures for creating brain visualizations.

Computerized imaging techniques – studying brain function using computer imaging to convert information into three-dimensional models of the brain, which can be viewed on a television monitor.

Computed tomography (CT) – imaging technique creating images from different angles.

Concept – a mental category that groups similar objects, events, qualities, or actions; an idea as the basis for a psychological theory.

Concordance – a technique for studying inheritance by examining individuals of known genetic relationships.

Concordance rate – the percentage of paired people with a trait or disorder.

Concrete operational period (*Piaget's stages of cognitive development*) – between ages seven and eleven, during which children better understand mental operations. Children begin thinking logically about concrete events but have difficulty understanding abstract or hypothetical concepts.

Concurrent validity – compares measures of the same phenomenon to determine whether they produce similar results in the same circumstances.

Conditional positive regard – acceptance and caring only for specific standards of behavior.

Conditioned response (*classical and operant conditioning*) – resembles an unconditioned response by pairing a conditioned stimulus with an unconditioned one.

Conditioned emotional response – an emotional response such as fear established through classical conditioning.

Conditioned reinforcer – stimuli that act as reinforcers but are not based on biological survival. *For example, attention, praise, or money.*

Conditioned reinforcers (*classical conditioning*) – neutral stimuli become reinforcers.

Conditioned response (*classical conditioning*) – a previously neutral stimulus becomes a conditioned stimulus by repeated pairing with an unconditioned stimulus.

Conditioned stimulus (*classical conditioning*) – a neutral stimulus evokes a response like an unconditioned response by pairing it with an unconditioned stimulus; a stimulus which, by repeated pairings with an unconditioned stimulus, elicits a conditioned response.

Conditioning – how events, stimuli, and behavior become associated.

Conditions for growth (*Rogers*, 1959) – for a person to grow, they need an environment that provides genuineness (openness), acceptance (unconditional positive regard), and empathy (listened to and understood).

Conditions of worth – restrictions imposed on self-expression to earn positive regard.

Conduct disorder – a pattern of repetitive behavior of children where the rights of others or the current social norms are violated. Symptoms include verbal and physical. *For example, aggression, cruel and destructive behavior, lying, truancy, vandalism, and stealing.*

Cones – photoreceptor cells in the center of the retina for color vision.

Confabulation – when a person thinks they remember something that did not happen.

Confederates – individuals who pose as participants in empirical research to produce responses from others, united in purpose.

Confidence – being sure that a hypothesis is correct or that the chosen actions are best given the circumstances.

Confidentiality – discretion in keeping secret information. The ethical concern is that information gathered during psychological research or therapy should not be divulged to others unless otherwise agreed in advance or unless there is a legal requirement to disclose it.

Configurationism – a theory emphasizing the importance of configurational properties.

Confirmation (*research*) – observations consistent with the proposed hypothesis.

Confirmation bias (*research*) – cognitive error based on the tendency to seek information supporting one's beliefs and ignore contradictory information. Seeking and accepting evidence supporting what one wants to believe and ignoring or rejecting evidence that refutes those beliefs.

Conflict – an open clash between two opposing groups; the experience of having two or more incompatible desires or motives.

Conflict theory (*Karl Marx*, 1848) – opposition between competing interests is the basic animating force of social change and society in general. See *Social conflict approach*.

Conformity – the tendency for people to adopt the behaviors, attitudes, and values of reference group members. The process of giving in to pressure from a group. Social influence is expressed through exposure and submission to majority views.

Confound (*experimental research*) – when two variables change simultaneously, making it impossible to determine their relative influence.

Confounding variable – an uncontrolled variable that produces an unwanted effect on the dependent variable. It obscures the effect of the independent variable.

Congruence (*Carl Rogers theory*) – the accurate match between self-concept and reality; a feeling of integration is experienced when the self and ideal self match.

Conjugal family (or *nuclear family*) – composed of parents and their biological or adopted children.

Conscience – a person's moral sense of right and wrong, chiefly as it affects their behavior.

Conscientiousness (*Big Five Personality Trait*)– a personality trait of being conscious of one's actions.

Conscious (*Freud's theory*) – aspect of the mind contains those thoughts and feelings of which the person is immediately aware at a given moment; area of the psyche in which a person's awareness operates and readily accessible memories reside. The part of the mind containing information that a person is paying attention to.

Consciousness – comprises qualities such as subjectivity, self-awareness, sentience, and the ability to perceive the relationship between oneself and one's environment; awareness of themselves and their environment. *It is a subject of much research in the philosophy of mind, psychology, neuroscience, and cognitive science.*

Consensual validation – mutual affirmation of conscious views of reality.

Consent – an ethical necessity whereby participants agree to the procedures and have the right to withdraw at any time.

Conservation (*Piaget's theory of development*) – the ability to recognize that measurable physical characteristics of objects can be the same even when objects look different. Understanding that physical characteristics of quantity do not change, even though the appearance may change, is demonstrated by children in the *pre-operational stage* of Piaget's theory of development.

Consequent control – a behavioral measure in which the intervention follows the behavior to be changed. Consequent procedures can affect behaviors by using pleasant or unpleasant consequences (positive or negative reinforcement or punishment) to make their performance more or less likely or by using feedback.

Consistency paradox – the observation that personality ratings across time and among observers are consistent, while behavior ratings across situations are inconsistent.

Consolidation – transfer of information into long-term memory.

Contact comfort – comfort derived from the infant's physical contact with the mother or caregiver.

Contact hypothesis – direct contact between hostile groups alone will reduce prejudice.

Constancy – the tendency to give rise to similar perceptual experiences.

Constant errors – uncontrolled variables acting on only one independent variable level. Their action may either be in the same direction as a predicted difference, exaggerating the apparent effect of the independent variable, or in the opposite direction, obscuring the effect of the independent variable.

Constructive theories of perception – top-down (or concept-driven) theories that emphasize the need for several sources of information to construct a perception of the world. In addition to the information available in the sensory stimulus, we need to use higher cognitive processes, according to this theory, to interpret the information appropriately.

Construct validity – an indicator of validity that aims to demonstrate that the phenomenon being measured exists, for example, *by justifying it with a model or theory*.

Contact comfort – derived from physical closeness with a caregiver.

Contact hypothesis – prejudice declines when people in an ingroup become more familiar with the customs, norms, food, music, and attitudes of people in an outgroup.

Contact hypothesis – direct contact between hostile groups alone will reduce prejudice.

Contagion – an incident in which an infectious disease is transmitted.

Contempt – lack of respect accompanied by a feeling of intense dislike.

Contemptible – deserving of scorn or disrespect.

Content analysis – examines certain media (e.g., books, TV, magazines, the Internet) to determine their effect on a person's perceptions or behavior. It involves the analysis of language, certain words, or specific activities that appear in the chosen media.

Content validity – the test's ability to measure all critical aspects of measured characteristics.

Context-dependent forgetting – failure to retrieve information from long-term memory due to the absence of appropriate contextual cues.

Context of discovery (*experimental design*) – the initial phase of research in which observations, beliefs, information, and general knowledge lead to a new idea or way of thinking about some phenomenon.

Context of justification – research phase in which evidence is brought to bear on hypotheses.

Contextual distinctiveness – assuming that the context and distinctiveness of the recalled experience can alter the serial position effect.

Contiguity (*behaviorism*) – reinforcer must occur immediately after a response for learning.

Contingency management – changing behavior by modifying consequences.

Contextual intelligence – effectively functioning in daily situations.

Contextual reinstatement (*criminal psychology*) – improving memory for an event by returning to where it happened or asking the witness to imagine that place and the same emotional state.

Contingency of reinforcement (*operant conditioning*) – the relationship between a response and reinforcer.

Continuity (*developmental theory*) – changes occur through a continuous gradual process rather than as a series of discrete stages; continuity is an assertion about the processes that underlie development and behavior changes. *For example, perceiving interrupted lines and patterns as continuous by filling gaps.*

Continuous reinforcement – a schedule in which reinforcement happens every time a particular response occurs. *For example, a reinforcer schedule following every response.*

Contrast processing (*visual perception*) – differentiating brightness levels in adjoining areas.

Control (*psychological*) – the sense that one can anticipate events in their environment – a feeling that one can accomplish things and is not at the mercy of forces beyond one's control. Types of control include informational, decisional, behavioral, cognitive, and retrospective.

Control group (*experimental design*) – the group used as a baseline to compare the effect of the independent variable in the experimental group. A group of experimental subjects receives the same treatment and is treated exactly like the experimental group, except for the independent variable.

Control procedures – consistent methods for giving instructions, scoring responses, and holding all other variables constant except those being systematically varied.

Controlled processing (or *attentional processing*) – a conscious mental operation, relatively slow and easily interrupted. Require attention; often difficult to perform more than one controlled process at a time.

Controls – limiting factors that could distort valid and reliable data collection.

Convenience sample (*quasi-random sampling*) – the potential sample pool differs from the population; the impact on representativeness (if any) often depends on the behavior studied. *For example, selecting university students instead of older people.*

Convergence – 1. the degree to which the eyes turn inward to fixate on an object. 2. the turning inward of eyes when an object is viewed close.

Convergent problem (*closed-end* or *well defined problems*) – a problem with a single solution, and all elements lead towards that solution.

Convergent thinking – when a person narrows a list of possibilities to arrive at a correct answer.

Conversion disorder – medically unexplained symptoms affect voluntary motor or sensory functioning.

Coping – efforts to manage stress and minimize, control, or tolerate demands exceeding their resources to fight or avoid; dealing with internal or external demands perceived as threatening or overwhelming.

Coprolalia – uncontrollable use of obscene language, often accompanied by mental disorders.

Cornea – the transparent outer membrane of the eye.

Corpus callosum – a band of fibers that divides the cerebrum into two halves. A wide band of nerve fibers connects the brain's two hemispheres.

Correlation – the degree of relatedness between two sets of scores. If two sets of scores are correlated, researchers can predict (with varying degrees of certainty) the approximate value of one score if the value of the other is known.

Correlational analysis – measures the extent of a relationship between variables that are thought likely to co-vary.

Correlation coefficient, *r* (*descriptive statistics*) – represents how closely two variables co-vary: the strength of the relationship between two variables. The degree of relationship between two variables; for positive correlations, it is a number that varies between 0.0 and + 1.0, and for negative correlations between 0.0 and -1.0; in both cases, the closer the value is to 1, the stronger the relationship between the two variables.

> **Positive correlation** – one variable increases as another increases (*directly related*). A positive correlation exists when high values on one variable are associated with high values on another.

> **Negative correlation** – one variable decreases as the other increases (*inversely related*). A negative correlation exists if high values on one variable are associated with low values on another.

Correlational research method (*descriptive research method*) – provides information about the relationship between variables, traits, or attributes.

Cortex – **the** brain's outer layer controls many higher functions like speech and perception.

Cortical activity – neural activity in the cortex of the brain.

Corticosteroids – hormones released by the adrenal cortex in response to stress; drugs that mimic the action of a group of hormones produced by adrenal glands; they are anti-inflammatory and act as bronchodilators.

Counseling psychologist – specializes in guiding in areas such as vocational selection, school problems, drug abuse, and marital conflict.

Counterbalancing – a systematic variation of the order of presentation of the levels of the independent variable. *For example, half of the participants first undergo Condition A, followed by Condition B, while the other half do vice versa. Repeated measures avoid order and fatigue effects.*

Counterconditioning – a therapy technique substituting new responses for maladaptive ones using conditioning procedures.

Counterfactual thinking – memories about events that did not take place. *For example, winning a competition when losing.*

Countertransference (*psychoanalytic therapy*) – the therapist may transfer feelings or conflicts onto the patient. The therapist must recognize this and guard against it. Circumstances in which a psychoanalyst develops personal feelings about a client because of the perceived similarity of the client to significant people in the therapist's life.

Couples therapy – a therapist helps couples identify and resolve conflicts.

Course – a connected series of events, actions, or developments.

Covariation model of attribution (*Kelley*) – people decide on the cause of behavior by weighing how consistent and distinctive the behavior is and how much consensus there is.

Covariation principle (or *analysis of variance*) – individuals attribute behavior to a causal factor if it existed while the behavior occurred but not when it did not occur.

Craik and Lockhart (1972) – *levels of processing model of memory* as a counterpoint to the multi-store memory model. Memory is a product of the depth of processing and encoding of information; for instance, shallow or deep processing (e.g., semantic processing).

Creativity – generating novel, practical ideas; the capacity to produce something unique, valuable, and appropriate to the circumstances.

Credibility – the quality of being believable or trustworthy.

Criminal psychology – studying the thoughts, intentions, and reactions of criminals.

Crisis – conflict needs to be resolved to move to the next stage of development.

Criterion – a standard by which things or people may be compared and judged.

Criterion validity (or *predictive validity*) – the degree to which test scores indicate a result on a specific measure consistent with another criterion of the assessed characteristic.

Critical period (or *sensitive period*; *developmental psychology*) – a critical period in developmental psychology when a particular process, such as filial imprinting, may occur. The absence of the required external stimuli can lead to incomplete development during this stage. *For example, for filial imprinting, if a moving object (e.g., their mother) is not witnessed during the critical period shortly after birth, a baby may not form a filial imprint of that stimulus.*

Critical value (*statistical test*) – quantity compared with the observed (calculated) value to determine significance. *The comparison with the observed (calculated) allows you to conclude if you have found a significant result. Each inferential statistical test has a table or tables of critical values.*

Cross-cultural study – conducted across two or more cultures to compare them.

Cross-sectional sample (*research design*) – selected so that the sample matches the population for characteristics such as age and income.

Cross-sectional design (*research design*) – groups of participants of different chronological ages are observed and compared at a given time.

Cross-sectional study (*research design*) – selecting representative groups who vary on a characteristic; when the characteristic is age, this design provides a means of making developmental comparisons.

Cross tolerance (*pharmacology*) – arises with some drugs, such as opiates (e.g., heroin, morphine) and tryptamines (e.g., LSD, mescaline, psilocybin), when prolonged use results in tolerance to others.

Crowd – a large, cohesive gathering of individuals or coming together to form a tightly spaced group. *In addition, crowding is the psychological perception associated with this increase in density.*

Crowding – being close; feeling uneasy if others violate expectations about the use of space.

Crystallized intelligence – knowledge and skills accumulated over a life span; already acquired by a person (e.g., arithmetic).

Cue-arousal theory – specific environmental cues trigger aggressive behavior.

Cue-dependent coding – all information is stored in memory as a set of relationships (i.e., context); remembering depends on restoring the cues that formed the original context.

Cue-dependent forgetting – failure to recall memory due to a lack of cues during memory encoding.

Cultural bias – a tendency in psychological theory and research to ignore the differences between cultures and impose understanding based on the study of one culture alone.

Cultural identity – the influence of culture on identity development. Individualist cultures stress the importance of personal achievement and independence, while collectivist cultures stress collective achievement and dependence.

Crystallized intelligence – the facet of intelligence involving the knowledge a person has already acquired and their ability to access that knowledge, measured by vocabulary, arithmetic, and general information tests.

Cultural imperialism – the influence of one society's cultural values over those of another.

Cultural integration – consists of aspects of society promoting order and stability.

Cultural lag – cultural elements change at different rates (nonmaterial changes faster than material), disrupting a cultural system (e.g., religion lagging the changes happening in science or technology, traditional gender roles persisting in an egalitarian, modern society).

Cultural perspective – psychological perspective focusing on cross-cultural differences in the causes and consequences of behavior.

Cultural pluralism – when smaller groups within a larger society maintain their cultural identities, whereby their values and practices are accepted by the dominant culture, provided such are consistent with the laws and values of society. See *Multicultural.*

Cultural relativism (*atypical psychology*) – the practice of judging a culture by its standards; all culture groups are valid and functional to those who function within them (i.e., there are no good or bad, inferior or superior, just different based on each group's cultural evolution).

Culture – the set of beliefs, values, behaviors, traditions, practices, and material objects learned, taught, or shared and defined by a people's way of life; everything a group can and does share in common (e.g., social norms, worldview).

Culture-bound disorders – psychological disorders limited to specific cultural contexts.

Culture-bound syndrome – a mental disorder confined to the members of a cultural group.

Culture shock – personal disorientation accompanying exposure to foreign cultures or unfamiliar ways of life different from one's own.

Cultural universals – customs and practices that are common to all societies.

Custom – a practice from the past that people continue to observe.

Cutaneous senses – skin senses that register sensations of pressure, warmth, and cold.

D

Dark adaptation – the process by which receptor cells become more sensitive to light; how the eyes adjust from a change in illumination from light to low light intensity.

Darwin, Charles (1809-1882) – English naturalist who proposed that species evolve through natural selection so that traits (or phenotypes) that enhance survival propagate.

Date rape – unwanted sexual violation by a social acquaintance in the context of dating.

Davis-Moore Thesis (1945) – social stratification is a universal pattern with beneficial consequences for the operation of society; it justifies the inequality in a class system (*functionalist theory*).

Daydream – a visionary fantasy (pleasant thoughts, ambitions, hopes) experienced while awake. Daydreaming is challenging to define because this psychological phenomenon has many variations. They may be related to an experience from the past or the future.

Daytime sleepiness – excessive sleepiness during daytime activities; the primary complaint of patients evaluated at sleep disorder centers.

Daze – confusion characterized by a lack of clarity.

Debriefing – a meeting in which someone reports on a task. An ethical procedure at the end of a study whereby participants are given as much information as possible about the study and are given the option to discuss their study experience to ensure that participants leave the experiment in the same emotional state as they entered.

Decay – the loss of information in memory over a long period.

Decay theory – memory traces fade with time.

Decentration – the ability to focus simultaneously on several aspects of a problem.

Deception (*research*) – intentionally misleading and misinforming participants about the aim of the study; a misleading falsehood.

Decibels (dB) – measures volume (or sound intensity).

Decision aversion – the tendency to avoid decision-making; the tougher the decision, the greater the likelihood of decision aversion.

Decision-making – weighing alternatives and choosing among them; reasoning that involves considering and choosing options.

Declarative knowledge – memory for facts (*semantic*) and events (*episodic* knowledge).

Declarative memory – the remembering of information; memory considered explicit.

Deductive reasoning – a conclusion drawn from a set of general premises or statements.

Deduction (or *deductive reasoning*) – a logical process of concluding a set of general principles. Thinking in which one draws a conclusion intended to follow logically from two or more statements or premises, tested through data collection.

Defense mechanism (*Freudian psychoanalytic theory*) – psychological strategies to distort or deny reality to cope with anxiety or a challenging situation.

Deindividuation – when group members cease to view themselves as individuals; the tendency of people in a large, arousing, anonymous group to lose inhibitions, sense of responsibility, and self-consciousness. Individual identity is replaced with group identity.

Deinstitutionalization – trend toward providing treatment through community-based outpatient clinics rather than inpatient hospitals.

Déjà vu (or *paramnesia*) – the experience of thinking about a new situation that occurred. Experience which a person feels sure happened, and the circumstances of the two experiences could be different.

Delinquency – criminal or antisocial activity.

Delirium – when a person loses focus and perception, abruptly followed by cognition. It is an acute syndrome that might develop quickly within hours or even a few days.

Delta waves – brain waves when a person is deeply asleep.

Delusion – unfounded and irrational beliefs held despite contrary evidence; an erroneous belief held in the face of contrary evidence. A belief fixed in a person's mind could be fanciful, false, or derived from deception. Characteristics of mental disorders, such as schizophrenia, can be manifested in delusions of grandeur (believing one is famous) or delusions of persecution (believing one is being chased or followed).

Delusions – false beliefs are held strongly despite contradictory evidence.

Demand characteristic – cues in an experiment that reveal information to participants about the aim and expected outcome, thereby influencing their behavior and subsequently confounding the results.

Dementia – characterized by several significant psychological deficits; a disorder characterized by considerable deterioration in cognitive function (e.g., memory loss). Dementia includes *cortical dementia* (e.g., Alzheimer's disease) and *sub-cortical dementia* (e.g., Huntington's disease).

Demographic – a socioeconomic or similar factor that defines a group or area.

Dendrite – a nerve fiber extending from a neuron; receives signals from neurons and sends them toward the cell body branched fibers at the end of the cell body of a neuron that receives incoming impulses.

Dendritic trees – highly branched fibers extending from neurons.

Denial – a defense mechanism whereby individuals reject aspects of reality, refusing to acknowledge something evident to others.

Deoxyribonucleic acid (DNA) – the molecule that forms the basis of heredity. *DNA holds all genetic information on the chromosomes.*

Department of Psychology – the academic department responsible for teaching and researching psychology.

Dependent personality disorder – when an individual is heavily reliant upon others and demonstrates feelings of inadequacy and helplessness when alone.

Dependent variable (DV) – a quantity whose value depends on another quantity observed in an experiment may be affected by manipulations of the independent variable. Experimentally, the values of the variable change due to the manipulation of the independent variable.

Depression (or *unipolar disorder*) – a mood disorder characterized by persistent feelings of great sadness, hopelessness, worthlessness, guilt, and a loss of interest in activities; characterized by low self-esteem, low mood, and lack of interest in daily activities.

Deprivation – a condition of having too little of something.

Depth/distance (visual) perception – the capability to view the world three-dimensionally, utilizing monocular and binocular cues to appraise depth and distance between objects.

Depth psychology – a set of techniques for exploring underlying motives and a method of treating mental disorders based on the theories of Sigmund Freud.

Descriptive statistics – the description and summation of sets of scores in statistics researchers use to describe their data so it can be organized and summarized.

Determinism – the assumption that all behavior has specific causes; the belief that genetic factors and external environmental influences determine cognitive processes and behavior. It negates the ability of humans to choose their behavior entirely of their own free will.

Development – the series of age-related changes throughout a person's life span.

Developmental delay – cognitive functioning gets impaired, and a person suffers from deficits in adaptive behaviors. Individuals with significantly below average intellectual functioning, IQ scores of 70-75 or below, and an inability to use adaptive skills.

Developmental norms – median-age children develop specific behaviors and abilities.

Developmental psychology (or *human development*) – studying social and mental development during a lifetime. The scientific study of the processes that underlie and control growth and change in behavior over time.

Deviant behavior – behavior recognized as violating social norms.

Diabetes – a condition caused by a deficiency of insulin.

Diagnosis – identification and classification of psychological disorder; distinguishing among disorders.

Diagnostic and Statistical Manual of Mental Disorders (**DSM**) – a reference for diagnosing psychological disorders. A multi-axial manual used to classify, define, and describe mental health disorders.

Dialectical reasoning – a process of going back and forth between opposing points of view to produce a satisfactory solution to a problem.

Diathesis – constitutional predisposition to a disease or abnormality.

Diathesis-stress hypothesis – a hypothesis about the cause of certain disorders, such as schizophrenia; suggests that genetic factors predispose an individual to a specific disorder, but environmental stress factors must impinge for the disorder to manifest itself.

Dichotic listening (*attention research*) – a different auditory message is simultaneously presented to each ear. Participants are required to repeat one of the messages while ignoring the other.

Didactic – informative with a focus on instructive teaching.

Diencephalon – a part of the forebrain containing the thalamus and the hypothalamus.

Difference threshold (*just noticeable difference*, or *JND*) – the smallest difference in stimulation detectable 50 percent of the time.

Differential psychology – studies measurable differences between individuals.

Diffusion of responsibility – the tendency to feel less responsible in the presence of others because responsibility is distributed among all the people present. In emergencies, the larger the number of bystanders, the less responsibility each feels. In groups, an individual feels less responsibility because accountability is diffused amongst the group.

Digit span – a test of short-term memory whereby participants are presented with a series of digits and asked to repeat them. The average digit span is 7 +/- 2.

Directional hypothesis (or *one-tailed hypothesis*; *statistics*) – states which of the two-condition means will be larger, most often used, one-tailed T-test.

Discovery learning (*Piagetian belief*) – children learn through self-discovery, aided by a teacher providing suitable materials, stimulating intrinsic satisfaction.

Discursive psychology – analyzes patterns of meaning to study language functioning.

Discrete variable – measurement using a discrete category (e.g., gender) instead of a continuous score (e.g., height, weight, intelligence).

Discrimination – unequal and unlawful treatment based upon race, color, creed, religion, sex, national origin, age, disability, veteran status, or sexual orientation.

Discriminative stimulus (*operant conditioning*) – a cue indicating consequences after the response.

Disease model of addiction – compelling behavior must be medically treated.

Disengagement theory – a mutual process of disengagement in activities by individuals and society.

Displacement – the act of taking the position of another.

Dispositional variables – the organismic variables or inner determinants of behavior within human and nonhuman animals.

Disorganized schizophrenia – the patient displays disorganized speech and behavior along with schizophasia.

Disorganized speech – one symptom of schizophrenia, a disturbance whereby speech is disjointed and incoherent.

Disorganized type (*a subtype of schizophrenia*) – characterized by disorganized behavior, disorganized speech, and emotional flatness or inappropriateness.

Disorientation – when a person is confused about place, time, direction, and identity. *For example, disorientation may be due to intoxication or delirium.*

Displacement – forgetting in short-term memory with new information replacing previous contents; a defense mechanism for transferring feelings to someone or something else.

Display rules – norms that tell people whether, how, and when emotions should be displayed.

Disposition – the usual mood of a person.

Dispositional attribution – when behavior is attributed to internal controllable factors. *For example, effort or ability, as opposed to external factors (situational attributions), such as weather or bad luck.*

Dissociative amnesia – an inability to remember extensive, crucial personal information, usually about something traumatic or painful.

Dissociative disorders – characterized by disturbances in consciousness, memory, identity, and perception; a condition often caused by trauma, in which a person disconnects from a full awareness of self, time, or external circumstances to defend against unpleasant realities or memories.

Dissociative fugue – a disorder in which a person suddenly and unexpectedly leaves home, fails to remember the past and becomes confused about their identity.

Dissociative identity disorder (DID) (or *multiple personality disorder*) – a person fails to remember important personal information and has two or more personalities controlling behavior.

Dissonance theory – people change their attitudes when they have attitudes that are inconsistent with one another.

Distal cause – indirectly affecting behavior, such as previous similar experiences.

Distal stimulus – in the processes of perception, the physical object in the world, as contrasted with the proximal stimulus (the optical image of it on the retina).

Distributed practice (or *spacing effect*) – learning material in short sessions over periods.

Divided attention – the ability to divide attentional processing between more than one task.

Divergent thinking – people's thoughts diverge as they try to generate many solutions to a problem.

Divorce – the legal dissolution of a marriage.

Dizygotic twins (or *non-identical twins*) – a fetus developing from different zygotes (i.e., fertilized eggs) and sharing about fifty percent of its DNA.

DNA (deoxyribonucleic acid) – the physical basis for transmitting genetic information.

Door-in-the-face technique – a method inducing compliance whereby individuals are first asked a large favor, followed by a smaller one, which is more likely to be followed.

Dopamine – a monoamine brain neurotransmitter essential for normal central nervous system functioning; essential for learning, experiencing pleasure and reward, voluntary movement, memory, and emotion. Pharmaceuticals to treat shock and hypotension.

Dopamine hypothesis – schizophrenia is based on the over-activity of dopamine synapses.

Double bind – an unresolvable dilemma.

Double-blind control (*experimental design*) – an experimental technique in which biased expectations of experimenters are eliminated by keeping the participants and the experimental assistants unaware of which participants have received which treatment.

Double-blind design (*experimental design*) – neither the subjects nor the experimenter knows which subjects belong to the experimental and control groups. Experimental control with the subject and experimenter uninformed about the purpose to reduce bias (*experimenter bias*).

Double-blind study (*experimental design*) – neither the subjects nor the persons administering the experiment know the critical aspects of the experiment.

Double-bind theory (*Bateson*, 1950s) – a model of schizophrenia proposing that faulty communication patterns within the family contribute to the onset of schizophrenia.

Down's syndrome (or *trisomy 21*) – a genetic disorder caused by abnormal cell divisions (i.e., nondisjunction) that results in an extra genetic chromosome 21 (i.e., trisomy 21). This genetic imbalance causes distinct facial appearance, intellectual disability, and developmental delays and may be associated with thyroid or heart disease.

Dramaturgical analysis (*Erving Goffman*, 1956) – investigation of social interaction in terms of theatrical performance (i.e., people are actors in society playing roles on different "sets" or "stages," adapting using role-appropriate "scripts").

Dream analysis – the psychoanalytic interpretation of dreams for insight into a person's unconscious motives or conflicts.

Dream work (*Freudian dream analysis*) – an internal censor that transforms the latent content of dreams into manifest content.

Dreaming – a stage of sleep typified by visual imagery and rapid eye movements (REM).

Drive reduction theory of motivation (*Clark Hull*, 1943) – people act to reduce needs and maintain a constant physiological state. All behavior is motivated and stems from the satisfaction of homeostatic drives (e.g., hunger and thirst). Stimuli (e.g., food and water) that decrease the drives reinforce the behavior that led to them.

Drives – internal state arising in response to disequilibrium in physiological needs.

Drug therapy (or *pharmacotherapy*) – treatment using medication.

Drug treatments – psychological disorders based on biological explanations of abnormal behavior. Treatment includes anti-anxiety drugs, anti-depressant drugs, and anti-bipolar drugs.

Dual-earner couples – both partners are employed outside the home; known as dual-income, two-income, two-earner, or dual-worker couples.

Dysfunctional – functioning incorrectly or abnormally.

Dyslexia (*developmental dyslexia*) – difficulties with written and spoken language (across differing levels of intellect) because of development, while acquired dyslexia occurs due to a stroke or similar injury, whereby language skills are impaired.

Dysphoria – abnormal depression and discontent.

Dysthymic disorder – involving depressed mood on most days for at least two years.

E

Early intervention in psychosis – the clinical interventional approach for early symptoms of psychosis. A psychotic condition, if detected early, helps provide treatment at the right time.

Eating disorders – problematic eating patterns, extreme concerns about body weight, and inappropriate behaviors aimed at controlling body weight.

Eccentric – conspicuously or grossly unconventional or unusual.

Echoic memory – auditory sensory memory.

Echolalia – the state in which a person repeats the vocalizations made by someone else. A condition often in autistic children and catatonic schizophrenics, whereby individuals demonstrate a pathological repetition of others' words, either immediately or delayed for hours or days. Disorders include Tourette syndrome, autism, Rubenstein-taybi syndrome, aphasia, schizophrenia, developmental disability, Alzheimer's disease, Asperger syndrome, and others may exhibit echolalia.

Echopraxia – when a person involuntarily imitates or repeats the movements of others. It is a behavioral phenomenon; thus, it differs from a 'tic.' Tics include sudden, non-rhythmic, repetitive vocalization or motor movements (throat clearing, eye blinking, toe crunching).

Ecological psychology – studying interactions and interrelationships between an individual and surroundings regarding information exchange, learning, problem-solving, etc.

Economic psychology – studies the cognitive, emotional, social, and human factors involved in decision-making (e.g., by consumers, investors, and borrowers). *For example, the effects of decisions made on returns, market prices, and allocation of resources are studied.*

Educational psychology – the scientific study of the learning process, the psychology of teaching, the effectiveness of educational interventions, and the social psychology of institutions like schools that impart education.

Efferent nerves – bundles of axons carry information from the central nervous system (CNS) to muscles and sense organs.

Efficacy – the effectiveness of medicine or psychotherapy treatments.

Egalitarian family system – both partners share power and authority fairly and equally.

Ego (Latin, I; *psychodynamic model*) – the component of personality managing the conflict among the id, the superego, and the constraints of the real world. In psychoanalysis, the part of the personality mediates between the id and superego by directing instinctual drives and urges into appropriate channels. The aspect of personality that attempts to satisfy the needs of the id but recognizes that not all its needs can be reasonably fulfilled.

Ego defense mechanisms – mental strategies (conscious or unconscious) by the ego to defend itself against conflicts experienced in life.

Ego psychology (*psychoanalysis model*) – derived from Freud's concept of 'id-ego-superego.' The objective of studying ego psychology is to understand the development of the ego, its management, and its adaptation to reality.

Egocentrism – the inability to take someone else's point of view; an individual is incapable of differentiating between self and the world. An egocentric person understands, analyzes, and interprets the world on their own terms.

Egocentricity (*Piaget*) – the preoperational stage, whereby a young child cannot take another's perspective. Piaget's 'three mountains' experiment tests egocentricity, as children cannot see how the 'mountains' would look to a child at a different location.

Elaboration – deep processing with information learned associated with meaningful material.

Elaboration likelihood model – how likely people focus cognitive processes on elaborating upon a message and, therefore, follow the central and peripheral routes to persuasion; changes in attitudes tend to be long-lasting when people think about the content of persuasive messages they receive.

Elaborative rehearsal – technique improves memory by enriching information encoding. Active processing of items to improve memory from focusing on sensory characteristics (visual appearance, sound) to emphasizing the semantic content (meaning) of information.

Electra complex (comparable to *Oedipus Complex* in Freudian psychology) – competition for the father's affection in females. This can lead to resentment of the mother, for whom the father demonstrates love. Electra Complex is named after *Electra* in Greek mythology, a character who plans with her brother, Orestes, to murder her mother, Clytemnestra, in revenge for her murdering Electra's father.

Electric stimulation of the brain – an invasive method of studying the brain in which an implanted electrode activates brain regions.

Electroconvulsive shock treatment (ECT) – electrical shocks to treat severe depression, passing small amounts of electric current through the brain, inducing a convulsion or epileptic seizure, as an effective treatment for severe depression.

Electrocardiograph (ECG or EKG) – records heart electrical activity.

Electrodermal response (or *galvanic skin response*) – an increase in the skin's rate of electrical conductivity; measures the change in electrical resistance of the skin, a standard measurement of autonomic reaction and arousal.

Electroencephalograph (EEG) – records the overall electrical activity of the brain via electrodes placed on the scalp.

Electromyograph (EMG) – records muscle activity.

Electrooculograph (EOG) – records eye movements.

Elimination by aspects – the process of eliminating alternatives in a decision based on whether they do or do not possess aspects or attributes the decision maker has deemed necessary or desirable.

Emancipation (*psychological*) – step-by-step personality development by a self-reliant mature individual. Worthy education guides toward mature self-reliance and self-realization.

Embryo – a ball of zygote-derived cells developing during the embryonic stage.

Embryonic stage – begins two weeks after conception and ends two months after conception.

Empirical – information based on observations, experiments, or experiences rather than ideology, religious beliefs, or intuition.

Empiricism – the doctrine that knowledge derives from experience.

Emotion – a complex, subjective experience accompanied by biological and behavioral changes. A pattern of extreme changes in physiological arousal, behavior, cognitive processes, and environmental influences expressed in subjective terms such as happiness, fear, or anger.

Emotion work – the process of acting out an emotion not presently felt.

Emotion-focused coping – aims to manage the adverse effects of stress on the individual by changing an emotional response.

Emotional development – developing a full range of emotions from sad to happy to angry and learning to address them appropriately.

Emotional intelligence – an ability that helps people perceive, express, understand, and regulate emotions; the ability to manage self-emotions and people in general.

Emotional reasoning – a cognitive error when a person decides in a state of anxiety and relies on emotional reactions to determine a course of action.

Empirically validated treatments – showing the effects more than placebo or no treatment.

Empty nest – the time in parents' lives when their children have grown and moved away.

Emotional state – a person's emotions (especially concerning pleasure or dejection).

Empathy – the ability to understand another's perceptions and feelings. Rogers cited it as a condition for growth.

Empirical data (or *experimental data*) – information derived from measurements made in "real life" situations (e.g., field data).

Encoding – the process of putting information into memory, changing sensory input into a mental representation in the memory system.

Encoding specificity – the principle that subsequent retrieval of information is enhanced if cues received at the time of recall are consistent with those present at the time of encoding.

Endocrine glands – secrete hormones into the bloodstream; a network of tissues that allows the body to communicate via hormones.

Endocrine system – a network of glands synthesizing and secreting hormones into the blood.

Endocrinologist – a specialist in the endocrine glands and hormone systems.

Endogenous – caused by factors within the body or mind or arising internally.

Endogenous biological rhythms – physiological cycles originating inside the body rather than depending on environmental cues.

Endogenous pacemakers – inherited mechanisms important for regulating biological rhythms, particularly in the absence of external cues. A group of hypothalamic cells (suprachiasmatic nucleus or SCN) are the principal endogenous pacemaker regulating melatonin production in the pineal gland.

Endogamy – the practice of selecting mates of the same social category or group (e.g., same religion, race, social class/caste, tribal group, ethnicity).

Endorphins – a group of neurotransmitters (e.g., α-endorphin, β-endorphin, and γ-endorphin) involved in pain, pleasure, and modulating the action of other neurotransmitters.

Engram – the physical memory trace for information in the brain.

Environmental stressors (or *aggressive behavior*) – environmental elements that give rise to anti-social behavior by increasing arousal, which may produce negative emotions and aggressive behavior. For instance, high temperatures, intense levels of noise, and crowding can produce high levels of aggression.

Environmental variables – external influences on behavior.

Epistemology (*philosophy*) – the philosophical theory of knowledge.

Episodic memory – long-term memories of personal experiences and the contexts in which they occur, remembering personal facts.

EQ (emotional intelligence) – the counterpart of IQ.

Equilibration (*Piaget's theory of cognitive development*) – maintaining a balance between the environment and mental structures (or *schemas*) representing that environment.

Equity theory – 1. a cognitive theory of work motivation that proposes that workers are motivated to maintain fair and equitable relationships with other relevant persons; 2. a model that postulates that equitable relationships are those in which the participants' outcomes are proportional to their inputs.

Erikson, Erik (1902-1994) – German-American psychoanalyst and proponent of developmental psychology. Proposed eight stages of psychosocial development from birth to death, for instance, identity *vs.* role confusion.

Ergonomics – the study of the 'fit' between humans and their workplace, designs working environments that maximize user efficiency and comfort.

Erogenous zones – areas of the skin surface that are especially sensitive to stimulation and give rise to erotic or sexual sensations.

Estimator variables (*witness testimony*) – affect the accuracy of witness testimony that the justice system has little control over, including weather and the amount of time the witness was at the scene.

Estrogen – the female sex hormone produced by the ovaries responsible for releasing eggs from ovaries and developing and maintaining female reproductive structures and secondary sex characteristics.

Ethical guidelines – prescriptive guidance (e.g., guidelines published by the BPS) on the conduct of psychologists in research and practice to oversee what is acceptable within the pursuit of a specific goal, including informed consent, right to withdraw, and debriefing.

Ethical hedonism – individuals engage in moral behavior, such as altruism, because it provides some personal advantage.

Ethics (*philosophy*) – a system of moral values; the study of principles relating to conduct (e.g., right and wrong). Morality governs conduct, especially a member of a profession.

Ethnicity – shared cultural heritage; group sharing a common language, religion, history, homeland, ancestry, and some remaining customs and traditions; today's ethnic groups often represent watered-down culture groups due to the assimilation pressures around them.

Ethnocentrism – from an ethnic, national, or cultural group perspective; judging another culture by the standards of one's culture; an attitude of superiority about culture or society.

Ethnomethodology (*Harold Garfinkel*, 1967) – studying how people construct and deal with reality; everyone learns shared definitions of reality to make everyday interactions possible.

Etiology – studying the causes or origin of a disease or mental disorder.

Euphoria – a feeling of great elation; a feeling of happiness, confidence, or well-being sometimes exaggerated in mood disorders such as mania.

Evaluation research – relies on standard data collection techniques to assess the effectiveness of social programs in both the public and the private sectors.

Evolution – a change in the frequency of genes in a population.

Evolutionary perspective – stresses the importance of behavioral and mental adaptiveness, based on the assumption that mental capabilities evolved over millions of years to serve particular adaptive purposes.

Evolutionary psychology – uses research methods to study psychological issues, including behavioral and mental adaptiveness over millions of years, to help explain human behavior.

Excitatory – that tends to excite or cause excitation.

Excitatory inputs – information entering a neuron that signals it to fire.

Excitatory postsynaptic potential – voltage change when neurotransmitter binds excitatory receptor.

Existential therapies (or *humanistic therapies*) – helping patients find meaning in their lives.

Exogamy (or *heterogamy*) – the practice of selecting a mate from outside one's social group; marriage between people of social categories.

Exogenous zeitgebers (*time givers*) – external events that help regulate biological rhythms, for instance, light and social stimuli (see *endogenous pacemakers*).

Expectancy approaches (or *incentive approaches*) – motivation-producing goal-directed behavior.

Expectancy effects – results when a researcher or observer subtly communicates to participants the kind of behavior they expect to find, thereby creating the expected.

Expectancy theory – a cognitive theory of work motivation proposes that workers are motivated when they expect their efforts and job performance to result in desired outcomes.

Expected value – the process of adding the value of winning times the probability of a win to the value of a loss times the probability of a loss to decide.

Experience-sampling method – an experimental method describing the specific contents of consciousness; participants record what they feel and think whenever signaled to do so.

Experiential intelligence – the ability to adapt to new situations and produce new ideas.

Experiment – a test under controlled conditions made to demonstrate truth, examine the validity of a hypothesis, or determine the efficacy of something previously untried.

Experimental group – subjects in an experiment for whom the independent variable is manipulated. The *control group* serves as a comparison group.

Experimental methods – systematically manipulating the independent variable to determine the effect upon the dependent variable.

Experimental psychology – typically involves laboratory research in basic areas of the discipline; aims to discover the processes of cognition and behavior by different means, such as studying emotions, motivating individuals, and understanding social psychology.

Experimental research – investigates causal relationships between variables.

Experimenter bias – a source of error arises when researchers' preferences or expectations influence the research outcome. Bias is introduced by an experimenter when outcome expectations are subtly communicated to participants in the experiment.

Experimenter effects – when behavior or characteristics influence participants through subtle cues or signals affecting the performance or response of subjects in the experiment.

Explicit attitudes – conscious beliefs that guide decisions and behavior.

Explicit memory – conscious, intentional remembering of information; requires a conscious attempt to recall memory.

Exposure therapy – aims to eliminate anxiety by having patients face accurate or imagined versions of feared stimuli.

Expressive language – the ability to use language to communicate.

Extended family – consisting of parents and children, as well as other kin, such as uncles and aunts, nieces and nephews, cousins and grandparents.

External attribution (or *situational attribution*) – inferencing a person's behavior due to situational factors.

External locus of control – believing circumstances are not within one's control but are due to luck, fate, or other people.

External validity – the extent by which research results can be generalized beyond specific situations studied.

Extinction (*conditioning*) – gradual disappearance of response after it stops being reinforced.

Extraneous variable – other than the independent variable affecting the dependent variable. It is not part of the hypothesis; it makes possible an alternative explanation of results, an uncontrolled variable.

Extrinsic motivation – to act for external rewards.

Extrovert – a person directed toward others instead of the self; a person concerned more with practical realities than inner thoughts and feelings.

Extroversion (*Big Five Personality Trait*) – personality traits of confidence, outgoing behavior, and assertiveness. A personality dimension characterized by sociability, engaging in conversations, and impulsiveness. Measured on the Introversion-Extroversion scale of the EPI (*Eysenck Personality Inventory*, 1964).

Eye movement desensitization and reprocessing (EMDR) – exposure therapy in which patients move their eyes back and forth while recalling memories to be desensitized.

Eyewitness testimony – evidence given by witnesses (e.g., court cases); studying the accuracy of memory following an accident (or crime) and exploring common errors. Psychologists question eyewitness testimonies' reliability and accuracy, which can be affected by false memories.

Eysenck Personality Inventory (EPI) (1964) – a personality test to measure traits of extroversion and neuroticism using the Introversion-Extroversion scale.

F

F scale (Adorno, 1947; *F stands for fascism*) – a personality test measuring an authoritarian personality; measures the authoritarian personality by exploring the extent to which people agree with statements such as 'Obedience and respect for authority are the most important virtues children should learn. F-scale measures components of authoritarianism (e.g., authoritarian aggression, conventionalism, authoritarian submission, superstition, anti-interception, cynicism, destructiveness, toughness, and projectivity).

Face perception – enables a person (mind and brain) to recognize and interpret a face.

Face recognition – comparing a perceived stimulus pattern with stored representations of familiar faces.

Face validity – the extent to which the measure evaluates what it claims.

Facial expression – nonverbal communication by humans and animals (primarily mammals) in conveying social information.

Facial-feedback hypothesis – brain uses facial muscle feedback to recognize emotions experienced.

Factitious disorders – people exaggerate or feign the symptoms of a disease.

Factor analysis – a statistical procedure clustering variables into dimensions depending on similarities among the variables.

Faculty psychology – the human mind is a collection of faculties performing tasks assigned.

False memory – a person falsely recalls a belief. False memories may be created inadvertently or intentionally, as demonstrated by the *Lost in the Mall Technique* (James Coan, 1997). Discovering false memories has had implications for using eyewitness testimonies in court cases.

False negative (or *Type II error*) – in inferential statistics, concluding that the observed results are due only to chance when a significant effect exists.

False positive (or *Type 1 error*) – in inferential statistics, concluding that an observed outcome is significant when it reflects only chance.

Falsifiability – the ability of a hypothesis to be rejected; it is a criterion to evaluate a theory, whereby the theory should state circumstances where it can be proven wrong.

Family – an intimate group of two or more people who are typically related, live together, care for the needs of each other, and share close emotional ties and functions.

Family stress model (*Salvador Munchin*) – separation and divorce are viewed as transactional processes in the evolution of a family's life cycle.

Family studies – researchers examine trait similarities among family members to determine whether the trait might be inherited.

Family systems theory – family as a set of interacting and interdependent components.

Family therapy – a therapist sees two or more family members simultaneously. The interactions between family members have an impact on their psychological health. Psychotherapy helps nurture the change and development in family relationships.

Fantasy – the imaginative thoughts, desires, or feelings far from reality or impossible altogether. Fantasies differ from imagination power as fantasies could be sexual.

Fatigue effects – when participants become tired or bored if a demanding or repetitive task is repeated, resulting in deteriorating performance.

Fear – an emotion in anticipation of some specific pain or danger; a basic survival mechanism or emotional response to a threat or specific stimuli. The stimuli or threat may be pain or danger of losing one's life. Fear is generally experienced for a worsening situation.

Feature detection theories – explain pattern recognition by proposing that images are processed in terms of their parts, which then match the features of a pattern stored in memory.

Feature detectors – specific features of the environment activate specialized neurons.

Feature processing (*visual perception*) – the ability to detect contours for object recognition.

Fechner, Gustav (1801-1887) – experimental psychology pioneer and psychophysics founder (techniques measuring the mind). He demonstrated the non-linear relationship between psychological sensation and the physical intensity of a stimulus, the Weber-Fechner law.

Feelings – the expression and sensation of emotion; created, expressed, and stored.

Feigned scarcity – implying a product is scarce, even when not, to increase demand for it.

Feminine – associated with women and not with men.

Feminine traits – tactful, quiet, aware of feelings, connection, empathy, caring.

Feminism – proposes that women and men often experience culture differently, and cultural values and norms increase inequality due to gender. Defines and establishes political, economic, personal, and social equality of the sexes. Feminism asserts that societies prioritize the male point of view and that women are treated unjustly.

Feminist theory – approaches explain the social, economic, and political positions of women in society to free women from traditional expectations, constraints, roles, and behaviors, both micro and macro sociological.

Feral children (or *wolf children*) – children living in the wild display animal-like behaviors, indicating wild animals have brought them up.

Festinger, Leon (1919-1989) – American social psychologist who developed theories of cognitive dissonance (whereby incongruity between beliefs or behaviors causes psychological discomfort) and social comparison theory.

Fetal alcohol syndrome – a collection of symptoms in babies of alcoholic mothers who drank heavily during pregnancy.

Fetal stage – last stage of prenatal development, two months from conception until birth.

Fictive kin – nonrelatives accepted as part of an African American family.

Field experiments – in a natural rather than a comparatively artificial laboratory setting. Consequently, extraneous variables are challenging.

Field research – data collected by systematically observing subjects in natural surroundings.

Fight-or-flight response (*Walter Bradford Cannon*, 1915) – a set of physiological responses triggered in stressful situations, including muscle contractions and pupil dilation in a state of heightened awareness in preparation to respond to a threat. A series of internal activities set off when an organism experiences a threat in preparation for defending or attacking (*fight*) or fleeing to safety (*flight*).

Figure – what stands out when people organize visual information.

Filial imprinting (*stamping in* or *imprinting*) – a process in the early stages of life when an infant observes a moving object and forms an attachment. When a young animal learns the characteristics of its parent, it is most apparent in nidifugous birds, which imprint on their parents and follow them. Initially described by Douglas Spalding as *stamping in*, the process was referred to as imprinting by Oskar Heinroth and demonstrated by his student, Konrad Lorenz, in graylag geese (*Lorenz*, 1935).

Filognosy – love for the knowledge of self-realization as inspired by Western and Eastern concepts for the integrity of views, logic, and intelligence in modern society on a global scale.

Five-factor model (or *Big Five*) – a comprehensive descriptive personality system mapping the relationships among common traits, theoretical concepts, and personality scales.

Five stages of grief (or *Kubler-Ross model*, 1969) – when people deal with tragedy and grief in five discrete sequential stages, *Denial*, *Anger*, *Bargaining*, *Depression*, and *Acceptance*.

Fixation (*psychoanalytic theory*) – an inability to progress normally from one developmental psychosexual stage to the next; a preference for gratification mode associated with a stage of psychosexual development due to too much or too little gratification.

Fixed-interval schedule – a technique when reinforcement happens after a set amount of time. *For example, reinforcement is applied systematically, for instance, every four minutes.*

Fixed ratio schedule – a reinforcement applied according to some predetermined responses; reinforcement happens after a set number of responses. *For example, one reinforcement for every three responses.*

Flashbulb memories (*Brown and Kulik*, 1977) – vivid, detailed memories of noteworthy events related to an emotionally arousing event.

Flooding (*behavioral therapy*) – treats phobias through exposure to the feared object for an extended period, with no opportunity for escape. Exposure therapy is when the patient is suddenly exposed to a feared stimulus rather than gradually.

Fluid intelligence – abstract intelligence analyzing complex relationships, reasons, and problems.

Flynn effect – phenomenon showing people's performance on IQ tests improved over time in industrialized countries.

Folkways – norms that members of a society (or a group within society) consider not critical and that can be transgressed without severe punishment.

Folk psychology – the collection of constructs, assumptions, and convictions that construct language used daily to discuss human psychology.

Follow-up study – continuing contact with participants after a study to examine long-term effects that may have arisen due to their participation.

Foolishness – exhibited by beliefs or actions indicating poor learning abilities or low intelligence.

Foot-in-the-door technique – compliance whereby people are more likely to comply if they initially agree to a small request, followed by a larger one later. Agreeing to a problematic request after first agreeing to an easy one.

Forced-choice item – respondents select one response, reducing socially desirable responses.

Forebrain – the anterior portion of the brain, the biggest and most complex part, includes structures such as the thalamus, the hypothalamus, the limbic system, and the cerebrum.

Forensic psychology (*criminal justice*) – the ability to testify in court and formulate the findings from psychology into legal language.

Forgetting – the inability to recall what was previously remembered; explained by several theories, such as dependent forgetting (the memory trace is lost), cue-dependent forgetting (the lack of necessary cues to retrieve the memory), repression (painful memories unconsciously repressed), or interference.

Forgetting curve – graphing how quickly learned information is forgotten over time.

Formal assessment – the systematic procedures and measurement instruments trained professionals use to assess an individual's functioning, aptitudes, abilities, or mental state.

Foundational theories – frameworks for initial understanding formulated by children to explain their experiences of the world.

Fovea – the center of the retina, where vision is the sharpest; a small area on the retina containing closely packed cones onto which light from an object is focused upon.

Frame – a particular description of a choice; the perspective from which a choice is described or framed affects how a decision is made and which option is chosen.

Frame of mind (or *state of mind*) – a temporary psychological state (i.e., mental or emotional or mood).

Framing – deciding between options based on whether they are presented with positive or negative connotations. Individuals tend to make risk-avoidant choices when options are positively framed while selecting loss-avoidant options when presented with a negative frame.

Fraternal – characteristic befitting a brother.

Fraternal twin – see *dizygotic twins*.

Free association (*psychodynamic technique*) – a patient is encouraged to freely talk about their thoughts, wishes, experiences, and mental images as they arise, hoping to allow preconscious content to surface in the consciousness.

Free will – the ability to decide and choose how to behave without external influences determining behavior; opposes *determinism*.

Free will *vs.* determinism – the debate between those who believe that external or internal factors acting upon the individual determine behavior (*determinism*) and those believing individuals respond actively to the outside world (*free will*).

Frequency (*statistical analysis*) – the number of times per second an output (e.g., sound wave) cycles from the highest to lowest amplitude.

Frequency distribution (*statistical analysis*) – data set reflecting how often each score occurs, represented in several graphical ways, including histograms.

Frequency theory – how people discriminate low-pitched sounds with a frequency below 1000 Hz. A tone produces a rate of vibration in the basilar membrane equal to its frequency, with a frequency for the neural response to code pitch.

Freud, Sigmund (1856-1939) – Austrian psychoanalyst who developed the psychodynamic theory in psychology. Founder of psychoanalytic psychology emphasizing the unconscious mind, childhood experiences, and repressed urges. Freud maintained that the Oedipus and Electra complexes and other desires motivate human behavior. His theory of psychosexual development outlines five stages; oral, anal, phallic, latent, and genital, according to the objects fixated upon at each stage. Freud focused on the structure and development of personality, comprised of three parts – the id, ego, and superego. Ego deals with conflicts between the id and superego, utilizing defense mechanisms such as denial.

Freud, though controversial, has impacted psychology through psychoanalysis and his therapeutic techniques (e.g., free association). Furthermore, he applied a range of his ideas to dreams to understand unconscious desires. *For example, repressed urges often manifest in dreams through symbolic images.*

Freud's defense mechanisms – 1) reaction formation, 2) projection, 3) displacement, 4) undoing, 5) isolation, 6) sublimation, and 7) denial.

Freudian psychology – the psychological theories of Sigmund Freud (1856-1939).

Freudian slip – a slip-up, either in speech, writing, or memory, reflecting the unconscious mind's hidden worries or focus. The accidental mispronunciation of, or unconscious use of, a word or phrase unintentionally reveals a person's true feelings.

Frontal lobe – the area of the cortex in front of the central fissure and above the lateral fissure; involved in motor control and cognitive processes.

Frontal lobotomy – a medical operation popular in the 1940s and 1950s, which involved sectioning or removing sections of the frontal lobes, often to treat cases of bipolar mood disorder or chronic pain.

Frustration – the experience of being thwarted while achieving a goal; an act of hindering someone's plans or efforts.

Frustration-aggression hypothesis – aggression is caused by frustration.

Frustration-aggression theory (*Dollard and Miller*, 1939) –

Fully functioning person – portrayed by Rogers as the ideal of growth; an openness, a high level of spontaneity, compassion, and self-direction demonstrate healthy growth.

Functional fixedness (*Gestalt theory*) – thinking only of an object's common use in solving a problem. Perceiving an object as having only one already established or associated use; an inability to identify a new use.

Functional MRI (fMRI) – a brain imaging technique that scans by measuring magnetic changes in blood flow to brain cells.

Functionalism (*psychology*) – mental processes are beneficial environmental adaptations.

Functionalist theory – social institutions and processes in society exist to serve a necessary function and work in harmony to maintain society in balance. Also, a macro-sociological theory states that similar beliefs bind people and create stability, sharing core values that unify society and promote cultural solidarity.

Fundamental attribution error (or *correspondence bias*) – the tendency to attribute other people's behavior to internal factors such as personality traits, abilities, and feelings. Attribution theory overemphasizes dispositional factors (e.g., personality) and underestimates situational factors (e.g., weather) on behavior.

G

GABA (gamma-aminobutyric acid) – the primary inhibitory neurotransmitter in the brain.

G factor – general intelligence underlying all intelligent performance (i.e., general intelligence or general mental ability factor).

Galton, Sir Francis (1822-1911) – English scientist (cousin of Charles Darwin) who explored many fields, including heredity, meteorology, statistics, psychology, and anthropology; founder of eugenics and first to use fingerprints for identification.

Galvanic skin response (or *electrodermal response*) – an increase in the skin's rate of electrical conductivity. A measure of the change in electrical resistance of the skin, a standard measurement of autonomic reaction and arousal.

Gambler's fallacy – a chance event is more likely if it has not happened recently.

Ganglion cells – visual system cells integrate impulses from bipolar cells in a single firing.

Gate-control theory – pain signals traveling from body to brain must pass a gate in the spinal cord.

Gender – a learned distinction between masculinity and femininity; properties distinguishing organisms based on sex. Commonly refers to the psychological characteristics (e.g., behavior and attitudes) of being male and female (in contrast to 'sex,' which refers to physiological characteristics).

Gender identity – an individual's perception of whether they are male or female. Awareness typically begins in infancy and is reinforced during adolescence, regarding individuality as male or female, male and female, or neither.

Gender narcissism – the over-perception or over-emphasis of gender or the difference between genders during childhood results in either the over-valuation or devaluation of one gender later in adulthood. The concept of gender narcissism can be explained based on theories like the 'castration complex' and 'penis envy' posited by Sigmond Freud.

Gender roles – a given culture's acceptable attitudes and behaviors for each gender.

Gender stereotypes – societal beliefs about the characteristics of males and females.

Gene – biological units of heredity, crucial for transmitting traits.

General adaptation syndrome (*Hans Selye*, 1936) – depicting physiological mechanisms in response to a stressor over an extended period. Three stages are 1) the alarm stage, which activates an arousal response (e.g., to fight or flee). 2) the resistance stage is when the body attempts to cope with the stressor. 3) the exhaustion stage occurs if the stressor continues over a prolonged period, leading to physical symptoms such as stomach ulcers.

General intelligence (g) (*Charles Spearman*, 1863-1945) – a mental attribute underlying a range of intellectual tasks. Charles Spearman proposed that people who performed well on one mental ability test tended to do well on other tests.

Generalizability – the extent to which findings based on a study using a sample of participants represent the target population or other populations.

Generalization (*psychology*) – transfer of a learned response to a similar stimulus.

General adaption syndrome (GAS) – the pattern of nonspecific, adaptational physiological mechanisms in response to a continuing threat by almost any severe stressor.

Generalized anxiety disorder – persistent and excessive anxiety lasting six months; characterized by uncontrollable, irrational, and excessive worry about daily life activities. The magnitude of worry experienced is in excess if compared with the cause.

Generalized other (*George Herbert Mead*, 1964) – cultural norms and values for evaluating oneself; society's roles become a part of one's identity and identity superimposed upon others. People who do not have close ties to a child but who will influence the child's internalization of society's norms and values (e.g., librarian, policeman, drill sergeant).

Generative – symbols of a language combined to produce unlimited messages.

Generativity – a commitment beyond one's self and partner to family, work, society, and future generations; typically, a crucial step in development in one's thirties and forties.

Genes – segments of DNA as hereditary units; the biological units of heredity; discrete sections of chromosomes responsible for the transmission of traits.

Genetic – hereditary information passed from parents through genes in sperm and egg cells.

Genetics – the study of heredity of physical and psychological traits.

Genetic psychology – studies the social and mental development of children.

Genius – a person with exceptional ability and creativity. *For example, an IQ over 140 is a genius.*

Genital personality (*psychoanalysis*) – the mature personality not dominated by infantile pleasure drives.

Genital stage (*psychoanalysis theory*) – the last stage of psychosexual development when the primary source of pleasure is the genitals.

Genocide – the systematic destruction of one group, often ethnic or racial group, by another.

Genotype – the genetic code inherited and carried in DNA.

Germinal stage – the two weeks after conception.

Gestalt (German, *configuration*) – emphasizes that the whole (whether person or image) is greater than the sum of its parts.

Gestalt law of organization – identifies factors leading to forms of perceptual organization.

Gestalt psychology – emphasizes the importance of configurational properties. The German school of thought studies how people organize visual information into patterns and forms. A theory that the brain functions as holistic, analog, and parallel. Emphasizes that 'the whole is greater than the sum of the parts. Psychological phenomena (e.g., perception, learning, and thinking) are organized, structured wholes. *For example, Gestalt problem-solving seeks a structural understanding of how parts of the problem fit to reach the goal.*

Gestalt therapy – considers all dimensions of a person's life and experience to stimulate personal growth and increase self–awareness in developing a sense of the whole person.

Glial cells – give structural support to neurons and nourish and insulate them.

Globalization – the growth and spread of worldwide investment, trade, communication, production, and new technology.

Global perspective – the study of the larger world and society's place in it, comparing one's thinking and behavior to other cultures.

Glucose ($C_6H_{12}O_6$) – a simple sugar acting as an energy source (ATP) for cells.

Glutamate – the primary excitatory neurotransmitter in the brain.

Gnosiology (*cognitive psychology*) – the study of gnosis (i.e., knowledge of infinite, uncreated, and divine).

Goal-directed selection – a determinant of why people select some parts of sensory input for further processing; reflects the choices made as a function of one's goals.

Goal state – the desired outcome for problem-solving.

Grandiose delusion – a belief centered around the idea that one is important or famous.

Gratification – the positive emotional response (happiness) to the fulfillment of desire.

Gratitude – positive emotion in response or acknowledgment of favor or benefit received.

Great Mother (*primary archetypes by Jung*) – embodies maternal qualities such as caring, understanding, and encouraging parents who may be consulted for advice or sought in times of need. Another contrasting side of this archetype is the Shadow of the Great Mother, whose destructive forces are to be feared. *For example, the concept of Mother Nature sees the positive, creative influence of the Great Mother in fertility, growth, and abundance of crops. Her Shadow is embodied in the destructive tendencies of storms, tsunamis, and earthquakes.*

Grimace – a facial expression displaying or exhibiting emotions like contempt, complacency, and disapprobation.

Ground – the background in which a figure stands when people organize visual information.

Group – a social unit composed of people interacting and depending on one another.

Group cohesiveness – the strength of the liking and commitment group members have toward one another and the group.

Group dynamics (*social psychology*) – studies psychodynamic interactions in social groups.

Group polarization – the tendency for a dominant point of view in a group to be strengthened to a more extreme position after a group discussion. The tendency for groups to shift to make more extreme decisions than decisions made independently by group members. If individual members of a group are already cautious in their attitude, they will demonstrate a shift toward an even more cautious attitude during like-minded group discussions. When individuals are less cautious before group discussion, they are likely to show a shift towards more risky decisions.

Group psychological abuse – psychological abuse systematically and frequently.

Group psychotherapy – psychotherapists treating a group. The interrelationships between a group are explored, examined, and developed using group processes or the group context.

Group synergy (or *collective intelligence*) – the intelligence that emerges from the shared efforts of competition and collaboration among a group.

Group therapy – when therapeutic sessions are in groups rather than individually, the therapist acts as a facilitator amongst the group. Group therapy can help individuals feel less isolated and, through fostering social interaction, can discuss with and help others.

Groupthink – decision-making by a group; close-knit group emphasizing consensus instead of critical thinking and rational decision-making. *Decision-making groups often reach an extreme, unwise, unrealistic conclusion because of discounting information inconsistent with their view and expressing disapproval against members who disagree.*

Guided search (*visual perception*) – a parallel search for single, basic attributes to guide attention to the likely locations of objects with more complex combinations of attributes.

Guilt – a higher development than shame; the emotional or cognitive experience that succeeds in the realization that one has violated a moral standard. Guilt has an internal punitive voice operating at the level of the superego (an internalized punitive harsh parental figure). Remorse and guilt are closely related. There is valid guilt and invalid guilt.

Gustation – the faculty of distinguishing sweet, sour, bitter, and salty properties in the mouth.

Gustatory – relating to the sense of taste.

H

Habit – an automatic pattern of behavior in reaction to a situation; a behavior due to experience and occurs automatically. *For instance, behaviors satisfying psychological cravings (e.g., chain-smoking).*

Habits – a repeated behavior occurring subconsciously (i.e., without active thinking or consciously). A habit is an activity performed without self-analysis, and most of the time, it goes unnoticed by the person exhibiting it.

Habituation – when an organism's response to repeated stimuli temporarily decreases.

Hall, G. Stanley (1844-1924) – American child psychologist whose theories of child psychology strongly influenced educational psychology.

Hallucinations – sensory or perceptual experiences without any external stimulus; false perceptions without relevant sensory stimuli, such as hearing voices.

Hallucinogens – drugs causing sensory and perceptual distortions.

Halo effect – a perceptual bias when rating a person on one characteristic as being positive or negative affects the ratings on other characteristics (similarly positive or negative). *For example, if an individual is rated intelligent, the rater also perceives them as friendly.*

Hardiness (*Susan Kobasa*) – responding to stressful situations with *control* (*vs.* powerlessness), *commitment* (*vs.* alienation), and *challenge* (*vs.* threat). Personality factors such as control, commitment, and challenges help mitigate against adverse effects of stress.

Harlow, Harry Frederick (1905–1981) – American psychologist, doctoral advisor to Abraham Maslow, known for his maternal separation, dependency needs, and social isolation experiments on rhesus monkeys, which manifested the importance of caregiving and companionship to social and cognitive development.

Hawthorne effect (1924-27) – modifying behavior by study participants in response to their knowledge of being observed.

Health – a general condition of soundness and vigor of body and mind, not simply the absence of illness or injury.

Health behaviors – activities maintaining or improving health.

Health promotion – strategies and tactics that help enable people to gain control of, and therefore enhance, their health through changes in lifestyle and preventative practices, significantly reducing the risk of illness.

Health psychology – the influence of behavior, illness, health, and biology are studied, why people become ill, how they stay healthy, and how they respond to illness. Focuses on the relationship between psychosocial factors and illness's emergence, progression, and treatment.

Hedonic relevance – the likelihood of making a dispositional attribution when involved and the consequences are severe. Therefore, it is likely to overstate the influence of dispositional factors and underestimate the importance of situational factors.

Hedonism – behavior is motivated toward pursuing pleasure and avoiding pain.

Hegemonic masculinity – societal practices encouraging men to place themselves in higher standing while keeping women in subordinate positions.

Heinroth, Oskar (1871-1945) – German biologist who re-discovered 'imprinting' during a critical development period (Douglas Spalding as 'stamping in'). Heinroth mentored Austrian ornithologist Konrad Lorenz, whose work imprinting graylag geese introduced a broader audience to imprinting (Lorenz, 1935).

Heider, Fritz (1896-1988) – Austrian psychologist focused on interpersonal relationships, proposing balance and attribution theories.

Helmholtz, Hermann von (1821-1894) – German physicist and physician who studied eyes, theories of vision, visual perception of space, color vision, the sensation of tone, perceptions of sound, and empiricism in perception physiology.

Helping behavior – see *altruism and bystander behavior.*

Heredity – the biological transmission of inherited characteristics from parents to offspring.

Heritability estimate (*statistics*) – a mathematical estimate indicating how much of a trait's variation in a population can be attributed to genetic factors. Estimates the degree of inheritance of a specific trait, measured by the similarity between individuals with differing amounts of genetic similarity.

Hermaphrodites (or *intersexual*) – when an individual, at birth, is not distinctly male or female; intersex individuals were previously referred to as *hermaphrodites*; however, the term today is considered stigmatizing or misleading.

Hertz (Hz) – measuring frequency in cycles per second.

Heterogamy (or *exogamy*) – selecting a mate from outside one's social group; marriage between people of social categories.

Heterosexism – the belief that heterosexuality is superior.

Heterosexuality – an attraction to the opposite sex.

Heuristic – used in learning, problem-solving, and discovery; a commonsense rule to help solve some problem. Cognitive *rules of thumb* provide informal strategies for problem-solving, usually more successful than random search but less effective than algorithms.

Hierarchical classification – the ability to classify according to more than one level.

Hierarchy of needs theory (*Abraham Maslow's model of basic human motives*; 1943) – Maslow diagrammatically explained a hierarchical pyramid with five needs levels ranging from physiological (e.g., food, water, shelter) to the highest level of self-actualization. Maslow believed people pay attention to higher needs only when lower needs are satisfied, and each level of the hierarchy must be met before achieving the next.

Higher-order conditioning (*classical conditioning*) – the process by which a neutral stimulus acts as a conditioned stimulus by being paired with another stimulus already evoking a conditioned response.

Hindbrain – the posterior portion of the brain, including the cerebellum and brainstem; the portion of the brain consists of the medulla, the pons, and the cerebellum.

Hindsight bias – the tendency to interpret the past to fit the present.

Hippocampus – part of the limbic system in the medial temporal lobe involved in memory. Essential for spatial orientation and navigation. Crucial for memory is the transfer of information from short-term to long-term memory.

Histogram (or *bar graph*) – a plot showing how data are distributed; a graph of the numerical distribution of scores for one data set, with no gaps between the bars.

Histrionic personality disorder – attention-seeking behavior and shallow emotions; a desire to be the center of attention and the tendency to be self-focused, excitable, highly open to suggestion, very emotional, and dramatic.

Hitch, Graham (*Baddeley and Hitch, Working Memory Model*, 1974) – a theory of memory consisting of a central executive, articulatory-phonological loop, and visuospatial sketchpad.

HIV (human immunodeficiency virus) – a virus that attacks white blood cells, reducing the body's ability to fight illness. HIV causes AIDS and can be transmitted by unprotected sex, by drug users who use similar equipment, and from an infected mother to an unborn child.

Holistic – an approach focusing on the whole person rather than their constituent parts, emphasizing the organic relation between parts and the whole.

Holmes and Rahe (*Social Readjustment Rating Scale*, 1967) – measure the impact of life events.

Homeostasis – a state of equilibrium of internal conditions, maintaining physiological equilibrium. Biological mechanisms maintain metabolic equilibrium.

Homeostatic drive theory (*of eating and drinking*) – eating and drinking is driven by homeostasis.

Homogamy (or *endogamy*) – selecting mates of the same social group (e.g., same religion, race, social class/caste, tribal group, ethnicity).

Horizontal cells – integrate information across the retina; rather than sending signals toward the brain, horizontal cells connect receptors.

Horizontal mobility – 1. movement from one job to another without change in social status; 2. cultural dissemination without change in social status (e.g., trends that move within economic classes).

Hormones – chemical messengers secreted by endocrine glands affecting metabolism and bodily functions. Chemicals produced in glands and released into the bloodstream regulate body functions. *For example, mood and sexual characteristics.*

Hostile aggression – aggression to cause intentional harm to another person or object.

Hostility – angry internal rejection; generally, a synonym for aggression or anger.

Hozho – a Navajo concept referring to harmony, peace of mind, goodness, ideal family relationships, beauty in arts and crafts, and body and spirit health.

Hue – dimension of color space capturing the qualitative experience of the color of light.

Human behavior – behaviors exhibited by humans and influenced by attitudes, cultures, values, emotions, authority, ethics, hypnosis, rapport, coercion, persuasion, etc.

Human behavior genetics – hereditary component of individual differences in behaviors and traits.

Human-potential movement – therapy encompasses those practices and methods that release the potential of the average human for greater levels of performance and experience richness.

Humanism – encourages seeing people's lives as those people would see them.

Humanistic perspective – emphasizes an individual's inherent capacity for making rational choices and developing to maximum potential. Every person is unique and possesses an inherent capacity for rational choices, growth, and maximum potential. *Focuses on the human aspect of the development of psychotherapy—for example, client-centered therapy. The therapist sees the world through the patient's perspective, and the patient views their situations with greater insight and acceptance, with a goal of growth and fulfillment.*

Huntington's disease (HD) is a fatal heredity disease that destroys neurons in brain areas involved in emotions, intellect, and movement.

Hyperactivity – a higher degree of inappropriate motor activity than typical for an age group. See *Attention Deficit Disorder (ADD).*

Hyperfocus – an intense mental concentration or visualization focusing consciousness on a narrow subject or beyond objective reality and onto subjective mental planes, daydreams, concepts, fiction, the imagination, and other objects of the mind.

Hypophysis – the primary gland of the endocrine system.

Hypothalamus – a part of the forebrain helps control the pituitary gland, the autonomic nervous system, body temperature, and biological drives. The basal part of the diencephalon governs the autonomic nervous system. Maintaining homeostasis, regulating motivated behavior (e.g., appetite), and hormonal functions.

Hypothesis – a testable prediction given a specific set of conditions; a testable statement predicting the relationship between two (or more) variables, which can be accepted or rejected because of experimental outcomes. A tentative insight has not yet been verified or tested.

Hypothetical – based on assumption rather than fact or reality.

Hypnosis – an altered state of awareness induced by relaxation and suggestion, allowing access to the subconscious. A state of mind in which a person enters a trance-like state induced artificially, manifested in a sleep-like state or deep relaxation. In this state, the suggestibility is heightened, and the memories might be suppressed. Consequently, changes in perception, memory, and self-control leave an individual more vulnerable to suggestions. Hypnosis in therapy remains controversial, particularly with false memories being recovered.

Hypochondriasis – a disorder in which a person constantly fears having a severe disease.

Hysteria – state of violent mental agitation; an individual loses self-control due to emotional excesses or unmanageable fear. The fear might result from multiple past events involving conflicts or imagined problems (e.g., diseases) associated with a body part.

I

ICD – see *International Classification of Disorders*.

Iconic memory – sensory memory in the visual domain for large amounts of information to be stored briefly.

Id (Latin, *it*) – the component of personality containing instinctual energy; human personality consisting of inborn biological instincts. The unconscious pleasure personality operates irrationally and pursues primitive drives such as anger and hunger. Instincts and energies causing psychic activity are included in the id. Id, ego, and super-ego are the three parts of the psyche, as given by Freud. The psychodynamic model is the aspect of personality expressing innate needs and demands instant gratification of those needs. Later in development, a person's id is tempered by the ego and, eventually, the superego.

Ideal culture – the beliefs, values, and norms people in society hold.

Ideal self (*Rogers's humanistic theory*) – an evolving construct of individual goals and aspirations.

Ideas of reference (or *delusions of reference*) – a symptom of schizophrenia and bipolar disorder, believing irrelevant or unrelated objects, people, or events are personally significant.

Identical twins – see *monozygotic twins*.

Identification – the act of designating something.

Identification and recognition – ways of attaching meaning to percepts.

Identity – the characteristics by which a thing or person is known.

Identity achievement – when a person commits to an identity after considering alternative possibilities.

Identity diffusion – confusion when a person lacks a clear sense of identity and has not yet begun exploring issues related to identity development.

Identity foreclosure – when someone prematurely commits to values or roles others prescribe.

Identity moratorium – a commitment to an identity is delayed while a person experiments with roles and values.

Idiographic – relating to the study of individuals.; focuses on the individual rather than developing general laws of behavior (nomothetic; *proposition of the law*).

Illogical – contrary to logic; lacking sense or sound reasoning.

Illusion – a misinterpretation of a sensory stimulus; perceptual experiences through the senses that do not accurately represent the physical event.

Illusory contours – perceived in a figure when no contours are physically present.

Illusory correlation – perceiving a relationship between variables where none exists.

Image – a personal facade one presents to the world.

Imagination – the ability to form mental images or spontaneously generate images.

Imaging techniques – *see* CAT, MEG, MRI, and PET scans.

Imitation (*modeling or observational learning*) – learning behavior by observing others; copying another's behavior. *For example, babies learn through imitation when they imitate their parents.*

Immediate memory (*working memory* or *short-term memory*) – a phase where information and images are stored only for a brief period.

Immune system – the body's defense against harmful agents (e.g., bacteria and viruses); cells and chemicals defend against infection and disease by targeting and destroying harmful pathogens.

Impermeable – preventing (e.g., liquids) from passing or diffusing through.

Implantation – the process by which the embryo becomes embedded in the uterus wall.

Implicit attitudes – beliefs are unconscious but can still influence decisions and behavior.

Implicit memory – unconscious retention of information affects thoughts and behavior.

Implicit uses of memory – the availability of information through memory processes without exerting any conscious effort to encode or recover information.

Implosion therapy (*behavioral therapy*) – reducing patient phobias by requiring them to imagine fearful stimuli. Proposes that experiencing the feared situation through imagination in the safe context of therapy removes the anxiety associated with the stimuli.

Impression management theory – a desire to make a favorable impression on others. Adjusting behavior to appear positive to others. *For example, by doing favors for others.*

Imprinting – primitive learning during the early part of an animal's life, whereby an enduring attachment is formed to another (*filial imprinting*). Early learning phase when a person or animal forms a specific pattern of behavior.

Impulsive aggression – emotion-driven aggression in reaction to situations in "the heat of the moment."

Inalterable – not capable of being changed or altered.

Incentive – a stimulus eliciting goal-directed behavior; an environmental stimulus that encourages people to act in a particular way.

Incentive approaches (or *expectancy approaches*) – motivation-producing goal-directed behavior.

Incest taboo – cultural norms and laws forbidding sexual relationships between close-blood relatives, such as siblings, parent and child, uncle/aunt, and niece/nephew.

Incidence – the relative frequency of occurrence of something.

Inclusive fitness – the reproductive fitness of an individual organism plus any effect that the organism has on increasing reproductive fitness in related organisms.

Incongruence (*Carl Rogers and humanistic therapists*) – a disparity between the self-concept and reality; a mismatch between self and ideal self results in conflict or unease.

Incubation (*Gestalt model of problem-solving*) – pausing actively to modify one's mental set.

Independent construals of self – conceptualization of the self as an individual whose behavior is organized primarily by reference to one's thoughts, feelings, and actions rather than by reference to the thoughts, feelings, and actions of others.

Independent group design (*between-subjects* or *unrelated design*) – when separate groups participate in distinct levels of the independent variable, so each data set is independent, comparisons are made between groups rather than within them.

Independent variable (*experimental design*) – manipulated in an experiment (e.g., participants receive in a memory experiment) and consequently affects the dependent variable. The value does *not* depend on changes in other values.

Individualism – the quality of being a single thing or person,

Individual psychology (*Alfred Adler*) – the primary motivations for human behavior are not sexual or aggressive urges but strivings for superiority.

Individuality – the quality of being a single thing or person.

Individuation (*Carl Jung*) – a process of realizing one's Self. Jung claimed that people's aspiration to live up to certain archetypes leads to repressing aspects of their Self. These must be allowed to surface and coexist (i.e., *integration*) for a person to understand who they are.

Individualistic cultures – when self-interest and individual rights are promoted with low levels of mutual interdependence between individuals rather than the collective needs and interests of others.

Induced motion – an illusion in which a stationary point of light within a moving reference frame is perceived as moving while the reference frame appears stationary.

Induction – reasoning based on forming general principles from specific observations; a conclusion about the probability of psychological phenomena, based on evidence and experience, from the specific to the general.

Inductive reasoning – drawing a general conclusion from premises or statements; using specific facts or past experiences to reach a specific conclusion. Inductive reasoning is reasoning based on facts and principles.

Industrial psychology – applying psychological principles to practical problems of education, industry, and marketing.

Inferences – missing information filled in by sample evidence or prior beliefs and theories.

Inferential statistics – determines the likelihood that a result is just due to chance. Procedures for analyzing empirical data to test if the independent variable has had a significant effect on the dependent variable to either accept or reject the hypothesis (thereby attributing the results to chance variation). *For example, it includes hypothesis tests, confidence interval, regression analysis, chi-square, binomial Sign, Wilcoxon Matched Pairs, Mann-Whitney U, and Spearman's Rho.*

Inferior colliculus – an essential auditory center in the midbrain.

Inferiority complex (*psychoanalysis*) – an exaggerated sense of inferiority; feeling inferior to others. Such feelings can arise from imagined or actual inferiority in the afflicted person.

Informational influence (or *social influence*) – an individual's tendency to conform because a group provides information; it occurs when seeking informational guidance from others in groups due to the desire to be correct.

Informed consent – a subject's voluntary agreement to participate in a research study after learning about the study to make a knowledgeable decision to participate. An ethical requirement for sufficient information about an experiment or therapeutic intervention to enable an informed judgment about whether to participate. *For example, permission by a patient to undergo surgical treatment after the patient understands the risks involved.*

Infradian rhythm – biological cycle less than every 24 hours. *For example, the menstruation cycle.*

Infundibulum – any of the funnel-shaped body parts.

Ingmar Bergman (1918-2007) – a Swedish film director who used heavy symbolism and explored characters' psychology.

Ingroup – a group to which one belongs; group perceived as a member based on global dimensions (e.g., race, religion) or specific localized dimensions (e.g., friendship).

In-group bias – an evaluation of one's group as being better than others.

Inhibition – 1. a synaptic message preventing the recipient neuron cell from firing. 2. restraint on instinctive impulses in behavior; conscious exclusion of unacceptable desires.

Inhibitory – stopping an action (e.g., muscle becoming stiff) by modifying sensory input.

Inhibitory inputs – information entering a neuron for signals *not* to fire.

Inhibitory postsynaptic potential – a change in voltage occurs when a neurotransmitter binds to an inhibitory receptor.

Innate – inherited or natural to an organism, existing at birth rather than acquired.

Innate abilities – abilities present from birth.

Innovation (*minority influence*) – social influence when a group's minority influences the majority. Several conditions must be met, including holding a clear and confident position.

Insanity – a legal term for a mental inability to take responsibility for one's actions. Insanity is a permanent condition; it can be defined as craziness or madness. Insanity is a symptom of schizophrenia or other psychotic disorders.

Insecure attachment – feelings between infant and caregiver developing due to the caregiver's lack of sensitivity in responding to the infant's needs. Two types of insecure attachment are insecure/avoidant (children who avoid social interaction with others) and insecure/resistant (seek and reject social interaction).

Insight therapies – treatments involve complex conversations between therapists and patients. Treatments help patients understand the nature of their problems and the meaning of their behavior, thoughts, and feelings.

Insomnia – a chronic problem with falling or staying asleep; the unusually prolonged inability to fall asleep or difficulty staying asleep.

Instinct – an inborn pattern of behavior often responsive to specific stimuli; "the spawning instinct in salmon"; "altruistic instincts in social animals."

Instinctive drift – the tendency for conditioning to be hindered by instincts.

Instinctual drift – the tendency for learned behavior to migrate toward instinctual behavior.

Instrumental aggression – cognition-based and goal-directed aggression carried out with premeditated thought to achieve specific aims.

Insulin – a hormone secreted by the pancreas.

Integral theory (*Ken Wilbur*, 1973) – attempts to integrate all human wisdom into a new, emergent worldview that can accommodate the perspectives of all previous worldviews, including those that appear to contradict one another.

Integrative approach – combining ideas and techniques of several schools of psychology.

Intellect – the faculty of reasoning, knowing, and thinking, distinct from feeling; a person's understanding or mental powers.

Intellectual development (*Piaget*) – emerges from hereditary and environmental factors. Knowledge is invented and reinvented as the child develops and constantly interacts with the world around them. Piaget's theory of intellectual development is grounded in biological sciences; cognitive growth is an extension of biological growth governed by the same laws and principles. Piaget argued that intellectual development controlled every other aspect of development – emotional, social, and moral.

Intelligence – the capacity to acquire and apply knowledge; an underlying ability to adapt and function effectively within a given environment. It includes benefitting from experiences, acting purposefully, solving problems, and adapting to new situations.

Intelligence quotient (IQ) – calculated by dividing mental age by chronological age (multiplying by 100 to give a whole number); compares the mental age of a child with their chronological age; now calculated as an IQ score.

Interbrain – the posterior division of the forebrain

Interdependence – when two or more things depend on each other.

Interdependent construal of self – conceptualization of self as part of encompassing social relationships; recognizing one's behavior is determined, contingent on, and organized mainly by what the actor perceives to be the thoughts, feelings, and actions of others.

Interference theory – people forget information because of interference from other learned information; it occurs when incoming information disrupts memory traces.

Intergenerational mobility – the change in social class or types of jobs between generations (e.g., when parents ensure their children will be better off than them).

Intermittent reinforcement (or *partial reinforcement*)– a schedule in which reinforcement happens only occasionally when a particular response occurs.

Internal attribution (or *dispositional attribution*) – an inference that an event or a person's behavior is due to personal factors such as traits, abilities, or feelings.

Internal consistency – a measure of reliability; the degree to which a test yields similar scores across its parts, such as on odd versus even items.

Internal locus of control – a belief that one controls one's circumstances.

Internalization – 1. according to Vygotsky, the process through which children absorb knowledge from social context; 2. learning cultural behaviors and expectations so profoundly that one automatically assumes they are correct and accepts them without question.

International Classification of Disorders (lCD) – mental disorders published by the World Health Organization (WHO). Patterns of symptoms, as opposed to etiology or treatment, are emphasized. ICD is not diagnostic.

Interneurons – brain neurons relay messages from sensory neurons to interneurons or motor neurons.

Inter-observer reliability – a measure of the extent to which individuals generate the same records when they observe the same behaviors. By correlating the scores of observers, inter-observer reliability is measured. Individuals (or groups) with highly correlated scores demonstrate good interobserver reliability.

Interpersonal attraction – positive feelings about another person; studying factors involved in the attraction between people. *Includes friendships, sexual attraction, and romantic love.*

Interpretation (*psychoanalytic technique*) – the hidden meanings of free association, dreams, feelings, memories, and behavior by the patient.

Interquartile range – the spread of scores for the middle 50 percent of scores.

Intersectional theory – meshes characteristics (e.g., gender and race) with the research.

Intersexual – when an individual, at birth, is not distinctly male or female; intersex individuals were previously referred to as *hermaphrodites*; however, the term today is considered stigmatizing or misleading.

Interval data – values with equal intervals but not absolute zero.

Interval schedule – when reinforcement happens at a time interval.

Interview – usually verbal research consisting of either open or closed-ended questions.

Intimacy – the warm, close, caring aspect of a romantic relationship; the capacity to commit (sexual, emotional, moral) to another.

Intragenerational mobility – the change in social class or job types occurring within a person's lifetime (e.g., moving from the working class to the middle class).

Intrinsic motivation – the motivation to act for the sake of the activity alone, taking pleasure in an activity rather than working towards an external reward. When a person is inwardly motivated to perform a specific activity, people are intrinsically motivated if they perform any activity for self-satisfaction rather than monetary or other gains.

Introjection – unconscious internalization of the world (especially aspects of persons) within the self, so the internalized representation takes over the psychological functions of the external objects.

Introspection – when a person looks inward to gain insight into their personalities; contemplation of thoughts, desires, and conduct.

Introversion (*Eysenck's personality theory*) – an introverted disposition; a personality trait characterized by quiet thoughtfulness and social aversion, particularly in large groups (contrast with extroversion). Introversion is associated with a reluctance to seek the stimulation of social contacts and to be more passive and controlled than extroverts.

Introvert – a personality of introversion; a timid person who tends to shun social contact. Characteristics often include reserved behavior, such as quietness and an aversion to social interactions. Introverts may prefer their own company or small groups and take a contemplative approach to problems. The opposite is an *extrovert*.

Intuition – a person's ability to acquire knowledge without inference or logical reasoning. Intuition is a natural tendency used by some to make decisions.

Ion – positively and negatively charged atom or molecule.

Ion channels – the portions of neurons' cell membranes that selectively permit specific ions (e.g., Na^+, K^+ and Ca^{2+}) to flow in and out.

IQ (*intelligence quotient*) – calculated by dividing mental age by chronological age (multiplying by 100 to give a whole number); compares the mental age of a child with their chronological age; now calculated as an IQ score.

Iris – the muscle ring surrounding the pupil in the eye.

Ironic processing (or *white bear principle*) – a psychological process wherein an individual is frequented by specific thoughts when deliberately attempting to suppress or avoid them.

Irrational – contrary to or lacking in reason or logic.

Irreversibility – the inability to mentally reverse an operation.

J

James-Lange theory of emotion – people experience emotion because they perceive their bodies' physiological responses to external events. The perception of an emotionally arousing stimulus leads to a behavioral response resulting in differing sensory and motor feedback to the brain, which is interpreted as an emotion.

Jealousy – typically refers to the thoughts, feelings, and behaviors when a person believes a rival threatens a valued relationship. This rival may not know they are perceived as a threat.

Jenkins activity survey (1979) – a questionnaire-type survey of behavior and famous for evaluating Type A behavior.

Jigsaw classrooms – use a technique of "jigsawing," in which each pupil is given part of the total material to master and then shares it with other group members.

Job burnout – a syndrome of emotional exhaustion, depersonalization, and a diminished sense of personal accomplishment, often experienced by workers in high-stress jobs.

Johari window (1955) – an exercise to understand interpersonal relationships. Psychologists Joseph Luft (1916–2014) and Harrington Ingham (1916–1995) created it for self-help groups and heuristic (*problem-solving and self-discovery*) exercises for corporations. In the exercise, someone picks several adjectives from a list, choosing ones they feel describe their personality. The subject's peers then get the same list, each picking an equal number of adjectives to describe the subject. These adjectives are inserted into a two-by-two grid of four cells for comparison and discussion.

Joy – the emotion of great happiness.

Judgment – a cognitive process of assessing a person, situation, or event and using evidence to decide. In psychology, judgment evaluates a person's adjudication capabilities.

Jung, Carl (1875-1961) – Swiss psychiatrist and founder of analytical psychology. Jung was a friend of Sigmund Freud but later disagreed with his theories. Jung proposed that humans inherited shared memories and ideas in a collective unconscious and noted numerous archetypes to which people relate to. Jung placed importance on a hypothetical *collective unconscious* and explored the symbolic nature of dreams. His work included exploring the psyche through three principles: the principle of *opposites*, *equivalence*, and *entropy* (1928).

Jungian psychology – the psychological theories of Carl Jung.

Justification of effort – if one works hard to reach a goal, one will likely value that goal.

Just noticeable difference (or *differential threshold*) – the smallest noticeable difference between the first and second level of sensory stimulus.

Just World hypothesis – believing the world is fair and people get what they deserve. Assumes the world is a fair and just place where people receive what they deserve.

K

K-line (Marvin Minsky in, *K-lines: A Theory of Memory*) – a mental agent who is an aggregated form of several mental agents actively involved in problem-solving or formulating new ideas.

Kelley, Harold (1921-2003) – a social psychologist focusing on interpersonal relationships and contributed to attribution theory, how individuals 'attribute' causes to events, for instance, a "situational" or "dispositional" factor.

Kin altruism (*evolutionary psychology*) – the concept that individuals help those who are close relatives because it fosters the transmission of their genes.

Kinesics – interpretation of body language, including gestures and facial expressions.

Kinesthetics – the response and feedback from movement sensations in the muscles or joints.

Kinesthetic sense – bodily position and movement relative to each other.

Kinesthesis – the sense of the position and movement of body parts.

Kinship (family) studies – examining correlations of traits or behaviors between individuals with differing degrees of genetic similarity.

Kleptomania – a condition in which a person cannot resist the urge to hoard or collect things.

Knowledge – the psychological result of perception, learning, and reasoning; understanding complex cognitive processes such as perception, communication, reasoning, and association.

Knowledge management – identifying, creating, representing, distributing, and adopting experiences and insights.

Kobasa, Susan (1979) – examined stress resistance, particularly "hardiness" to stress, characterized by commitment, control, and challenge.

Kohlberg's stages of moral development – moral reasoning, the basis of ethical behavior, develop in six stages. Each successive stage is more efficient than the earlier one in dealing with moral dilemmas an individual faces.

Korsakoff's syndrome (or *Alcohol amnestic disorder*) – amnesiac common in chronic alcoholics, a deficiency of thiamine (vitamin B_1) with symptoms including retrograde amnesia, anterograde amnesia, confabulation, apathy, and lack of insight.

Kubler-Ross model (or *five stages of grief*; 1969) – when people deal with tragedy and grief in five discrete sequential stages: *Denial, Anger, Bargaining, Depression*, and *Acceptance*.

L

Laboratory experiments – conducted in a rigorously controlled environment, whereby the independent variable is manipulated while all other extraneous variables are controlled.

Laboratory observation – an observational research method in which information about subjects is collected in a laboratory setting.

Lacunar amnesia – the subject loses memory about an event, resulting in a gap or lacuna.

Language – system of how information is encoded and decoded; a system of symbols and rules for meaningful communication.

Language acquisition – how children acquire or develop human language.

Language Acquisition Device (LAD) – an innate mechanism aiding language development through recognizing grammatical structure.

Language development – the study of language acquisition, emphasizing the development of four sub-systems of language: 1) semantics, 2) pragmatics, 3) tense, and 4) gender.

Language disorders – linguistic information related to semantics and grammar.

Language-making capacity – innate operating principles children bring to learn a language.

Language production – what people say, sign, and write, as well as the processes they go through to produce those messages.

Lapsus – an involuntary mistake made while writing or speaking. As per the psychoanalytic theory proposed by Sigmond Freud, lapsus represents a deed that hides a desire in the unconscious mind.

Lapsus linguae – an error in memory, speech, or physical action because of an unconscious conflict, wish, or train of thought interfering with healthy functioning.

Latah – when an individual enters a trance-like state, enacting physical or verbal automatisms that result from a startle reflex.

Latent content (*Freud's stages of psychosexual development*) – the underlying or hidden content represented in dreams.

Latent functions – functions unintended or unrecognized (e.g., a newspaper as a flyswatter).

Latent learning – knowledge not initially expressed overtly; things learned stay in the subconscious mind and might be expressed in response to specific experiences or events.

Latency stage (*Freud's fourth stage of psychosexual development*) – sexual preoccupations are repressed; children focus on interacting with same-sex peers.

Lateralization – the difference in specialization between the two hemispheres of the brain.

Lateral thinking – a creative (or indirect) approach to problem-solving instead of following step-by-step logic, examining problems from different perspectives to find the best solution.

Lateralization of function – the distribution of functions across the brain's two hemispheres. For instance, language ability is localized in the left hemisphere.

Law of common fate (*grouping*) – elements moving in the same direction at the same rate are grouped.

Law of Effect (*Edward Thorndike; behavioral psychology*) – behavior with good consequences tends to be repeated, and behavior with adverse consequences tends to be avoided. Consequences select behaviors. When a reward follows a response, it is strengthened and more likely to be repeated. Behavior carrying a reward is 'stamped in' - associated with the reward and so conducted more often - and behavior that was punished or produced no reward would be 'stamped out' and reduced.

Law of proximity (*grouping*) – the nearest elements are grouped.

Law of similarity (*grouping*) – the most similar elements are grouped.

Lazarus, Richard (1922-2002) – American psychologist focused on the study of cognition, in the appraisal of emotion and stress, and coping mechanisms in response to stress.

Leadership – the ability to influence others to achieve goals. Characteristics contributing to successful leadership include cognitive ability, charisma, and motivation.

Leading questions – subtly communicate for respondents to answer in a particular way, which results in a biased answer or recall of an event. Illustrates how memory can be altered after eyewitness testimony.

Learned – non-responsiveness demonstrated when there is a perception of possessing a lack of control over a situation after an experience of non-contingent, unavoidable negative stimuli.

Learned helplessness – a tendency to give up passively in the face of unavoidable stressors. A general pattern of nonresponding in the presence of noxious stimuli often follows after an organism has previously experienced noncontingent, inescapable aversive stimuli.

Learning – a change in behavior or knowledge resulting from experience.

Learning model – disorders result from the reinforcement of abnormal behavior.

Learning model of addiction – addiction is a way of coping with stress.

Learning-performance distinction – the difference between what has been learned and what is expressed in overt behavior.

Least preferred co-worker theory (LPC) – how a leader prioritizes work tasks and relationships by asking leaders to either favorably or unfavorably evaluate the person they found challenging to work with. High LPC leaders used more favorable terms to describe the LPC, and vice versa for the low LPC. High LPC leaders commonly have close and warm relationships, often prioritizing a relationship before a task. In contrast, low LPC leaders often put the task first and only consider relationships once work is acceptable.

Legal psychology – research conducted empirically concerning legal institutions, law, and the people who encounter the legal system.

Lens – part of the eye behind the pupil and iris; adjusting shape to focus light from near or far objects.

Leptin – a hormone secreted by fat cells.

Lesion – any localized abnormal structural change in a bodily part

Lesioning – injury or destruction of brain tissue.

Lesioning studies – invasive surgical method of studying the brain where a small area is destroyed.

Level of measurement – the type of data (e.g., nominal, order, interval, or ratio) affects the inferential statistic used.

Levels of processing theory (*Craik and Lockhart's theory*) – the 'deeper' information is processed, the more likely it is to be retained in memory.

Lexicon – the vocabulary of a person, language, or branch of knowledge.

Liberation theology – a fusion of Christian principles with political activism, often Marxist.

Libido (*psychoanalysis*) – energy from the *id*, typically driven towards achieving sexual pleasure.

Lie scales (*statistics*) – information about the likelihood of a subject lying.

Life-change units (LCUs) – in stress research, measure stress to changes during a given period.

Life events – require a significant adjustment in a person's life (e.g., divorce or moving). Quantified on the Holmes and Rahe *Social Readjustment Rating Scale*, respondents indicate the events (differing scores allocated according to greater adjustment required) experienced over the previous twelve months.

Light adaptation – the process by which receptor cells become less sensitive to light; the eye adjusts to increasing light intensity levels, and pupils shrink.

Light intensity – the amount of light emitted or reflected by an object.

Lightness constancy – the tendency to perceive the whiteness, grayness, or blackness of objects as constant across changing illumination levels.

Likert scale (*Rensis Likert*, 1932) – survey response format; items have responses on a continuum and response categories such as "strongly agree," "agree," "disagree," and "strongly disagree."

Limbic system (*mammals only*) – a part of the forebrain involved in emotional experience and memory; a series of subcortical structures connecting the cortex with other parts of the brain essential in regulating emotional and motivational behavior and memory. Structures within the limbic system include the thalamus, hypothalamus, amygdala, and hippocampus.

Linguistic relativity hypothesis (*Benjamin Lee Whorf*, 1956) – language determines how people think.

Link method – the process of associating items with one another to remember them.

Lithium – a drug prescribed for treating bipolar disorders.

Lobotomy – a surgical procedure severing nerve tracts in the frontal lobe, formerly used to treat certain psychological disorders but now rarely performed.

Localization of function – actions (e.g., movement control, language production) associated with specific brain areas.

Locus of control – people's perception of whether they have control over circumstances in their lives; the extent to which people believe they have control over situations. An internal locus of control is the belief that actions and consequences are under individual control (e.g., through hard work). In contrast, an *external locus of control* refers to consequences resulting from external circumstances.

Logic (Classical Greek, *word, thought, idea, argument, account, reason, or principle*) – the study of the principles and criteria of valid inference and demonstration.

Logical empiricism (*philosophy of science*) – comparing and evaluating theories regarding how well they account for the evidence.

Logical positivism (*philosophy of science*) – empiricism that bases knowledge on perceptual experience (not intuition or revelation).

Logotherapy (*Viktor Frankl*, 1946) – finding meaning in life is crucial for individual growth and happiness. It focuses on finding the meaning in one's life rather than emphasizing the doctrine of 'will to pleasure' or 'will to power.'

Long-term memory (LTM) – permanently stores an unlimited amount of information. Long-term memory includes episodic memory (personal episodes), semantic memory (knowledge), and declarative memory (knowing 'that' and procedural memory of knowing 'how). Enduring memories are retained and preserved for retrieval over extended periods.

Long-term potentiation – a lasting change at synapses occurs for long-term memories.

Longitudinal study – a research method examining changes in a group of participants through repeated testing over an extended period.

Long-term memory (LTM) – the preservation of mental information for retrieval later.

Looking-glass-self – Cooley's assertion that the self is based on how others respond to us.

***Lost in the Mall* Technique** (*James Coan*, 1997) – a method of implanting false memories of an event that never occurred. The technique was popularized by an experiment in which James Coan provided family members with reminiscing stories. He told his brother that he was lost in a shopping mall as a child - it was invented, but when questioned, the brother believed it had happened to him. The *Lost in the Mall* technique demonstrates the effect of retroactive interference on memories.

Loudness – a perceptual dimension of sound influenced by the amplitude of a sound wave; large amplitudes are generally experienced as loud, and those with small amplitudes as soft.

Lowball technique – making an attractive proposition and revealing its downsides after a person agrees.

Lucid dreams – dreams in which people are aware that they are dreaming; a conscious awareness of dreaming is a learnable skill enabling dreamers to control the direction and content of their dreams.

M

Macrosociology – examines large-scale and broader aspects of society (e.g., functionalist and conflict theories and, to some extent, feminism).

Magnetic resonance imaging (MRI) – a method for studying the brain using magnetic fields and radio waves to visualize the brain. A noninvasive and painless diagnostic tool that uses a magnetic field and radio waves to see inside the body without X-rays or surgery, a computer interprets the radio waves. It creates a picture of the internal body tissues.

Magnetoencephalography (MEG) – a non-invasive technique for visualizing (imaging) the brain by recording small magnetic fields produced by active neurons.

Major depressive disorder – diagnosed after at least one major depressive episode; at least two weeks marked by sadness or irritability and loss of interest in activities. Other symptoms may include changed sleeping or eating patterns, low energy, feelings of worthlessness or guilt, difficulty concentrating, and recurrent thoughts about suicide.

Maladaptive – showing faulty adaptation.

Maladaptive behavior – actions bringing stress.

Maleficence – doing or causing evil.

Mamillary body – one of two small round structures on the undersurface of the brain that form the terminals of the anterior arches of the fornix.

Managed care – an arrangement for health care in which an organization, such as a health maintenance organization, acts as an intermediary between a person seeking care and a treatment provider.

Mania – an emotional state typified by intense elation, general euphoria, hyperactivity, excessive talkativeness, grandiose feelings or thoughts, and disrupted thought processes. An irrational but irresistible motive for a belief or action; elevated mood, unusual thought patterns, and psychosis.

Manic depressive disorder (or *bipolar disorder*) – alternating between periods of depression and mania; a mood disorder characterized by extremes of mania and depression. A person suffers from elevated mood and depression since an individual is subject to extreme conditions such as mania (elevated mood) and depression.

Manic episode – a component of bipolar disorder characterized by extreme elation, unbounded euphoria without sufficient reason, and grandiose thoughts or feelings about personal abilities.

Manifest content (*Freudian dream analysis*) – the plot of a dream; the simple, symbolic form of a dream in which the conscious mind is aware, both during sleep and on waking, which is assumed to hide the true meaning.

Manifest functions – intended or recognized (e.g., a newspaper reading to learn about the news); see *Latent functions*.

Marriage – a socially approved mating relationship that is expected to be stable and enduring.

Marriage market – a process in which prospective spouses compare the assets and liabilities of eligible partners and choose the best available mate.

Mann-Whitney U test (*non-parametric inferential statistical test*) – tests whether two samples are likely to derive from the same population (i.e., two populations have the same shape) and whether two sample means are equal.

Masculine – associated with men and not with women.

Masculine traits – aggressive, independent, dominant, competitive, active.

Maslow, Abraham (1908-1970) – proposed humanistic psychology as a third force in reaction to the perspectives of psychoanalysis and behaviorism and believing humans are essentially good. Maslow's hierarchy of needs proposes a psychological structure of needs and tendencies whereby basic needs (e.g., hunger) must be satisfied before higher needs (e.g., self-esteem) can be achieved towards self-actualization.

Masochism – a feeling of gratification from inflicting pain or humiliation upon oneself.

Mass hysteria (*sociopsychological phenomenon*) – a manifestation of similar symptoms of hysteria. The common form is when a group believes they are suffering from a disease.

Mass media – communication designed to reach large numbers.

Massed practice (or *cramming*) – the process of learning material over a brief period.

Master status – an ascribed or achieved status that determines a person's identity.

Matched pairs design – participants in different conditions are matched according to specific characteristics. *For example, age or gender.*

Matching hypothesis – picking partners who are about equal in attractiveness.

Material culture – the tangible objects society makes, uses, and shares; see *Nonmaterial culture*.

Matriarchal family system – the oldest females (usually grandmothers and mothers) control cultural, political, and economic resources and consequently have power over the males.

Matrilocal residence pattern – newly married couples living with the wife's family.

Maternal deprivation hypothesis (*Bowlby*, 1953) – children deprived of maternal care and love in early childhood will likely suffer emotional, social, or intellectual delays in later life. Bowlby proposed prolonged separation (resulting in an attachment bond breaking) to cause deprivation syndrome.

Mathematical psychology – research using mathematical modeling of cognitive, perceptual, and motor processes.

Maturation – genetically programmed growth and development; development relatively independent of environmental influences, such as depth perception and walking; implied is the assumption that the characteristics are governed by heredity.

Maturational – relating to or involved in total development.

Mean (*descriptive statistic*) – the arithmetic average of a set of scores; an average computed by adding some function of the numbers. A measure of central tendency, the total sum of all the scores divided by the total number of scores.

Means-ends analysis – a problem-solving strategy in computer programs whereby problems are broken down into constituent parts and solved until finalized.

Measures of central tendency (*descriptive statistic*) – the mean, median, and mode.

Measure of dispersion – measuring the spread (or *variability*) in a set of scores.

Measures of variability (*statistics*) – a statistic, such as a range or standard deviation, indicating how tightly the scores in a set of observations cluster together.

Median (*descriptive statistic*) – the middle score in a set of scores arranged from lowest to highest; a measure of central tendency utilizing the mid-point of the ranked data.

Medical model – a theory of abnormal behavior assuming such disorders have physiological causes, describing and explaining psychological disorders as diseases.

Medical model of abnormality – views mental disorders as having physiological causes. *For example, genetics, biochemistry, and physiology.*

Meditation – the practice of focusing attention; promotes a state of calmness so the mind and body can be brought into greater harmony to facilitate health and healing.

Medulla oblongata – lower or hindmost part of the brain; controls essential functions not under conscious control, such as breathing; a small region of the brain stem regulating basic bodily processes, including breathing and the heartbeat.

MEG (magnetoencephalography) – a non-invasive technique for visualizing (*imaging*) the brain by recording small magnetic fields produced by active neurons.

Melancholia – a mood disorder with low levels of eagerness and enthusiasm in performing activities of daily life. Described by the Greeks and Romans and characterized by deep and persistent sadness, it corresponds closely to depression.

Melatonin – a hormone regulating the sleep cycle.

Memory – the cognitive process whereby experience is remembered; the capacity to encode, retain, store, and retrieve information.

Menarche – a woman's first menstrual period.

Menopause – the gradual, permanent cessation of menstruation.

Mental – refers to the mind, the collective aspects of intellect and consciousness.

Mental age (*Alfred Binet*, 1905) – the chronological age typically corresponding to a level of intellectual functioning and measures performance on intelligence tests. Typically, mental age is equivalent to chronological age, but if a child is of lower/higher intelligence, the mental age will be accordingly lower/higher than chronological age. IQ is the ratio of *mental age* to *chronological age*, with 100 being average. For example, an 8-year-old who passes the 10-year-old's test would have an IQ of $10/8 \times 100 = 125$.

Mental block – when a person cannot continue thoughts or when painful thoughts are repressed.

Mental condition – qualities of a state are constant even though the state may be dynamic.

Mental disorders – anxiety disorders, conduct disorder, depressive disorders, oppositional defiant disorder, pervasive development disorder, or Tourette's syndrome.

Mental health – emotional and cognitive well-being or the absence of any mental disorder. Psychological and emotional well-being enables individuals to work, love, relate to others effectively, and resolve conflicts.

Mental hospitals – institutions specializing in the treatment of psychological disorders.

Mental management – the activity in which mental processes are explored, described, and studied in their diversity.

Mental process – the performance of some composite cognitive activity.

Mental set (*Gestalt theory*) – a schema to organize perception of a new problem; a tendency to use only solutions that worked in the past. The qualities of a state are relatively constant, even though the state itself may be dynamic.

Mental strain – nervousness resulting from mental stress.

Mere exposure effect – the tendency to like novel stimuli more if encountered repeatedly; the higher the exposure to a stimulus, the stronger and more likely the attraction to it.

483

Mesencephalon – the middle portion of the brain.

Meta-analysis (*statistics*) – combining and analyzing data from independent studies. a Statistical technique for evaluating hypotheses by providing a formal mechanism for detecting the general conclusions from data from many experiments.

Metabolic – biomolecular bodily functions; extracting and converting energy for bodily processes.

Metalinguistic awareness – the capacity to think about how language is used.

Metamemory – implicit or explicit knowledge about memory abilities and effective memory strategies; cognition about memory.

Metamotivation (Abraham Maslow) – describes the motivation of self-actualized individuals striving to reach their full potential beyond the scope of their basic needs. See *Reveral theory*.

Metapsychology – systematically examines the philosophical study of psychology. Metapsychology describes the concepts and principles that lie beyond the laws of psychology.

Method of loci (or *mnemonics*) – imagining oneself physically in a familiar place to remember. Increases memory effectiveness through memorizing a series of distinct locations (such as rooms in a house) and then imagining an item remembered at each location. Items are recalled by mentally "walking through" the house and "seeing" the item.

Metric – based on a decimal unit of measurement.

Microsociology – studies why people act in a certain way in a particular situation (e.g., symbolic interactionism and, to some extent, feminism).

Midbrain – the brain between the hindbrain and forebrain participates in locating events in space and contains a dopamine-releasing system of neurons. The middle portion of the brain relays sounds to the auditory cortex.

Midlife crisis – a time of doubt and anxiety in middle adulthood.

Milieu therapy – a humanistic approach to treating psychological disorders emphasizing the importance of an institution in recovery. An environment is created whereby staff and patients are viewed as equal, and an atmosphere is fostered of self-respect.

Milgram, Stanley (1933- 1984) – an influential social psychologist, conducted a controversial study on obedience to authority under conditions whereby obeying conflicts with personal conscience.

Miller's Magic Number (1956) – *The Magical Number Seven, Plus or Minus Two: Some Limits on Our Capacity for Processing Information* is one of psychology's most highly cited papers. Cognitive psychologist George A. Miller (1920-2012) of Harvard University's Department of Psychology published in *Psychological Review* (1956).

Mind – collectively, the aspects of intellect and consciousness manifested as combinations of thoughts, perception, memory, emotion, will, and imagination; the mind is the stream of consciousness. Consciousness and intellect use perception, thoughts, emotions, memory, imagination, and will. It includes all the brain's conscious processes.

***Minnesota Multiphasic Personality Inventory* (MMPI)** – a test developed to help clinical psychologists diagnose psychological disorders.

Minority influence – when a persuasive minority exerts pressure to change the majority's attitudes, beliefs, or behaviors. Minorities are influential when they appear consistent and principled.

Misattribution – a mistaken attribution of emotional response to a cause it did not produce.

Misinformation effect – the tendency for recollections of events to be distorted by information given after the event.

Mitosis – when cells divide, each with a complete set of chromosomes (i.e., genetic material). Each of these cells receives an exact copy of the original chromosomes. During development, mitosis occurs until the adult organism is created.

Mnemonics (or *method of loci*) – strategies for improving memory, often through using existing familiar information (e.g., imagery) while encoding new information to aid later retrieval and access.

Mock juries (or *shadow juries*) – participants investigate factors affecting the decision-making process.

Mode (*statistics*) – the score most frequent within a data sample.

Modeling (*Albert Bandura*) – learning and socialization by observing and imitating others.

Monism – viewing mind and body as a single unit.

Monoamine oxidase inhibitors (MAOI) – antidepressants increasing levels of norepinephrine and serotonin.

Monocular cues – depth perception cues that require only one eye.

Monogamy – when one person is married exclusively to another person.

Monogenic traits – physical characteristics (traits) determined by a single gene.

Monozygotic (identical) twins – fetuses develop from the same zygote (i.e., fertilized egg) and share 100% genes.

Mood – mental or emotional state.

Mood disorders – marked disturbances in an emotional state, which affect thinking, physical symptoms, social relationships, and behavior. A mood disturbance characterized by emotional extremes, alternating between extreme depression and mania.

Moral development – when children learn to understand the differences between right and wrong and make independent decisions on moral issues.

Morality – what is innately regarded as right or wrong. A system of principles and judgments shared by cultural, religious, and philosophical concepts and beliefs, by which humans subjectively determine whether given actions are right or wrong. A system of beliefs and values ensures that individuals will keep their obligations to others in society and behave in ways that do not interfere with the rights and interests of others.

Moral realism (*Piaget's theory of moral development*) – when children understand adult rules as firm and unquestionable.

Moral reasoning – the processes causing people to think about right and wrong.

Morality – governs conduct, especially a member of a profession.

Moratorium (*Erikson*) – a period during which adolescents consider values and goals to understand and establish their identities.

Mores – to standards of behavior or customs appropriate within a society and accepted by the majority. Norms that members of a society consider very important because they maintain moral and ethical behavior.

Morpheme – the smallest significant unit of language that conveys meaning.

Motivated forgetting (or *psychogenic amnesia*) – forgetting what is desired.

Motivation – an internal state that arouses, drives, and directs behavior accounted for by physiological explanations (e.g., internal drives such as hunger), behavioral explanations, and psychological explanations (e.g., for complex human behaviors, such as the need for achievement).

Motive – an impulse that causes a person to act; a specific need or desire, such as hunger or achievement, which energizes and directs behavior.

Motor development – the increasing coordination of muscles that makes physical movements possible.

Motor neurons – transmit messages from the central nervous system (i.e., spinal cord or brain) to muscle cells.

Muller-Lyer illusion (1889) – when two lines of the same length appear to be different because of different diagonal lines attached to the end of each line.

MRI – *magnetic resonance imaging*.

Multiaxial diagnosis (*DSM classification system of mental disorders*) – patients are assessed on a variety of axes (e.g., clinical conditions, psychosocial and environmental factors)

Multicultural – the coexistence of several cultures in the same geographic area without one culture dominating the other; see *Cultural pluralism*.

Multiculturalism – promoting the equality and coexistence of many varied cultural traditions; the government's willingness to accommodate the broadest cultural diversity (e.g., multilingualism, multi-religious, multicultural history); see *Pluralism.*

Multimodal therapy (*Lazarus*) – a cognitive behavioral therapy considering all aspects. Seven dimensions represent behavior, affects, sensations, images, cognitions, interpersonal relationships, and biological functioning that must be focused on and treated to be effective.

Multiple personality disorder (MPD) – a dissociative disorder when two or more distinct and separate personalities manifest, each displaying different interests, memories, and behavior patterns.

Multi-store model of memory (or *Atkinson and Shiffrin's model of memory*, 1968) – memory with three sequential stages: 1) short-term memory, 2) long-term memory (7+/- 2 "chunks" of information), and 3) sensory memory.

Mutations – small genetic changes in genes.

Myelin sheath – a layer of fatty tissue covering the axons of nerve cells, insulating the axon from other axons, and increasing the conduction of nerve impulses along the axon.

Myelencephalon – posterior part of the hindbrain forms the medulla oblongata in adults.

N

Name-calling – a strategy of labeling people to influence their thinking.

Napoleon complex – an inferiority complex experienced by men with short stature. Men with this complex try to overcompensate for their efforts in other aspects or areas of life for their short stature.

Narcissism – a personality trait characterized by self-love, associated with ego or self-image.

Narcissistic personality disorder – marked by self-love and self-absorption; when a person has an exaggerated sense of importance, a strong desire to be admired, and a lack of empathy.

Narcolepsy – a tendency to fall asleep periodically during the day; an uncommon sleep disorder, narcolepsy is marked by recurring irrepressible attacks of sleep during regular waking hours, as well as by cataplexy, sleep paralysis, and hallucinations.

Narcotics (*opiates*) – drugs that relieve pain.

Narrative method – the process of making up a story to remember something.

Narrative therapy (*psychotherapy*) – the therapist engages with the patient and aims to discover the richer or positive narratives originating from disparate descriptions of experiences.

Nativism – aspects of cognitive processes and behavior are innate.

Natural experiment – the researcher cannot control the independent variable nor participant allocation to conditions.

Naturalistic observation – collecting information about subjects in a natural setting without external intervention. When the observer does not manipulate variables within a natural setting, behavior occurs by merely observing and recording. The observational technique can be divided into *participant observation* (where the researcher contributes to a group's behavior while participants are unaware of the observer's true purpose or identity) and *non-participant observation* (whereby the researcher remains inconspicuous).

Natural selection (1859) – a process in which organisms evolve to adapt to the environment. Darwin's theory of evolution is that animals have adapted better to their environment, allowing members of a species to produce more offspring than others due to possessing advantageous traits that improve survival chances and increase reproductive success.

Nature *vs.* nurture – a debate within psychology exploring the extent to which specific aspects of behavior are inherited or learned due to environmental influences.

Necrophilia – an irresistible sexual attraction to dead bodies.

Need – a necessary physical or emotional item that helps humans lead a healthy life. Needs could be physical, objective, and subjective.

Need for achievement – an assumed basic human need to strive to achieve goals motivating a wide range of behavior and thinking.

Negative correlation – a relationship between two measured variables in which one variable increases as the other decreases.

Negative emotions – any feeling that causes misery and sadness. These emotions make people dislike themselves and others, taking away their confidence.

Negatively skewed distribution (statistics) – data distribution with very low scores.

Negative punishment (*operant conditioning*) – removes stimulus after a response so the response will be less likely to occur.

Negative reinforcement (*operant conditioning*) – removes a stimulus after a response so that the response is more likely to occur. A method to increase the probability and strength of a response by removing or withholding an aversive stimulus (negative reinforcer)

Negative-state relief – people assist others in alleviating negative feelings, for instance, to lessen guilt or sadness.

Negative symptoms (*abnormal psychology*) – indicated by an absence or reduction of normal behavior, particularly concerning schizophrenia, deficits in functioning that reveal the absence of expected behaviors, for instance, flat affect and limited speech.

Negativism – when a person has a negative perception of life, specifically events in the future.

Neoencephalon – the part of the brain with the recent phylogenetic origin; the cerebral cortex and related parts.

Neo-Freudian – characterizes a group of Freudian-influenced psychologists who, while accepting the concept of unconscious conflict, disagree over the extent of the influence of bodily pleasures or frustrations and have placed greater emphasis on other aspects of behavior and experience. Famous neo-Freudians include Adler and Jung.

Neolocal residence pattern – when newly married couples have their residence.

Neonate research – investigations using newborn infants.

NEO Personality Inventory – measures the Big Five traits: extraversion, openness to experience, agreeableness, conscientiousness, and neuroticism.

Neuromodulator – any substance that modifies or modulates the activities of the postsynaptic neuron.

Neuropsychology – behaviors and psychological processes related to brain structure and functions.

Nerve impulse – the electrical signal produced when a neuron is active, passing from the dendrites along the axon to the specific terminals.

Nerves – bundles of axons extending from many neurons.

Nervous opticus – the cranial nerve serving the retina.

Nervous strain – nervousness resulting from mental stress.

Nervous system – complex coordinated network of tissues communicating via electrochemical signals.

Neurons – nervous system cells that communicate via electrochemical signals.

Neuropsychology – concerned with the physiological bases of psychological processes.

Neurological disorder – disturbance in the structure or function of the nervous system resulting from developmental abnormality, disease, injury, or toxin.

Neuron (or *nerve cell*) – a nervous system cell receives and communicates with other cells.

Neuropathic pain – pain caused by the abnormal functioning or overactivity of the nerves; results from an injury or a disease of the nerves.

Neurophysiology – the study of the nervous system, including brain function.

Neurotic disorder – when a person does not have signs of brain abnormalities and does not display grossly irrational thinking or violate basic norms but does cause them to experience subjective distress.

Neuroscience (*physiological psychology*) – the functioning of the nervous system, which includes the structures and functioning of the brain and its relationship to behavior.

Neurosis – a disorder not attributable to any known neurological or organic dysfunction.

Neuroticism (*Big Five Personality Trait*) – a fundamental personality trait; it is an enduring tendency to experience negative emotions. An anxious mentality often leads to stress or anger.

Neurotransmitter – biomolecules (chemicals) messengers released by the terminals of a neuron between synapses to excite or inhibit adjacent neurons.

Neutral stimulus (*classical conditioning*) – a stimulus that initially fails to elicit a response but becomes a conditioned stimulus as conditioning continues.

Nietzsche, Friedrich (1844-1900) – nineteenth-century philosopher with writings on morality, truth, language, cultural theory, aesthetics, history, nihilism, power, consciousness, and the meaning of existence have enormously influenced Western philosophy and intellectual history.

Nightmare – an unpleasant dream with an emotional response primarily associated with fear or horror.

Nirvana – the beatitude that transcends the cycle of reincarnation.

Nociceptive pain – pain induced by a noxious external stimulus; specialized nerve endings in the skin send this pain message from the skin through the spinal cord to the brain.

Nocturnal emissions (or *wet dreams*) – a signal of the onset of puberty for children.

No–fault divorce – state laws do not require a partner to establish wrongdoing by another for a divorce.

Noetic psychology – finding meaning and purpose, integrating cognition (thinking) with affect (emotion), and resolving existential angst.

Nominal data – data organized based on category.

Nomothetic – searching for abstract universal principles; a perspective to establish general behavior patterns extended to all members.

Non-conformity – withstanding tendency to conform to the majority's attitudes, judgments, or behavior.

Nonconscious – information not typically available to consciousness or memory.

Non-directional hypotheses (or *two-tailed hypotheses*) – the independent variable affects the dependent variable but does not specify direction (e.g., higher/lower scores) of effect upon the dependent variable.

Non-invasive procedures – imaging without direct contact or interference (e.g., MRI and PET scans).

Non-participant observation – observer remains inconspicuous, so participants' behavior is unaffected.

Nonprobability sample – a sample chosen with little or no attempt to get a representative cross-section of the population.

Non-REM (NREM) sleep – the period during which a sleeper does not show rapid eye movement; characterized by less dream activity than during REM sleep.

Nonmaterial culture – the shared set of meanings society uses to interpret and understand the world. See *Material culture.*

Non-verbal communication (or *body language*) – communication not conveyed through verbal or written language, for instance, posture and facial expressions.

Norepinephrine (or *noradrenaline*) – a catecholamine precursor of epinephrine secreted by the adrenal medulla and released at synapses. A neurotransmitter involved in learning, memory, dreaming, awakening, emotion, and responses to stress, important in regulating mood; disturbances in its tracts have been implicated in depression and mania.

Norm crystallization – the convergence of the expectations of a group of individuals into a common perspective as they talk and carry out activities together.

Normal curve – the symmetrical curve representing the distribution of scores on attributes; allows researchers to judge how typical or atypical an observation or result is.

Normal distribution – a theoretical distribution with finite meaning and variance; a frequency distribution represented by a symmetrical, bell-shaped curve, whereby the mean, mode, and median all lie at the highest point of the curve; characteristics such as IQ are distributed in a large population.

Normative influence – conformity due to a desire for group acceptance and liking by others; group effects arise from members' desire to be liked, accepted, and approved of by others.

Normative social influence – an individual's tendency to conform because of a need to be accepted or not rejected by a group.

Norms – data providing information about how a person's test score compares with the scores of other test takers. Written and unwritten rules, guidelines, and expectations by which a society guides the behavior of its members (e.g., "right" and "wrong," proper social interaction).

Norms (*social*) – written and unwritten rules, guidelines, and expectations by which a society guides the behavior of its members (e.g., "right" and "wrong," proper social interaction).

Norms (*testing*) – standards based on measurements of large groups, comparing an individual's scores with those of others within a well-defined group.

Nuclear family (or *conjugal family*) – a family unit composed of parents and their biological or adopted children.

Nucleotides – biochemical units (Adenine, Cytosine, Guanine, and Thymine) comprising deoxynucleic acid (DNA) and genes.

Null hypothesis – differences between the independent and dependent variables merely occur because of chance rather than as any significant effect of the independent variable.

O

O, Anna – a patient of Josef Breuer who suffered from hysteria with symptoms of hydrophobia, partial paralysis, and involuntary eye movements. Breuer claimed these were caused by events earlier in life and could be alleviated by expressing them in psychoanalytic sessions. The case of Anna O later influenced the theories of Sigmund Freud.

Obedience – compliance with commands given by an authority figure; the trait of being willing to follow commands or guidance.

Object permanence – an understanding that objects continue to exist despite being hidden from sight or awareness. A crucial cognitive concept that, according to Piaget, does not develop until infants are eight months old or more.

Objective personality tests – consist of self-report inventories; objective tests include the MMPI-2, the 16PF, and the NEO Personality Inventory.

Object relations theory (Melanie Klien, 1882-1960) – a psychoanalytic theory that the building blocks of how people experience the world derive from their relations to loved and hated objects (significant people in their lives).

Objective test – a standardized test to assess a psychological disorder.

Objectivity – investigating and collecting data without influence by personal interpretation.

Object permanence – the ability to recognize that an object exists even when the object is not present and not perceived.

Object relations – the relationships people have with others, who are mentally represented as objects with specific attributes.

Obsessive-compulsive personality – a strong need to repeat certain acts or rituals.

Observation – receiving knowledge from the outside world using the senses. An observation does not manipulate an independent variable but allows the observation of relationships between variables as they occur. *When an observer records behavior demonstrated by a participant, these include naturalistic, participant, and non-participant observations.*

Observational learning (or *vicarious conditioning*) – a change in behavior or knowledge that happens by watching. When a person first observes, retains, and then replicates or imitates the behavior. Socialization occurs from observing and imitating the behavior of others who serve as a model instead of through direct experience. See *modeling*.

Observational psychology – aims to understand behavior and learn through observation.

Observer bias – a tendency for observers to record data biased due to personal expectations (e.g., awareness of the hypothesis) or motives rather than recording what happens.

Obsessions – persistent ideas, thoughts, impulses, or images causing anxiety or distress; irrational thoughts and images that are usually unfounded but over which a person may appear to have little control, ultimately affecting everyday functioning.

Obsessive-compulsive disorder (OCD) – when an individual suffers from anxiety from intrusive thoughts; involves obsessions, compulsions, or both. Behavior characterized by obsessions (uncontrollable, persistent, irrational thoughts or wishes) and compulsions (repetitive, ritualistic acts).

Occam's razor (or *principle of parsimony*) – the principle of applying the simplest possible explanation to any set of observations.

Occipital lobe – the rearmost region of each cerebral hemisphere, behind the parietal lobe and above the temporal lobes. Crucial for the processing of visual information.

Occupational health psychology – the psychosocial causative agents or factors associated with the workplace responsible for health-related problems.

Occupational psychology – focuses on humans in the workplace, including job satisfaction, leadership, selection and recruitment, and the effect of working conditions on performance.

Occupational psychosis – when individuals gain a biased attitude influenced by career or occupation.

Occupational therapy – aimed at incorporating purposeful and meaningful occupation to enable individuals with impairments or other limitations to participate in the activities of day-to-day life.

Oedipal conflict (*Freud's theory of development*) – the central conflict associated with the phallic stage, which challenges the developing ego, named after the Greek story of Oedipus, who unknowingly killed his father and married his mother.

Oedipus complex (*Freudian psychoanalytic theory*) – the intense sexual love that a young boy develops toward his mother, followed by jealousy and rivalry with his father to seek the attention and affection of the mother. A male child's sexual desire for his mother and his hostility toward his father, whom he considers a rival for his mother's love. A complex in males leads to competing for the attention and affection of their mother. This demand is often in competition with their father, who may become the focus of feelings of resentment or jealousy. The son subsequently demonstrates castration anxiety, fearing that his father might castrate him for his incestuous feelings towards his mother, so he represses and identifies with his father. Oedipus Complex is named after a character in Greek mythology whose competition for his mother's affection, Jocasta, leads him to murder his father, Laius. In females, *Oedipus Complex* may be compared to *Electra Complex*.

Offender profiling – a technique based on examining the crime scene, including how the crime was committed, and considering previous offender profiles to build and predict a detailed description (including socio-demographic characteristics) of a criminal offender.

Olfactory – relating to the sense of smell.

Olfactory bulb – the center where odor-sensitive receptors send their signals, located just below the frontal lobes of the cortex.

Onset – the beginning or early stages.

One-tailed hypothesis (or *directional hypothesis*; *statistics*) – states which of the two-condition means will be larger, most often used, one-tailed T-test.

Ontogeny – the evolution (i.e., origin and development) from conception to death.

Open-ended questions – do not contain fixed, pre-determined responses, allowing respondents to answer relatively freely.

Openness to experience (*Big Five Personality Trait*) – open-minded towards new ideas.

Operant – having influence or producing an effect.

Operant behavior – a network of factors involved in the behavior of humans and animals.

Operant conditioning – a type of learning in which responses come to be controlled by their consequences, modifying the form and occurrences of behavior by using the consequences. *Learning is determined by consequences that either reinforce or punish behaviors, increasing or decreasing the probability of the behavior.*

Operant extinction – when a behavior returns to the occurrence level before operant conditioning and no longer produces the desired consequences.

Operation – the performance of some composite cognitive activity; the act of something.

Operational definition – a way of stating precisely how a variable will be measured; a variable or condition based on the same operation or procedure determines its existence and makes it usable. Variables are manipulated or measured.

Operationalization – defining a fuzzy concept to make it measurable by variables consisting of specific observations.

Opponent-process theory – a neurological and psychological model that accounts for behaviors, including color vision. Color vision is when the visual system receptors respond opposite to wavelengths associated with three pairs of colors. Proposed by Leo Hurvich (1910-2009) and expanded by Richard Solomon (1918-1995) of the University of Pennsylvania.

Opportunity sample – a technique not based on random selection or probability; the researcher selects convenient respondents.

Oppositional defiant disorder – a disruptive pattern of behavior of children and adolescents with defiance, disobedience, and hostility toward adults in positions of authority.

Optic disk – the *blind spot* in the retina at which the optic nerve leaves the eye.

Optic nerve – a bundle of ganglion cell axons originating in the retina; a group of nerve fibers comprised of axonal ganglion cells leaving the eyeball, carrying information from eye towards brain.

Optic tract – the cranial nerve that serves the retina.

Optimal mismatch theory (*Piaget's theory of intellectual development*) – accelerates learning by 'mismatching' a child's current level of competence with problems slightly more complex than this level. If there is a correct, optimal difference between what they can do and what they are asked to do, children experience a cognitive conflict and seek solutions through their actions.

Optimism – the tendency to expect positive outcomes.

Oral personality (*Freud's Stages of Psychosexual Development*) – characterized either by great optimism or aggressive and ambitious selfishness. It forms in early childhood by fixation during the oral stage of development.

Oral stage (*Freud's Stages of Psychosexual Development*) – the first stage from birth to about 15 months, when the primary source of gratification is stimulation of the mouth and lips. Occurs in the first year, when the need to feed is satisfied orally. Irregularities experienced during the oral stage, such as food deprivation, can lead to an oral fixation, manifesting as a need for oral satisfaction (e.g., chewing gum) later in life.

Order effects – differences in participants' performance due to participants experiencing conditions in a specific order. Subsequently, learning and practice effects can arise (whereby participants adapt and improve on later measurements) or fatigue effects (decreased performance on later measures).

Ordinal data – can be rank-ordered, but intervals between ranks are not necessarily equal.

Ordinate – when plotting data on a graph, the ordinate refers to information on the vertical y-axis. The dependent variable is plotted on the y-axis.

Organ of Corti – an inner ear sensory organ where sound is transduced into nerve impulses.

Organic disorder – with a known physiological cause. For instance, schizophrenia has been linked to enlarged brain ventricles and excessive dopamine.

Organismic variables – the inner determinants of an organism's behavior.

Organizational psychologists – study aspects of the human work environment (e.g., communication among employees, socialization or enculturation of workers, leadership, job satisfaction, stress and burnout, and overall quality of life).

Orientation – functionality of the mind that creates awareness of time, person, and place.

Orientation constancy – the ability to perceive the actual orientation of objects in the real world despite their varying orientation in the retinal image.

Origin of Species (*Charles Darwin*, 1859) – theory of evolution in a book with the same title, presenting evidence that the diversity of life arose by common descent through a branching pattern of evolution. Populations evolve (i.e., more adept for the environment) for generations through natural selection (i.e., differential survival and reproduction of individuals due to differences in physical characteristics).

Ossicles – three bones (i.e., the hammer, anvil, and stirrup) in the middle ear.

Outcome study – exploring how successful a therapeutic intervention has been. For instance, an experimental group was given a drug compared to a control group that received a placebo.

Out-group – 1. a social or cultural group with which one feels they do not identify, are in competition with or in opposition to; 2. an outside group whose cultural practices are avoided or are behaved in contrast to (e.g., if Jewish Israelis constitute one's *in-group*, then Palestinians would be one's *out-group* and vice-versa).

Overlearning – continuing to practice material to increase retention even after it is learned.

Overcompensation (*Alfred Adler*) – the attempt to cover up a sense of inferiority by focusing on outward signs of superiority such as status, wealth, and power. When an individual attempts to offset weakness in an area of their lives by focusing on another aspect.

Overconfidence effect – the tendency for people to be too sure that their beliefs, decisions, estimates, and recall accuracy are correct.

Overregularization – a grammatical error usually appears during early language development, when rules of the language are applied too broadly, resulting in incorrect linguistic forms.

P

Pain – the body's response to noxious stimuli intense enough to cause, or threaten to cause, tissue damage.

Panic disorder – an anxiety disorder in which sufferers experience unexpected, severe panic attacks that begin with intense apprehension, fear, or terror.

Pain management – measures and techniques employed to control and reduce pain.

Paleocerebellum – the anterior lobe of the cerebellum was among the earliest parts of the hindbrain to develop in mammals.

Panic attack – periods of intense anxiety, fear, physiological arousal, discomfort, and other issues that occur suddenly and are discrete. A period in which a person has uncomfortable and frightening physical and psychological symptoms, including heart palpitations, trembling, fear of dying, and a perceived loss of control. Panic attacks are associated with a variety of cognitive and somatic symptoms.

Panic disorder (*DSM classification)* – characterized by recurrent, unexpected panic attacks, unpredictable attacks of intense feelings of apprehension, anxiety, and fear, and physiological symptoms of chest pain, dizziness, and heavy breathing.

Papillae – small bumps on the tongue holding taste buds, which hold taste receptors in the tongue and throat, inside the cheeks, and on the roof of the mouth.

Paradox of Choice (*Barry Schwartz*, 2004) – an overabundance of options can lead to anxiety, indecision, paralysis, and dissatisfaction.

Paralinguistics – how it is said rather than what is said, including pauses and tone of voice.

Parallel forms – different versions of a test to assess test reliability; the change of forms reduces the effects of direct practice, memory, or the desire of an individual to appear consistent on the same items.

Parallel processing – two or more mental processes conducted simultaneously.

Paranoia – disturbed thoughts characterized by excessive anxiety or fear, with irrationality and delusion. A thought process characterized by excessive fear or anxiety. The degree or extent of paranoia could be so high that it might sometimes lead to the patient suffering from delusions and thought processes affected by irrationality.

Paranoid type (*schizophrenia subtype*) – marked delusions or hallucinations and relatively normal cognitive and emotional functioning.

Paranoid schizophrenia – a subcategory of schizophrenia with an organized and systematic set of delusions or hallucinations, including persecution or jealousy.

Parapsychology – seeks to explain the paranormal (i.e., it cannot be explained by typical sensory experiences). Directed at discovering the existence and causes of psychic abilities and the concept of '*life after death*' with scientific methods.

Parasympathetic – relating to the parasympathetic nervous system.

Parasympathetic division – the subdivision of the autonomic nervous system that monitors the routine operation of the body's internal functions and conserves and restores body energy.

Parasympathetic nervous system (PNS) – combined with the sympathetic nervous system, comprises the autonomic nervous system. PNS is antagonistic to the sympathetic nervous system by conserving and restoring bodily energy to restore the organism to calm and relaxation (i.e., homeostasis). Part of the autonomic nervous system conserves energy active during relaxation.

Parental investment – the sum of resources utilized to produce and raise offspring.

Parenting styles – how parents rear their children; an authoritative parenting style balances demandingness and responsiveness is the most effective.

Parietal lobe – the cortex region behind the frontal lobe and above the lateral fissure, containing the somatosensory cortex, necessary for the sense of touch.

Parkinson's disease – a degenerative neurological disorder typified by difficulties in movement, for instance, a continual rapid tremor in the limbs, a lack of sensory-motor coordination, and a tendency to be continually tired. The condition may involve the production of the neurotransmitter dopamine.

Parsimonious – excessively unwilling to spend.

Parsimony (*personality*) – extreme stinginess.

Parsimony (*philosophy of science*) – the simplest explanation is favorable.

Partial reinforcement (*operant conditioning*) – a contingency of reinforcement whereby a response is rewarded or punished only some of the time. A phenomenon in which responses resist extinction because of partial or intermittent schedules of reinforcement.

Participant (or *subject*) – an individual who is the subject of or participates in an experiment.

Participant modeling – a therapeutic technique in which a therapist demonstrates the desired behavior, and the client is aided by supportive encouragement to imitate the modeled behavior.

Participant observation – a research method using direct participation by the researcher in the events studied. A data collection method where the researcher becomes a participant in a real-life research setting in order to observe what happens in that setting; its strengths are an in-depth understanding and flexibility; ideally, it does not disrupt the subjects' lives; its weaknesses are that it can be expensive and, in some settings, dangerous, or there is little control over the data.

Participant variables – confounding effects resulting from the characteristics of the participants influencing the results, such as differences in age, memory, gender, state of hunger, or level of arousal.

Passion – an intense emotion exhibiting an eager interest or desire for the same.

Passionate love – sexual desire and tenderness for, and intense absorption in, a person with whom one is romantically involved.

Pastoral counselor – a religious order member specializing in treating psychological disorders, often combining spirituality with practical problem-solving.

Paternal deprivation – loss of the father or growing up without a steady father figure may have deprivation effects, including emotional and social disturbances depending on the nature and length of the absence.

Pathological – the quality of being diseased or dysfunctional. Sigmund Freud's psychological theories describe and diagnose the sources of pathological social behavior.

Pathological – relating to the study of diseases.

Pathology – the branch of medical science that studies diseases.

Patriarchal family system – the eldest men (grandfathers, fathers, uncles) control cultural, political, and economic resources and consequently have power over the females.

Patrilocal residence pattern – newly married couples living with the husband's family.

Pattern recognition – transforming and organizing raw sensory information into a meaningful whole.

Pavlov, Ivan (1849-1936) – Russian physiologist demonstrated classical conditioning, a fundamental tenet of the behaviorist approach; received the 1904 Nobel Prize in Physiology and Medicine for *recognition of his work on the physiology of digestion.*

Pavlov's dog experiments – classical conditioning by salivation in dogs.

Pavlovian conditioning (*classical conditioning* or *respondent conditioning*) – learning in which a subject responds to a neutral stimulus as they would to another stimulus by learning to associate the two stimuli. Learning when a neutral stimulus is repeatedly paired with an unconditioned stimulus (UCS) produces an unconditioned response (UCR). After several trials, the neutral stimulus is a conditioned stimulus (CS) and thus produces a conditioned response (CR).

Peak experience (*Maslow*) – a temporary, profound, and intense experience of enhanced awareness, frequently accompanied by feelings of feeling fully alive.

Peer – equal to a person compared to regarding a specific dimension.

Peer group – a social unit of (typically) same-age peers sharing values and behaviors.

Peg word method – a process of remembering a rhyme by associating numbers with words and words with the items to be remembered.

Penis envy (*psychoanalytic theory*) – a sense of discontent and resentment Freud thought women experience, resulting from their wish for a penis.

Perceived control – the belief that one can make a difference in the course or consequences of some event or experience; often helpful in dealing with stressors.

Percentile score – percentage who achieved the same or lower score.

Perception – selection, meaningful organization, and interpretation of sensory information. The processes that organize information in the sensory image and interpret it as having been produced by properties of objects or events in the external, three-dimensional world.

Perceptual constancy (*psychology*) – perceived objects give similar perceptual experiences despite variations in observation conditions. Objects tend to provide the same perceptual experience despite changes in the retinal image (e.g., size constancy). The ability to recognize that an object is the same even when it produces different images on the retina.

Perceptual defense – words with a high degree of emotional content or might be 'taboo' are perceptually recognized less easily than neutral valence words.

Perceptual development – systematic progress and maturation of perceptual abilities and processes over time.

Perceptual organization – combining incoming sensory information into a coherent, meaningful perceptual experience. *For example, the ability to perceive patterns and to judge size and distance in a three-dimensional scene.*

Perceptual set – the readiness to see based on expectations, experiences, emotions, and assumptions.

Perceptual speed – the time to perceive and discriminate between stimuli accurately.

Performance psychology – the study of factors allowing individuals and societies to flourish. The study of knowledge and psychological skills required for developing the performing guidelines in business, sports, performing arts, and fitness.

Peripheral nervous system (PNS) – nervous system outside the brain and the spinal cord, including the somatic nervous system and the autonomic nervous system; central nervous system (CNS).

Perpetuate – cause to continue or prevail.

Persecution – to be badly treated, oppressed, or harassed because of beliefs, gender, race, religion, or sexual orientation.

Persecutory delusion – a belief centered on being oppressed, pursued, or harassed.

Perseverate – repeat a response after cessation of the original stimulus.

Persona – an image of oneself presented to others.

Persona (*Jungian psychology*) – the image of the self-projected onto others. Some traits of personality are negative and suppressed from persona. Therefore, a persona may not represent a person's genuine inner Self and may be influenced by the model personalities or archetypes a person aspires to.

Personableness – the complex of attributes that make a person socially attractive.

Personhood – being a person.

Personal identity – the distinct personality of an individual regarded as a persisting entity.

Personal space – the physical region around a person and from interactions with others.

Personality – the collection of characteristic thoughts, feelings, and behaviors that make up a person. Qualities that make a person (or thing) distinct from others. The unique psychological qualities of an individual influence characteristic behavior patterns (overt and covert) in different situations over time.

Personality disorders – pathological trends in personality structure; stable patterns of experience and behavior differing noticeably from patterns considered normal (or typical) by a person's culture. It may manifest as a lack of good judgment or poor relationships with others, accompanied by little anxiety and no personal sense of distress.

Personality inventory – a self-report questionnaire to measure personality characteristics through questions on personal thoughts, feelings, and behaviors. Eysenck Personality Inventory (EPI) measures personality along the dimensions of neuroticism – stability and extroversion – introversion.

Personality types – distinct patterns of personality characteristics assign people to categories; qualitative differences, rather than differences in degree, discriminate among people.

Personal unconscious (*Jungian psychology*) – an individual's unique unconscious. A psyche component repressing experiences, thoughts, or feelings. The contents of the Personal Unconscious can affect the subject matter of dreams and can emerge in other forms, such as irrational fear.

Person-centered theory (*Carl Rogers*) – self-concept is the most important feature of personality.

Person-centered therapy – See *client-centered therapy.*

Person perception – forming impressions about other people.

Persuasion – efforts to alter attitudes; communication intended to induce belief or action.

Pervasive development disorder (PDD) – five disorders characterized by delays in developing multiple essential functions, including socialization and communication. *For example, autism is a common PDD.*

PET (positron emission tomography) scans – a technique for imaging brain activity by recording the extent of metabolic activity in different brain regions during different cognitive or behavioral activities through injecting a radioactive substance.

Phallic stage (*Freud's Stages of Psychosexual Development*) – the third stage from about 3 to 5 years of age, during which the source of gratification is focused on the genitals; follows the Oral and Anal stages and typically occurs between the ages 3 to 6 years. During the Phallic Stage, the erogenous zone moves from anal/bowel movements to the genitals. The child may experience the Oedipus Complex or Electra Complex at this stage.

Phantom limb phenomenon – experienced by amputees who often continue to experience sensations that seem to originate from the missing limb.

Pharmacotherapy (or *drug therapy*) – treatment using medication.

Phenomena – an observable occurrence, pattern, or relationship between events.

Phenomenological – how things appear or are experienced; the humanistic approach emphasizes perceptions and feelings as defining the meaning of their behavior.

Phenotype – observed characteristics manifested from genetic and environmental influences. The observable characteristics of an organism result from the interaction between its genotype and environment.

Pheromones – chemical signals released by organisms that other species members instinctively perceive; often serve as long-distance sexual attractors.

Phi phenomenon (or *stroboscopic movement*) – an illusion of movement that arises when a series of images is presented very quickly, one after another.

Philosophy – the study of general and fundamental problems concerning the existence, knowledge, truth, justice, beauty, validity, mind, and language.

Philosophy of mind – studies the nature of the mind, mental events, mental functions, mental properties, consciousness, and their relationship to the physical body, particularly the brain.

Philosophy of perception – how mental processes and symbols depend on the world, internal and external to the perceiver.

Philosophy of science – the study of assumptions, foundations, and implications of science.

Philosophical – about philosophy; a certain critical, creative way of thinking.

Phobia – an anxiety disorder characterized by irrational fear; the fear experienced about situations, things, activities, or people that could be intense, irrational, and persistent.

Phobic disorder (or *phobia*) – anxiety of persistent and irrational fear of an object or situation often unreasonable and unfounded in proportion to the threat, which may interfere with daily functions.

Phoneme – a distinct speech sound in language; the smallest distinguishable unit in a language. Minimal units of speech create differences in speech production and reception.

Phonemic encoding – encoding verbal information that emphasizes how words sound.

Photochemical – relating to or produced by the effects of light on chemical systems.

Photoreceptor – eye cells specialized for receiving light stimuli.

Phylogeny – the evolution and development of a species. Compare ontogeny, which is the evolution and development of an organism.

Physical dependence (or *physiological dependence*) – addiction based on a need to avoid withdrawal (*physically painful and unpleasant symptoms*). A state where the body has adapted and become dependent on drugs, and sudden absence can result in withdrawal.

Physical development – the bodily changes, maturation, and growth in an organism starting with conception and continuing throughout the lifespan.

Physiological – relating to how living things function rather than shape or structure.

Physiological dependence (or *physical dependence*) – the process by which the body becomes adjusted to and dependent on a drug. Addiction is based on a need to avoid withdrawal (*physically painful and unpleasant symptoms*); the body adapts and becomes dependent on drugs, and sudden absence can result in withdrawal.

Physiological psychology – the physiological basis of psychological processes.

Physiologists – scientists who study living organisms and how their parts work.

Piaget, Jean (1896-1980) – Swiss developmental psychologist whose work has enormously influenced psychology and education. Piaget defined four sequential stages of cognitive development: 1. sensorimotor, 2. preoperational, 3. concrete operational, and 4. formal operational stage. Different thinking characterizes each stage. A child develops through development, and the schema changes to solve new experiences (*accommodation*).

Piagetian – relating to Jean Piaget writings, theories, or methods, especially for child development.

Piliavin (*subway experiment*, 1969) – famous experiment demonstrating diffusion of responsibility by exploring factors that influence helping behavior toward bystanders.

Pineal eye – a sensory structure for light reception on the dorsal diencephalon in reptiles.

Pitch – sound quality of highness or lowness; primarily dependent on sound wave frequency.

Pituitary gland – the primary gland of the endocrine system next to the hypothalamus, which regulates endocrine functions, including the secretion of growth hormones, and secretes hormones that trigger hormone secretions in other glands. For instance, the adrenocorticotropic hormone (ACTH) is released during stress, which triggers the release of steroids from the cortex of the adrenal glands.

Pinna – the visible part of the ear.

Place theory – different frequency tones produce maximum activation at different locations along the basilar membrane, with the result that pitch can be coded by the place at which activation occurs; how people discriminate high-pitched sounds with a frequency greater than 5000 Hz.

Placebo – a chemically inert substance administered instead of a therapeutic to test subjective effects by the participant. An innocuous or inert medication.

Placebo control – an experimental in which treatment is not administered; see *Placebo effect*.

Placebo effect – when participants display improvements after being administered a placebo, believing it has beneficial powers even though it has none. Expectations of improvement contribute to placebo effects when a subject receives a fake drug or treatment.

Placebo therapy – independent of specific clinical procedures that result in improvement.

Placenta – the tissue passes oxygen and nutrients from the mother's blood into the fetus and removes waste materials from the fetus.

Pleasure principle (*Freud*) – the drive to achieve pleasure and avoid pain; the operating principle of the id. An assertion that actions are motivated by the pursuit of maximum pleasure and enduring the least amount of pain possible. Freud proposed that humans are motivated to achieve immediate and maximal pleasure, regardless of the cost.

Pluralism – a state in which independent cultures coexist while maintaining their cultural differences; see *Multiculturalism.*

Polarization – having a relationship between two opposite attributes.

Polyandry – a marriage where the wife has more than one husband simultaneously.

Polygamy – a marriage in which one spouse of either sex may have more than one mate at the same time; a family unit with more than two partners; see *Polyandry* and *Polygyny.*

Polygenic traits – physical characteristics influenced by several genes.

Polygraph (or *lie detector*) – a device that detects changes in autonomic arousal.

Polygyny – a mating system in which a single male mates with many females.

Pons – a part of the hindbrain involved in sleeping, waking, and dreaming. A nerve fiber band links the medulla oblongata and the cerebellum with the midbrain.

Pons Varolii – a nerve fiber band linking the medulla oblongata and cerebellum with the midbrain.

Popular culture – the beliefs, practices, activities, and products widely shared among a population.

Population (or *target population*) – the entire group to which the study results are intended to apply and from which those selected to participate in the study will be drawn. The collection of individuals from which a sample is populated.

Positive correlation (*statistics*) – a relationship between two measured variables in which as one variable increases, the other does too.

Positively skewed distribution (*statistics*) – data distribution with a few very high scores.

Positive punishment (*operant conditioning*) – the presentation of a stimulus after a response so that the response will be less likely to occur.

Positive regard (or *unconditional positive regard*) – complete acceptance and caring of an individual without imposing conditions; a broad acceptance and support of an individual irrespective of what the individual says or does. A therapist's quality is crucial in patient-centered therapy. It involves nonjudgmental acceptance of the patient.

Positive reinforcement (*operant conditioning*) – the presentation of a stimulus after a response so the response is more likely to occur. Increasing the likelihood of a response by immediately following the response with a desirable stimulus (a positive reinforcer).

Positive symptoms – indicated by the presence of altered behaviors. Behaviors related to a mental disorder that does not occur in healthy persons (e.g., hallucinations in schizophrenia).

Positron emission tomography (PET) is a method for studying the brain that involves injecting a radioactive substance that collects in active brain areas.

Possible selves – the ideal selves that a person would like to become, the selves a person could become, and the selves a person is afraid of becoming, components of the cognitive sense of self.

Posthypnotic amnesia – a subject's inability to remember something that happened while they were hypnotized.

Post-traumatic stress disorder (PSTD) – an anxiety disorder arising because of the experience of a traumatic event, such as a life-threatening event. Symptoms typically involve a persistent re-experience of the event through hallucinations, recollections, flashbacks, increased anxiety, and guilt.

Postsynaptic (*neurology*) – neuronal cells with dendritic receptors for neurotransmitters released into the synaptic cleft by the presynaptic neuron.

Postsynaptic neuron – at a synapse, the neuron receives a neurotransmitter.

Postsynaptic potential – the voltage change at a receptor site of a postsynaptic neuron when a neurotransmitter molecule links up with a receptor molecule.

Posthypnotic amnesia – when a person who has been hypnotized and instructed to forget what happened during hypnosis accordingly claims not to remember what happened.

Predictive validity (or *criterion validity*) – how well a test or scale can foretell the measure of some criterion (e.g., a cognitive test for an occupation compared to a subject's later performance reviews).

Precipitate – bring about abruptly.

Precipitating – bringing on suddenly or abruptly.

Preconscious – thoughts, experiences, and memories not in a person's immediate attention but put into awareness at any moment. Part of the mind contains information outside one's attention, which is not currently addressed but is readily accessible if needed.

Predictive validity – indicates if a test can accurately predict future performance.

Predisposed – made susceptible.

Prefrontal lobotomy – a surgical operation severing nerve fibers connecting the brain's frontal lobes with the diencephalon, especially those fibers of the thalamic and hypothalamic areas; the best-known form of psychosurgery.

Prejudice – a negative belief about individuals. A learned negative attitude with stereotypes towards people; behavioral manifestation is *discrimination*.

Prenatal period – the time between conception and birth.

Pressure – a sense of being compelled to behave in a particular way because of expectations set by oneself or others.

Presynaptic – the axonal end of the neuron where the synapse may be inhibited or stimulated to release neurotransmitters.

Presynaptic neuron – at a synapse, the neuron that releases a neurotransmitter.

Prevalence – the quality of being widespread.

Primacy effect – information presented first to a participant is more likely to be remembered than material subsequently presented; improved memory for items at the start of a list.

Primary auditory cortex – in the temporal lobe of the cerebrum, the brain part processes auditory information.

Primary caregiver – the person responsible for caring for an infant, often the biological mother.

Primary motor cortex – in the frontal lobe of the cerebrum, the brain part controls muscle movement.

Primary prevention – strategies to prevent disease by developing good health habits and discouraging poor ones.

Primary process thinking – irrational, illogical, and motivated by a desire for immediate gratification of impulses.

Primary punisher (*operant conditioning*) – a consequence naturally unpleasant.

Primary reinforcer (*operant conditioning*) – positive stimuli based on innate biological urges (e.g., food or water); a consequence naturally satisfying.

Primary somatosensory cortex – in the parietal lobe of the cerebrum, the part of the brain involved in handling touch-related information.

Primary visual cortex – in the occipital lobe of the cerebrum, involved in handling visual information.

Priming – 1. memory retrieval by activating information associated with that memory. Previous exposure to a word or situation improves implicit memory and increases the activation of associated thoughts or memories, the advantage conferred by prior exposure to a word or situation. 2. the act of making ready.

Principle of closure (*Gestalt psychology*) – people interpret familiar incomplete forms as complete by filling in gaps.

Principle of continuity (*Gestalt psychology*) – people perceive interrupted lines and patterns as continuous by filling in gaps.

Principle of parsimony (*Occam's razor*) – applying the straightforward explanation to observations.

Principle of proximity (*Gestalt psychology*) – people perceive objects as a group when they are close together.

Principle of similarity (*Gestalt psychology*) – people tend to group similar objects.

Principle of simplicity (*Gestalt psychology*) – perceiving forms as simple, symmetrical figures rather than irregular ones.

Prison study (*Philip Zimbardo*, 1971) – a famous study showing the influence of roles. Participants were assigned roles of prison guards or prisoners. Participants assigned as prison guards undertook increasingly cruel behavior in the belief of conforming to their social role.

Proactive interference – forgetting new information because of earlier learned information.

Pro-attitudinal behavior – a tendency to behave in a manner consistent with existing, underlying attitudes.

Probability – a numerical measure of chance, expressed as a number between 1 (certainty) and 0 (impossibility). A probability of 0.05 represents the probability of an effect occurring if the null hypothesis is true. The results are purely due to chance factors.

Probability sample – a sample for which each person (or thing, such as an email address) has an equal chance of being selected because the selection is random.

Problem-solving – the thought processes involved in solving a problem; the active effort people make to achieve a goal that cannot be easily attained.

Problem space – the elements of a problem: the initial state, the incomplete information or unsatisfactory conditions the person starts with; the goal state, the set of information or state the person wishes to achieve; and the set of operations, the steps the person takes to move from the initial state to the goal state.

Procedural memory – the memory of how to do things. *For example, how to ride a bike. Procedural memory is usually considered implicit.*

Process – the performance of some composite cognitive activity.

Prognosis (*clinical psychology*) – the expected eventual outcome of a disorder; a prediction about the probable course and outcome.

Projection – a defense mechanism of attributing one's unacceptable thoughts or feelings to someone else when unwanted thoughts are externalized or projected onto someone else.

Projective hypothesis – people interpret ambiguous stimuli in ways that reveal their concerns, needs, conflicts, desires, and feelings.

Projective personality tests – require subjects to respond to ambiguous stimuli, such as pictures and phrases, that can be interpreted differently.

Projective test – requires psychologists to make judgments based on a subject's responses to ambiguous stimuli to assess a psychological disorder. A personality assessment during which an individual interprets an ambiguous, abstract stimulus, and the response reveals unconscious and hidden feelings, motives, and conflicts.

Proprioception – sensing the body's position, location, orientation, and movement.

Prosencephalon – the anterior portion of the brain.

Prosocial behavior – actions believed to help others.

Prosody – the study of poetic meter and the art of versification.

Protection of participants – an ethical requirement whereby researchers must minimize risk or harm to participants.

Prototype – a typical example of a concept.

Proximal cause – a direct influence on behavior, such as one's attitude or an aspect of the immediate situation.

Proximal stimulus – the optical image on the retina, contrasted with the distal stimulus (the physical object in the world).

Proximity – the property of being close; the tendency to perceive close objects as groups.

Psychoactive drugs – drugs that affect sensory experience, perception, mood, thinking, and behavior.

Psyche (*Carl Jung*) – the totality of each person's psychic contents. The totality of the human mind, including the conscious and subconscious. The role of the psyche is the focus of the psychoanalytic approach, whose proponents include Sigmund Freud and Carl Jung.

Psychiatrists – medical doctors with an M.D. degree and completed postdoctoral specialty training in mental and emotional disorders; may prescribe medications to treat psychological disorders.

Psychic determinism – the assumption that experiences determine mental and behavioral reactions.

Psychoactive drugs – chemicals that affect mental processes and behavior by temporarily changing one's conscious awareness of reality.

Psychoanalysis (*Sigmund Freud*) – therapy to treat mental disorders. The study of behavior and functioning of human psychology by investigating the mind. Psychoanalysis systematizes the theories of human behavior and treats psychological and emotional illnesses. *It focuses on the importance of unconscious forces, childhood experiences, and the psyche's division into the id, ego, and superego.*

Therapy with the assumptions of unconscious conflict and psychosexual development. It aims for the patient to better understand their unconscious thoughts and feelings through free association and transference. It consists of a range of techniques that attribute abnormal feelings and behaviors to the internal conflicts of the mind. Psychoanalysts, beginning with Sigmund Freud and later Carl Jung, may use techniques such as hypnosis and regression to uncover repressed memories and thoughts in the subconscious mind, believing that by enabling them to surface in the conscious mind, a person can overcome problems.

Psychoanalyst – an individual who has earned either a Ph.D. or an M.D. degree and has completed postgraduate training in the Freudian approach to understanding and treating mental disorders.

Psychoanalytic theory – concerned with the definition and dynamics of personality development. Provides a conceptual framework more-or-less independent of clinical practice rather than based on empirical analysis of clinical cases. Sigmond Freud proposed the psychoanalytic theory, which has undergone many modifications.

Psychobiography – the use of psychological (especially personality) theory to describe and explain an individual's course through life.

Psychodrama (*human development*) – explores issues, problems, dreams, concerns, and aspirations of groups, organizations, systems, and people in general through dramatic action.

Psychodynamics – focuses on underlying human behavior systematically. The emphasis is on the interplay between conscious and unconscious motivation. The processes and emotions that determine psychology and motivation. The interrelation of conscious and unconscious processes and emotions determines personality and motivation.

Psychodynamic approach (*Freud's Stages of Psychosexual Development*) – views behavior from childhood experiences and the influence of unconscious processes, drives, and conflicts; focuses on internal processes of the psyche. Originating from the theories of Freud, the psychodynamic approach looks at 'dynamics' that influence feelings, thoughts, and behavior, including conflicts between the subconscious and conscious and the effect of earlier experiences. *For example, fixation during Freud's Stages of Psychosexual Development.*

Psychodynamic model – disorders result from maladaptive defenses against unconscious conflicts.

Psychodynamic personality theories – theories of personality sharing the assumption that powerful inner forces shape the personality and motivate the behavior.

Psychodynamic perspective – a psychological model in which behavior is explained regarding past experiences and motivational forces; actions are viewed as stemming from inherited instincts, biological drives, and attempts to resolve conflicts between personal needs and social requirements.

Psychodynamic psychotherapy – alleviates psychic tension by revealing the unconscious content of a patient's psyche.

Psychodynamic theories (*Sigmund Freud*) – emphasize unconscious motives and desires and the importance of childhood experiences in shaping personality.

Psycholinguistics – relating to the psychology of language; studies the psychological basis of linguistic competence and performance. The study of neurobiological and psychological factors enabling humans to acquire, use, comprehend, and produce a language.

Psychological – 1. how organisms function (i.e., mental, emotional, not physical). 2. mental or emotional as opposed to physical. 3. relating to the science of mental life.

Psychological assessment – using specified procedures to evaluate people's abilities, behaviors, and personal qualities.

Psychological condition (or *psychological state*) – when the qualities of a state are relatively constant even though the state is dynamic.

Psychological dependence – addiction based on cravings; reliance upon when addicted.

Psychological diagnosis – the label given to psychological abnormality by classifying and categorizing the observed behavior pattern into an approved diagnostic system.

Psychological disorder – a psychological disorder of thought or emotion; atypical thoughts or emotions; a more neutral term than mental illness.

Psychologically – regarding the science of the mind and mental processes.

Physiological psychology (or *biological psychology*) – studies the neural mechanisms of perception and behavior through direct manipulation of the brains of nonhuman animal subjects in controlled experiments.

Psychological state (or *psychological condition*) – when the qualities of a state are relatively constant even though the state is dynamic.

Psychological test – 1. generalizations about an individual are inferred based on sample behaviors. 2. an instrument for collecting information about personality traits, emotional states, aptitudes, interests, abilities, values, or behaviors.

Psychologist – a person who, by study, training, and experience, has achieved professional recognition and standing in clinical psychology; a specialist in the science of mental life.

Psychology – the scientific study of behavior and mental processes.

Psychology of learning – studying the effects of conditioning, environment, and reinforcement provides psychologists with the best information about human behavior.

Psychometric approach – a method of understanding intelligence by emphasizing people's performance on standardized aptitude tests.

Psychometric function – a graph plotting the percentage of detections of a stimulus (on the vertical axis) about stimulus intensity (on the horizontal axis).

Psychometric testing – measures competence in a specific area of cognitive testing and functioning (e.g., intelligence, personality).

Psychometrics – concerned with quantitative psychological measurements.

Psychometry – concerned with psychological measurements.

Psychoneuroimmunology – research investigating interactions between psychological processes (e.g., responses to stress) and the functions of the immune system

Psychonomic – uses experimental methods to study psychological issues.

Psychopath (or *antisocial personality disorder*) – individuals who lack regard for others, are impulsive, and behave in a socially unacceptable manner; characterized by a lack of conscience and respect for other people's rights, feelings, and needs, beginning by age fifteen. Behavior that harms or offends another lacks judgment and consideration for others. *For example, a person might cause damage to the property of others. Such behavior is the manifestation of anti-social personality disorder.*

Psychopathological functioning – emotional, behavioral, or thought disruptions that lead to personal distress or block one's ability to achieve important goals.

Psychopathology –concerned with abnormal (i.e., unusual, and atypical) behavior.

Psychopharmacology – the study of the effects that drugs have on behavior.

Psychophysics – the study of the relationship between the physical properties of stimuli and people's experience of the stimuli. The relationship between physical stimuli and the mental events that arise from these stimuli. Concerns quantitative relations between physical stimuli and their psychological effects. The methods developed are fundamental to sensation and perception.

Psychophysiology – concerned with the physiological bases of psychological processes and the physiological bases of psychological processes.

Psychosis – any major mental disorder involving loss of contact with reality, usually including delusions or hallucinations.

Psychotic – a person who has psychosis.

Psychotic belief – an erroneous belief held even with contrary evidence.

Psychosocial – psychological or social aspects of health, disease, treatment, or rehabilitation.

Psychosocial stages (*Erik Erikson*, 1950) – successive developmental stages that focus on an individual's orientation toward the self and others; these stages incorporate both the sexual and social aspects of development and the social conflicts arising from the interaction between the individual and social environment.

Psychosomatic disorders – physical disorders aggravated by or primarily attributable to prolonged emotional stress or other psychological causes.

Psychosurgery – surgical procedures on brain tissue to alleviate symptoms of severe psychological disorders.

Psychotherapy – treatment for abnormal behavior primarily verbal rather than biochemical (e.g., pharmaceuticals); psychological treatment through confidential verbal communications with a mental health professional.

Psychosexual development (*psychoanalytic theory*) – how a child progresses through set stages according to gratification (oral, anal, genital) and by the person towards which this feeling is directed.

Psychotic disorders – severe mental disorders with impairments testing manifested by thought, emotional, or perceptual difficulties; no longer a diagnostic category after DSM-III.

Puberty – the beginning of adolescence, marked by menarche in girls and the beginning of nocturnal emissions in boys.

Pubescence – a young person who has just reached puberty or sexual maturity. A child at the end of childhood and beginning of adulthood, including being nearly old enough physically to reproduce or have babies.

Public territory – a place with low occupation and perception of ownership (e.g., a park or beach).

Punisher (*operant conditioning*) – any stimulus that, when made contingent upon a response, decreases the probability of that response recurring.

Punishment (*operant conditioning*) – a response followed by a negative reinforcer, which decreases the probability of the response. Delivering a consequence decreases the likelihood of a response.

Pupil – the opening in the eye's lens, letting light into the back of the eye.

Pure light – electromagnetic energy (light) of a single wavelength.

Q

Q-sort – a tool occasionally used in therapy. A pack of cards containing statements is presented to the patient, who then sorts these into categories (for example, 'very like me,' 'not at all like me,' and so on). If therapy is successful, there will be a shift from a great distribution of negative cards to positive cards to reflect a positive self-image.

Quantitative psychological research – includes mathematical modeling with statistical estimation or interference.

Qualitative research (*data*) – using mathematics and statistics to study techniques and ways to measure human attributes and mathematical and statistical patterning of psychological processes and analysis of psychological data. Information in a nonnumerical form (e.g., speech, written words, pictures) places importance on the meaningful interpretation of data rather than simply converting data to numbers. *For example, material gathered from a case study.*

Quantitative research (*data*) – information in numerical form. *For example, the number of students in a class or the average score on a quiz.*

Quantum psychology – using awareness of automatic responses and triggers in addition to the inherent mechanism of those responses.

Quasi-experiment (*research design*) – the experimenter does not influence participant allocation to different conditions but instead utilizes existing groupings.

Questionnaire (*survey*) – a research method with different formats of questionnaires. *For example, the Likert scale and open- and closed- questions.*

Quota sampling – a technique for obtaining participants by a quota in proportion to a frequency in the population.

R

Race – a category composed of people who share certain inheritable phenotypical traits that members of society deem socially significant.

Racism – discrimination against people based on their skin color or ethnic heritage.

Radical behaviorism – the basic philosophy in the experimental analysis of behavior.

Radicalization – a transformation from activism or passiveness to militant, revolutionary, or extreme posture.

Rage – a mental state when an individual reaches an extreme position of the intensity spectrum of anger.

Random allocation – how experimenters divide participants into each experimental condition to reduce bias in the distribution of participant characteristics.

Random assignment (*experimental design*) – placing subjects into an experimental or control group so that subjects have an equal chance of being placed in either one or the other.

Random sample – the selection of a random sample; obtaining participants whereby every member of the population has an equal chance of being selected.

Range (*descriptive statistic*) – the difference between the highest and lowest scores in a set of scores and between the highest and lowest scores in a data set.

Rapid eye movement (REM) sleep (or *paradoxical sleep*) – a stage of deep sleep when brain wave activity is similar to waking. Eye movements and dreaming characterize REM. In adults, REM sleep alternates with other periods of sleep (non-REM sleep) over a 90-minute cycle. REM sleep is accompanied by increased heart rate, blood pressure, and faster and more irregular breathing patterns.

Rapport –when a person is *in sync* or *on the same wavelength* as another.

Rating scale – the appraisal of a person or behavior along a specific scale.

Rational – consistent with or based on or using reason. *For example, rational behavior.*

Rational-emotive sleep (or *paradoxical sleep*) – a stage of deep when brain wave activity is similar to that in the waking state. The rapid movement of the eyes during the sleep cycle. REM is commonly associated with dreaming. Characterized by eye movements and dreaming. In adults, REM sleep alternates with other periods of sleep (non-REM sleep) over a 90-minute cycle. REM sleep is accompanied by increased heart rate, blood pressure, and faster and more irregular breathing patterns.

Rational-emotive therapy (*cognitive-behavioral therapy*, Albert Ellis) – aims to identify catastrophic thinking and to change the irrational assumptions that underlie it.

Rational-emotive therapy (*cognitive therapy* or *cognitive behavioral therapy*) – identifying and changing maladaptive thinking patterns that can result in negative emotions and dysfunctional behavior; focusing on the role of faulty beliefs and thought patterns in abnormal behavior; it encourages testing beliefs *via* behavioral strategies.

Rational-legal authority (or *bureaucratic authority*) – power legitimized by legally-enacted rules and regulations (e.g., the majority rules, the chain of command).

Rationalism – the doctrine that reason is the basis for regulating conduct.

Rationalization – a defense mechanism using incorrect but self-serving explanations to justify unacceptable behavior, thoughts, or feelings.

Rationalization of society (*Max Weber*, 1864-1920) – the historical change from tradition, emotion, and spirituality to more scientifically based rationality as the dominant mode of human thought and decision-making.

Ratio schedule – when reinforcement happens after a certain number of responses.

Reaction formation – a defense mechanism involving behaving opposite to behavior, feelings, or thoughts considered unacceptable. *For example, a man deals with homosexual feelings by displaying external resentment towards gays.*

Reaction range – the limits that heredity places on characteristics such as IQ.

Reaction time – the time a subject takes to respond to a stimulus, the interval between the stimulus and the response.

Readiness – being temporarily ready to respond in a particular way.

Real culture – the actual, everyday behavior of people in a society.

Realistic conflict theory – prejudice and discrimination that proposes intergroup conflict and antagonism occur when groups compete for scarce resources.

Reality principle (*Freud's theory analytical approach*) – behavior is informed not only by inner desires (contrast *Pleasure Principle*) but by recognizing external realities and what is reasonable or acceptable. The awareness that gratification of impulses must be delayed to accommodate real-world demands. It acts as the operating principle of the ego; constraints and rules governing the ego delay id gratification by recognizing the demands of the real world.

Reasoning – the mental (cognitive) process of looking for reasons for beliefs, conclusions, actions, or feelings. The process of thinking in which conclusions are drawn from a set of facts; thinking is directed toward a given goal or objective.

Rebound – the symptoms medicine was going to cure return when stopping the medicine and sometimes extra much so during the time just after one has gone off the medicine.

Recall (*human memory*) – the process of remembering without any external cues.; the active retrieval of information. Successful memory recall depends on several factors. The ability to access a memory when needed. *For example, Craik and Lockhart (1972) claimed that increased effort spent thinking over or rehearsing information can lead to an increased recall.*

Recency effect – improved memory for a list of words at the end of a list than earlier.

Receptive language – the ability to understand language.

Recentering (*Gestalt theory*) – developing an alternative target for a situation (e.g., solving problems).

Receptive field – the visual area from which a given ganglion cell receives information.

Recidivism – reverting to crime. *For example, an offender commits a crime after released from prison.*

Reciprocal altruism (*evolutionary psychology*) – individuals perform altruistic behavior if the expected benefit of future help from strangers surpasses the short-term cost of helping, helping others at the expense of one's resources, in the expectation that the favor will be repaid. *For example, vampire bats feed related bats blood and expect they will do the same when requested.*

Reciprocal determinism – the interaction process between a person's characteristics and the environment. This interaction results in personality.

Reciprocity norm – an implicit rule in many societies that tells people they should return favors or gifts given to them.

Recognition (*memory*) – identifying presented information as familiar and having been experienced before. The process of identifying learned information by using external cues and recalling a fact, incident, or other items from long-term memory.

Reconstructive memory – an account of piecing together and reassembling stored information during recall and stored knowledge, expectations, and beliefs to fill gaps and produce a coherent memory representation. Adults recover early repressed memories (often sexual abuse), which are often cited as the cause of a problem (e.g., eating disorder)

Reductionism – human processes presented in a simplified manner, often criticized by humanistic theories for de-humanizing subjects by considering them on an atomistic level.

Regression (*psychotherapy*) – a therapeutic technique to take a subject back to an earlier point in their life, hoping to find causes of present problems. During regression, thoughts are pushed from consciousness to unconsciousness. Defense mechanism when the *ego* temporarily reverts to an earlier stage of development.

Reflex – an innate response to a stimulus; an unlearned response triggered by specific stimuli. *For example, a baby sucking on an object in their mouth.*

Reflexology – the study of reflex action as it relates to the behavior of organisms.

Refractory period – when the nerve cell has been depolarized and cannot be stimulated after an action potential until repolarization.

Regression (*Freudian theory*) – a defense mechanism reverting an earlier developmental period behavior to prevent anxiety and satisfy current needs, a more immature state of psychological development.

Regression toward the mean (*statistics*) – the tendency for extreme states to move toward the average when assessed a second time. The relation between selected values of x and observed values of y (from which the probable value of y can be predicted for any value of x).

Regulatory Focus Theory – studies the relationship between motivation and goal fulfillment.

Rehabilitation – methods to retrain the neural pathways to improve or regain neurocognitive functioning damaged by traumatic injury or disease.

Rehearsal – the process of practicing material to remember it. A cognitive process of repeating an item to maintain it in short-term memory.

Reinforcement – a stimulus strengthening the behavior that produced it; the delivery of a consequence increases the likelihood that a response will occur.

Reinforcement contingency – a consistent relationship between a response and the changes in the environment it produces.

Reinforcement schedule – the pattern in which reinforcement is given over time.

Reinforcer (*conditioning*) – any stimulus that, after following a response, increases the probability of a response. A stimulus strengthens or weakens the behavior that produced it.

Reinforcing stimulus – strengthens or weakens the behavior that produced it.

Relapse – 1. return to behavior after the recovery. 2. the symptoms that the medicine was going to cure return when one stops taking medicine and sometimes extra much so during the time just after one has gone off the medicine.

Related t-test (*parametric inferential statistical test*) – used with interval or ratio data, a repeated measure (or *matched pairs*) to investigate differences in the effect each level of the independent variable has on the dependent variable.

Relative motion parallax – a source of information about depth in which the relative distances of objects from a viewer determine the amount and direction of their relative motion in the retinal image.

Relative poverty – not having enough money to maintain an average standard of living.

Relaxation response – when muscle tension, cortical activity, heart rate, and blood pressure decrease and breathing slows.

Relaxation training – procedures reducing and relaxing muscle tension, heart rate, and cortical activity. This is evident in systematic desensitization.

Relearning – a method for measuring forgetting and retention, which involves assessing the time it takes to memorize information a second time.

Reliability – the ability of a test to produce the same result when administered separately to the same groups. A measure of consistency to represent the degree to which replications of a test or method produce similar data scores.

Religion – a social institution involving beliefs and practices based upon a conception of the sacred and the possible rituals that surround the sacred.

REM rebound effect – the tendency to spend more time in the REM stage of sleep after a period of REM sleep deprivation.

Remorse – personal regret felt after committing a hurtful, shameful, or violent act.

Repeated measures design (*within-subjects* or *related design*) – each participates in every independent variable level.

Replicability – ability of research to repeatedly yield same results when done by different researchers.

Representative sample – corresponds to the population from which it is drawn in terms of age, sex, and other qualities of the studied variables.

Representativeness heuristic – a probability estimate for an event based on how typical that event is.

Repression – a defense mechanism keeping unpleasant thoughts, memories, feelings, or ideas associated with pain or guilt blocked from conscious awareness. The concealment of memories, thoughts, or feelings which cause anxiety or discomfort. These repressed ideas reside in the unconscious (according to Carl Jung, the *Personal Unconscious*). They may surface in dreams or influence a person without them being aware, such as in the case of Josef Breuer's client, Anna O. Therefore, repressed thoughts and their effect on a person are often subjects of psychoanalysts.

Reproductive advantage – the outcome of a characteristic that helps an organism mate successfully and thus pass on its genes to the next generation.

Research – gaining knowledge by examining appropriate theories or empirical data; an investigative process such as an experiment or a case study in psychology.

Residual stress pattern – a chronic syndrome in which the emotional responses of posttraumatic stress persist over time.

Resistance (*psychoanalysis*) – the patient's inability or unwillingness to accept the analyst's interpretations of behaviors or to discuss specific experiences. A patient's usually unconscious efforts block the progress of treatment.

Resocialization – the process of unlearning old ways of doing things and adopting new attitudes, values, norms, and behaviors.

Resource allocation model of divided attention (or *capacity models of divided attention*) – proposes processing resources allocated according to demands and environmental factors.

Respiratory center – the region in the medulla oblongata and pons that integrates sensory information about the level of oxygen and carbon dioxide in the blood and determines the signals to be sent to the respiratory muscles.

Respondent conditioning (*classical conditioning* or *Pavlovian conditioning*) – learning in which a subject responds to a neutral stimulus as they would to another stimulus by learning to associate the two stimuli. Learning whereby a neutral stimulus is repeatedly paired with an unconditioned stimulus (UCS) that naturally produces an unconditioned response (UCR). After several trials, the neutral stimulus is a conditioned stimulus (CS) and thus produces a conditioned response (CR).

Responder bias (or *participant reactivity*) – participant's tendency to produce biased responses from wanting to appear socially desirable or to be in line with what the experimenter wants.

Response bias – the systematic tendency due to non-sensory factors for an observer to favor responding in a particular way.

Response tendency – a learned tendency to behave in a particular way.

Resting potential – the slight negative charge inside an inactive neuron.

Resting state – when the inside of a neuron has a slightly higher concentration of negatively charged ions than the outside. The neuron during this time is inactive.

Restoration accounts of sleep – hypothesis that the purpose of sleep is to restore and repair the body.

Retention – the proportion of learned information retained or remembered.

Reticular activating system (RAS) – network in reticular formation with an arousal function.

Reticular formation (RF) – a complex neural network in the brainstem's central core; monitors bodily functions in such processes as arousal, sleep, attention, and muscle tone. A brain structure that includes regions of the hindbrain and midbrain and participates in sleep, wakefulness, pain perception, breathing, and muscle reflexes. A diffuse network of nerve fibers in the brain stem and limbic system, with connections up to the cortex and down to the spinal cord, alerts the cerebral cortex to incoming sensory signals and serves to regulate arousal levels, maintain consciousness, and awaken from sleep.

Retina – a thin layer of neural tissue in the back of the eye. The light-sensitive region of the eye has three layers of neural tissue, including photoreceptors that convert light into neural responses to be passed to the brain via the optic nerve.

Retinal disparity – the difference between the images picked up by the two eyes.

Retrieval – the process of getting information out of memory; recovery of a stored item from memory.

Retrieval cues – internal or external stimuli aiding memory retrieval; stimuli help to get information out of memory.

Retroactive interference – forgetting old information because of newly learned information; the impact of information on the recall of memories that have already been stored. Interference can include the wording of research questions, as demonstrated in a 1978 experiment that manipulated participants' recall of the events in a video using different questions.

Retrograde amnesia – an inability to remember events before a traumatic brain event; the affected person cannot recall or retrieve the events that occurred before the amnesia.

Retrospective study – assesses the impact of early experience on later development, looking back from the time of the specified effect *to* the early experience.

Reuptake – the process by which neurotransmitter molecules return to presynaptic neurons.

Reversal theory – explains human motivation in terms of reversals from one opposing meta-motivational state to another; see *Metamotivation*.

Reverse psychology – a persuasion technique using falsely advocating beliefs and behaviors instead of what should be advocated.

Reversibility – the ability to reverse actions mentally.

Reversible figure – an ambiguous drawing that can be interpreted in several ways.

Reward – a satisfying or pleasurable event (for example, food to a hungry animal)

Rewards-cost model (*Piliavin theory*) – altruistic behavior is determined by evaluating the rewards and costs of helping and not helping.

Rhetoric – one of three ancient arts of discourse, with logic and grammar for persuasion.

Rhombencephalon – the posterior brain portion, including the cerebellum and brainstem.

Risky shift – the tendency for a group's dominant, risky point of view to be strengthened to an even riskier position after a group discussion. People tend to make riskier decisions when they are group members than if they make the same decision independently.

Ritalin – a drug whose action resembles amphetamines; controversially used in treating children suffering from attention deficit (hyperactivity) disorder.

Ritual healing – ceremonies that infuse a particular emotional intensity and meaning into the healing process.

Rogers, Carl (1902-1987) – a founder of the humanistic perspective. His theories encompassed the importance of unconditional and conditional positive regard for developing the self-concept and conditions of worth set by others. His work has been applied to several domains through his development of patient-centered therapy.

Rods – photoreceptor cells in the eye's retina to see in dim light. Rods are critical for sight during dim illumination, whereas *cones* are more active in good light conditions. Individuals who lack rods (or have dysfunctional rods) suffer from night blindness and cannot see correctly in dim light.

Role – behavior expected of someone who holds a status (i.e., expected behavior).

Role conflict – occupying two roles simultaneously, where each is incompatible with the expectations of the other.

Role model – a person whose behavior is observed and imitated.

Role performance – the actual behavior of a person with a status (i.e., expected behavior).

Role set – roles attached to a person (e.g., mother, husband, realtor, Catholic).

Role strain – the frustrations and uncertainties a person experiences when coping with the requirements of two or more statuses.

Role-taking – assuming someone else's perspective for learning purposes.

Rorschach test (1921) – a projective test with a series of ten bilaterally symmetrical inkblots that subjects describe. Psychologists then use complex scoring systems to interpret the subjects' responses. Responses and interpretations are assumed to reveal characteristics such as emotional responsiveness and personality.

Rules – behavioral guidelines for acting in specific ways in certain situations.

S

SAD – see *seasonal affective disorder*.

Sadism – the enjoyment an individual derives by inflicting pain on others.

Sadness – the state of experiencing sorrow.

Salience – the distinctiveness or importance of something. *For example, when thirsty, images of drinks.*

Sample – a collection of subjects drawn from a population that a researcher studies. The group was selected from a population to participate in a study so research could generalize about the original population.

Sampling bias – a source of error arises when the sample is not representative of the population the researcher wants to study.

Sampling error – due to a non-representative sample.

Sampling method – a group of population participants; includes random, stratified, opportunity, and quota sampling.

Sanctions – rewards for good or appropriate behavior or penalties when bad or inappropriate.

Sapience – to apply knowledge, experience, understanding, common sense, and insight.

Sapir-Whorf hypothesis (1929) – people perceive the world through the cultural lens of their unique language; habits of speech and reading create habits of perception and, to some extent, a unique reality.

Satanic ritual abuse – physical or psychological mistreatment using satanic rituals.

Saturation – dimension of color capturing the purity and vividness of color sensations.

Sauce-Bearnaise syndrome – conditioned taste aversion when an individual associates the taste of a specific food item with the symptoms caused by a toxic or spoiled substance.

Savant syndrome – a disorder wherein a person with diminished mental skill demonstrates extraordinary proficiency in one specific isolated skill.

Scaffolding – a child's learning advances by providing a framework for the child to develop.

Scalloped response pattern – when responses are slow at the beginning of the interval and faster just before reinforcement happens. It occurs because of a fixed-interval schedule.

Scapegoat – a person or category of people, typically with little power, whom people unfairly blame for their mistakes or inadequacy.

Schachter and Singer (1962) – proposed a two-factor theory of emotion, whereby an emotion is experienced as a combination of *arousal* and *attribution* (labeling).

Schedule of reinforcement (*operant conditioning*) – sequence of presenting and withholding reinforcement.

Schema – a mental model that includes knowledge, beliefs, and expectations; a mental structure representing aspects of the world. Mental frameworks structure knowledge, beliefs, and expectations of objects, people, and situations to guide cognitive processes and behavior.

Schemes *(Piaget)* – cognitive structures that develop as infants and young children learn to interpret the world and adapt to their environment.

Schizoid personality disorder – social withdrawal and restricted expression of emotions; characterized by extreme shyness, reclusive nature, discomfort with other people, and incapability of forming close relationships.

Schizotypal personality disorder – unconventional beliefs, odd behavior, thinking, and a need for social isolation. Severe psychopathology with the breakdown of integrated personality functioning, withdrawal from reality, emotional distortions, and disturbed thought processes.

Schizoaffective disorder – with symptoms of a major mood disorder and schizophrenia.

Schizophrenia – a severe psychiatric disorder characterized by problems with perceptions or expressions of reality, significant social problems, disorganized thinking, and delusions or hallucinations. A disorder involving a loss of contact with reality and symptoms that may include hallucinations, delusions, disorganized speech or behavior, emotional flatness, social withdrawal, decreased richness of speech, and lack of motivation.

Schizophrenia in remission – a diagnosis indicating the patient is free of schizophrenic symptoms but has had periods of schizophrenia.

Schizophreniform disorder – identical to schizophrenia, with the duration of prodromal, active, and residual phases being shorter than six months.

Schizophrenogenic family – a family with faulty communication patterns and conflict between members has been implicated in schizophrenia development.

School refusal – when children and adolescents demonstrate severe anxiety symptoms and refuse to attend school.

Scientific method – a standardized process of making observations, gathering data, forming theories, testing predictions, and interpreting results. 1. a research process that includes careful data collection, exact measurement, accurate recording and analysis of the findings, thoughtful interpretation of results, and, when appropriate, a generalization of the findings to a larger group; 2. the set of procedures for gathering and interpreting objective information to minimize error and yield dependable generalizations.

Scientific research – the effort to reduce uncertainty about some aspect of society through the science of observation.

Seasonal affective disorder (SAD) – a mood disorder associated with changes in season; a bout of depression occurring during certain times of the year when there is less sunlight, usually during the winter months.

Second cranial nerve – cranial nerve serving the retina.

Secondary analysis – a data collection method examining the data collected by someone else; includes historical materials, public records, and official statistics; its strengths are convenience and inexpensive; its weakness is gathering all information a researcher needs.

Secondary process thinking – logical and rational.

Secondary punisher (or *conditioned* punisher; operant *conditioning*) – a consequence unpleasant because it has become associated with a primary punisher.

Secondary reinforcement – acts as a reinforcer by association with primary reinforcement.

Secondary reinforcer (or *conditioned reinforcer*) – operant conditioning when a consequence is satisfying because it has become associated with a primary reinforcer.

Secondary sex characteristics – differences between the sexes, other than reproductive organs, such as body hair, facial hair, and voice pitch. Sex-specific physical traits not essential to reproduction include breasts, widened hips, facial hair, and deepened voices.

Secondary territory – space and items with a medium degree of occupation and perception of ownership. *For example, a classroom seat.*

Secularization – the historical decline in the importance of the supernatural and the sacred; the declining influence of religion in everyday life.

Secure attachment – a bond between mother (or primary caregiver) and infant, whereby the mother is sensitive and responsive to the child's needs, who will not experience significant distress at separation from the caregiver but seek comfort from a caregiver when frightened. *Secure attachment relates to healthy subsequent cognitive and emotional development as adults, including high self-esteem and maintaining loving, trusting relationships.*

Security blanket – an item (e.g., blanket, toy) a child uses to reduce anxiety.

Sedative – drugs slow the nervous system, producing drowsiness and reduced sensory-motor skills by reducing central nervous system functioning.

Selective abstraction (or *cognitive bias*) – when only one detail is chosen from the context and believed, while everything else is ignored.

Selective attention – focusing on some sensory information and ignoring others; a perceptual process of focusing on specific stimulus elements.

Selective distortion – interpreting information in a particular way to support existing beliefs.

Selective optimization with compensation – a strategy for successful aging in which one makes the most of gains while minimizing the impact of losses that accompany normal aging.

Selective serotonin reuptake inhibitors (SSRI) – antidepressants to increase serotonin levels.

Selective social interaction theory – as people age, they become more selective in choosing social partners who satisfy their emotional needs.

Self – an awareness of one's social identity.

Self-acceptance – an acceptance of self as self, even with shortcomings.

Self-actualization (*Maslow's hierarchy of needs*) – an individual's desire to grow, reach their potential, and realize their full potential. A holistic approach toward life, thus allowing oneself to reach the highest potential without greed for success. According to Maslow, self-actualization is a human's highest need, which arises after satisfying more basic needs. The process of becoming a person is psychological emancipation (Carl Rogers).

Self-annihilation (or *suicide*) – the act of killing oneself.

Self-awareness – explicit understanding that one exists with a top-level of consciousness; cognizance of the autobiographical character of personally experienced events. Includes the concept that one exists as an individual, separated from others, with private thoughts.

Self-categorization theory – people are likely to be influenced by those perceived to be similar to themselves (i.e., in-group members).

Self-criticism – critically scrutinizing one's beliefs, thoughts, actions, and behavior.

Self-concept (*Rogers*) – the most important feature of personality; a mental representation of individuality and interdependence, including self-understanding and self-esteem. The self-concept includes all the thoughts, feelings, and beliefs people have about themselves.

Self-disclosure – the tendency to reveal gradually more personal information when knowing others better.

Self-effacing bias – a tendency in certain cultures to attribute their successes to situational factors rather than to personal attributes and to attribute their failures to lack of effort.

Self-efficacy – confidence in one's ability to meet challenges effectively; belief in the ability and performance of a task or situation.

Self-esteem – evaluative attitude towards the self of how much an individual likes themselves, influencing personal and social behaviors; a feeling of pride.

Self-fulfilling prophecy – expectations affect interactions and elicit an anticipated response.

Self-handicapping – the process of developing, in anticipation of failure, behavioral reactions and explanations that minimize ability deficits as possible attributions for the failure.

Self-help groups – therapy groups without a therapist.

Self-image – an enduring mental perception depicting not only details potentially available to an objective investigation by others (height, weight, hair color, sex, I.Q. score) but items learned, either from personal experiences or by internalizing the judgments of others.

Selfishness – the act of placing one's interests or desires above the needs of others.

Self-loathing (or *self-hatred*) – characterized by extreme dislike of oneself.

Self-motivation – the ability to motivate oneself without requiring influence from another.

Self-perception theory – observations and perceptions shape attitudes and characterizations.

Self-realization – the emancipation towards self-reliance in respect of integrity, filognosy (*love of knowledge*), different views, forms of logic, and intelligence in society. Self-actualization is the more specific humanist conception of self-realization.

Self-report – data by asking people to report and identify their behavior or mental state.

Self-report data – information that people being surveyed give about themselves.

Self-report inventory –a test requiring people to answer questions about their typical behavior.

Self-serving – interested only in self.

Self-serving bias – the tendency to attribute successes to internal factors and failures to situational factors; the tendency to influence judgments of behavior by emphasizing external factors for failure but attributing success to ability or effort.

Selye, Hans (1907-1982) – endocrinologist who explored physiological responses to stress, illness, and disease. Selye's article in Nature (1926) entitled, *A Syndrome Produced by Diverse Nocuous Agents*, identified a set of symptoms of being exposed to threats in rats as general adaptation syndrome and later labeled *stress*. *General Adaptation Syndrome* has three stress stages: an alarm state, a resistance state, and an exhaustion state.

Semantic dyslexia – an inability to attach words to their meanings when reading.

Semantic encoding – formatting verbal information that emphasizes the meaning of words.

Semantic memory – remembering general facts; the initial memory processes involved in the momentary preservation of fleeting impressions of sensory stimuli.

Semantic memory (*long-term memory*) – the memory of meanings, understandings, and other concept-based knowledge; general knowledge of the world, including facts.

Semantic slanting – a way of making statements to evoke specific emotional responses.

Semicircular canals – three fluid-filled tubes in the inner ear; main structures in the vestibular system.

Sensation – when physical energy from objects or the body stimulates the sense organs.

Senses – physiological methods of perception. The senses and their operation, classification, and theory are overlapping topics studied in neuroscience, cognitive psychology (or cognitive science), and the philosophy of perception.

Sensitive period (or *critical period*) – a time in development when an organism can best develop a response. *For example, the development of language.*

Sensitive responsiveness – how a primary carer responds to an infant's signals.

Sensitivity – the ability of the organism to respond to any physical stimuli.

Sensitization – 1. becoming overly sensitive to specific events or situations (especially emotional ones). 2. the process of becoming highly responsive to situations.

Sensory adaptation –the decrease in sensitivity to an unchanging stimulus.

Sensory memory – a memory system storing incoming sensory information for an instant; a modality-specific memory involved in temporarily preserving sensory stimuli, serving as a buffer between the senses and short-term memory.

Sensory nerves – neural pathways in the parasympathetic nervous system (PNS) that transfer information from the sensory receptors to the central nervous system (CNS).

Sensory neurons –carry messages from sense receptors toward the central nervous system (CNS).

Sensory preconditioning (*classical conditioning*) – facilitates learning an association between two conditioned stimuli.

Sensory physiology – how biological mechanisms convert physical events into neural events.

Sensory receptors – specialized cells that convert physical signals into cellular signals processed by the nervous system.

Sensory threshold (*psychophysics*) – the theoretical concept of detecting minimum stimulation.

Sentience – state of being conscious; feelings are distinguished from perception or thought.

Sentient – self-aware, choice-making consciousness. Humans and cetaceans (dolphins and whales) are the two sentient species on Earth.

Separation anxiety disorder – an individual experiences excessive anxiety regarding separation from home or from people with whom they are closely attached; the emotional distress babies show when separated from their caregivers.

Serial monogamy – marrying several people but one at a time.

Serial-position curve – a graphical representation of memory retrieval, whereby recall is highest for beginning *(primacy effect)* and end items *(recency effect)* listed than in the middle.

Serial position effect – a characteristic of memory retrieval in which the recall of items at the beginning and the end of a list is often better than recalling items in the middle.

Serial processes – two or more mental processes carried out in order, one after the other.

Serotonin –a neurotransmitter involved in sleep, wakefulness, appetite, aggression, impulsivity, sensory perception, temperature regulation, pain suppression, and mood. Produces an inhibitory effect.

Set – being temporarily ready to respond in a particular way.

Set point –a genetically influenced determinant for body weight.

Sex – a biological distinction between males and females.

Sex chromosomes – contain genes encoding male or female characteristics.

Sex differences – commonly observed differences between males and females that may be primary (associated with reproduction), secondary (biological, but not associated with reproduction), and differences in mental, emotional, or behavioral characteristics.

Sex-linked trait – any genetically determined characteristic linked to one sex more than the other. *For example, male performance at spatial ability tests is superior to women.*

Sexism – prejudice and discrimination against one sex by members of the other, for instance, in employment.

Sexual arousal – the arousal of sexual desires as preparations for sexual behavior.

Sexual imprinting – a process of observation of one's parents, which influences a person's sexual orientation later in life. Sexual imprinting can, for example, affect the traits an animal will seek in a potential mate (Gallagher, 1977).

Sexual orientation – the pattern of emotional, romantic, and sexual attractions between males and females; preference for sexual partners of the same or opposite sex.

Sexual response cycle – a four-phase model of physiological responses (excitement phase, plateau phase, orgasmic phase, and resolution phase) triggered during sexual stimulation.

Sexual script – implicit rules for people to judge sexual behavior appropriately in a given situation.

Sexual selection – a process in which females choose their mates based on specific characteristics that will be passed to their male offspring. Individuals have features that make them attractive to members of the opposite sex (intersexual selection) or help them to compete with members of the same sex for access to mates (intrasexual selection).

Sexuoerotic tragedy – an intense, memorable, and meaningful event that is pivotal in changing the person's perception of what is sexually arousing and what is not.

Shadow (*Jungian psychology*) – an archetype representing the side of a person hidden from the persona. The Shadow contains a person's anxieties and traits which they consider, correctly or incorrectly, to be negative. *For example, it may contain a person's sensitivity and humility, which to some is a positive attribute but, to the person, maybe a sign of weakness.*

Shadowing (*attention studies*) – listening to and repeating a message presented in one ear.

Shamanism – a spiritual tradition involving healing powers and actual or assumed contact with the spirit world.

Shame – a negative effect elicited by a perceived loss of self-esteem related to behavior.

Shape constancy – perceiving the shape of an object despite variations in the size of the retinal image.

Shaping (*operant conditioning*) – a procedure in which reinforcement guides response closer to a desired response.

Shaping by successive approximations (*operant conditioning*) – a behavioral method that reinforces responses that successively approximate and match the desired response.

Shell shock battle fatigue – a disorder caused by the excessive stress of active warfare.

Shock value – the potential of a communication medium, such as an image or text, to provoke a reaction, such as disgust, shock, anger, or fear.

Short-term memory (STM) – retaining a small amount of information in an active, easily accessible for a brief period; stores a limited amount of information for a brief period; preserves recent information over relatively brief intervals of limited capacity, and information is stored for only a short time without rehearsal.

Shyness – an individual's discomfort or inhibition in interpersonal situations interfering with pursuing interpersonal or professional goals.

Sibling rivalry – inevitable rivalry between children for parental affection and resources.

Siege mentality – the shared feeling of helplessness, defensiveness, or victimization.

Signal detection theory (SDT) – predicts when a weak signal will be detected. A systematic approach to the problem of response bias allows an experimenter to identify and separate the roles of sensory stimuli and the individual's criterion level in producing the final response.

Sign language – gestural communication for people who are hard of hearing.

Significance level (*statistics*) – the probability that an observed outcome is due only to chance.

Significance tests (*statistics*) – whether observed results reflect real differences due to the manipulation of variables rather than chance variations.

Significant difference (*statistics*) – comparison between experimental groups or conditions that would have occurred by chance less than an accepted criterion; in psychology, the criterion most often used is a probability of fewer than 5 times out of 100, or $p < 0.05$.

Similarity – the tendency to group similar objects.

Simplicity – perceiving forms as simple, symmetrical figures rather than irregular ones.

Simultaneous conditioning (*classical conditioning*) – when unconditioned (UCS) and conditioned stimuli (CS) are presented simultaneously rather than one (UCS) preceding the other (CS).

Simultaneous discovery – when two or more parties make a discovery independently. For example, American psychologist Edwin Twitmyer (1873-1943) produced theories like classical conditioning when Ivan Pavlov (1849-1936) demonstrated them in Russia.

Simulation heuristic – a specialized adaptation of heuristics for counterfactual thinking and regret.

Single-blind (*experimental procedure*) – a procedure in which subjects do not know whether they are in an experimental or control group.

Single-blind design experiment – subjects are uninformed of the purpose and aim of the study to avoid bias.

Situational attribution – attributing behavior to be caused by factors outside one's control. *For example, task difficulty or weather.*

Situation awareness – the perception of environmental elements within a volume of time and space, comprehension of their meaning, and the projection of their status.

Situational variables – confounding effects due to environmental influences, such as lighting, noise levels, and temperature.

Sixteen Personality Factor Questionnaire (16PF) – assesses sixteen personality dimensions.

Size constancy – the tendency to perceive objects as being closer to their actual size rather than the physical size registered on the eye's retina.

Size-weight illusion – the tendency to underestimate the weight of a bigger object compared to a similar smaller object of the same mass.

Skewed distribution – an asymmetrical frequency distribution whereby the median is usually more representative than the mean as a measure of central tendency.

Skill – the ability to perform a task successfully and competently.

Skinner, B. F. (1904-1990) – *American psychologist, Harvard professor, and proponent of the behaviorist theory of learning. Skinner described differences between informal learning, which occurs naturally, and formal education, depending on the teacher creating optimal patterns of stimulus and response (reward and publishment; operant conditioning). Learning is a process of stimulus conditioning, reward, and punishment.*

Skinner box – a device to study operant conditioning.

Skinner box (*operant conditioning chamber*) – a laboratory apparatus created by B.F. Skinner analyzed the behavior of animals. *For example, experiments on animals like pigeons, rodents, and primates.*

Skinnerian – relating to B. F. Skinner or his behaviorist psychology.

Sleep – a natural and periodic state of rest during which consciousness is suspended.

Sleep apnea – a temporary suspension of breathing repeatedly occurring during sleep that often affects overweight people or those having an obstruction in the breathing tract, an abnormally small throat opening, or a neurological disorder.

Sleep cycle – circadian biological rhythm oscillating between sleep and awareness.

Sleep disorders – include insomnia, sleep apnea, and narcolepsy.

Sleeper effect – persuasive messages may not have an immediate effect but may be revealed in a behavior change after some time.

Sleep-learning – conveying information to a sleeping person, usually with a sound recording.

Sleep spindles – short bursts of brain waves occur during stage 2 sleep.

Smooth muscles – involuntary muscles help organs such as stomach and bladder functions.

Sociability – a child's inclination to interact with others and seek their attention or approval.

Social anxiety –a psychiatric disorder characterized by a persistent, intense, and chronic fear of being judged, embarrassed, or humiliated by others owing to one's actions.

Social behavior – any behavior which involves others or is oriented toward others.

Social categorization – the process by which people organize the social environment by categorizing themselves and others into groups.

Social clocks – social and cultural norms indicate the typical ages at which people experience life events, behaviors, and issues.

Social cognition – the mental processes involved in how individuals perceive and react to social situations; studying how people process social information, emphasizing encoding, storage, retrieval, and application in social situations.

Social comparison – a tendency to judge behavior against that of others.

Social-conflict approach – a framework for building a theory based on the assumption that society is characterized by inequality and conflict that generate change; where functional theory addresses what works in a cultural group or society, the social-conflict theory looks for the dysfunction, mostly the structures that reinforce inequality; see *Conflict theory*.

Social desirability – behaving to bring social approval from others or responding in a self-evaluative situation (e.g., interview, questionnaire) to present ourselves to reveal more socially desirable characteristics (while potentially hiding undesirable characteristics).

Social desirability bias – a tendency to describe themselves in socially approved ways and respond to a question so that people view the answer favorably. The social desirability bias could take two forms: a respondent exhibits an overreporting of good behavior or an underreporting of bad behavior displayed.

Social development – growth of social behaviors, such as forming attachments, developing healthy self-esteem, and forming successful relationships; individuals' social interactions and expectations change over their lifespan.

Social drift theory (hypothesis) – explaining the relationship between social class and severe mental illness by suggesting that seriously mentally ill 'drift' down the socio-economic scale.

Social exchange theory – people help each other because they want to gain as much as possible while losing as little as possible.

Social facilitation – a tendency for individuals to perform better in the presence of others.

Social facilitation and inhibition (SFI) – an improvement in performance due to the presence of others (*social facilitation*) or an impairment in performance due to the presence of others (*social inhibition*).

Social identity theory – individuals categorize themselves and others into in-groups and out-groups. Unfavorable comparisons are made between groups due to a need to maintain a positive social identity, subsequently giving rise to competition and discrimination.

Social influence – how a person's behavior is affected by others (e.g., conformity pressures and group dynamics); a condition wherein an individual's thoughts or actions are affected or altered by others.

Social inhibition – the conscious or unconscious constraint of behavior objectionable in social settings; a drive that keeps humans from becoming involved in potentially objectionable actions or expressions in a social setting.

Social intelligence – a theory of personality for the expertise people bring to life experiences.

Social interactionist theory – a micro sociological theory that shared-meaning orientations and assumptions form the basic motivation behind people's actions.

Social learning – learning through imitation and modeling of the behavior of role models.

Social learning theories – people learn new attitudes, beliefs, and behaviors through social interaction, especially during childhood.

Social-learning therapy – clients observe reinforced desirable behaviors.

Social loafing – people working on a task make less effort than if working alone; the reduced effort people invest in a task when working with others.

Social mobility – a person's ability to move up and down the social ladder; see *Horizontal, Intragenerational,* and *Intergenerational mobility.*

Social norms – societal rules about appropriate behavior; expected standards of appropriate behavior and attitudes for members of a group or society.

Social perception – the process by which a person comes to know or perceive the personal attributes of themselves and others.

Social phobia – characterized by intense anxiety when exposed to certain social or performance situations.

Social psychology – studies individuals and their relationships with others, groups, and society; it attempts to understand and explain how thoughts, feelings, and behavior are influenced by the actual, imagined, or implied presence of others.

Social Readjustment Rating Scale (SRRS) (Holmes and Rahe, 1967) – scores important life events and changes according to psychological impact and degree of adjustment required. Higher scores on the SRRS indicate a higher risk of stress-related ill health.

Social responsibility norm – a societal rule that tells people they should help others who need help, even if it is costly.

Social rhythm therapy (*behavioral therapy*) – the disruptions in circadian rhythms are treated. This therapy adopts the biopsychological treatment model instead of using medications only.

Social roles – behavior patterns considered appropriate for a person in context.

Social schemas – mental models that represent and categorize social events and people.

Social skills training (*behavioral therapy*) aims to enhance a patient's relationships with others; a program to teach people to improve social skills, such as making eye contact.

Social stratification – ranking the members of a society into a pattern of superior and inferior ranks, such as wealth, prestige, power, etc. (e.g., caste or class systems).

Social support – people or supportive services during difficult periods, including information (e.g., advice) or emotional support (e.g., reassurance that one is cared for).

Social trap – a situation in which one harms oneself and others by acting in self-interest.

Socialization – sociologists, social psychologists, and educationalists refer to learning culture and how to live within it. It provides individuals with the necessary resources to act and participate in society.

Socially sensitive research – may have direct social consequences for participants or the population represented. *For example, research into racial differences.*

Society – people who interact in a defined territory and share common interests and values (i.e., some aspects of culture and leadership that bring them together).

Sociobiology – focuses on evolutionary explanations for the social behavior and social systems of humans and other animal species.

Sociocultural evolution (*Lenski*) – the change process resulting from a society's gaining cultural information, particularly technology, that may have a good or destructive impact on society.

Socio-demographic – a combination of sociological and demographic characteristics.

Socioeconomics – the relationship between economic activity and social life.

Sociologist – a social scientist studying institutions and the development of human society.

Sociology – the scientific or systematic study of society, including patterns of social relations, social stratification, social interaction, and culture.

Soma (or *cell body*) – the central area of a neuron, containing the nucleus and cytoplasm.

Somatic – bodily (physical) characteristics as opposed to the mind or spirit.

Somatic nervous system – part of the peripheral nervous system (PNS) connected to skeletal muscles and sense organs.

Somatic therapies (*biomedical* or *biological therapies*) – treating mental disorders with physical or chemical methods, such as medication or psychosurgery, rather than psychotherapy.

Somatic treatments – procedures for mental disorders employing physical and chemical methods. *For example, Electroconvulsive Shock Treatment (ECT).*

Somatization disorder (*hysteria* or *Briquet's syndrome*) – a disorder in which psychological conflicts present in the mind are expressed unconsciously as physical symptoms that do not have any actual or physical origin behind them. Characterized by physical symptoms, such as pain and gastrointestinal, sexual, and pseudo-neurological problems. The disorder begins before age thirty and continues for many years.

Somatoform disorders – a psychiatric disorder characterized by physical symptoms that mimic disease whose physical cause cannot be identified.; characterized by symptoms that a medical condition cannot explain, the effects of a drug, or another mental disorder.

Somatosensory cortex – a part of the brain that processes stimulation from the skin, body wall, muscles, bones, tendons, and joints; determines pain intensity.

Somatotherapy (or *somatic therapy*) – treating mental illness physically, such as medication or psychosurgery, rather than psychotherapy.

Sound waves – changes in pressure generated by vibrating molecules.

Source amnesia (*source misattribution* or *source monitoring error*) – the inaccurate recall of the origin of information in memory.

Spalding, Douglas (1841-1877) – English biologist who noted the concept of *stamping in* with newborn chickens (Spalding, 1873). As imprinting, Spalding's observations were developed in the 20th Century by German biologist Oskar Heinroth. Heinroth's student, Konrad Lorenz, popularized the concept by imprinting himself as a parent for graylag geese.

Spatial memory – the ability of animals to form an internal representation or map of familiar areas or home range.

Spatial memory (*cognitive psychology*) – the part of memory assigned to record information about one's environment and spatial orientation.

Spatial-temporal reasoning – the ability to visualize spatial patterns and manipulate them mentally in a time-ordered sequence of spatial transformations.

Spearman, Charles (1863-1945) – English psychologist focused on intelligence research, proposing the theoretical underlying general factor (g) of intelligence and statistics, establishing Spearman's rank correlation coefficient and factor analysis.

Species-specific behavior (or *instincts*) – characteristic of all species members. *Response patterns (popularly called instincts) apply to behaviors. For example, mating, defense, and raising offspring.*

Specific phobia – feeling intense anxiety when exposed to a particular situation.

Specious present – the time duration in which one's perceptions are in the present.

Speech perception – the process by which humans interpret language sounds.

Spinal cord – connects the brain to the body.

Spinal fluid – the clear liquid produced in the ventricles of the brain.

Spinal reflexes – automatic behaviors requiring no input from the brain.

Spiritual psychology (or *transpersonal psychology*) – transpersonal or spiritual aspects of human experience.

Split half reliability – an evaluation of a test's internal consistency by randomly splitting test items into two halves and comparing participants' performance on the two halves. The two scores should correlate highly if the test is internally dependable.

Split-brain studies – split-brain operations on epileptic patients involve cutting the corpus callosum, separating the brain's two hemispheres.

Split-brain surgery – the corpus callosum is cut, separating the brain's two hemispheres.

Spontaneous recovery (*classical conditioning*) – an extinguished conditioned response will be spontaneously produced after extinction; the re-emergence of a conditioned response previously extinguished by numerous factors, including injury.

Spontaneous remission (*psychotherapy*) – improvement in condition without professional intervention often serves as a baseline criterion to compare the effectiveness of therapies.

Sport psychology – the scientific study of sports and practical application of such knowledge.

Stable attribution – an inference that behavior is due to stable, unchanging factors.

Stage – a period in development when people show typical behavior patterns and capacities.

Stages of sleep – human sleep is divided into five stages according to electroencephalographic (EEG) recordings. 1) REM sleep with rapid eye movements and includes dreaming. 2) Stage 1 with a 50% reduction in alpha waves compared to awake resting with eyes closed. The stage is somnolence or "drowsy sleep." It appears at sleep onset and can be associated with *hypnagogic hallucinations* (i.e., during stages of entering sleep). 3) Stage 2 with "spindles" (12-16Hz) and "K-complexes." 4) Stage 3 with delta waves (1-2Hz) 20%-50% of the time. 5) Stage 4 with delta waves over 50% of the time

Stamping in (*Edward Thorndike's Law of Effect*) – the association of a particular type of behavior with a subsequent reward. Thorndike proposed that this association would produce similar behavior because of the reward.

Stamping out (*Edward Thorndike's Law of Effect*) – the association of a specific behavior with a punishment, or at least the absence of any reward. Over time, the behavior would be 'stamped out' - gradually decreasing because of the association.

Standard deviation (*statistics*) – the square root of the variance. Indicates the degree to which scores vary around the mean of a distribution. A measure of dispersion and the average difference of a set of scores from the mean measure.

Standardization – a set of consistent procedures to treat participants in an experiment or record data using uniform procedures when administering and scoring tests.

Standardized instructions – directions given to study participants so each participant receives the same information to minimize variation.

Standardized tests – exams with uniform procedures for administration and scoring.

Standardization sample – people representing the population of potential test takers.

Stanford Prison Experiment (*Philip Zimbardo*, 1971) – an experiment with participants assigned roles of correctional officers or prisoners. Participants assigned as correctional officers undertook increasingly cruel behavior in the belief of conforming to their social role.

States – temporary behaviors or feelings.

Statistical infrequency – any rare behavior viewed as abnormal.

Statistical significance – the likelihood that a result was not due to chance. A conclusion is drawn from the results of a research study whereby the effect of the independent variable upon the dependent variable is not due to chance.

Statistics – the analysis and interpretation of numerical data.

Status – a social position or identity a person occupies in a society; see *Status set*.

Status set – a collection of social statuses that an individual occupies at a given time (if one has a *Role set*, then they will often have a status set).

Stepfamily – a household in which two adults marry or cohabit and one or both have a biological or adoptive child/children from a prior relationship.

Stereoscopic vision – the perceptual experience of a three-dimensional image by combining two different views of the same scene from the two eyes.

Stereotype – beliefs about people based on their membership in a group. An oversimplified, generalized, and often inaccurate perception based on membership in a group often underlies prejudice and discrimination.

Stereotype threat – associated with being at risk for confirming a negative stereotype of one's group.

Steroids – any natural (e.g., testosterone) or synthetic substances regulating body function.

Stigma – 1. a powerfully negative social label that radically changes a person's self-concept and social identity; 2. adverse reaction to others because of assumed inferiority or source of difference denigrated.

Stimulants – drugs activating the central nervous system (CNS). A drug that increases activation of the central nervous system (CNS) and the autonomic nervous system (ANS) decreases fatigue, increases physical activity and alertness, and reduces hunger, resulting in a temporary mood elevation.

Stimulus (plural, *stimuli*) – any event acting to arouse action.; something effectively impinging upon the sensory system. Any event, situation, object, or factor may affect behavior; in the behaviorist approach, a stimulus must be a measurable environmental change.

Stimulus discrimination (*classical conditioning*) – the tendency *not* to have a conditioned response to a new stimulus like the original conditioned stimulus. An organism learns to differentiate between stimuli that differ from the conditioned stimulus, the tendency for a response only when a stimulus is present.

Stimulus-driven capture – a determinant of why people select some parts of sensory input for further processing; occurs when features of specific stimuli (objects in the environment) automatically capture attention, independent of the local goals of a perceiver.

Stimulus generalization (*conditioning*) – transfer of a response learned from one stimulus to a similar stimulus; the tendency to respond to a new stimulus as if it is the original conditioned stimulus.

Stimulus-response learning – involves an association between a stimulus and a response.

Storage – the retention of encoded information in memory over time; the process of maintaining information in memory.

Strain (*psychology*) – nervousness resulting from mental stress.

Strange situation – an experiment devised for studying attachment behavior.

Stratified sample – the group reflects the composition of the population. For example, 20 percent of left-handed and 80 percent of right-handed individuals would determine a selection of participants using the exact percentages.

Stream of consciousness – continuous flow of ideas facilitating an individual's conscious experience.

Stress (*psychology*) – 1. a state of mental or emotional strain or suspense. The experience of being threatened by taxing circumstances, circumstances threatening the well-being, or the process of evaluating and coping with threatening circumstances. 2. emphasis attached to something. A mismatch between the perceived demands of the environment and an organism's perceived ability to cope.

Stress moderator variables – change the impact of a stressor on a given stress reaction.

Stress reduction – techniques to cope with stress and reduce its adverse effects.

Stressors – circumstances psychologically or physically demanding; any event or stimulus (internal or external) that triggers a stress response.

Stroop effect (1930s) – reaction delay between congruent and incongruent stimuli; a demonstration of interference in the reaction time of a task. *For example, when a word such as red is printed differing from the color expressed by the word's semantic meaning (e.g., "red" printed in blue ink), a delay occurs in the processing of the word's color, leading to slower test times and increased mistakes.*

Structural encoding – encoding verbal information emphasizing how words look.

Structural Family Therapy (*Salvador Munchin*) – explores invisible rules governing family functioning, mapping the relationships between family members or between family subsets, and ultimately disrupting dysfunctional relationships, stabilizing them into healthier patterns. Minuchin contends that pathology rests not with the individual but the family system.

Structural-functional approach – a theoretical framework based on the assumption that society is a complex system whose parts work together to promote stability; humans work toward functional organization, order, and stability, and their cultural norms and institutions reflect that goal; therefore, there are logical reasons for why people do the things they do and organize themselves the way they do; see *Functionalist theory.*

Structuralism – studying the structure of mind and behavior; the view that mental experience can be understood as a combination of simple elements (or events).

Subconscious – level of consciousness beneath awareness that cannot be accessed at will. According to psychodynamic theory, the subconscious may contain repressed thoughts and memories and influence dreams. Attempts to access the subconscious have been made using hypnosis and regression.

Subconscious (*Freud's theory*) – portions of the mind below conscious awareness.

Subcortical – the brain portion immediately below the cerebral cortex, which is part of the brain responsible for most higher functions (e.g., sensation, voluntary muscle movement, thought, reasoning, memory)

Subculture – cultural patterns that distinguish some segment of a society's population; variations within a society regarding some aspects of religion, language, traditions, and customs or outward symbols and appearance setting them apart from the mainstream or dominant culture (e.g., intercity gangs, the Amish of Pennsylvania, hippies of the 1960s, etc.).

Subject – A person or animal that a researcher studies.

Subject bias – results from the subject's expectations or the subject's changing behavior.

Subjective – an assessment based on criteria that exist only or principally in the assessor. *Two subjective assessors assessing the same item might differ widely in their assessment.*

Subjective Units of Disturbance Scale or Subjective Units of Distress Scale (SUDS) – a scale of 10 measuring the subjective intensity of disturbance experienced by an individual.

Subjective utility – deciding by estimating the personal value of a decision's outcome.

Subjective well-being – perception about happiness and satisfaction with life.

Subliminal message – communication unrealized on a conscious level but understood on a subliminal level.

Sublimation (*Freud's theory*) – making the expression of an impulse socially acceptable. A defense mechanism whereby energy is redirected (*channeling unacceptable thoughts*) toward socially acceptable behavior.

Submissiveness – the trait of willingly yielding to another's will or a superior force.

Substance abuse (according to *DSM*) – a maladaptive pattern of drug use resulting in repeated negative consequences (e.g., legal, social, work-related, or school-related). Relying excessively on a substance (e.g., alcohol or opioids) often interferes with daily functions.

Substantia nigra – a layer of deeply pigmented grey matter in the midbrain.

SUDS (Subjective Units of Disturbance Scale or Subjective Units of Distress Scale) – a scale of 10 that measures the subjective intensity of disturbance experienced by an individual.

Suicide (or *self-annihilation*) – the act of killing oneself.

Suicidology – studying suicide, including psychology, physiology, psychiatry, and sociology.

Superego (*Freudian theory psychodynamic model*) – a portion of the psyche governed by moral constraints. The superego represents conscience, recognizing the needs of those in the external world, and is responsible for feelings of guilt; the moral component of the personality—more developed aspects of personality than the id and the ego.

Superior colliculus – an essential visual center between the retina and the striate cortex.

Superiority complex – the subconscious neurotic mechanism of compensation developed by the individual owing to extensive feelings of inferiority. The unhealthy belief that everyone can perform the task except oneself.

Superordinate goal – a higher and more important goal than usually pursued by individuals within a group.

Superstition – irrational belief, fear of consequences arising from another, unlinked behavior, or absence of behavior.

Suppression – the conscious exclusion of unacceptable thoughts or desires.

Suprachiasmatic nucleus (SCN) – a bilateral brain region in the hypothalamus controlling endogenous circadian sleep rhythms; neuronal and hormonal activities regulating body functions over 24 hours.

Survey – a method of getting information about a specific behavior, experience, or event using interviews or questionnaires with several participants.

Surveys – a data collection method using questionnaires and interviews; its strengths are that it can be inexpensive, easy to administer, have a fast turnaround, and easy to acquire sensitive information; its weaknesses are low response rate and the possibility of respondents giving inaccurate (or dishonest) answers.

Survival advantage – the outcome of a characteristic helping an organism to live long enough to reproduce and pass its genes to offspring.

Sustainable ecosystem – the human use of the natural environment to meet the needs of the present generation without threatening the prospects of future generations; economic growth without further or irrevocable damage to natural ecosystems.

Syllogism – deductive reasoning where the conclusion is derived from two premises.

Sylvia Plath effect – the theory that creative writers are more susceptible to mental illness.

Symbol – a sound, gesture, or written character representing an object, action, event, or idea.

Symbolic-interaction approach – a theoretical framework based on the assumption that society is the product of the everyday interactions of individuals; therefore, the focus of research should be on the actual viewpoints, perspectives, and interpretations of people (the culture and its institutions as they see it, not necessarily as social scientists see it).

Symbolic interactionist theory – cultural symbols forge identities (that change over time), and culture (norms and values) helps people merge into society despite differences.

Symbolic thought – the ability to represent objects in terms of mental symbols.

Symbolic violence – actions with discriminatory or injurious implications (e.g., gender dominance or racism.

Symbols – anything that stands for something else and has a meaning for people who share a culture (e.g., apple pie, American flag).

Symbiosis – a relationship between two animals where each animal benefits.

Sympathetic nervous system – part of the autonomic nervous system that prepares the body for action and expends energy.

Symptom – a change from typical structure, function, or sensation; indicative of disease.

Synapse (*neurology*) – the junction between the axon of one neuron and the cell body or dendrite of a neighboring neuron. The flow of neurotransmitter chemicals connects a small physical gap between two neurons.

Synaptic cleft – the gap between two cells at a synapse.

Synaptic transmission – the relaying of information from one neuron to another across the synaptic gap; when a nerve impulse passes across the synaptic cleft from the *presynaptic neuron* to the *postsynaptic neuron*.

Synaptic vesicles – tiny sacs in a neuron's terminus that store and release neurotransmitters.

Syndrome – an association of several clinically recognizable features, signs, symptoms, phenomena, or characteristics.

Synonym – a word expressing the same or similar meaning.

Syntax – the study of the rules for forming admissible sentences. A system of rules that governs how words can be meaningfully arranged to form phrases and sentences.

Systematic desensitization (*behavioral therapy*) – counterconditioning to decrease anxiety, treating phobias and anxieties, whereby a patient is gradually exposed to more anxiety-provoking situations until fear is replaced by relaxation. Behavioral therapy effectively helps overcome phobias and anxiety disorders with a user embracing relaxation and coping techniques.

System variables (*witness testimony*) – variables affect the accuracy of witness testimony and over which the police (and justice system) have influence, including interviewing techniques.

Systems intelligence – human actions connecting sensitivity to the systemic environment with systems thinking, thus enhancing a person's problem-solving capabilities.

Systems psychology (*Roger Barker, Humberto Maturana*, and *Gregory Bateson*) – human behavior concerning complex systems inspired by systems thinking and theory.

Systems theory – a theoretical framework using multiple interrelated elements, where the properties of the whole are different from properties of the parts; systems are governed by negative feedback (which promotes stability) and positive feedback (which promotes instability). Explains a range of phenomena and situations. *For example, Minuchin's family systems theory.*

T

Taboo – something avoided, banned, or not allowed because of a cultural belief.

Tabula rasa (Latin; *blank slate*) – humans are influenced by environmental, rather than innate, influences. Behaviorists propose that human behavior is infinitely plastic and malleable and, therefore, can be explained through learned experiences rather than genetic predispositions.

Talking cure (*somatoform disorders* or *talking therapy*) – used in psychiatry to relieve the subject from hysterical symptoms.

Tarantism – a nervous disorder characterized by an intense urge to dance, attributed to a tarantula bite.

Tardive dyskinesia – occasionally a side-effect of antipsychotic drugs, typified by the involuntary tongue, lips, jaw, and facial movements. It is usually a permanent condition characterized by involuntary movements.

Taste aversion – learning formed after one trial, whereby an association is formed between feelings of sickness and (usually) food, resulting in avoidance.

Taxonomy – a classification of organisms based on similarities.

Telegraphic speech – contains no articles or prepositions; reduced sentences (resembling telegrams) that distinguish children's speech patterns from around 18 months to two years, demonstrating the basics of early grammar by containing crucial nouns and verbs.

Telencephalon – the anterior division of the forebrain.

Telepathy – transferring thoughts or feelings from one mind to another without sensory perceptions.

Telic state – a motivational state in which arousal is avoided.

Temperament – innate personality features or dispositions; aspects of personality existing at birth and are believed to result from genetic influences. The inborn component of an individual's personality.

Template theories – an account of pattern recognition; incoming information is matched with templates (miniature representations) of patterns stored in long-term memory.

Temporal lobe – cortex region below the lateral fissure; contains the auditory cortex.

Tend-and-befriend response – a response to stressors hypothesized for females; stressors prompt females to protect their offspring and join social groups to reduce vulnerability.

Tenseness – a state of mental or emotional strain or suspense.

Tension (*psychology*) – a state of mental or emotional strain or suspense.

Tension myositis (*John Sarno, MD*, 1923-2017) – patients exhibiting psychosomatic (*psychological causes*) musculoskeletal and nerve symptoms characterized by back pain.

Teratogen – an agent such as a virus, a drug, or radiation causing deformities in an embryo or fetus.

Terminal buttons – vesicular nodules at the end of axons that release neurotransmitters. Bulblike structures at the branched endings of axons contain exocytotic vesicles with neurotransmitters.

Ternus illusion (1926) – a mirage of visual perception regarding apparent motion in humans.

Territoriality – the tendency of animals to defend (e.g., through scent markings) a geographical area from other members of their species to gain access to and increase control over a resource.

Testosterone – a male sex hormone produced by the testes responsible for the production of sperm and the development of secondary sexual characteristics associated with aggression.

Test-retest reliability – measurement consistency by correlating (the same) test performance on two occasions. Produces the same results when given to the same group at different times.

Thalamus – part of the brain through which sensory information goes to the cerebrum. Large egg-shaped structures of grey matter form the dorsal subdivision of the diencephalon, part of the forebrain that transmits nerve impulses up sensory pathways to the cerebral cortex. Damage to the thalamus can result in anterograde amnesia.

Thalmencephalon – the posterior division of the forebrain.

Thanatos (*Freudian*) – represents the death instinct, characterized by aggressive behavior and a rejection of pleasurable stimuli.

Thematic Apperception Test (TAT) (*projective personality test*) – subjects generate stories about a set of ambiguous pictures. The subject is given a series of pictures depicting scenes that are ambiguous enough to trigger a variety of interpretations but still push the subject in a particular direction, making an association with a specific thing or event. A projective test whereby individuals are presented with ambiguous pictures and asked to generate a story reveals personality characteristics such as motivation for power, achievement, affiliation, and underlying emotional problems, often used to measure the need for achievement.

Theoretical psychology – an interdisciplinary field with theoretical and philosophical aspects involving specialists from clinical to critical psychology.

Theory – an explanation coherently organizing separate pieces of information; a well-substantiated explanation. A structured set of concepts to explain a phenomenon.

Theory of Cognitive Development (*Jean Piaget*) – children pass four stages of mental representation on the way to an adult level of intelligence.

Theory of deadly initials – suggests a link between the lifespan of males and their initials.

Theory of mind – a child's understanding of the emotions and motives of others. It stresses the ability to understand that others have beliefs, desires, and intentions that may differ.

Theory of multiple intelligences – defines intelligence and addresses whether methods that claim to measure intelligence are scientific.

Theory of natural selection (*Charles Darwin*, 1859) – explains the process of evolution; inherited characteristics that give an organism a reproductive or survival advantage are passed more often to future generations than other inherited characteristics.

Theory of ecological optics – perception emphasizes the richness of stimulus information and views the perceiver as an active explorer of the environment.

Therapeutic – having a beneficial effect on mental or physical health.

Therapeutic window – the amount of a drug required for effect without toxicity.

Therapy – any process aiding understanding and recovery from psychological difficulties. A variety of therapies is divided into *psychotherapies* (*using discussion or action*) and *somatic therapies* (*using medical or biological intervention*).

Theta waves – brain waves when a person is lightly asleep.

Think-aloud protocol – comments made by experimental participants on the mental processes and approaches used while working on a task.

Thinking – a mental process allowing humans to model their surroundings and deal with the situation according to their goals, plans, and desires.

Third eye – a sensory structure capable of light reception on some reptiles' dorsal side of diencephalon.

Third force – humanistic perspective as an alternative to psychoanalytic and behaviorist.

Thomas Theorem (*W.I. Thomas*, 1863-1947) – asserts that situations defined as accurate become real in their consequences, even if all the facts are not considered.

Thorndike puzzle box – a laboratory apparatus used by Skinner to demonstrate trial-and-error learning.

Thought – an idea, an instance of thinking, the state or condition of thinking.

Thought broadcasting – a delusion that a person can insert thoughts into another or that others can perceive their thoughts.

Thought disorder (*abnormal psychology*) – a pattern of disordered language use that is assumed to be related to disordered thinking. Describes disturbance of thought or speech that might be symptomatic of a mental disorder. *For example, incoherent thought and speech patterns.*

Thought disturbances (*abnormal psychology*) – distortions of thought (e.g., incoherent speech).

Thought field therapy (*psychotherapy*) – an innovative therapy to solve psychological problems developed from extensive knowledge about the body's energy system.

Thought insertion – delusions that thoughts are being inserted into their mind by another.

Thought withdrawal – delusion that makes a person feel thoughts have been 'taken out' of their mind.

Thorndike, Edward (1874-1949) – renowned animal researcher exploring *trial and error* learning (or instrumental learning) in animals by developing the *Thorndike puzzle box.*

Thousand-yard stare – the unfocused gaze, a characteristic combat stress reaction of a battle-weary soldier.

Three Mountains test (*Piagetian task*) – to demonstrate egocentricity, children are shown a model of three mountains and watch as a doll is positioned at a different point around the mountains. Pre-operational egocentric children cannot see the mountains from the doll's perspective.

Three-term contingency – how organisms learn that, in the presence of some stimuli but not others, their behavior is likely to have a particular effect on the environment.

Timbre – quality of sound; dimension of auditory sensation reflecting the complexity of sound waves.

Tip of the tongue phenomenon – when a word is known yet cannot be retrieved.

Token economy (*operant conditioning*) – behavior modification based on operant conditioning; a form of operant conditioning by which a subject is 'taught' to behave in a particular manner through rewards. It encourages behavior by employing secondary reinforcers (tokens) after desirable behavior, which can be collected and exchanged for primary reinforcers (a meaningful object or privilege).

Tolerance – 1. the need for more of a drug to get the same effect over time. 2. the ability to tolerate beliefs or practices followed by others.

Tolman, Edward (1886-1959) – American psychologist, the theory of *Sign Learning* focuses on stimuli instead of responses and concentrates on learning (escape, latent, avoidance, approach, and choice-point learning) in rats, commonly in mazes.

Top-down approach (*offender profiling*) – examines evidence from the crime scene considering existing classifications and theories of serious crimes (*the top*) and appraises which category a crime fits (*American criminal profilers*).

Top-down processing – perceptual processing in which previous experiences, existing knowledge, expectations, motivations, or the context in which perception occurs affect how a perceived object is interpreted and classified.

Touch illusions – exploit the sense of touch, one of the five senses humans depend on.

Tourette's syndrome – a neurological disorder characterized by facial grimaces, tics, upper body movements, grunts, shouts, and coprolalia.

Trace-dependent forgetting – information no longer stored in memory.

Traffic psychology – a behavioral study of road users and their psychological processes.

Trait (*personality*) – an aspect of personality; a personal characteristic or attribute occurring consistently and influencing behavior across situations. Behaviors and feelings are consistent and long-lasting (e.g., agreeableness).

Trance – relaxed state of mind ordinary in hypnosis; a psychological state induced by incantation.

Transactional analysis (*Eric Berne*; 1910-1970) – theory of personality with a humanistic, Neo-Freudian approach focusing on interpersonal *transactions* and communication.

Transcranial magnetic stimulation (TMS) – a noninvasive procedure for treating severe depression with brain stimulation using a magnetic coil.

Transduction – transforming one form of energy into another; when a transducer accepts energy in one form and returns related energy in a different form.

Transference (*psychoanalysis*) – passing emotions from one person to another; patients relate to their therapist as they would to prominent figures. A patient attaches feelings toward the therapist that were previously unconsciously directed toward a significant person who may have been involved in emotional conflict.

Transfer-appropriate processing – suggests memory is best when the type of processing carried out at encoding matches the processes carried out at retrieval.

Transference neurosis (*Sigmund Freud***)** – analysand infantile neurosis observed during the psychoanalytic process.

Transfer of training – when skills learned in one situation may be transferred to a second, related situation. Knowledge or abilities acquired in a specific area are used to solve problems or acquire knowledge in other areas.

Transformation – a series of changes to achieve a specific goal.

Transgender – general term for tendencies to diverge from the gender norm of society; individuals who are transsexual or intersexual.

Transpersonal experience – an intense shift in consciousness while experiencing the feeling of being one infinite or unbroken life.

Transpersonal psychology – stresses the transpersonal (spiritual) aspects of humans.

Transexual – an adjective describing someone who identifies with a physical sex different from the sex assigned at birth.

Transvestic fetishism – a person's sexual or erotic interest in cross-dressing.

Transvestism – the practice of acquiring the sexual role or adopting the clothes and behavior of the opposite sex.

Transvestite – people who cross-dress but do not necessarily identify with the opposite sex.

Trauma – emotional shock often characterized by long-lasting effects, a physical injury (due to an external force), or a psychological injury (caused by an emotional event).

Tree of Knowledge (ToK) system (*Gregg Henriques*) – a theoretical approach to unifying subjects.

Treisman, Anne (1935-2018) – British psychologist specializing in visual attention and object perception, renowned for proposing the feature integration theory of attention.

Trial (*experimental psychology*) – a single unit of experimentation where a stimulus is presented, an organism responds, and a consequence follows.

Trial and error – experiment with different solutions until one works.

Trial-and-error learning (*Thorndike*) – responses that do not achieve the desired effect are gradually reduced, and those that do are gradually strengthened.

Triarchic theory of intelligence (*R. Sternberg*) – distinguishes three aspects of intelligence.

Trichromatic theory (or *Young-Helmholtz theory*) – color vision originates from three types of cones in the retina, which are sensitive to light of three different wavelengths.

Tricyclics – antidepressant drugs that increase levels of norepinephrine and serotonin.

Trust metric – measures how much the other members trust a group member.

Tulving, Endel – Estonian-born Canadian experimental psychologist and cognitive neuroscientist known for research *Levels of Processing* in memory (Craik and Tulving, 1975).

Turing test – determines how closely computers mimic the human cognitive process.

Tutelary – providing protective supervision.

Two-factor theory of emotion (*social psychology*) – emotions have two components (*factors*) of physiological arousal and cognition. People's experience of emotion depends on 1. physiological arousal and 2. cognitive interpretation. When people perceive physiological symptoms of arousal, they look for an environmental explanation of this arousal. Accordingly, "cognitions interpret the meaning of physiological reactions to outside events."

Twin studies – studying monozygotic and dizygotic twins to assess the relative contributions of genetic and environmental influences on a characteristic. A typical psychology research approach to identifying variations among subjects whose genetic makeup is similar, therefore eliminating hereditary factors as an influence on a disorder or other issue.

Twins, mono-zygotic – identical twins.

Type 1 error (or *false positive*) – rejecting the null hypothesis when it should be accepted.

Type 2 error (or *false negative*) – accepting the null hypothesis when it should be rejected.

Type A personality – a set of personality characteristics, including a sense of competitiveness, hostility, constant time pressure, and impatience, which result in an increased risk of coronary heart disease.

Type B personality – relaxed, patient, easygoing, amiable behavior.

Type C behavior pattern – a constellation of behaviors predicting who may develop cancer or have cancer progress quickly; behaviors include passive acceptance and self-sacrifice.

U

Ultradian rhythm – a biological cycle occurring more frequently than 24 hours. One cycle repeats in less than twenty-four hours, for instance, stages of sleep several times during a single night's sleep.

Unconditional positive regard (or *positive regard*) – complete acceptance and caring of an individual without imposing conditions; a broad acceptance and support of an individual irrespective of what the individual says or does. A therapist's quality is crucial in patient-centered therapy. It involves nonjudgmental acceptance of the patient.

Unconditioned response (*classical conditioning*) – a naturally occurring response without previous conditioning. A reflexive response elicited by an unconditioned stimulus, such as pupil contraction to bright light, without prior learning.

Unconditioned stimulus (*classical conditioning*) – evokes an innate response; a stimulus elicits a reflexive (unconditioned) response.

Unconscious (*Freudian theory*) – the part of the mind containing thoughts, feelings, desires, and memories of which people have no awareness but influencing people's behavior. A portion of the psyche that cannot be accessed by the unconscious, repressing urges, impulses, and thoughts, which may filter into conscious awareness directly or in symbolic form.

Unconscious inference (1867) – a perception occurring outside of conscious awareness, reported by Hermann von Helmholtz.

Unconscious mind – a part of the mind triggering a collection of thoughts inhibiting the mind without the subject being aware.

Unconscious motive – behavior resulting from influences outside conscious awareness and manifests in defense mechanisms or other symbolic ways.

Understanding – the cognitive condition of someone who comprehends. *It is the possession of knowledge coupled with the capability of reasoning and making judgments relating to the applicability of the knowledge.*

Undifferentiated schizophrenia – when the person does show psychotic symptoms but without meeting the criteria for paranoid or catatonic types.

Undifferentiated type (*schizophrenia*) – diagnosed if a patient does not meet the criteria for paranoid, disorganized, or catatonic subtypes of schizophrenia.

Unfalsifiable – if data cannot disprove it and thus is not valid for predictions.

Unipolar depression (*unipolar disorder* or *depression*) – persistent feelings of great sadness, hopelessness, worthlessness, guilt, and a loss of interest in activities. It manifests in low self-esteem, low mood, and lack of interest in the activities to be performed in daily life.

Unitization (*psychology*) – configuring smaller information units into large, coordinated units.

Universal – characteristic applied to all members, despite experiences and development.

Universal Law of Generalization – probability a response to one stimulus is generalized to another.

Universalization – supportive intervention by therapists to reassure or encourage patients.

Unstable attribution – an inference that behavior is due to unstable, temporary factors.

Unstructured interview – when the interviewer does not have pre-determined questions but instead asks questions spontaneously as topics arise.

Upper quartile – the data point at the 75 percent point when data are rank-ordered.

Use – an automatic pattern of behavior in reaction to a situation.

Utilitarianism – what is ethically acceptable produces the greatest pleasure and happiness (*vs.* pain and suffering) for the greatest number.

V

Valence (*psychology*) – the positive or negative emotional charge of an event, object, or situation. For emotions, it means an event, object, or situation's intrinsic attractiveness (*positive valence*) or aversiveness (*negative valence*).

Validity (*psychological research*) – the ability of a test to isolate the characteristic it is designed to measure; the extent to which it measures what it claims and intended. The quality of an argument or degree to which an experiment is accurate and may be generalized.

Values – perceptions of what is important in life; involves principles, standards, or judgments about what is valuable or essential. Culturally defined standards by which people judge desirability, goodness, and beauty serve as broad guidelines for social living and public policies; core values are a high priority in society (e.g., individualism or personal freedoms in the U.S.).

Value theory – how people appraise things and concepts, the reasons for this evaluation, and the scope of applications of honest evaluations across society.

Vanity – a narcissistic personality trait with a focus on oneself.

Variable – something likely to change; any measured factor shows variation across cases or conditions. An event, characteristic, behavior, or condition is studied and measured.

Variable-interval schedule – a reinforcement schedule in which reinforcement happens after a particular average amount of time.

Variable interval schedule – in operant conditioning, a schedule of reinforcement is determined by the average time interval that must elapse since the last reinforcer before a response will be reinforced.

Variable ratio schedule (*operant conditioning*) – a schedule of reinforcement is determined by the average number of responses required to receive a reinforcer.

Variability (*descriptive statistics*) – the dispersion (spread) of scores within a data set.

Vegetotherapy – psychotherapy involving physical manifestations of emotions.

Ventromedial hypothalamus – a section of the hypothalamus, when lesioned in rat brains, demonstrates abnormal appetitive behavior.

Vermis – the narrow central part of the cerebellum between the two hemispheres.

Vermis cerebelli – the narrow central part of the cerebellum between the two hemispheres.

Vertical thinking – a distinct approach to problem-solving using selective, analytical, and sequential methods.

Vestibular – relating to the sense of equilibrium.

Vestibular sense – indicates how one's body is oriented with respect to gravity.

Vestibular system – the sensory system involved in balance.

Vicarious – experienced at secondhand.

Vicarious learning (or *observational learning*) – a change in behavior or knowledge by watching. Socialization occurs from observing and imitating the behavior of another person who serves as a model instead of through direct experience. When a person first observes, retains, and then imitates the behavior. See *modeling*.

Vicarious reinforcement – learning by observing others rewarded for their behavior.

Vigilance – watching or anticipating something; to watch for danger, to be precise.

Vision logic (*Ken Wilber*, 1977) – a post-formal but personal level of cognitive development in Wilber's integral theory.

Visual agnosia – disorders due to disruption of visual recognition.

Visual cliff – an apparatus to assess an infant's perception of depth, comprised of a thick glass pane covering a small and deep drop. Both surfaces are covered with the same checkered pattern; however, children six months and older will not explore the deep side, demonstrating depth perception.

Visual cortex – the region of the occipital lobes in which visual information is processed.

Visual hallucination – a visual perception triggered in a conscious state without a source of external stimuli.

Visual learning – learning wherein the ideas and concepts are presented as images and techniques.

Visual pathways – the routes nerve impulses travel from the retina to the brain's visual areas.

Visual perception – the brain's ability to interpret the images seen through the eyes to eventually make sense of what is being seen.

Visual thinking –processing information visually instead of linguistically or verbally.

Volition – one of three primary human psychological faculties that stresses the study of will, choice, and decision.

Volitional – with deliberate intention.

Volley principle – an extension of frequency theory proposing peaks in sound waves come too frequently for a single neuron to fire at each peak; several neurons fire as a group at the frequency of the stimulus tone.

Volume – an increase in the magnitude of vibration in the air (measured in decibels). Sounds increase in volume as the amplitude of the waves increases.

Voluntary response – a response controlled by the individual rather than elicited by specific stimuli as reflexes are.

Volunteer bias – participants who volunteer for a research investigation may differ in characteristics from non-volunteers, comprising a non-representative sample.

Voodoo death – used in stress literature as being *scared to death*.

Voyeurism – an act of perversion that helps an individual obtain sexual gratification by seeing the genital organs of others or watching them indulge in a sexual act.

Vulnerability – susceptibility to physical or emotional injury or attack.

Vulnerability-stress model – individuals with a biological vulnerability to a disorder will have the disorder only if specific environmental stressors exist.

Vygotsky, Lev (1896-1934) – *Zone of Proximal Development* by Belarusian psychologist whose theory of the development of cognitive abilities through social interaction learning gained supporters during the 20th Century. He was known for childhood development theories emphasizing society's role in development. In *Thought and Language*, Vygotsky observed the significance of vocalizing one's *thought process*, which later internalized to become an *inner voice*.

W

Wada test – technique to anesthetize one hemisphere of the brain by injecting a short-acting anesthetic (e.g., sodium amytal) into the carotid artery serving one hemisphere, repeating the procedure for the other hemisphere to identify which hemisphere is essential for language.

WAIS – see *Weschler Adult Intelligence Scale*.

Wakefulness – a recurring phase characterized by consciousness, wherein behaviors necessary for survival are executed.

Watson, John (1878-1958) –American psychologist and founder of *methodological behaviorism*. Famed for the Little Albert classical conditioning experiment.

Wavelength – the distance between the peaks of waves.

Waxy flexibility – a psychomotor symptom of catatonic schizophrenia characterized by a decreased response to external stimuli, due to which the individual remains immobile.

Weapon focus effect – the tendency for witnesses to a crime involving a weapon (e.g., gun) to recall details of the weapon but to be less accurate on other details (e.g., perpetrator's face). A factor affecting the reliability of eyewitness testimony because the attention of the witness is focused on the weapon the criminal is holding, which makes them ignore other aspects and leads to memory impairments when recollecting crime scene details.

Weber, Ernst (1795-1878) – German physician who studied sensation and touch; emphasized good experimental techniques as guidance for new directions and areas of study for future psychologists, physiologists, and anatomists.

Weber's Law (1860, *psychophysics*) – the amount a stimulus must change to be noticeable is proportional to the intensity of that stimulus. Thus, more potent stimuli must be increased more than weaker stimuli for a noticeable change.

Wernicke's aphasia (*Carl Wernicke*, 1848-1905) – the inability to communicate verbally owing to impairment of sensory abilities; caused by damage to Wernicke's area in the brain, resulting in disruptions in processing and comprehension of speech input, while speech production remains unimpaired. See *Broca's aphasia*.

Wernicke's area – part of the left temporal brain lobe cortex involved in understanding language. Wernicke proposed to be the center of language comprehension, whereby sound patterns of words are stored to convert speech sounds into words.

Weschler Adult Intelligence Scale (WAIS) – measures elements of adult intelligence, including verbal intelligence and performance intelligence, which are then divided into specific abilities so that performance and deficiencies can be assessed; released in 1955 as a revision of the Wechsler-Bellevue test (1939).

Wechsler Intelligence Scale for Children (WISC) – a general intelligence test completed without reading or writing, designed for children aged 6 to 16.

Wechsler Preschool and Primary Scale of Intelligence (David Wechsler, 1967) – an intelligence test for children between 2 years, 6 months, and 7 years, 3 months.

Westermarck effect (1891) – Finnish anthropologist Edvard Westermarck proposed a tendency for people to develop a sexually passive attitude toward those in their social circle and to seek a partner outside of that circle.

Westermarck, Edvard (1862-1939) – Finnish anthropologist, *Westermarck Effect* (1891).

Wilber's integral theory (1973) – attempts to integrate all human wisdom into a new, emergent worldview accommodating the perspectives of all previous worldviews, including those appearing to contradict one another.

Will – the capability of conscious choice, decision, and intention. Nietzsche defines will similarly to *"any internally motivated action,"* but more narrowly. In this sense, will is more of a "creative spark," a certain independence and stubbornness.

Wellness – optimal health incorporating the ability to function fully and actively over physical, intellectual, emotional, spiritual, social, and environmental health domains.

Wisdom – expertise in the fundamental pragmatics of life.

Wise Old Man (*Jungian psychology*) – represents archetype stoic contemplation and reasoning. The Wise Old Man is reclusive but reaches thought-out decisions.

Wish fulfillment (*Freud's theory*) – a symbolic manifestation of drives as dream fantasies.

Withdrawal (or *abstinence syndrome*) – physically painful and unpleasant symptoms (e.g., vomiting, shaking, headaches, convulsions) suffered by a physically dependent drug user as the drug wears off.

Withdrawal from investigation – an ethical requirement of psychological research that participants have the right to withdraw at any time during the study.

Withdrawal symptoms – sweating, nausea, or shakiness when drug usage ceases.

Within-subjects design (*repeated measures design* or *within-subjects*) – experimental design in which each participates in every level of the independent variable.

White Bear Principle (or *ironic processing*) – a psychological process wherein an individual is frequented by specific thoughts when deliberately attempting to suppress or avoid them.

Wolf children (or *feral children*) – children living in the wild often display animal-like behaviors, indicating wild animals have brought them up.

Womb envy (*Karen Horney*; 1885-1952) – the alleged unconscious, unexpressed desire of man to possess a womb; discontent and resentment men experience because of their inability to bear children.

Word recognition threshold – the minimum exposure of a word necessary to recognize and identify it when recognized 50 percent of the time.

Word salad (*schizophasia*) – the utterance of a jumble of meaningless words and phrases.

Working memory – an active recall process that holds information while processed or examined; the ability to hold some information in memory for a brief period while simultaneously processing the same or any other material.

Working memory model (*Baddeley and Hitch*, 1974) – a flexible reasoning and language comprehension system comprised of the phonological loop, visuospatial sketchpad, and central executive. Human memory is divided into an *Articulatory Phonological Loop* and *Visuo-Spatial Sketchpad*, which communicates with a *Central Executive.*

Working through – repeating, elaborating, and amplifying interpretations in psychotherapy.

Workplace stressors – aspects of the working environment (e.g., impending deadlines) experienced to be stressful, including physical stressors (such as noise, length of the working day, and inherent danger) and psychosocial stressors (such as relationships with co-workers, organization of work, and role responsibility).

World Health Organization (WHO) – an office of the United Nations (UN) overseeing international efforts to improve general health conditions and to address international threats such as pandemics.

World system theory (*Immanuel Wallerstein*) – a macro-scale approach to social analysis in which the world system (not nations themselves) is the means to understanding social changes and historical events; in this system, there are "core" (First World) countries, "semi-periphery" (industrializing) countries and "periphery" (poorer) countries that interrelate, with some inevitably taking advantage of others.

Wundt, Wilhelm (1832-1920) – German philosopher and a founder of modern psychology.

Y

Yerkes-Dodson law (1908) – a relationship between arousal and performance derived from experiments and observation by psychologists Robert Yerkes and John Dillingham Dodson.

Young-Helmholtz theory (or *Trichromatic theory*) – color vision originates from three types of cones in the retina, which are sensitive to light of three different wavelengths.

Z

Zeitgeber (German; *time* and *giver*) – an endogenous (*environmental*) cue that helps animals' internal pacemakers regulate biological rhythms. *For example, daylight is a zeitgeber helping to regulate daily (circadian) rhythms.*

Zener cards – a set of twenty-five cards, each featuring one of the five symbols, used by experts to test claims like extra sensory perceptions.

Zero-defects mentality – when a command-and-control structure stops tolerating mistakes.

Zimbardo, Philip (1933-) – American psychologist conducted the Stanford Prison experiment (1971), investigating how people conform to social roles.

Zone of Proximal Development (1930s) – Belarusian psychologist Lev Vygotsky proposes that a person's cognitive abilities are central to a 'zone,' further out of which one finds their potential abilities developed through social learning.

Everything You Always Wanted to Know About...

Chemistry

Physics

Cell and Molecular Biology

Organismal Biology

American History

American Law

American Government and Politics

Comparative Government and Politics

World History

European History

Psychology

Environmental Science

Human Geography

Visit our Amazon store

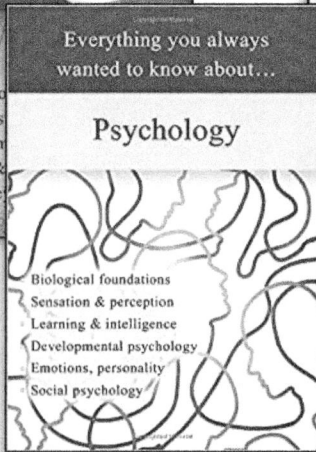

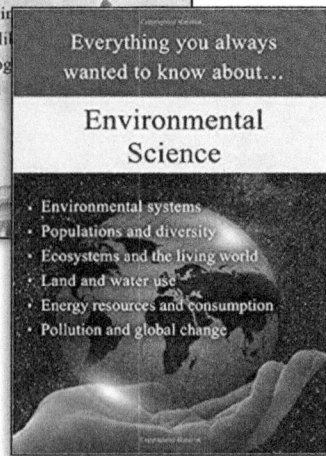

Everything you always wanted to know about...

American History

- Political histo
- Economic his
- Social movem
- Intellectual &
- Foreign polic

Everything you always wanted to know about...

American Government and Politics

Constitutional foundations
Governmental i
Civil rights & li
Political ideolog
Interest groups
Mass media
Public policy

Everything you always wanted to know about...

Psychology

- Biological foundations
- Sensation & perception
- Learning & intelligence
- Developmental psychology
- Emotions, personality
- Social psychology

Everything you always wanted to know about...

Environmental Science

- Environmental systems
- Populations and diversity
- Ecosystems and the living world
- Land and water use
- Energy resources and consumption
- Pollution and global change

Essential Biology Self-Teaching Guides

Eukaryotic Cell & Cellular Metabolism

Molecular Biology & Genetics

Nervous & Endocrine Systems

Circulatory, Respiratory & Immune Systems

Digestive & Excretory Systems

Muscle, Skeletal & Integumentary Systems

Reproduction & Development

Microbiology

Plants & Photosynthesis

Evolution, Classification & Diversity

Ecology & Population Biology

Visit our Amazon store

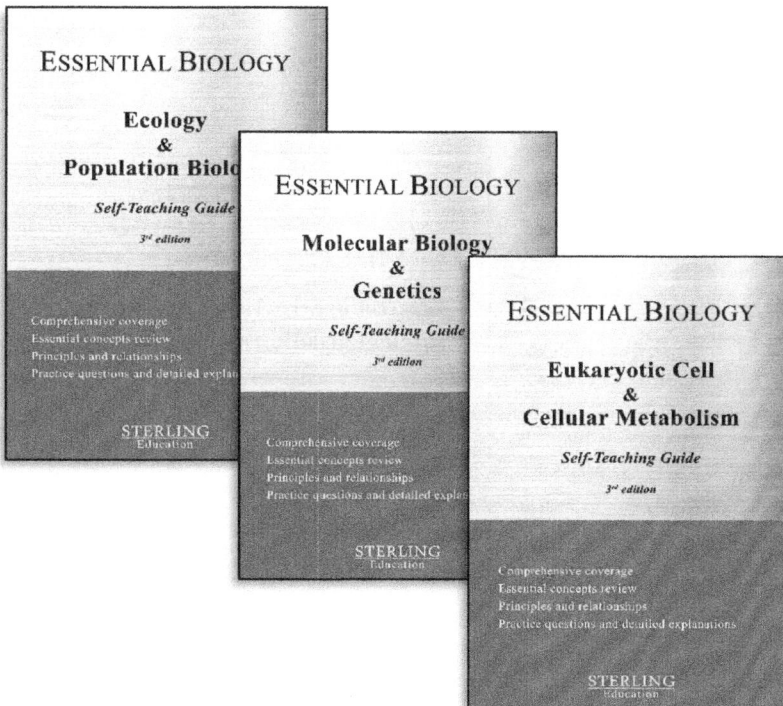

ESSENTIAL BIOLOGY

Ecology
&
Population Biology

Self-Teaching Guide

3rd edition

Comprehensive coverage
Essential concepts review
Principles and relationships
Practice questions and detailed explanations

STERLING
Education

ESSENTIAL BIOLOGY

Molecular Biology
&
Genetics

Self-Teaching Guide

3rd edition

Comprehensive coverage
Essential concepts review
Principles and relationships
Practice questions and detailed explanations

STERLING
Education

ESSENTIAL BIOLOGY

Eukaryotic Cell
&
Cellular Metabolism

Self-Teaching Guide

3rd edition

Comprehensive coverage
Essential concepts review
Principles and relationships
Practice questions and detailed explanations

STERLING
Education

Essential Chemistry Self-Teaching Guides

Electronic Structure & Periodic Table

Chemical Bonding

States of Matter & Phase Equilibria

Stoichiometry

Solution Chemistry

Chemical Kinetics & Equilibrium

Acids & Bases

Chemical Thermodynamics

Electrochemistry

Visit our Amazon store

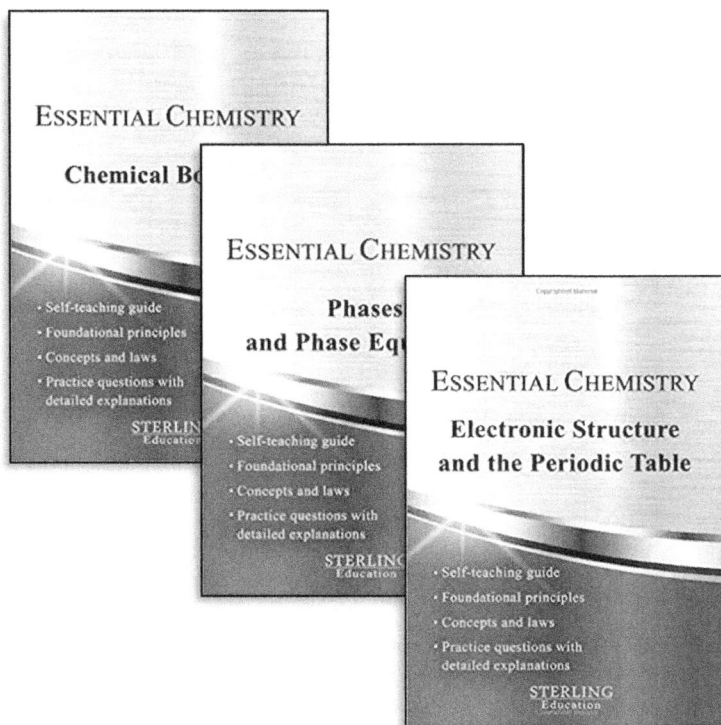

Essential Physics Self-Teaching Guides

Kinematics and Dynamics

Equilibrium and Momentum

Force, Motion, Gravitation

Work and Energy

Fluids and Solids

Waves and Periodic Motion

Light and Optics

Sound

Electrostatics and Electromagnetism

Electric Circuits

Heat and Thermodynamics

Atomic and Nuclear Structure

Visit our Amazon store

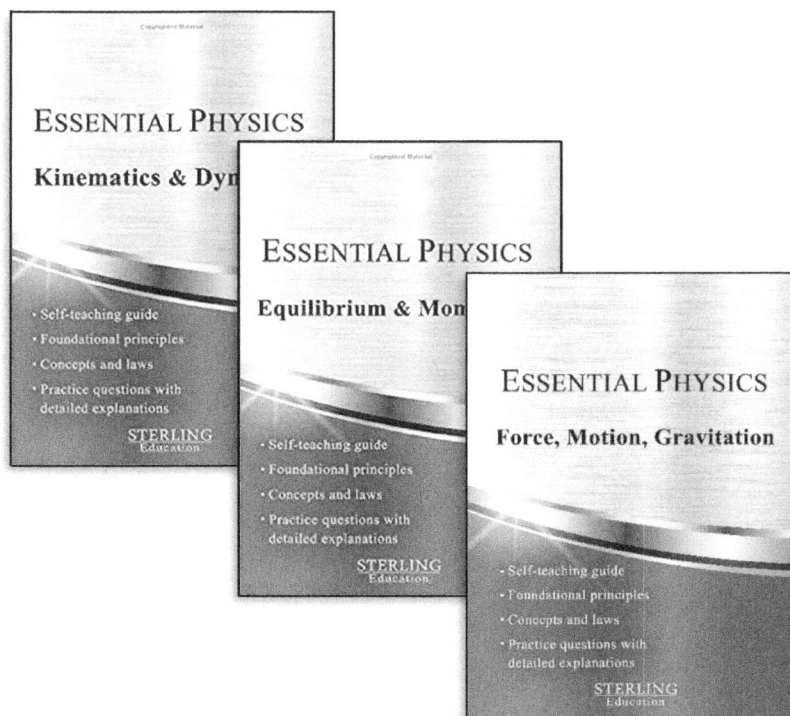

Made in the USA
Las Vegas, NV
02 May 2025